Emerging Issues in Intellectual Property

QUEEN MARY STUDIES IN INTELLECTUAL PROPERTY

Series Editors: Uma Suthersanen, *Reader in Intellectual Property Law and Policy, Centre for Commercial Law Studies, Queen Mary, University of London*, Graham Dutfield, *Centre for International Governance, University of Leeds* and Ilanah Simon Fhima, *Faculty of Laws, University College London, UK*

Editorial Board

Jonathan Moskin, *White & Case LLP, New York, USA*
Christopher Wadlow, *Norwich Law School, University of East Anglia, UK*
Thomas Dreier, *Professor, University of Karlsruhe, Germany*
Marshall Leaffer, *Professor, Indiana University School of Law, USA*
Ysolde Gendreau, *Professor, Université de Montréal, Canada*

The Centre for Commercial Law Studies at Queen Mary, University of London, has teamed up with international social science publisher, Edward Elgar Publishing Ltd, to re-launch its prestigious book series, Queen Mary Studies in Intellectual Property. Already established as an important forum for acute and relevant debate in the field of intellectual property, the series aims to build further upon its success, publishing books by renowned guest editors who will commission original and often provocative work by both leading scholars and specialist practitioners on key subjects and issues in IP. Combining volumes that are theoretical in their analysis with others that seek to explore the issues from a more practical perspective, all will be rigorous, as well as international in origin, outlook and appeal. The scope of the series will be wide-ranging and its approach will be to synthesize insights from a range of disciplinary backgrounds. The books in this series will not only provide unique sources of reference for researchers and students in IP, but will offer a level of insight to lawyers, policymakers and legislators that is consistent with the reputation of the Centre.

Titles in the series include:

US Intellectual Property Law and Policy
Edited by Hugh Hansen

Emerging Issues in Intellectual Property
Trade, Technology and Market Freedom: Essays in Honour of Herchel Smith
Edited by Guido Westkamp

Emerging Issues in Intellectual Property

Trade, Technology and Market Freedom:
Essays in Honour of Herchel Smith

Edited by

Guido Westkamp

*Queen Mary Intellectual Property Research Institute,
Centre for Commercial Law Studies, Queen Mary,
University of London, UK*

QUEEN MARY STUDIES IN INTELLECTUAL PROPERTY

Edward Elgar
Cheltenham, UK • Northampton, MA, USA

Published by
Edward Elgar Publishing Limited
Glensanda House
Montpellier Parade
Cheltenham
Glos GL50 1UA
UK

Edward Elgar Publishing, Inc.
William Pratt House
9 Dewey Court
Northampton
Massachusetts 01060
USA

A catalogue record for this book
is available from the British Library

Library of Congress Cataloguing in Publication Data

Emerging issues in intellectual property : trade, technology, and market freedom / edited by Guido Westkamp.
      p. cm. — (Queen Mary studies in intellectual property)
   Includes bibliographical references and index.
   1. Intellectual property. 2. Smith, Herchel, 1925–2001. I. Smith, Herchel, 1925–2001. II. Westkamp, Guido.
   K1401.E44 2007
   346.04′8—dc22   2007000717

ISBN 978 1 84542 775 7

Typeset by Cambrian Typesetters, Camberley, Surrey
Printed and bound in Great Britain by MPG Books Ltd, Bodmin, Cornwall

Contents

Contributors

Michael Blakeney, Herchel Smith Professor, Queen Mary Intellectual Property Research Institute, Centre for Commercial Law Studies, Queen Mary, University of London.

John Cahir, Solicitor with Matheson Ormsby Prentice, Dublin, and former Doctoral Associate, Queen Mary Intellectual Property Research Institute, Centre for Commercial Law Studies, Queen Mary, University of London.

Graham Dutfield, Professor of International Governance, University of Leeds and former Herchel Smith Senior Research Fellow, Queen Mary Intellectual Property Research Institute, Centre for Commercial Law Studies, Queen Mary, University of London.

Gail Evans, Reader in International Trade and Intellectual Property Law, Queen Mary Intellectual Property Research Institute, Centre for Commercial Law Studies, Queen Mary, University of London.

Alison Firth, Professor of Commercial Law, Newcastle University and former Senior Lecturer, Queen Mary Intellectual Property Research Institute, Centre for Commercial Law Studies, Queen Mary, University of London.

Johanna Gibson, Herchel Smith Professor, Queen Mary Intellectual Property Research Institute, Centre for Commercial Law Studies, Queen Mary, University of London.

Gary Lea, Senior Lecturer in Business Law, Australian Defence Force Academy, University of New South Wales, Canberra and former Lecturer and Herchel Smith Research Fellow, Queen Mary Intellectual Property Research Institute, Centre for Commercial Law Studies, Queen Mary, University of London.

Florian Leverve, Doctoral Associate, Queen Mary Intellectual Property Research Institute, Centre for Commercial Law Studies, Queen Mary, University of London.

Muriel Lightbourne, Visiting Scholar, University of Illinois at Urbana-Champaign, USA and former Research Scholar, Queen Mary Intellectual

Property Research Institute, Centre for Commercial Law Studies, Queen Mary, University of London.

Marcelin Tonye Mahop, Doctoral Associate, Queen Mary Intellectual Property Research Institute, Centre for Commercial Law Studies, Queen Mary, University of London.

Spyros Maniatis, Professor, Queen Mary Intellectual Property Research Institute, Centre for Commercial Law Studies, Queen Mary, University of London.

Duncan Matthews, Reader, Queen Mary Intellectual Property Research Institute, Centre for Commercial Law Studies, Queen Mary, University of London.

Jeremy Phillips, Intellectual Property Consultant, Olswang, Solicitors, Visiting Professor, Faculty of Laws, University College London (UCL) (since 1998) and Esteemed Associate, Queen Mary Intellectual Property Research Institute (since 2007).

Mira Sundara Rajan, Canada Research Chair in Intellectual Property Law, University of British Columbia and former Herchel Smith Research Fellow, Queen Mary Intellectual Property Research Institute, Centre for Commercial Law Studies, Queen Mary, University of London.

Noam Shemtov, Doctoral Associate, Queen Mary Intellectual Property Research Institute, Centre for Commercial Law Studies, Queen Mary, University of London.

Uma Suthersanen, Reader, School of Law, Centre for Commercial Law Studies, Queen Mary, University of London and former Herchel Smith Research Fellow.

Guido Westkamp, Senior Lecturer, Queen Mary Intellectual Property Research Institute, Centre for Commercial Law Studies, Queen Mary, University of London.

Daphne Zografos, Lecturer, University of Reading and former Doctoral Associate, QMIPRI.

Foreword

Dr Herchel Smith, in whose honour this Festschrift has been prepared, through his generous endowments created the Herchel Smith Chairs in Intellectual Property and Herchel Smith Research Fellowships in Intellectual Property at both Queen Mary, University of London and the University of Cambridge. Annual public lectureships in intellectual property are delivered at both universities.

Born in Plymouth, in 1925, Herchel Smith was educated at Exeter College, Oxford and at Emmanuel College, Cambridge, where he took the Natural Sciences Tripos. He worked at both universities, with Professor Lord Todd at Cambridge and as a post-doctoral fellow in the Dyson Perrins Laboratory at Oxford. Appointed a university lecturer in organic chemistry at Manchester University, he invented and patented new chemical reactions for the synthesis of novel steroids. Dr Smith emigrated to the United States in the 1950s to work for Wyeth Pharmaceuticals. Herchel Smith's work on new methods for the total synthesis of steroids led to the development of commercially feasible methods for the industrial production of estrone, equilin (an important constituent of treatments for post-menopausal syndrome), 19-nor-testosterone, and Norgestrel (a novel progestogen). Norgestrel was found to be a potent contraceptive and formed the basis for a range of contraceptive drugs.

Dr Smith retired in 1973 and started a new career as a philanthropist in which he returned to the academic community the major part of the substantial fortune that had accrued from his patent and licensing fees. On his death on 20 December 2001, in addition to the intellectual property gifts to Queen Mary, University of London and the University of Cambridge, he endowed the Herchel Smith Laboratory for Medicinal Chemistry, a leading centre for the research and development of magnetic resonance imaging, a Chair of Immunology and the Herchel Smith Chairs of Medicinal Chemistry and Organic Chemistry. Harvard University received similar endowments. The University of Pennsylvania Medical Center in Philadelphia and Williams College in Williamstown, Massachusetts, were also beneficiaries of his generosity.

This Festschrift is a celebration of the contribution which Herchel Smith made to establishing Queen Mary, University of London as one of the foremost intellectual property research institutes in the world.

Michael Blakeney

PART I

Technology, market freedom and the public domain

1. The confusing case of Mr Smith – Herchel Smith as litigant

Jeremy Phillips

This chapter is dedicated to the memory of a man to whom the intellectual property community owes a great debt. He was a man of intellect and of learning, of generosity and of foresight; he was, above all, a man who rose above the handicap of starting life with an utterly unmemorable surname, indeed one of the most common surnames in the world. The fact that there are so many Smiths was only partially mitigated by our subject's unusual forename Herchel. For, even taking a 'global appreciation' of the name, it was still perfectly possible to confuse it with the names of others. This author recalls his own confusion when Gerald Dworkin, a gentleman, a scholar and the second incumbent of the endowed Chair in what was then Queen Mary and Westfield College, moved to King's College, forsaking the Regent's Canal for the River Thames and incidentally changing his title from Herchel Smith Professor to Herbert Smith Professor.

HERCHEL SMITH THE LITIGANT

In addition to being an inventor and a philanthropist, Herchel Smith was also an intellectual property litigant. Although records in the United Kingdom reveal no extant record of his having participated in copyright or trade mark litigation, he made his mark in British patent litigation.

In *Roussel-Uclaf's Application*[1] the United Kingdom Patent Office had held that a patent application by the French company Roussel-Uclaf had been partially anticipated by claims contained in a patent granted to Herchel Smith. The company's patent claimed what it maintained to be a novel steroid, the 13-beta-n-propylenantiomer of 18-nor-estrone. Herchel Smith opposed,[2]

---

[1]   [1971] FSR 656 (PAT).

[2]   Both the application and the opposition were made under the Patents Act 1949, which was superseded by the Patents Act 1977 on 1 June 1978 but continued to apply in numerous situations for many years thereafter.

maintaining not only that his earlier patent[3] covered the same subject but that the applied-for patent was void for insufficiency, in that it failed to contain a warning that Roussel-Uclaf's patent could not be put to use without infringing his own patent. The French company appealed to the Patent Appeal Tribunal.

For Roussel-Uclaf B. W. Budd QC and William (later Lord Justice) Aldous, citing General Electric Co. Ltd's patent,[4] argued that both objections would be met by amending the patent application by inserting a statement that the applicant was 'aware of the prior claim' and that they had published grounds which, if established, would invalidate the prior claim. For Herchel Smith, the formidable Stephen Gratwick QC maintained that this amendment was insufficient: it was not enough for the applicant to state that it had published grounds upon which the earlier claim could be invalidated: those grounds of putative invalidity had to be reasonable.

Graham J, sitting as the Patent Appeal Tribunal, dismissed the appeal, holding it was indeed necessary for the applicant to state reasonable grounds upon which the earlier claim might be invalidated, but allowing the applicant to submit a further amendment to the Comptroller. The only issues before the court were technical legal issues: the court made little reference to the technical content of the invention and no reference to Herchel Smith.

Smith as a Surname

If Herchel Smith had sought, in keeping with his celebrity status, to monopolise his name by registering it as a trade mark, he would almost certainly have found that it was registrable on the basis of its inherent distinctiveness. This distinctiveness would depend however on the highly unusual nature of his forename. The etymology of 'Herchel' is not entirely certain, but the name appears most likely to be a homophone of the not uncommon Jewish name 'Herschel'.[5]

Some scientists are known solely by their surnames. Examples include Einstein, Copernicus, Galileo, Marconi, Ohm and Watt – all of whom have secured perpetuity for their reputation, if not actual immortality, by reason of their registration as trade marks. It is improbable that Herchel Smith would ever have been able to achieve that end, on account of the highly commonplace nature of his surname. Let us now review its character and quality.

---

[3]   UK Patent 1,010,051.

[4]   [1959] RPC 103 and 109.

[5]   'Herschel' is itself derived from 'Hirsch', a deer, which is the German translation of the common Hebrew name Tzvi.

The original English meaning of the word 'smith' is that of a person who works in metal.[6] The word has however long since absorbed its principal secondary connotation, that of a surname. Apart from its pervasive nature – presumably a consequence of generations of males of that surname producing male offspring that bore their father's name – another remarkable feature of the name Smith is its utter classlessness in English society. Some names may peg a person's position within the traditional scale of English social hierarchy, indicating descent from nobility,[7] their peasant roots[8] or their craft[9] or professional calling.[10] The surname Smith, however, may be found at every level of British society and is absolutely classless.[11]

The fact that Smith is the most common surname in the English-speaking world[12] does not prevent it from being registered as a trade mark. This was recently confirmed by the European Court of Justice in *Nichols*,[13] in which the court emphasised that even common surnames were judged by the same criteria for registration as were all and any other words, logos, slogans, shapes, colours or sounds.[14] In any event, the frequency with which the name Smith is found in almost all walks of commerce does not preclude particular Smiths from becoming entirely distinctive in relation to goods, services, celebrity and so on. Well known trade marks including the word 'Smith' include SMITH'S CRISPS, W. H. SMITH, SAMUEL SMITH beer, the corporate names Smith Aerospace, Smith & Nephew, GlaxoSmithKline, Smith Barney, Smith & Wesson, Herbert Smith, Reed Smith and the Adam Smith Institute. Individual Smiths of repute include Stevie Smith,[15] Harvey

---

[6]   'Derived from the Anglo-Saxon "smitan", to smite or strike, SMITH and its derivations are an occupational name for a man who works with metal (smith or black-smith), one of the earliest jobs for which specialist skills were required. It is a craft that was practised in all countries, making the surname and its derivations the most common of all surnames': http://genealogy.about.com/library/surnames/s/bl_name-SMITH.htm (verified 1 July 2005).

[7]   Fitz- anything suggests Norman nobility; see also Cholmondeley, Fiennes. Compound names also suggest upper-class affiliation. See, for example, M. Python, 'Upper Class Twit of the Year', http://www.jumpstation.ca/recroom/comedy/python/twit.html (verified 3 July 2005), offers such instantly identifiable class-specific names as Gervaise Brook-Hampster, Oliver St John-Mollusc and Nigel Incubator-Jones.

[8]   For example Shepherd, Swain.

[9]   Archer, Fletcher, Thatcher.

[10]   Priest, Scrivener.

[11]   Thus M. Python, n. 7 supra, also offers as a recognisably upper-class *nomen* the name Vivian Smith-Smythe-Smith.

[12]   http://en.wikipedia.org/wiki/Smith#Family_name (verified 3 July 2005).

[13]   *Nichols Plc v Registrar of Trade Marks* Case C-404/02 [2005] ETMR 21.

[14]   See paras 28, 34.

[15]   British poet, 1902–71. For a brief biography see http://www.strange-attractor.co.uk/stevibio.htm (verified 4 July 2005).

Smith,[16] Granny Smith,[17] Delia Smith,[18] Zadie Smith[19] and, to name one of the sharpest legal wits to grace the planet, Lord Birkenhead.[20] In short, *homo sapiens* has demonstrated a remarkable and persistent skill in distinguishing one possessor of the Smith surname from another.

A Smith By Any Other Name

'Smith' may be a ubiquitous surname but it is by no means without its mutations. Variant spellings such as Smyth, Smythe and Psmith[21] may be found, as well as hybrid forms such as Goldsmith, Shoosmith and Naismith. In its Smyth and Smythe form, the name may be pronounced either as 'Smith' or as 'Smeith' (with 'ei' as in 'eiderdown'). The name is also recognisable in its German translation, Schmidt, and in that name's own many variations.[22] Variants, hybrids and translations are all significant from the perspective of trade mark law.

ISSUES IN MODERN TRADE MARK LAW

The success of a trade mark infringement action and also the nature of the legal ground upon which it is based depend on the relationship of the defendant's trade mark to that of the proprietor who sues him for trade mark infringement. Effectively the position looks like this:

  If the two parties' marks are identical, the trade mark owner is on very

---

[16]   British show-jumper who, in 1971, made a rude two-fingered gesture after winning the British Show Jumping Derby which is now referred to as 'doing a Harvey Smith'. See http://news.bbc.co.uk/onthisday/hi/dates/stories/august/15/newsid_2534000/2534107.stm (verified 4 July 2005).

[17]   Born Maria Anne Sherwood, cultivator of the apple known today as the 'Granny Smith': see http://www.ryde.nsw.gov.au/ryde/msherwood.htm (verified 4 July 2005).

[18]   Best-selling British cookery author, who has sold more than 16 million copies of her books. See http://www.hub-uk.com/chefsbios/delia-smith.htm (verified 4 July 2005).

[19]   British novelist and intellectual; author of *White Teeth* and *The Autograph Man*: see http://en.wikipedia.org/wiki/Zadie_Smith (verified 4 July 2005).

[20]   F. E. Smith, First Earl of Birkenhead, Lord Chancellor. Some of his *bons mots* are related in the excellent entry on him at http://en.wikipedia.org/wiki/Frederick_Edwin_Smith,_1st_Earl_of_Birkenhead (verified 4 July 2005).

[21]   Ronald Eustace Psmyth is a creation of the author P. G. Wodehouse: see http://en.wikipedia.org/wiki/Psmith (verified 1 July 2005). The 'P' is silent, as in 'ptarmigan'.

[22]   For example, Grossschmidt, Kupferschmidt, Messerschmidt.

strong ground. Where their goods are similar, the trade mark owner will win his action against a defendant whose goods are similar, only on bringing proof that relevant consumers are likely to be confused between them. But if the parties' respective goods are identical, the owner will win his infringement action without even needing to prove any likelihood of confusion at all. Further protection is available in respect of a trade mark that has attracted a reputation through its having been used, where the defendant has sought to gain an unfair advantage from it or is acting to that trade mark's detriment.

If the two parties' marks are similar, the trade mark owner's position is still relatively strong. As in the instance described above, if two parties' goods or services are also similar, the owner will win his infringement action on proof of a likelihood of confusion resulting from the similarity, while further protection remains available in respect of a trade mark that has attracted a reputation through having been used, where the defendant has sought to gain an unfair advantage from it or is acting to its detriment. It is only where the two parties' marks are dissimilar, that the trade mark owner has no protection at all.[23]

This classification only works if it is possible for a court to adjudicate as to whether competitors' trade marks – in this case the words SMYTH, SMYTHE or PSMITH – are identical, similar or dissimilar to the registered mark SMITH.

Identity of Marks

The determination as to whether trade marks are similar or dissimilar has generated a substantial body of case law,[24] but it was initially assumed that there would be no problems in determining whether marks were identical or merely highly similar.

A problem soon emerged, though. If my mark is the word SMITH and a competitor uses the sign HERCHEL SMITH, has he used a sign that is identical to mine? Obviously the two are different, but there is a 100 percent correspondence between my word SMITH and the second word of HERCHEL

---

[23] Unless his application for relief came before the late Mr Justice Hart: see *L'Oréal SA and others v Ballure NV and others*, unreported, 26 January 2005. The claimant's trade marks were TRESOR, MIRACLE and NOA. The defendant was selling CREATION LAMIS, COFFRET D'OR, LA VALEUR, PINK WONDER and SWEET PEARLS. Dismissing an application by the defendant for summary judgment, Hart J held that, while the initial impression was that there was a lack of any relevant similarity in the packaging of the perfumes, it did not follow that the question of similarity should be considered in a vacuum and should be determined in an application for summary judgment on the information before the court.

[24] See for example *SABEL v Puma* Case C-251/95 [1997] ECR I-6191, [1998] ETMR 1 and subsequent cases of the ECJ.

SMITH – the two SMITHs are identical. Case law in the UK was clear. In *Asprey*, Jacob J (as he then was) took the view that 'William R. Asprey' was identical to ASPREY, a conclusion from which the Court of Appeal did not dissent. Likewise, in *AAH Pharmaceutical Ltd v Vantagemax Plc*,[25] Pumfrey J held that 'Vantage Rewards' was identical to VANTAGE. However, on a reference from France in *LTJ Diffusion v Sadas*[26] as to whether ARTHUR was identical to ARTHUR ET FELICIE the European Court of Justice gave firm guidance as to how it expected courts to determine whether marks were identical or merely similar:

> . . . a sign is identical with the trade mark where it reproduces, without any modification or addition, all the elements constituting the trade mark or where, viewed as a whole, it contains differences so insignificant that they may go unnoticed by an average consumer.

The first part of this statement tells us only that the word SMITH is identical to SMITH. But do SMYTH, SMYTHE and PSMITH contain 'differences so insignificant that they may go unnoticed by an average consumer'? All three variant spellings are homophones of SMITH, but the fact that any variant spelling of the name 'Smith' may be seen as an affectation would rather suggest that even small variants of spelling will be regarded as conspicuous.

For the record, the ruling in *LTJ Diffusion v Sadas* has since been considered in at least three British decisions:

Reed Executive Plc v Reed Business Information Ltd[27]   Pumfrey J, following his own lead in *AAH Pharmaceutical v Vantagemax*, found that a logo containing the words 'Reed Business Information' was identical to the trade mark REED since the words 'business information' would be seen as descriptors of the defendant's business, not as being part of their trade mark. The Court of Appeal, led by Lord Justice Jacob disagreed: there was no use of an identical mark because the defendant's use of the word 'Reed' had always been accompanied by other material. By the same reasoning, a descriptive corporate name such as 'Smiths Industries Ltd' would be regarded as non-identical to the trade mark SMITH.

Compass Publishing BV v Compass Logistics,[28]   where Laddie J held that COMPASS LOGISTICS was not identical to COMPASS: the differences

---

25   [2002] EWHC 990 (Ch), [2003] ETMR 18.
26   *LTJ Diffusion v Sadas Vertbaudet* Case C-291/00, [2003] ECR I-2799, [2003] ETMR 83.
27   [2004] EWCA Civ 159, [2004] ETMR 56.
28   [2004] EWHC 520 (Ch), [2004] RPC 41.

between the two were apparent and would be identified without difficulty or prior coaching by members of the public. He added that there was nothing in *LTJ Diffusion* or in *Reed v Reed* to suggest that noticeable differences should be ignored because they had only limited trade mark significance. On the same basis, SMITH'S CRISPS would not be identical to SMITH'S.

International Business Machines Corporation v Web-Sphere Ltd[29]   Lewison J determined that the sign Web-Sphere was identical to the Community trade mark WEBSPHERE, notwithstanding the presence of a hyphen between its two constituent words, because a global appreciation of the respective marks would result in their being regarded as effectively identical. The judge observed that. in deciding whether a mark and a sign were identical the overall impression, including visual, aural and conceptual similarities, was crucial: in this case the presence of a hyphen was deemed an insignificant difference, notwithstanding the fact that the average consumer was a sophisticated computer user who would be aware of the importance of the hyphen when searching for names on the internet. On this basis, we may presume that GOLDSMITH, GOLD-SMITH and GoldSmith would be regarded as identical.[30]

The conclusion that can be drawn from this is that minor differences can be disregarded when considering the issue of identity, except for those circumstances in which they cannot.

CONFUSING SIMILARITY

The principles upon which trade marks are compared with a view to their similarity are well entrenched in European Community and national law.[31] In sum, courts and national trade mark authorities are charged to make that comparison on a global basis,[32] assessing each mark as a whole and paying particular attention to their visual, aural and conceptual similarity.[33] The comparison is made through the eyes of the average consumer of the type of goods or services for which the marks are used,[34] that consumer being a fairly ordinary

---

[29]   [2004] EWHC 529 (Ch), ETMR 94.

[30]   It appears to be impossible to search for words with internal hyphens on Google and on the UK Trade Mark Registry website (empirical search, 1 July 2005).

[31]   For a lengthy review of these principles see, for example, Jeremy Phillips, 'Strong trade marks and the likelihood of confusion in European law', [2006] *Journal of Intellectual Property Law and Practice* 385.

[32]   Tenth recital to the preamble of Council Directive 89/104; *SABEL v Puma* Case C-251/95 [1997] ECR I-6191, [1998] ETMR 1, para. 22.

[33]   SABEL, supra, para. 14.

[34]   SABEL, supra, para. 23.

sort of person who is endowed with an imperfect memory[35] and who may be required to view the marks one at a time rather than simultaneously.[36]

Four cases involving SMITH-related trade marks have surfaced in recent years, including three before the Boards of Appeal of OHIM, the Office for Harmonisation in the Internal Market. They are as follows:

Aguirre y Compañia SA v Paul Smith Ltd[37]   Paul Smith applied to register as a Community trade mark the words PAUL SMITH for goods in ten different classes. Aguirre opposed, citing its earlier Spanish figurative registered trade marks incorporating the words JOHN SMITH. After Aguirre's opposition was dismissed, an appeal was lodged to the Board of Appeal but the parties reached their own settlement. The appeal was then withdrawn, each party bearing its own costs. Following the settlement, Paul Smith notified the Office that the appeal had been withdrawn. Aguirre confirmed that this was so and that it expected the PAUL SMITH mark to proceed to registration.

Teddy Smith SA v JLB Marketing Inc.[38]   JBL Marketing applied to register as a Community trade mark the words BETTY SMITH for goods in Class 25 (men's, women's and children's clothes; hats; shoes, tennis shoes etc.). Teddy Smith SA, opposed, citing its earlier French registration of the TEDDY SMITH trade mark for goods in Classes 18 and 25 (leather; imitation leather; products made from those materials and from animal skins; hats etc.). The Opposition Division dismissed the opposition.

Sotorock Holding Ltd v Laurence E. Gordon and Gayle Gordon[39]   Sotorock's predecessor in title applied to register as a Community trade mark a figurative mark containing the words GORDON & SMITH for goods in Classes 25 and 28 (clothing; footwear; headgear; articles for gymnastics and sport). The Gordons opposed, citing four earlier United States registered trade marks for the words GORDON & SMITH and G & S. The Opposition Division allowed the opposition. The question of likelihood of confusion with an earlier mark did not fall to be determined, since a United States registered trade mark is not an 'earlier mark' for Community trade mark opposition purposes.[40] However, the application had been filed by the opponents' trade mark agent without their

---

[35]   *Lloyd Schuhfabrik Meyer GmbH v Klijsen Handel BV* Case C-342/97 [1999] ECR I-3819, [1999] ETMR 690, para. 26
[36]   Ibid.
[37]   Case R 88/2000-3, Third Board of Appeal, 7 March 2001.
[38]   Case R 1037/2000-1, First Board of Appeal, 18 June 2001.
[39]   Case R 336/2001-2, Second Board of Appeal, 7 July 2003.
[40]   Council Regulation 40/94, Art. 8(2).

consent and was therefore unlawful.[41] The fact that the opponents had not immediately objected to the filing did not constitute consent.

Aguirre y Compañia SA v Smith Sport Optics, Inc.[42] Smith Sport Optics applied to register as a Community trade mark the word SMITH for goods in Classes 18 and 28 (walking sticks; hiking sticks; ski poles etc.). Aguirre opposed, citing earlier Spanish registrations of figurative marks containing the words JOHN SMITH for a wide variety of goods that included walking sticks, sporting articles and, indeed, Christmas tree decorations, and maintaining that there existed a likelihood of confusion. The Opposition Division rejected the opposition on the basis that, among other things, there was no visual, aural or conceptual similarity between the marks. Aguirre appealed. The Board of Appeal dismissed the appeal. Even though some of the goods for which Aguirre's mark was registered were identical to those for which Smith Sport Optic sought registration, there was insufficient similarity to cause any likelihood of confusion at all, stating: 'The consumer who is familiar with the mark JOHN SMITH will not necessarily assume that any walking stick sold under the mark SMITH comes from the same source'.[43]

These four decisions show how popular is the name SMITH as all or part of a trade mark even in Continental Europe. In contrast no Smith-related disputes in the United Kingdom – the 'home jurisdiction' of the name – appear to have reached the law reports.

Attacks on the Reputation of a Mark that has been Used

Council Directive 89/104[44] (on the approximation of national trade mark law in the European Union) and Council Regulation 40/94 (on the Community trade mark)[45] both provide that

> The proprietor shall be entitled to prevent all third parties not having his consent from using in the course of trade . . . any sign which is identical with or similar to the [Community] trade mark in relation to goods or services *which are not similar to those* for which the [Community] trade mark is registered, where the latter has a reputation [in the Community] and where use of that sign without due cause takes unfair advantage of, or is detrimental to, the distinctive character or the repute of the [Community] trade mark. (emphasis added)

---

41 Council Regulation 40/04, Art. 8(3).
42 Case R 895/2002-2, Second Board of Appeal, 7 September 2004.
43 Ibid., at para. 19.
44 Art. 5(3).
45 Art. 9(1)(c).

The corresponding version of this provision in the United Kingdom read as follows:

> (3)   A person infringes a registered trade mark if he uses in the course of trade a sign which –
> (a)   is identical with or similar to the trade mark, and
> (b)   *is used in relation to goods or services which are not similar to those for which the trade mark is registered,*
> where the trade mark has a reputation in the United Kingdom and the use of the sign, being without due cause, takes unfair advantage of, or is detrimental to, the distinctive character or the repute of the trade mark.[46] (emphasis added)

In two momentous decisions[47] the European Court of Justice ruled that this protection of the reputation of trade marks against the use of identical or similar marks on quite dissimilar goods and services applied equally to identical and similar goods too. Following these decisions the United Kingdom government decided to amend the Trade Marks Act 1994 by deleting the words which are marked in italics in the preceding quote.[48] This amendment may have been unnecessary, given the imperative need to interpret legislation that implements European Union legislation in the manner in which it is interpreted by the European Court of Justice.[49]

This amendment, together with a corresponding amendment which enables the proprietors of marks with reputations to oppose applications,[50] has been welcomed by trade mark owners as a major improvement in their lot, since it plugs a lacuna that was perceived to exist in the previous statutory regime. Whether owners of SMITH-related marks will be able to derive much benefit from it, however, remains to be seen. This is because the scope of operation of this provision is unclear where, as in the case of a ubiquitous term such as SMITH, it may not be easy for a trade mark owner to satisfy the burden of proof that it is his trade mark, rather than another Smith-related mark, to which the objectionable use or proposed registration refers.

---

[46]   Sect. 10(3).
[47]   *Davidoff & Cie SA v Gofkid Ltd* Case C-292/00 [2003] ECR I-389, [2002] ETMR 99; *Adidas-Salomon AG v Fitnessworld Trading Ltd* Case C-408/01 [2004] ETMR 10.
[48]   Trade Mark (Proof of Use, etc.) Regulations 2004 (2004 No. 946), r.7(2).
[49]   Per Geoffrey Hobbs QC, sitting as a Deputy Judge in *Electrocoin Automatics Ltd v Coinworld Ltd* [2005] ETMR 31.
[50]   Trade Mark (Proof of Use, etc.) Regulations 2004 (2004 No. 946), r.7(1).

FINAL WORD

It is fitting that this tribute to the late Herchel Smith should conclude with a mention of a most apposite fact. After spending more than two decades in Mile End but before settling in Lincoln's Inn Fields, the Queen Mary Intellectual Property Research Institute sojourned in premises in Charterhouse Square, slightly to the west of the Barbican, in the historical area known to its habitués as – Smithfield.

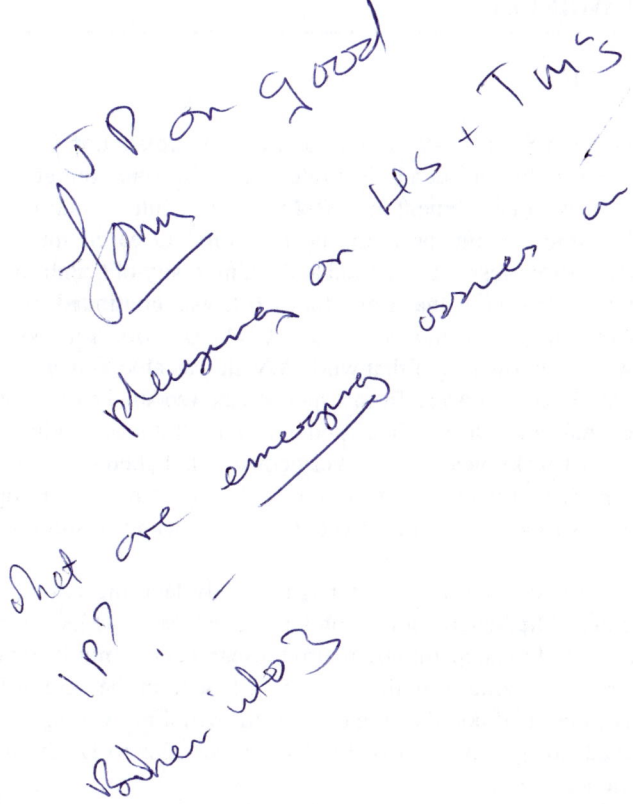

2. Auditing intellectual property rights by public research institutes

Michael Blakeney

1. INTRODUCTION

The career of Dr Herchel Smith may provide part of the explanation of why universities and other public research institutes have become obliged to involve themselves in the management and exploitation of intellectual property (IP) rights. Dr Smith commenced his post-doctoral research into the synthesis of steroids with Professor Lord Todd at the University of Cambridge. In the 1950s, as was common at that time, this work was continued in the private sector, when Dr Smith moved to the USA to work for Wyeth Pharmaceuticals. As a consequence of that work, Wyeth was able to develop a blockbuster contraceptive, *Norgestrel*, from which Wyeth received a considerable amount of revenue and Dr Smith earned many millions of pounds in revenue. This Festschrift acknowledges the very considerable bequests by Dr Smith both to Queen Mary, University of London and Oxford and Cambridge Universities, as well as to a number of universities and research institutes in the USA.

A lesson which the public research sector is belatedly learning is that, in addition to relying upon the benefaction of philanthropists such as Dr Smith, the sector is better advised to keep entrepreneurial researchers within its ranks and to capture some of the value from their research. Indeed in the case of Dr Smith, Wyeth Pharmaceuticals could be regarded as the beneficiary of the very considerable value added by a number of English universities to Dr Smith's capacity as a researcher.

A recent illustration of the change in attitude in the UK is the adoption in 2005 by the Council and General Board of Cambridge University of a Report recommending that the University extends its existing IP policy and 'asserts ownership of all intellectual property generated by its employees in the normal course of their duties, from 1 January 2003'.[1] Acknowledging the controversy

---

[1]   Para. 1.

which this decision generated, the University claimed that there was 'no intention of attempting to commercialize inventions without the willing support and co-operation of inventors' and in the University, 'knowledge transfer through commercialization should remain secondary to the primary objectives of teaching and research'.[2]

The Cambridge Report identified a number of objectives underpinning its new policy. Hearkening back to Dr Smith's experience, the University referred to the role of its IP policy in attracting and retaining academic staff,[3] the necessity to 'maintain and encourage a culture of entrepreneurship' and protecting such staff from 'predatory external parties'.[4]

A blunt reality which Cambridge, like all UK universities, is obliged to confront is the fact that Government structural funds for universities and public research institutes have substantially declined and in place of these funds research funding is made available on a competitive basis by the funding councils.[5] Funding charities, as well as the European Commission and private sector funders and collaborators, require universities and public research institutes to capture and manage the IP which they generate, as a precondition for the grant of research funding.

Although universities like Cambridge assure their staff that the primary objectives of the academy have not changed, patent applications now rank with books and articles as publications to be taken into consideration in assessing the academic merit of employees. An observation made in a number of studies is that the increased involvement in IP by the public research sector is diverting an increasing number of researchers away from basic to applied research.[6] As a consequence, public research institutes have to develop new administrative capacities to deal with this new reality. This chapter addresses a number of the practical implications for the IP-agile public research institute.

---

[2]   Ibid.
[3]   Ibid., para. 6.
[4]   Ibid.
[5]   A. Geuna, 'The changing rationale for European university research funding: are there negative unintended consequences', (2001) 35 *Journal of Economic Issues* 607–32.
[6]   For example, OECD, 'Draft final report on the strategic use of intellectual property by public research organisations in OECD countries', DSTI/STP (2002) 42/REV1; A. Geuna and L. Nesta, *University Patenting and its Effects on Academic Research*, Paper no. 99, Science Policy Research Unit, University of Sussex, June 2003.

2.   THE IP AUDIT

Until the last decade the subject of IP rights had not been an issue which had been addressed by the public research community. This situation was decisively changed by the developments in recombinant biotechnology and in patent law which made it possible for individuals to establish proprietary rights over genetic material. Among the consequences of this development have been the privatization of genetic materials previously thought of as being in the public domain, which on the one hand has depleted the genetic material available for public research and on the other has rendered the biological assets of those institutes vulnerable to misappropriation. The assertion of IP rights by private proprietors over enabling biotechnologies compromised the abilities of public research institutions to participate in modern biotechnological research programmes. The reduction of funding to public research institutes in the context of this privatization of genetic resources and enabling technologies has brought it home to those institutes that they have to take an active role in IP management.

As part of that management IP institutes have been obliged to conduct audits of their IP assets. The purposes of these audits are to identify the IP which is generated by researchers with a view to conserving that IP as an asset of the institute and to identifying the IP of third parties which passes through its doors, with a view to avoiding any liability for misuse of that IP. In addition to a public research institute undertaking IP audits as a matter of best management practice, these audits may be mandated by the donors and funders of those institutes. In the USA a decisive influence upon this process was the passage in 1979 of the Bayh-Dole Act, which encouraged the privatization of the IP generated by federally funded research institutes. This legislation precipitated the establishment of technology transfer offices at universities and research institutes for the purpose of commercializing the IP generated by their research. This development has been emulated in Europe such that institutes are unable to obtain European Commission funding for research where an IP exploitation plan is not in place.

3.   AUDIT METHODOLOGY

The objectives of an IP audit may be various. However, at the heart of an audit is the desire to identify relevant IP for the purpose of securing the ownership of that IP, with a view either to commercializing it or making it available to the research community and its clients. An IP audit will also make a significant contribution to the formulation and execution of the IP policy of the research institute. Finally, an IP audit will identify any third party IP which is being utilized by an institute, with a view to ensuring its security and minimizing any liability to third parties.

Initially the auditor will concentrate on identifying the IP assets. This is usually achieved by conducting interviews with key personnel, including company officers and managers, and staff who make and/or implement decisions in departments such as engineering, operations, marketing and finance. The interview process offers insight into the history and direction of research and business plans that may not be apparent from documentation.

A review of the institute's documents, such as contracts, licence agreements and material transfer agreements (MTAs) will be undertaken to identify existing IP assets, as well as third party IP. An analysis of the IP portfolio is carried out to determine which assets require protection. The auditor can also determine where gaps in protection lie or where competitors could potentially challenge IP rights.

An audit report will categorize the IP and identify any deficiencies in it. The report will often include: (i) a register of relevant agreements; (ii) a review of those research projects which might generate IP capture; and (iii) recommended in-house procedures for the capture and management of IP.

IP audits should be conducted regularly by all research institutions as part of their general management strategy. Evidence of IP management will be required not only by donors and funding bodies, but also by potential research collaborators and research funders from the private sector.

4. OWNERSHIP AND CONTROL OF IP

4.1 Introduction

A key issue in any IP audit is to establish the ownership and control of IP by the audited research institute. This will entail an examination of all documents relevant to: (i) the legal status of the institute; (ii) the obligations of personnel under their service agreements and employment contracts, together with their obligations under the institute's IP policy; (iii) agreements with research collaborators; (iv) agreements with funding bodies and donors; and (v) documents relevant to the research institute's status within any research network.

The capacity of a research institute to assert ownership and control over any IP is going to depend in the first instance upon its legal capacity. In the case of an institute which is incorporated, its powers of ownership and control will be set out in its constitution and by laws (memorandum and articles of association). These documents will usually have legal power conferred by the corporations law of the place of incorporation. On the other hand where the research institute has international status, its powers may be derived from a headquarters agreement between the host state, donor bodies and the institute, recognizing the legal personality of the institute.

Once invested with the legal power to exercise dominion over property, including IP, the institute will then have the power to contract with employees. Typically, IP clauses will be inserted in contracts of employment or in an institute IP policy or code which is incorporated by reference in the contract of employment.

4.2   Operating Agreements

In the case of international research institutes established by an agreement between donors and host governments, there will usually be a statement about the sort of legal personality which the institute will have. For example such an institute will usually be designated to be 'an autonomous, philanthropic, tax-free, non-profit, non-stock benevolent corporation'. There will usually be a term for which it is to exist, such as fifty years from the date of incorporation, with the possibility of renewal. At the end of the term there will usually be an indication of the right of ownership of the assets of the institute. In the case of an institute which establishes a collection of biological resources which are collected from other countries, there may be biopiracy objections if the ownership of these resources is lost on termination.

As was seen above, in relation to the Bayh-Dole Act, in return for public funding, an institute will be obliged to commercialize its research, or otherwise make it available to stakeholder communities. The operating agreement will usually indicate the power of the institute to 'receive and acquire by donation, grant, exchange, devise, bequest, purchase, or lease, either absolutely or in trust, contributions of such properties, real and personal, as may be necessary to carry out the objects and purposes' of the institute. This provision will have no operative effect, as the power will be conferred by incorporation.

4.3   Incorporation

Typically a research institute will be incorporated under the companies law of the host country. This law will contain provisions concerning the types of corporations and the powers of those companies. Companies are usually divided into non-profit and profit-making enterprises. The ownership and assets structure of each may differ. Invariably, the voting rights of the company will be allocated by reference to shares. Its management will be allocated to a board under a panel of directors and chief executive officer. The powers of the company are usually set out in a constitution or a memorandum of association and detailed in its by-laws or articles of association. These documents should be scrutinized to see the powers which the institute has to own and deal with IP. They will also set out the powers of relevant officers of the corporation to enter into transactions on behalf of the corporation. These documents will also set out the procedures for terminating the existence of the institute and the disposal of its assets on termination.

It will not be uncommon for the constitutive documents of a corporation to be silent on the fate of intangible property, such as IP, which might have been generated by the corporation during its life. This is because IP has only relatively recently become a corporate concern. However, where the tangible property is specifically disposed of, there is a good argument that the intangibles will follow the same route.

4.4   Charter of the Institute

It is not uncommon for public research institutes to indicate their public service function in a governing charter. This charter will usually be promulgated as an exercise of the power of the board under the by-laws of the corporation. As such, the charter will be subordinate to the general operation of the Articles of Incorporation and can confer no powers that are greater than those defined by the Articles of Incorporation.

4.5   Personnel Documents

Typically the persons working at a public research institute will comprise: national staff, internationally recruited staff, visiting scientists, consultants, affiliate scientists, project scientists, collaborative research fellows, doctoral and post-doctoral students. The assertion of ownership and control over any IP which they may generate will depend upon the terms of their engagement. For convenience we can categorize these persons as staff and non-staff.

4.6   Staff

The ownership and control of IP generated or held by staff will be dealt with by a combination of personnel contracts and the personnel policies and procedures of the institute. These will usually be gathered in a personnel manual. In some institutes, following the burgeoning of concern about IP, staff have been requested to sign an IPR statement by which staff agree that 'all inventions, improvements, data, processes, technologies, discoveries and other intellectual properties' generated by them while employed by the institute 'that relate to the research and development programs of the institute or result from tasks' assigned to them 'are the sole property of the institute'.

For an institute to exercise dominion over the IP which is generated within it, staff should be obliged to disclose their potentially protectable and protected discoveries, inventions, designs, plant varieties, trade marks, publications, software and data to the institute. In addition to the obligation of disclosure, most institutes will oblige employees to do all things necessary, including executing documents to assist it in obtaining legal protection for its IP.

A final obligation imposed upon institute employees will be that confidential information will be used only in the performance of duties to the institute and not be disclosed to unauthorized persons both during employment with the institute and for a reasonable period after the termination of employment.

In most UK universities rights to books, articles and other publications by employees are invariably waived. Ownership will be asserted in relation to inventions and plant varieties which are perceived to be more likely to return sizeable profits. A different attitude from that taken to conventional publications is taken to teaching materials. These are now being sold by universities in lucrative distance learning courses, particularly on-line. Consequently, copyright in teaching materials is increasingly being retained by universities and tertiary institutes.

An increasingly difficult publication issue is that as universities and research institutes look to exploit the inventions of their employees, they are concerned about disclosures of inventions which may impair the patentability of those inventions. This censorship appears at first blush to be antithetical to the educational mission of the university. However, it is not untypical for licence agreements, for example of genetic materials or enabling technologies with private sector enterprises, to require proposed articles to be vetted by the licensor and publication delayed until a patent application can be filed. Such licence obligations, which are assumed by a university or research institute as licensee, can only be discharged, if the licensee has a capacity to control the publications of its employees.

A particular problem which public research institutes may have with disgruntled employees is illustrated by the facts of *Madey v Duke University*.[7] Duke University employed Madey as a laboratory director. Prior to his appointment at the university, he owned two patents over some experimental equipment. This equipment was used in his work at the university. After his services were terminated, Madey successfully sued Duke University for infringement of his patents. This case illustrates the necessity for a university to put in place an agreement with its employees to cover any IP which they may bring to an appointment and upon which a research programme may be based.

Prior to *Madey* a university could have availed itself of the experimental

---

7   307 F.3d 1351 (Fed. Cir. 2002).

use exception defence in US patent law. The Federal Circuit Appeals court refused to allow this exception to exempt university research activities from infringing a patent, as it held that these research activities 'unmistakably further the institution's legitimate business objectives, including educating and enlightening students and faculty participating in these projects'. It also disregarded the non-profit status of Duke University. With universities in other countries becoming more entrepreneurial through the exploitation of their IP, the *Madey* case is a salutary lesson in the necessity to put in place appropriate IP management agreements with employees.

4.7 Non-Staff

A particular problem for the ownership and control of IP by a research institute is that it will frequently be hosting various categories of non-staff such as visiting scientists, consultants, project scientists, collaborative research fellows and students. Without an agreement with these non-staff the institute will not be able to assert control over any IP which these visitors may generate or use. There have been examples where visiting scholars, with the blessing of an institute, have been allowed to take away biological materials which subsequently have been patented by their home institutions.[8]

It is not uncommon in a number of countries for non-staff to execute an IP and confidentiality agreement. Problems have arisen from the uncertain status of visiting researchers, who in some instances have acquired patent rights over the subject of their research while a visitor. Confusion has also arisen where a research institute accommodates researchers who may be funded by outside donors. Uncertainty about the ownership of the research of such donors can also be clarified in the institute's IP policy.

A particular problem at universities has been the status of any IP generated by students during their postgraduate studies. This is exacerbated when a student has commenced research at one institution and concludes it at another. Best practices suggest that the student is placed under a contractual obligation through the enrolment process, when the student can be obliged to sign a declaration concerning any IP which may be generated.

5. POLICY ON IP

Given the burgeoning problems with IP for public sector institutions, most universities and research institutes have formulated IP policies to deal with the

---

[8] See M. Blakeney, 'Bioprospecting and Biopiracy' in B. Ong, ed., *Intellectual Property and Biological Resources*, Singapore: Marshall Cavendish, 2004.

ownership and control of IP. As a general principle, the public research institutes as a matter of policy emphasize the free availability of information, inventions and biological material which they develop, subject to the necessity to seek IP protection in order to secure the availability to developing countries of advanced biological technologies or biological materials. Some institutes declare that they will exceptionally apply for IP protection of the technologies or materials which they develop in the interests of their client communities or to prevent third parties obtaining IP rights over its innovations. For example, by filing a provisional patent application knowledge about an institute's innovations will be placed in the public domain. This is intended to destroy the novelty, and hence patentability, of those innovations which are required for the benefit of developing countries.

In a number of public research institutes an IP policy may be included in a policy on partnership with the private sector. This policy will often concede that to have access to biotechnology-derived products, and to make advanced biotechnologies available to developing nations, it may be necessary to enter into special agreements that accept some limitations on the distribution of the derived and associated materials. Within the context of this policy, the institute may assemble a list of IP which it is willing to share with the private sector in exchange for access to its IP, under mutually acceptable terms.

5.1   Contractual Arrangements Dealing with IP Ownership

Listed above are the various ways that an institution secures ownership of the IP generated by its staff. This situation may be varied by contracts with third parties. For example, a joint research or joint venture agreement with a third party may specifically provide for the ways in which IP generated by a project may be distributed between the parties. For example, if a research project is to be funded by a third-party donor, it will often have considerable influence upon the way that the fruits of the research are distributed between the parties. In some cases the funder may reserve to itself the right to exploit any IP which might be generated by a project. The research institute may have merely a right to any royalties which are generated by the exploitation of the IP. For this reason, the IP audit will have to examine closely all funding contracts.

In some countries, legislation may over-ride private contractual arrangements for the distribution of research output. For example, in Europe, the legislation dealing with research funding requires the approval of the European Commission for such agreements.

5.2   Identification of IP Generated by a Research Institute

An IP audit obviously has to identify all the IP generated by the research institute, whether existing in a registered or unregistered form. This would require the analysis of questionnaires completed by management and research staff and the examination of contracts, Material Transfer Agreements (MTAs), licences, collaboration agreements, memoranda of understanding, collaborative work plans, employment contracts and other legal arrangements to: (a) clarify the terms under which IP is being accessed and to determine whether the terms of access impose restrictions on the institute's ability to distribute products and services produced with the help of this IP; (b) identify ownership of relevant IP; (c) identify the source of IP in order to identify areas in which IP access and ownership issues may have to be re-examined to ensure compliance with the institute's current IP policy; (d) assess the importance of the IP to the institute's activities; and (e) to identify all new IP being developed at the institute (specifically, the IP opportunities perceived by the institute, for its own and third-party IP).

Typically an audit will identify the following principal potential sources of IP generated by an institute:

- patents associated with the genetic assets of an institute;
- plant variety rights associated with the germplasm conserved and developed by an institute;
- patents and confidential information associated with the enabling technologies and research and experimental techniques of an institute;
- copyright, database rights and know-how associated with publications, computer programs, databases and websites generated by the institute;
- trade marks;
- industrial designs.

5.2.1 Biological assets
The principal biological assets located at a scientific research institute will include:

- germplasm collection;
- DNA collection;
- microbial collection;
- biological tools for gene discovery;
- markers;
- enabling technologies, for example, marker genes and probes;
- advanced mapping populations;
- near isogenic lines;
- introgression lines;
- gene pyramids;
- advanced lines from conventional breeding;

- inbred lines for hybrids;
- varieties/cultivars;
- hybrids;
- transgenic lines.

These biological assets represent a considerable investment by the institute and its partners and collaborators. They also represent various levels of added value, utility and inventiveness. These biological tools will contain potentially patentable or licensable information. Given the expense of acquiring biological material from the private sector for an institute's researchers, its own biological assets represent bargaining chips which may be exchanged for that material in a cross-licensing arrangement.

Where an institute is involved in creating assets to be placed in the public domain, such as the innovations of the research institutes comprising the Consulting Group on International Agricultural Research (CGIAR),[9] the dangers of the unauthorized propertization of these assets by third parties has resulted in them identifying and placing those assets in the public domain, through the filing of provisional patent applications.

5.3   Patents, Utility Models and Industrial Design Rights in Equipment

A medical or agricultural research institute is likely to develop equipment and tools which could be the subject of IP protection. Given that protection is imperilled by any public demonstration of that equipment, it is necessary that the development of these devices is disclosed to the institute for evaluation.

5.4   Confidential Information

An important unregistered category of IP, particularly in the fields of agricultural and medical research, is confidential information. For example, the effects of a particular strand of DNA might be identified only after considerable experimentation. Where such research has been conducted in parallel,

---

[9]   These centres are: Centro Internacional de Mejoramiento de Maiz y Trigo (CIMMYT), the Centro Internacional de Agricultura Tropical (CIAT), Center for International Forestry Research (CIFOR), Centro Internacional de la Papa (CIP), International Center for Agricultural Research in the Dry Areas (ICARDA), International Center for Research in Agroforestry (ICRAF), International Crop Research Institute for the Semi-Arid Tropics (ICRISAT), International Livestock Research Institute (ILRI), International Institute of Tropical Agriculture (IITA), International Plant Genetic Resources Institute (IPGRI), International Rice Research Institute (IRRI) and the West Africa Rice Development Association (WARDA), World Fish Centre.

patent ownership may be problematical and so the research institutes may prefer to protect their work through confidential agreements. More conventionally, confidential information is often an adjunct to registered IP rights. For example, patent protection is conferred in exchange for the disclosure of sufficient information in a patent application to permit the invention, which is the subject of the application, to be worked. Inevitably, to protect its competitive advantage, the applicant will withhold information concerning the ways in which an invention will be effectively commercialized. This information, or know-how, may include: plant design and set-up, training, marketing plans, customer lists, and accounting and survey methods. Similarly, a protected trade mark is of limited commercial utility without an associated scheme for the advertising, licensing, franchising and marketing of goods or services under that mark. Ensuring control of the quality of licensed goods will usually entail the application of trade secrets.

At the centre of the action to protect confidential information are attempts to restrain the disclosure of trade secrets by former employees or researchers. A particular difficulty in these cases is in drawing a distinction between information which can be regarded as part of the stack of expertise of a skilled employee or researcher and other information gained during employment, such as secret industrial formulae or processes which may properly be regarded as belonging to the employer. Generally speaking an objective test is applied in which if the information in question can fairly be regarded as a separate part of the employee or researcher's stock of knowledge which a person of ordinary honesty and intelligence would recognize to be the property of the employee. In applying this objective test, the courts have tended to look, among other things, at the nature of the employment, the nature of the information and whether the information was capable of being isolated from other unprotected information. Chemical formulae and recipes, engineering drawings and designs are usually considered to be discrete categories of undisclosed information falling within the heartland of protectable confidential information. Typically, an institute's IP policy will oblige its researchers to maintain confidentiality through its contract of employment.

There are some national differences in laws protecting confidential information. The TRIPs Agreement, in Article 39, deals with preserving the confidentiality of test data submitted to government approval agencies. Given the long approvals process, particularly for pharmaceutical products, the opportunities for wrongful appropriation of such data by competitors was self-evident. Article 39.3 provides that

> Members, when requiring, as a condition of approving the marketing of pharmaceutical or of agricultural chemical products which utilize new chemical entities, the submission of undisclosed test or other data, the origination of which involves

a considerable effort, shall protect such data against unfair commercial use. In addition, Members shall protect such data against disclosure, except where necessary to protect the public, or unless steps are taken to ensure that the data are protected against unfair commercial use.

5.5 Copyright, Database Rights and Know-How Associated with Publications, Computer Programs and Databases

Copyright arises in relation to: publications, CD ROMs, databases, on-line displays and in relation to software developed by researchers. Copyright laws are territorial, governing the protection of works created within the country. However, through international agreements, a particular country's laws will be respected outside its territory. Most countries are signatories to the WTO Agreement on Trade Related Aspects of IP Rights (TRIPs), which affirms the Berne Copyright Convention and adds some additional protection.

Most copyright laws provide protection for print works, such as books, conference proceedings, research reports and journals. Copyright protection is also available for research notes, provided that these are in a written form. Copyright protection is also available for films, photographs, sound recordings and CDs. Under the Berne Convention and TRIPs Agreement, computer programs are treated as if they were literary works. Finally, copyright protection is available for on-line materials and screen displays.

5.5.1 Publications

Copyright will exist in the textual material, photographs, graphic designs, diagrams, charts and in the compilation or arrangement of a publication. A research institute will publish: scientific books, including monographs, conference proceedings, manuals and field guides; discussion papers, proceedings of conferences, meetings and workshops, and technical bulletins; and scientific posters.

5.5.2 CD ROMs

A number of different copyright interests may arise in respect of material on a CD ROM. Copyright may arise with respect to text, artistic works (such as photographs, drawings, diagrams), musical works, sound recordings and films, and in relation to the compilation of material contained in the CD. CD ROMS may be produced by an institute as part of its training materials. For example, the Asynchronous Internet-based courses in Experimental Design and Data Analysis and in Agricultural English are available on CD ROM. A number of different copyright interests may arise in respect of material on a CD ROM. Copyright may arise with respect to text, artistic works (such as photographs, drawings, diagrams), musical works, sound recordings and films, and in relation to the compilation of material contained in the CD.

Where materials have not been generated at the institute the audit should ascertain whether permission or clearance has been obtained from the author or original source prior to publication and that the author or original source is acknowledged. When material appearing on CD ROM is generated at the institute the CD ROM should carry a copyright notification with respect to the compilation and the individual elements of the CD.

5.5.3 Video materials

Video materials may be produced for the purpose of training and are protectable as copyright. Thus video materials produced at the institute should acknowledge it as the source and carry a copyright notice. If desired, this could be accompanied by a notice authorizing reproduction or copying of the material provided the institute is acknowledged as the source. If videos are to be produced involving material generated outside the institute then procedures will have to be put in place to obtain copyright authorization and copyright indemnities.

5.5.4 Copyright databases and know-how

The various research projects undertaken or underwritten by an institute generate considerable bodies of data. Under current copyright law, raw data or information is not protectable as a copyright work. Legislation is being considered in a number of countries under which the arrangement of databases, and possibly that raw data itself, may become the subject of sui generis, or special, IP protection. However, while raw data contained in databases is not capable of attracting copyright protection, the way in which information is expressed may be capable of attracting copyright. For example, a passage of text or a diagram or chart contained in a database may be protected by copyright. It is also possible that in certain circumstances, where sufficient originality or creativity in the arrangement of data is present, the database as a whole may be protected by copyright on the basis that it is a compilation. The fact that individual components of the database may be protected by copyright raises the issues of the assertion of copyright ownership in those components and of the need for mechanisms and procedures to ensure that the database does not contain material which infringes the copyright of others. These problems are of particular concern where the creation of a database is collaborative. This is because, first, where copyright exists in individual entries it may be unclear whether the copyright belongs to one collaborator or to all the collaborators jointly. Secondly, where material is being contributed from diverse sources each collaborator may become liable as an infringer where one collaborator inserts material which infringes the copyright of a third party.

5.5.6 On-line materials

The copyright principles which apply to print works and CD ROMs apply with equal force to on-line materials. Thus an institute would have to secure permission and indemnities in relation to the use of copyright material which it displays on its website. A matter which has arisen in recent copyright cases concerns IP approval for hypertext links to other World Wide Web sites. The institute home page may make available a large number of linked Internet resources. It should be ensured that the proprietors of those on-line resources have no objections to those linkages.

Mirroring occurs when a site is duplicated on another server. Framing occurs when one website imports material from another site and makes it part of its own site. Where such framing or mirroring occurs, it is essential that copyright clearances and indemnities are obtained.

5.5.7 Computer programs

Copyright subsists in both source and object codes of computer programs. Where commercially available programs are used or are incorporated in larger programs developed by the institute, licences are available from the suppliers of those programs. It should be noted that a licence to use commercially available software will not necessarily authorize the development or improvement of that software. The development or improvement of commercially available software for the purposes of, for example, facilitating or improving the accessibility of information stored on a database will infringe the copyright in such a program unless a licence to develop the program has been obtained. Where programs are written in-house by institute employees, copyright problems do not arise.

In order to provide evidence that computer programs have been generated in-house, it is recommended that when institute personnel generate such material they complete a Declaration of Originality. It is suggested that this Declaration be made in electronic form in order to facilitate and centralize collection and storage.

5.5.8 Trade marks

It will not be uncommon for a research institute to seek trade mark protection for its name and key research products. Thus the acronym and name of a research institute could be registered in Class 16 of the Nice trade mark classification in relation to 'research and educational materials'. Registrations can be obtained in each country in which research is undertaken.

Where an institute produces products such as seeds, in the case of an agricultural institute this could be registered in Class 30, in relation to '[plant] variety/breeding lines'.

Trade marks can also be sought for equipment and tools, for example in Class 7, covering agricultural equipment.

5.5.9 Confidential information

Research data compiled in institute projects by institute researchers may be protectable as confidential information. To be protected, the institute has to impose the cloak of confidentiality. This is achieved through confidentiality agreements with employees and researchers which will inform them that the institute attaches the quality of confidence to its research data and to its research methods. For the most part, a public research institute will waive its rights to the confidential information which it generates in its research findings. However, in those agreements where the institute undertakes to share unpublished research findings and data with its collaborators, some enforcement of confidentiality agreements will be necessary to ensure that the research findings can be shared and not dissipated. As awareness of IP protocols becomes more widespread, research collaborators will begin to insist upon an enforceable confidentiality regime. This means that it will be important to put in place mechanisms and procedures which ensure that confidential material is not publicly disclosed.

5.5.10 Biodiversity rights

The Convention on Biological Diversity (CBD) seeks to establish an international programme for the conservation and utilization of the world's biological resources and for the 'fair and equitable sharing' of the benefits arising from the utilization of genetic resources. A similar policy animates the International Treaty on Plant Genetic Resources for Food and Agriculture. For example, the CBD contains provisions dealing with access to genetic resources. Article 15 requires contracting parties to 'endeavour to create conditions to facilitate access to genetic resources for environmentally sound purposes' by other contracting parties on mutually agreed terms and conditions on the basis of 'prior informed consent'. A detailed code of access to biotechnology is prescribed in Article 16. Access and transfer are stated to be 'provided on terms which recognize and are consistent with the adequate and effective protection of IP rights'. The Article provides that developing countries which provide genetic resources shall be granted 'access to and transfer of technology which makes use of those resources'. Article 19.2 provides for the grant of access on a fair and equitable basis, and on mutually agreed terms, to contracting parties, 'particularly developing countries', to the results and benefits arising from biotechnologies based upon genetic resources provided by those contracting parties. Additionally, Article 8(j) of the CBD envisages that where the knowledge, innovations and practices of indigenous and local communities are utilized, there should be an equitable sharing of benefits arising from the utilization of such knowledge, innovations and practices.

A number of developing countries have introduced legislation which seeks to give effect to the benefit-sharing provisions of the CBD. Thus where a

patentable invention results from institute germplasm, contributed by indigenous persons or local communities, or collected as a result of the utilization of
the knowledge of those persons or communities, a liability for compensation
may arise. Indigenous groups and local communities have begun to insist upon
the collection of samples under the terms of bioprospecting agreements, which
invariably define the distribution of benefits from any royalties which may
result from patents. In a number of developing countries, the entry into
bioprospecting agreements is becoming mandatory.

6.   THIRD-PARTY IP

6.1   Patents and Know-How Associated with Biological Technologies

Most research institutes will have third-party proprietary technology licences.
The basis of the proprietary claims made by most of the licensors will be the
confidentiality of the biological materials or know-how which is licensed.
Additionally there may be the licensing of patented gene sequences. The
following are the salient features of these licences:

- permissible use of the licensed material confined to scientific research;
- confidentiality of licensed material to be preserved;
- all information concerning improvements in the material, or inventions
  associated with the material to be reported to the licensor;
- research progress to be reported periodically;
- use of material only by identified institute scientists;
- advance copies of manuscripts of publications to be provided to licensor.

The various obligations imposed by these agreements with third parties
emphasize the importance of an IP management facility at a research institute.

6.2   Genetic Material

Medical and agricultural research increasingly utilizes genetic material which
is provided to an institute under a material transfer agreement (MTA) or under
a confidentiality agreement. The terms of that MTA may restrict the use which
is to be made of that material. For example, it may be on condition that IP
rights are not sought in relation to that material, or that it is not to be used for
commercial purposes. Sometimes the MTA will require that material derived
from that supplied should also be supplied under those conditions. In each of
these cases, the responsibility to observe those conditions will be imposed on
the institute and it will be the purpose of the audit to identify these obligations
and how they are being managed.

On occasion genetic material is made available on an informal basis by a scientist from a third party, acting without the authority of that third party. In this case, the unauthorized use could involve the research institute in liability. Consequently the audit should identify the terms of all accessions of third-party genetic material.

6.3 IP Rights Associated with Equipment Utilised by the Research Institute

A number of items of research equipment obtained from commercial suppliers may generate IP obligations. For example the *Bio-Rad Biolistic PDS-1000/He* apparatus is often supplied subject to an agreement that it be used 'for research purposes only'. The *Hybaid PCR Express Thermal Cycler* is also supplied subject to a licence 'to practise the PCR process for internal research and development'.

These licence obligations may imperil the development of any IP resulting from the use of this equipment.

7. IP MANAGEMENT

A critical feature of effective IP management by a research institute and one that underpins an IP audit is the existence of a research culture in which awareness of the IP is communicated to researchers. With the increasing significance of IP for scientific research, it would seem to be important to establish an IP coordination office or officer for an institute. This office would be responsible for coordinating both IP administration and procedures within the institute and would be responsible for external IP liaison. The coordination of IP procedures would include: securing the IP compliance of staff and visitors; ensuring the inclusion of IP provisions in relevant third-party agreements; ensuring the utilization of appropriate MTAs by the institute, both as a recipient and distributor of germplasm and biological tools; maintenance of a central repository of IP documents; maintenance of the institute's IP database; as well as general responsibility for IP consciousness raising. Externally, the IP coordinator would provide an IP dimension to negotiations with research collaborators, as well as liaising with the IP officials of other institutes. The IP coordination office would ensure that:

- staff and visitors sign and adhere to IP and confidentiality agreements;
- copyright permissions and indemnities are secured for various publications;
- copies of MTAs and other IP agreements are filed centrally and copies of those agreements provided to appropriate staff members;

- proper research records are made, maintained and filed;
- coordination of the MTA granting procedure;
- supervision of the IP provisions of other agreements;
- liaison and updating on IP matters with the institute's legal advisers.

Providing for a central point of expertise to manage intellectual property is one way to assist university research institutes to deal with the complexities of the legal protection of intellectual property rights and commercial arrangements needed for the acquisition and the exploitation of those rights. Additionally, some research may depend upon the acquisition of a third party's intellectual property rights. For example, a private company may wish to contribute a patented gene. This may be on the basis that it is exclusively for the use of the institute or on condition that any improvements or applications are jointly patented. This will also be more conveniently managed centrally. Given that the right to patent an invention can be lost through premature disclosure, it may be incumbent upon an agricultural research institute to institute a system for the management of the publication activities of its researchers.

The research institute may choose between a specially dedicated research liaison office (RLO) or an official within the institute with intellectual property responsibilities. The decision will usually be made on the basis of funds available to pay salaries and to house relevant staff. A critical factor will be the revenues which are expected to be generated from IPR by the research institute. Where the research institute is associated with a university, it will usually be able to avail itself of the services of a central university institution. Where a research institute is not able to avail itself of the facilities offered by an associated university or government body, it will probably be advised to deploy one of its officers to perform the intellectual property coordination function.

The RLO may decide not to exploit ownership of certain intellectual property, in which case the rights will be released to the innovator(s), usually subject to a non-exclusive licence to use the intellectual property for research in the research institute. In those cases where the RLO forms the view that the research institute should be involved in the exploitation of the intellectual property, it will work with the innovator(s) in market evaluation and in finding commercial collaborators to exploit their intellectual property. Each case differs, and an appropriate strategy must be devised in conjunction with the research staff involved. The RLO will be responsible for securing professional assistance under appropriate conditions of secrecy. The ultimate vehicle for commercialization may be the research institute, through the RLO, or through the institute's commercial arm. The RLO will ensure the coordination of commercialization activities and prevent conflicts of interest.

To enable the RLO to evaluate the commercial potential of inventions and discoveries, researchers should be obliged to divulge their research activities in an appropriate form. This form will capture all preliminary information required for initial evaluation. Initial evaluation will involve assessing the invention's patentability (or other intellectual property protection) and commercial potential and fulfilling any obligations to research sponsors. For example, companies supporting specific research projects may have under the relevant research agreement the first right to negotiate licences for any inventions resulting from that research. Non-profit research sponsors may also have certain rights under previously negotiated research agreements. These rights and obligations must be fully defined and resolved before the invention can be made available for licensing.

Due to the high cost of prosecuting and then maintaining patents the RLO will usually have to delay filing of patent applications until strong commercial potential interest in technologies has been confirmed. In many cases initial filing is authorized only when companies commit to inventions through letter or option agreements. During the course of the patenting and licensing process multiple patent applications may be filed to maximize patent coverage for a given technology and cover developments made during the preparation period. Applications also may well be filed in foreign countries. Again, the commercial potential of the invention must be considered when making subsequent decisions to file or maintain patents.

Where commercialization of intellectual property rights is decided upon, the RLO will approach the most appropriate firms from a list prepared in conjunction with the innovators. The RLO will prepare executive summaries of inventions and submits these to relevant publications and databases. Marketing packages can be targeted at potential licensees identified through discussions with inventors and the use of various internal and external resource lists. The RLO will negotiate agreements in conjunction with the innovators, to ensure conformity with the role and mission of the research institute.

Once potential licensees have been identified negotiations proceed in a variety of ways. Short-term letter agreements may be used to confirm company interest in technologies and establish their commitment to pay patent costs during an evaluation and negotiation period. Option agreements define each of the two parties' rights and responsibilities and grant licensees the right to utilize the institute's intellectual property.

Depending on the nature of individual technologies and the estimated resources necessary for development and commercialization, the research institute may grant licensees exclusive rights, rights exclusive for a particular field of use, or non-exclusive rights. For example, most inventions in the health care field require very large investments of time and resources to develop and commercialize. Companies will often only make the necessary investment within the context of an exclusive licence agreement. In contrast, plant varieties will have already been tested and are ready for commercialization; thus they are licensed (typically) non-exclusively to multiple companies.

8.   CONCLUDING REMARKS

The principal objective of the intellectual property management policy of a research institute is to further the research mission of the institution. This is achieved by creating a fruitful climate for innovation and invention and facilitating the establishment of strategic linkages with researchers in other research institutes and with the private sector. The management of an institute's intellectual property resources may be through a specially established research liaison office (RLO) or by utilizing the intellectual property services which may be offered by an equivalent office within an associated institution, such as a university. Through its RLO a better understanding of the rights which the law gives for the protection of creative effort will be communicated to researchers and funding will be secured through collaborative research and development agreements. The RLO will be responsible for protecting and maintaining the intellectual property assets of the research institute and assist in developing an awareness and appreciation of the use of patent documents and registered plant variety data as research resources.

   An IP audit should also analyse the management of IP at a research institute from the perspective of the adequacy of management structures and procedures and in terms of the awareness of the IP obligations of staff and of the institutional mechanisms for dealing with institute and third-party IP.

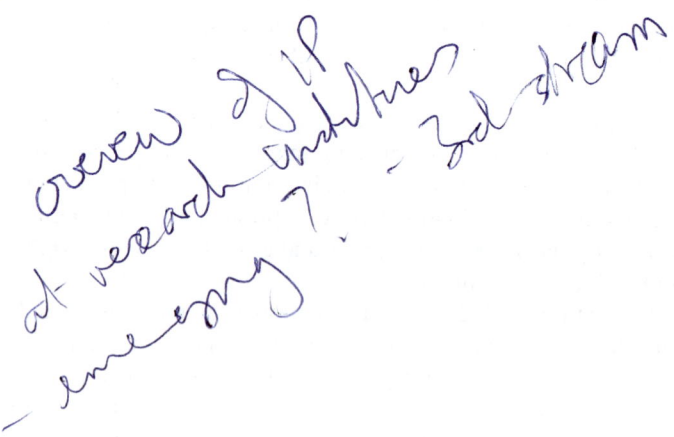

3. Some initial thoughts on copyright, human rights and market freedom

Uma Suthersanen

INTRODUCTION

The current nature of copyright law is often accepted as being the necessary and efficient response to the need of authors and publishers to appropriate the economic value of copyright works from users. Digital technology has simultaneously expanded and curtailed access to and usage of informational products, such as scientific, educational and academic works. Moreover, in the late twentieth century, some far-reaching provisions were introduced into international copyright law which may prove to have irrevocably tipped the balance towards the rights owners and away from the general public interest.

There is now a growing realisation of the potential impact of current copyright law on educational and knowledge policies. Can countries, especially developing countries, take advantage of the flexibilities provided in existing international copyright treaties to establish strong and reliable exceptions for the research, educational and scientific usage of copyright material? Should countries develop a more positive rights approach so that educational and developmental needs can be met? Should we now turn to international human rights law which encourages member states to have public interest policies which allow users 'freely to participate in the cultural life of the community, to enjoy the arts and to share in scientific advancement and its benefits'? Will such a general international 'public interest' rule be of any assistance or is more needed? We can perhaps reconcile all these potentially conflicting policies when we consider these issues from the perspectives of the relevant local and global stakeholders.

1. RATIONALE FOR COPYRIGHT LAW

The legal and economic rationales for copyright law have been in formation for the last 350 years. Early writers, such as Locke, Kant, Mill and Hegel offered a bifurcated perspective of copyright rationales: property rights should be granted either on the principle of rewarding or incentivising labour or on the more deontological and humanist principle of a person's right to personality and dignity. In later years, the arguments were couched in Romantic rhetoric, with authors pursuing a more egotistical agenda and advocating authorial rights as being the natural and just result of either the author's persona or the author's labour. In the twentieth century, a twin focus began from the human rights perspective, and from the economic perspective. The fundamental freedoms included a right to be recognised and rewarded for moral and material interests resulting from any scientific, literary or artistic production.[1] Copyright was also justified in economic terms – either in terms of welfare economics (Arrow) or neo-Schumpeterian economics.[2]

The result of this continuous stream of justifications has been to strengthen the proprietary component within copyright law over the public interest component. This strengthening, in turn, produces a steady proliferation of legal instruments which allow the author of a work (or the owner, in reality) to control exploitation of and access to the work. This chapter accepts that there are numerous individual principles within copyright law which deserve continued, if not greater, support and promotion, such as moral rights for authors.[3] Justificatory rhetoric defending copyright employs exciting if

---

[1]   This culminated, during the post WWII and Cold War eras, in copyright being embraced internationally by human rights rhetoric in the Universal Declaration of Human Rights and the 1966 International Covenants. For a discussion on human rights within international copyright law, see Uma Suthersanen, 'Towards an International Public Interest Rule? Human Rights and International Copyright Law', in *Copyright and Free Speech,* J. Griffiths and U. Suthersanen (eds), Oxford: Oxford University Press, 2005, chapter 5.

[2]   For a discussion on innovation, economics and intellectual property rights, see Graham Dutfield and Uma Suthersanen, 'The Innovation Dilemma: Intellectual Property and the Historical Legacy of Cumulative Creativity', [2004] 4 *Intellectual Property Quarterly* 379, at 381–3.

[3]   Article 6*bis*, Berne Convention (Paris revision, 1971), and Article 27(2), Universal Declaration of Human Rights (UDHR). For example, under international copyright and human rights laws, all authors, irrespective of the type of work created and irrespective of their labour status (i.e. whether they are employees or commissioned authors), should enjoy the basic fundamental human and moral rights of attribution and integrity. There are no easily acceptable reasons as to why moral rights should be denied to literary and artistic authors of traditional works; yet, countries such as the United Kingdom and the United States, which traditionally promote strong copyright laws, adopt a very conservative and lukewarm approach to moral rights. This approach manifests itself clearly in the World Trade Organization-administered Agreement on Trade-Related Aspects of Intellectual Property Rights (TRIPS) Agreement where the moral rights provisions are expressly not adopted for the benefit of authors, despite the fact that all other major provisions of the Berne Convention have been incorporated.

somewhat unilluminating terms such as 'natural rights', 'reward', 'unfair competition', 'incentives', 'human rights', 'public goods', 'theft' and 'allocation of resources'. The various justifications are not discrete but rather form one continuous and overlapping line of defence against the non-believers. Thus one can say that copyright is a means for authors to claim their 'natural right' to a 'reward' for their creative efforts, whilst simultaneously acting as a deterrent against 'theft' of the author's 'fundamental right' to enjoyment of his 'property'.

We can, nevertheless, categorise the copyright justifications into three broad balancing equations:

- the balance between property as capital reward and the public domain;
- the balance between property and ethics (for example, public education and public computing projects);
- the balance between property, market and fair competition (against societal, scientific and technological development).

It is clearly accepted within the international copyright laws that copyright is not an absolute right. There are intrinsic measures within copyright law which ensure the preservation of all these balances between rights holders and societal usage of copyright works; in addition, there are extrinsic measures within competition law and constitutional law which guard the balance between property and society.

2. INTRINSIC LIMITATIONS WITHIN INTERNATIONAL COPYRIGHT LAW

Intrinsic tools subsist within intellectual property laws and within copyright law, such tools including the following:

- the idea-expression rule;
- the threshold of originality;
- general statutory defences such as fair dealing, private use and fair use;
- specific statutory defences for educational, archival and library usage; and
- the Berne Appendix 1971 (which is now part of the TRIPS Agreement), which specifically allows compulsory licensing in relation to mass reproduction and translation of works for educational purposes.

2.1 Berne Convention and the TRIPS Agreement

The international copyright norms under the Berne Convention and the TRIPS

Agreement have developed in a lopsided fashion, with economic rights being broadened and extended consistently over the last 120 years and at an unaccountably accelerated pace. However, we have not seen a commensurate growth of limitations or exceptions in international copyright law. Indeed, the ones we still have are being eroded with the 'digital agenda'.

Historically, the rationale has been that it would be impossible to rationalise and harmonise the disparate set of exceptions existing within the different member states. For example, the 'fair use' defence under United States copyright law differs markedly from the 'fair dealing' defence under the United Kingdom copyright law. The historical reason is that exceptions and limitations were viewed reflecting national concerns and priorities. Thus, as Okediji states, 'minimum rights were developed internationally through consensus, while specific exceptions and limitations remained the domain of the State'.[4] Ricketson, in respect of the Berne Convention, remarks that as the Berne Convention matured, 'it came to reflect and incorporate limitations and exceptions that had evolved over time in a large number of states'.[5]

How often are these exceptions and limitations employed within negotiations and national laws, and how broadly are they interpreted by national legislators, courts and users? Take, for example, the Berne Appendix. How many countries have actually taken advantage of the Berne Convention Appendix provisions? The general consensus is that very few countries use the provisions, and yet the Berne Appendix 1971 is probably the only generally accepted bulk access tool in international copyright law. This is an increasingly urgent question in light of the further obligations that have been placed on users under the World Intellectual Property Organisation (WIPO) Treaties 1996.

2.2   The 'Digital Agenda' and the WIPO Treaties 1996

During the last decade of the twentieth century, copyright holders and managers argued that the international copyright laws had to be revised to accommodate new technologies and to incorporate a 'digital agenda'. Although some of the so-called digital problems were resolved within the 1994 TRIPS (for example, computer programs and databases), nothing was

---

    4   Ruth Okediji, 'The International Copyright System: Limitations, Exceptions and Public Interest Considerations for Developing Countries in the Digital Environment', ICTSD Working paper, available at http://www.iprsonline.org/unctadictsd/docs/Okediji_Copyright_2005.pdf.
    5   Sam Ricketson, *The Berne Convention for the Protection of Literary and Artistic Works: 1886–1986* (Centre for Commercial Law Studies, Queen Mary, University of London/Kluwer, 1987).

said within the TRIPS Agreement in relation to satellite broadcasting or Internet communications or the like. The possibility of introducing new international copyright norms to deal with the digital problems were discussed within the WIPO committees, and the result was the two WIPO 'Internet' treaties which serve to provide an additional layer of protection for copyright rights holders. The WIPO Treaties have been implemented in the United States and in the European Union, and it is interesting to note that the United States and the European Union versions of the implementation are vastly different. This in itself is a clear indicator that the WIPO Treaties provide much flexibility in interpretation and implementation, and that developing countries should exploit this flexibility.[6]

Can countries, especially developing countries, take advantage of the wide flexibilities provided in the WIPO Treaties by establishing strong exceptions for the research, education and scientific usage of copyright material?

3. THE NEW COPYRIGHT LANDSCAPE V GLOBAL EDUCATIONAL NEEDS

The concern, especially from developing countries, is that the digital agenda has mapped a new copyright landscape. The query is whether this is a *de facto* rather than a *de jure* landscape. Is this landscape a consequence of consensual mapping, done with the knowledge of all interested stakeholders, or is the digital agenda setting down new norms which were never really envisaged?

The following issues are of particular concern, especially in relation to educational needs of individuals and countries.

3.1 Controlling Access and the Progress of Technology

The WIPO Treaties introduce new rights for authors to protect their technological protection measures (TPMs)[7] and to prevent any modification of rights management information contained in works.[8] These new provisions on TPMs allow copyright owners to limit reproduction or communication of a locked copyright work; it can, sometimes, extend further and stop third parties accessing works which have been digitally locked up (either by encoding, scrambling, encryption or other tools). Is this a new 'right of access'? Copyright has

---

[6] United States Digital Millennium Copyright Act (DMCA), EU Directive 2001/29/EC (protection for anti-circumvention technologies and rights management technologies).

[7] Article 11, WIPO Copyright Treaty (WCT).

[8] Article 12, WCT.

traditionally been concerned with acts of copying and misappropriation, and rights of access are not part of this tradition. Moreover, can this new right be abused to digitally lock up non-copyright works, especially compilations or databases of public domain materials? A second and related concern is that TPMs can be employed to stop the progress of technology by allowing rights holders to sue manufacturers and suppliers of decryption and decoding hardware and software tools. Are there adequate checks and balances to ensure that encryption and other related technological research and study are not stifled?

3.2   Overriding Copyright Limitations

A particular concern associated with the new provision on technological protection measures (TPMs) is that, if unchecked, they may overprotect works by being employed to work against other copyright principles such as the private copying, fair use or fair dealing defences. Thus, TPMs may not only prevent copying or downloading of copyright works, but they can also prevent access to works which are excepted under general copyright principles. For example, the TPMs provision, as implemented in some countries, exposes a lawful purchaser of a digital product to both civil and criminal sanctions if such a lawful purchaser circumvents a technological lock to access forbidden material on the digital product: is this right if the product comprises the following types of material or data:

- the product comprises wholly or substantially pure data or ideas;
- the product comprises materials which are not subject to copyright protection under certain jurisdictions such as laws, government reports and court judgments (specific exceptions which are allowed under the Berne Convention and the TRIPS Agreement);
- the product comprises materials which have fallen out of copyright protection;
- the product comprises educational or historical documents which may be used in normal circumstances under a fair use or fair dealing or educational or a public interest defence?

We can take the scenario one step further. The TPMs provision, as implemented in some countries, can also be used to prevent a lawful purchaser from copying any part of the digital product even where the lawful purchaser of the physical product wishes to copy insubstantial parts of the work (which is a non-infringing act under copyright law) or where the user has a valid defence for copying parts of the work (for example, educational or library or archival usage).

Finally, the TPMs can be used by rights holders to allow a lawful purchaser of the digital product to access (and maybe to copy) the product, but limits the number of times this may be done. There are a variety of permutations which allow the rights holders to wield the TPMs as a Damocles' sword over traditional copyright principles. The question then is: should we be allowing provisions on TPMs to override traditional copyright defences? This relegation of copyright principles to the second division is already being accepted by courts in some jurisdictions.[9]

3.3   Is There a Digital South?

The TPM issue is but one concerning the continued access to and reliance on Internet and other digital resources. It is also undeniable that users, in both developed and developing countries, perceive a new age of information goods, which has little or no relationship with the previous world of copyright and access in relation to analogue materials.

It has been argued that the digital agenda, and its attendant problems, are concerns for the North or developed countries, as developing countries are more concerned with pricing of software and books, and mass reprography. It may be that developing countries are still at the analogue stage, demanding physical copies of educational goods, and tape and video reproductions of entertainment goods. However, such usage may be increasingly defunct. Digital usage has certainly increased, as has Internet usage. One study reveals that the majority of users in the world originate from North America, Asia and the European Union regions, with little increase in the number of users in Africa due to the lack of telecommunications infrastructure in this region.[10]

---

[9]   The Court of Rotterdam has ruled that it is unlawful to offer for sale DVD-copying software capable of making copies of DVDs that contain an anti-copying device. The case clarifies that under Dutch law the right to make private copies for personal use is outweighed by the prohibition against circumventing technological protection measures (TPMs). The software circumvented the anti-copying device contained on the DVDs, and thus, the sale of the software was held contrary to the recently introduced Article 29A of the Dutch Copyright Act, based on Article 6 of the EU InfoSoc Copyright Harmonisation Directive, which in turn is based on Article 11, WIPO Copyright Treaty 1996.

[10]   A May 2002 report stated that the countries with the highest level of Internet penetration were located primarily on the European continent: Sweden (64.6%), Denmark (60.3%), Netherlands (58.07%), United Kingdom (56.88%) and Norway (54.4%); in the Asian region: Hong Kong (59.58%); and in North America: United States (59.22%) and Canada (52.79%). See Nua Internet Surveys, at http://www.nua.com/surveys. Moreover, in Africa, if the more developed South African and North African markets are excluded, the average user figure in 2002 was one in 250 African Internet users as opposed to one in two North American/European Internet users.

Other cost-benefit analyses may show differing results. Putting aside the Internet revolution, there is definitely a high global demand for affordable hardware and software in all countries, which in turn is linked to a demand for digital educational goods.

The increased availability and attraction of digital works, as well as public domains and public commons projects and organisations such as Open Source, IP Justice, the Electronic Frontier Foundation, the Global Internet Liberation Campaign, the Digital Divide Network, the Digital Libraries project by Google and Microsoft, the Adelphi Charter, the BBC Creative Archive, and Creative Commons licence project, have merely highlighted the growing public interest need for a review of the balance which copyright law has hitherto attempted to achieve *vis-à-vis* access and learning.

Simply put, as access to the Internet becomes more globalised, concerns about access and fair use have grown. For developing countries with heavy reliance on foreign materials, the new international copyright law arena appears hostile in relation to attempts to harness resources at zero or little cost. This in turn is viewed as being a threat to the educational and developmental needs (and rights) of citizens of such countries.

3.4   Developing Countries and their Educational Needs

The public education systems in many developing countries are dependent upon foreign publications. The pricing of books, journals and on-line databases is an important consideration. This is especially true of academic and educational works, as opposed to fictional or populist works. Educational and research materials cover a much wider range of goods such as electronic databases comprising digital journals and teaching and research software. The cost of academic journals, for instance, is not only an issue in developing countries but also in developed countries with established publishing industries like the UK.[11]

One reason for concern is that the market for academic journals, especially in certain areas like medicine and science, is controlled by a very few publishers, who use their copyright and database right to extract high rents. Economists have always argued that intellectual property protection should be

---

[11]   *Universities UK (formerly Committee of Vice-Chancellors and Principals of the Universities of the United Kingdom) v Copyright Licensing Agency Limited, and Design and Artists Copyright Society Ltd,* Copyright Tribunal Case Nos CT 71/00, 72/00, 73/00, 74/00, and 75/01, unreported. The decision can be accessed at http://www.patent.gov.uk/copy/tribunal/triabissued.htm; and U. Suthersanen, 'Copyright and Educational Policies: A Stakeholder Analysis' (2003) 23(4), *Oxford Journal of Legal Studies* 585–609.

limited in such circumstances where the rights holder gains an excessive control over a specific product market or where the consumer is left with no alternative competing substitute product.[12]

Thus, it is all too probable that consumers can get locked into certain suppliers due to the unavailability of affordable informational resources. This is problematic for public schools and universities which cannot afford imported copyright-protected texts. The problem is further exacerbated by the fact that many developed countries refuse to accept international exhaustion principles. These principles were accepted in Australia and New Zealand due to the heavy costs of importation of foreign books, and the fact that copyright law was being used to prevent competitive importation and sale of legitimate books.[13] Such educational users may have no alternative but to allow the copying of texts by students, schools and colleges without payment or authorisation. This creates a difficult dilemma for developing countries: should they clamp down on copyright infringers but allow textbook prices to be prohibitively high for schools, most students and higher education institutions? Or should they allow mass copying but risk being placed on the US Watch List or being threatened with trade sanctions by copyright exporter countries?[14]

3.5 What's Wrong with the Educational Exceptions under Copyright Law?

3.5.1 Berne Convention Appendix

The 1971 Paris Act of the Berne Convention contains an Appendix (part of the TRIPS Agreement) which allows compulsory licensing in relation to mass reproduction and translation of works for educational purposes. Specifically, the Appendix provides that, subject to compensation to the copyright owner, there is a possibility of granting non-exclusive and non-transferable compulsory licensing in respect of (i) translation for the purpose of teaching, scholarship or

---

[12]   Thus, if one publishing house manages to capture and control a disproportionately large number of journal titles in several disciplines, an increase in the subscription price will not necessarily cause the user to switch to another publisher unless there is a meaningful substitute. The more extreme scenario arises where the publishing house in question is the sole source of certain types of information, for example, industry statistics or case reports which are used in 'official' citations. For example, some law reviews in the UK, and several courts in the US require citations to specific publishers' reports of court decisions. See especially *Matthew Bender & Co. v West Publishing Co.*, 158 F.3d 693 (2nd Cir. 1998).

[13]   Kerrin Vautier, 'The Economics of Parallel Imports', in *Industrial Property in the Bio-medical Age*, C. Heath and A. Kamperman Sanders (eds), Kluwer Law International, 2003, pp. 185–218.

[14]   Policy paper.

research, and (ii) reproduction for use in connection with systematic instructional activities of works protected under the Convention.[15]

A main complaint is that the Annex's provisions are complicated and have been very rarely employed.[16] Only eight or nine developing countries have adopted one or both options.

3.5.2   Berne Convention Article 10(2)

One may also argue that Article 10(2), Berne Convention (which is incorporated into the TRIPS Agreement), also provides authorisation to developing countries to permit reproductions for educational purposes as the provision stipulates that:

> It shall be a matter for legislation in the countries of the Union, and for special agreements existing or to be concluded between them, to permit the utilization, to the extent justified by the purpose, of literary or artistic works by way of illustration in publications, broadcasts or sound or visual recordings for teaching, provided such utilization is compatible with fair practice.

However, the wording within the provision is ambiguous. For example, is there a limit on the amount that may be copied from any given work? What do the words 'to the extent justified by the purpose' mean? It is arguable that there is no necessity to copy a whole work in order to convey the information required for the teaching purpose. On the other hand, the phrase does not preclude copying the whole of a work in appropriate circumstances. Ricketson suggests that Article 10(2) also permits the preparation for teaching purposes of compilations anthologising all or parts of a variety of works.[17] The term 'provided such utilization is compatible with fair practice' also suggests that one has to refer back to the three-step test.

3.5.3   Berne Convention/TRIPS Agreement 'three-step test'

It is also clear that Article 13, TRIPS (the three-step test) is a recognition of the fact that copyright is limited inherently by the public interest, and that exceptions and limitations must exist.[18] Can Article 13 allow for a more posi-

---

    [15]   World Intellectual Property Organization (1998), *Intellectual Property Reading Material*, Geneva, WIPO, pp. 260–1.

    [16]   C.M. Correa, *Intellectual Property Rights, the WTO and Developing Countries: The TRIPS Agreement and Policy Options*, London, New York and Penang: Zed Books and Third World Network, 2000.

    [17]   S. Ricketson, *The Berne Convention for the Protection of Literary and Artistic Works 1886–1986*, Centre for Commercial Law Studies, Queen Mary, University of London/Kluwer, 1987, p. 499.

    [18]   Sam Ricketson, 'US Accession to the Berne Convention: An Outsider's Appreciation', (1993) 8 *Intellectual Property Journal* 87; R. Okediji, 'The International Copyright System'.

tive rights approach so that developing countries can implement clear exceptions which allow full access to educational and scientific information?

Countries should learn how to apply the broad principles within international copyright law in a manner which suits their own constitutional, development and socio-economic needs. It is not suggested that the whole of the TRIPS Agreement or the WIPO Treaties be interpreted employing this approach. Nevertheless, one can only discern the meaning of certain phrases, provisions and principles, such as the 'three-step test' by looking at these provisions contextually within specific factual and political circumstances, rather than in an abstract fashion by looking at the intention of the parties to the treaty.

The three-step test comprises a triptych of constraints on the limitations and exceptions to rights under national copyright laws. It was first applied to the exclusive right of reproduction under Article 9(2), Berne Convention in 1967. Since then, it has been transplanted and extended into the TRIPS Agreement, the WIPO Copyright Treaty, the WIPO Performances and Phonograms Treaty and the European Union Copyright Directive.[19] It has also become a feature in both the European Union and United States driven FTA programmes. The test may prove to be extremely important if any nations attempt to reduce the scope of copyright law, because unless the WTO decides that their modifications comply with the test, such states are likely to face trade sanctions. Nevertheless, there is very little guidance on how this provision should be interpreted.

The test basically states that countries can introduce any limitation or exception to the economic rights granted under Berne, TRIPS and the WIPO Treaties as long as the limitation/exception complies with three conditions: (1) it must be limited to certain special cases; (2) it must not conflict with the normal exploitation of the work; (3) it must not unreasonably prejudice the legitimate interests of the author. All three steps have to be satisfied cumulatively. The test covers only those economic rights covered by the international treaties (and the FTAs). It does not apply to optional rights such as the *droit de suite* or to non-TRIPS sanctioned moral rights.[20] Neither does the three-step test apply to extrinsic measures such as human rights or competition laws.

From the outset it is clear that it is difficult, if not impossible, to apply either the literal or the 'intention of the parties' approaches to this provision. What *do* phrases such as 'normal exploitation of the work' or 'unreasonable prejudice' actually mean? The definitive interpretation of the three-step test under Article 13, TRIPS is the European Union–United States performing

---

19 Article 9(2) Berne Convention; Article 13, TRIPS Agreement; Article 30, TRIPS Agreement; Article 10, WIPO Copyright Treaty.
20 Article 13, TRIPS Agreement, Article 10, WIPO Copyright Treaty.

rights case before a World Trade Organisation (WTO) dispute settlement.[21] The dispute involved US copyright exemptions allowing restaurants, bars and shops to play radio and TV broadcasts without paying licensing fees.[22] The Panel held the United States in breach of Article 13 TRIPS. One of the exceptions did not pass the test as the factual information presented to the Panel indicated that a substantial majority of United States eating and drinking establishments and close to half of retail establishments would have been covered by the exemption. In relation to the interpretation of the test, the Panel offered an extremely literal explanation of the terms within the test. For instance, the term 'special' was defined as connoting 'having an individual or limited application or purpose' according to the English Oxford Dictionary, hence, an exception or limitation should be limited in its field of application or exceptional in its scope.

Secondly, in relation to the term 'normal exploitation of the work', the Panel observed that an exception or limitation in domestic legislation would conflict with a 'normal exploitation' if uses that in principle are covered by that right but exempted under the exception or limitation enter into economic competition with the ways that right holders normally extract economic value from that right to the work (i.e. the copyright) and thereby deprive them of significant or tangible commercial gains. On the facts of the case, it is quite understandable why the Panel found as it did – the exception was targeted at three major classes of users, and in some cases, about 70% of these users were being exempted from paying a licence fee. Moreover, although the court did not state this, there was clearly no overwhelming public interest or policy reason why these groups of users would be exempted from payment (as opposed to other users of the same type of copyright works).

Nevertheless, what if there are broad public interest grounds, which are in tandem with the policy and objectives as set out under Articles 7 and 8, TRIPS Agreement? A more teleological approach would then ensure that where circumstances dictate, the public interest may require a broader approach to the three-step test. Moreover, it is arguable that the Panel decision can be looked on as being much broader as limitations or exceptions would only be deemed unacceptable if the use was in 'economic competition'. It is clear that a literal interpretation of the three-step test is narrow and has the power to exclude many limitations and exceptions. Some domestic courts are already looking at the three-step test as a means of testing traditional defences against the new digital landscape. It is argued here that domestic courts should avoid

---

[21]   Report on Section 110(5) of the United States Copyright Act, WT/DS160/R. For the decision, see http://www.wto.org/english/tratop_e/dispu_e/1234da.pdf.

[22]   United States Copyright Act s.110(5)(A) and (B).

this literal approach and adopt alternative interpretative methods. As a matter of principle, it cannot be right to concede that any limitation which allows competitive usage of the work falls foul of the three-step test. Copyright law, by allowing for exceptions or limitations, is based on the tenet that certain types of usage do not allow right holders to extract any economic value, let alone normal or significant or tangible values or gains.

Moreover, it should be noted that the discussion has focused on the TRIPS version of the three-step test. And the TRIPS Agreement does refer to the competing and complementary objects and purposes of the agreement under Articles 7 and 8. This is not so under the Berne Convention where it is very clear that the object and purpose of the Berne Convention are solely concerned with the protection of the rights of authors, without reference to other kinds of competing objects and purposes, such as education and research or the promotion of public access to information.[23]

An interesting discussion on this topic is to be found in Ricketson's study on the three-step test.[24] His view is that the second step cannot be interpreted from a solely economic perspective as this would mean 'very little, if any, work left for the third step' to perform. Moreover, he acknowledges that the great bulk of uses that fall within the three-step test could be, in a narrow and economic interpretation, regarded as being within the scope of the normal exploitation of a work. Ricketson argues that the three-step test, especially at the second stage, must consider 'non-economic normative' factors. Moreover, Ricketson argues that because such factors would render the three-step test 'open-ended and uncertain', a balance, involving value judgements, would have to be struck by national legislation between the rights holder's interest and the needs of society and culture. Not only does he advocate a strong public interest ethos when applying the three-step test, he also advocates a teleological (evolutionary) approach by concluding that the three-step test is dynamic and should not become a 'grandfathering' clause that confers an immunity for all time on an exception under national law. By the same token, it is possible that new kinds of exceptions may arise that will fit within the second condition. It is not only economic issues that are relevant to the assessment required by the second step. '"Normative" issues of a non-economic kind also are relevant;

---

[23] Article 1, Berne Convention.

[24] See S. Ricketson, *The Three-Step Test, Deemed Quantities, Libraries and Closed Exceptions – A Study of the Three-Step Test in Article 9(2) of the Berne Convention, Article 13 of the TRIPS Agreement and Article 10 of the WIPO Copyright Treaty, with Particular Respect to its Application to the Quantitative Test in Subsection 40(3) of the Fair Dealing Provisions, Library and Educational Copying, the Library Provisions Generally and Proposals for an Open Fair Dealing Exception*, Centre for Copyright Studies Ltd, 2002.

that is, it must be determined whether the use in question is one that the copyright owner should control, or whether there is some other countervailing interest that would justify this not being so. In light of the other exceptions allowed under the Convention, such an interest would need to be one of some wider public importance, rather than one pertaining to private interests.'[25]

3.5.4 National laws and education exceptions

National copyright law has always sought to strike a balance between the rights of the owners and the rights of users by allowing – within certain limits – unauthorised reproduction or communication of protected works. This is called private use (EU and other civil law jurisdictions) or fair use (US) or fair dealing (UK and other Commonwealth jurisdictions).

One solution for developing countries is to refuse to pay for any educational usage of copyright material by relying on the exceptions within national copyright laws. Section 107 of the US Copyright Act, for example, sets out the scope of the fair use exception:

> Notwithstanding the provisions of sections 106 and 106A, use by reproduction in copies or phonorecords or by any other means specified by that section, for purposes such as criticism, comment, news reporting, *teaching (including multiple copies for classroom use), scholarship, or research*, is not an infringement of copyright. (emphasis added)

It is clear that non-commercial use, especially by educational institutions, will be given much more latitude in making use of copyrighted materials than commercial use of the same materials.[26] But how much more? As discussed above, strengthened international copyright law means that the concept of fair use, as set out in the US copyright law, may have become more restricted. Under international copyright law, it may be argued that such a no-payment copyright policy in relation to educational works falls foul of the three-step test set out in Art. 13, TRIPS Agreement. All exceptions must comply with this test, and the foremost rule is that exceptions to copyright protection can only be granted in 'special circumstances'. Usage for educational purposes may be too widespread to count as a 'special circumstance'.

Secondly, the fair dealing or fair use defence is usually limited to the person actually engaged in study or research, and does not extend to the person or firm facilitating these activities for others. Thus, copy shops or university libraries with photocopying machines which enable such educational usage

---

25   S. Ricketson, 'U.S. Accession to the Berne Convention: An Outsider's Appreciation', (1993) 8 *Intellectual Property Journal* 87.

26   *Basic Books, Inc. v Kinko's Graphics Corp.* 758 F. Supp. 1522 (SDNY 1991).

cannot avail themselves of such defences.[27] The reservation of the defence for a private individual, however, does not take into account the commonplace and economically dictated practice of multiple copying within educational institutions and copy shops caused by the high ratio of students to library resources, and the widened selection of reading material today as opposed to 30 years ago.

3.6 Developing Countries' Experiences of Collective Management[28]

It is clear that public policy favours access to works for educational usage, and this is true in both developing and developed countries. In the latter countries, a balance has been reached by allowing complete reliance on the private use/fair dealing exceptions but only in conjunction with some sort of payment of a licensing fee. Works are freely available for educational copying but local collecting societies, representing authors and/or publishers, negotiate with user groups and collect a fee.

There are three types of fees:

- compulsory licence fee;
- voluntary collective licensing fee; and
- equipment levy.

Collecting societies or rights management organisations have become an essential practical and economic ingredient within the copyright regime. If educational usage is to be compensated for, the most common approach is for a collective agreement between the rights owners and the main users of the works, i.e. the relevant government authorities in charge of schools and universities. A blanket licence obliterates the need to determine whether the usage in question is inside or outside the fair use or fair dealing exceptions. For a user, it is more expedient to be directed to one entity which manages the rights in relation to a specific category of work, thus saving him incurring transactional costs in terms of search and negotiation in obtaining licences

---

[27]   Under US law, see *American Geophysical Union v Texaco, Inc.* 60 F.3d 913 (2nd Cir. 1995); for UK law, see *Sillitoe & ors v McGraw-Hill Book Co. (UK) Ltd* [1983] FSR 545 (Ch.D.); for Australia, see *University of New South Wales v Moorhouse & Anor* [1976] RPC 151 (High Court, A'lia).

[28]   This section is summarised from U. Suthersanen, 'Collectivism of Copyright: The Future of Rights Management in the European Union', in *Oxford Yearbook of Copyright and Media Law*, E. Barendt and A. Firth (eds), Oxford: Oxford University Press, 2000, pp. 15–42; and A. Story, *Study on Intellectual Property Rights, the Internet, and Copyright*, London: Commission on Intellectual Property Rights, 2002.

from different authors in respect of different works. Collective management and blanket licensing are the common means by which reprographic copying in the educational sector is controlled.

The burden of administration and proof, however, should be placed on rights owners rather than users. That there is a high transactional cost involved in collective management is clear from the evidence tendered by Denise Nicholson, Copyright Services Librarian at the University of the Witwatersrand in South Africa to the UK Commission on Intellectual Property Rights study. She highlighted the following problems which are likely to be experienced by other universities not only in the developing world, but also in the developed world:[29]

- getting copyright clearance imposes a heavy administrative burden;
- obtaining permission directly from publishers for works excluded from or not mandated to the collecting society is time-consuming, expensive (payable in foreign currency) and difficult;
- in respect of translation, in some developing countries many languages may be spoken, and permission normally has to be sought for all translations;
- public domain material such as government documents are not easily accessible and must often be reproduced from published versions of the documents which involves having to get copyright clearance and paying high copyright fees;
- obtaining permission to transfer print into other formats, for example onto CDs, websites, etc. creates problems as publishers are reluctant to give permission, or they charge exorbitant fees; medical lecturers, for example, wishing to use anatomical diagrams from websites or wanting to scan them into other formats, cannot do this without going through the whole process of getting permission, which is often not given or is levied with high copyright costs. In many instances, rural medical personnel do not have access to computers, etc. and their only source of information is programmes prepared and provided by medical institutions and academic teaching hospitals;
- using material from multimedia or online resources for educational and other programmes creates problems as users do not always know where to obtain permission as often no response is received or strict conditions are applied and high levies are charged for use of the material;

---

[29]   Quoted verbatim from Story's study for CIPR. See A. Story, *Study on Intellectual Property Rights, the Internet and Copyright*, London: Commission on Intellectual Property Rights, 2002.

- copyright fees for electronic databases are usually incorporated in the subscription fee; however, each database has its own contract and conditions as to what can and cannot be copied, which makes it difficult for users and library staff to know how to respond.

The above evidence testifies to the further problems which will ensue when the international community adopts *sui generis* protection of databases as has been the case within the EU. Where publishers release digital versions of journals as part of a larger database, the user may have to contend with the database right which is independent of copyright, which will inevitably reside with the publisher, and for which the author will not necessarily have an implied licence with which to use the work.[30] The alternative licensing programme is the Continental European levy system where a 'tax' is placed on all copying machines (including scanners) and accessories (such as blank tapes, paper and diskettes). This is the system in place in most European countries. This would have the effect of directly targeting, and taxing, the manufacturers of such devices as opposed to placing the whole burden of usage of materials on educational users.

3.7 Technological Devices and Challenges

Information technology provides both opportunities and threats for the copyright industries that include the publishing industry, the main supplier of educational content. It sometimes appears, though, that these industries would prefer to emphasise the threats when lobbying governments to reform the law to accommodate technological changes. It has been argued that technological developments make it difficult for both authors and publishers to control the dissemination and use of works, and to enforce their exclusive rights. Technological developments, however, enable the digitisation of copyright works and now facilitate access to many works which hitherto may have been denied to many consumers. Technology can be further employed to assist rights owners in tracking their works, in collecting and distributing monies payable to authors, and in allowing enhancements to the educational sector such as easier clearance for the use of both paper and electronic material; bibliographic material on journals which will include not only ISBN numbers, names of publishers but also the names of the authors of individual articles; on-line sale of extracts or individual chapters of books, or journal articles rather than whole books or whole series of titles; offer a site licence for certain

---

[30] Directive 96/9/EC of the European Parliament and of the Council of 11 March 1996 on the legal protection of databases.

books or chapters to be placed on-line on closed or locked university websites.[31]

4.   THE RIGHT TO KNOWLEDGE

The scope of copyright protection is also limited by other types of laws such as human rights, competition and constitutional laws. These laws emulate the role of limitations and exceptions within intellectual property law by ensuring the balance between property and society.

For example, Article 27(1), Universal Declaration on Human Rights states that all citizens should have a right 'to participate in the cultural life of the community, to enjoy the arts and to share in scientific advancement and its benefits'. The issue then is whether we can write this fundamental right into copyright law and thereby enable users to participate, enjoy and share in the arts and sciences.[32] This has occurred, to a certain extent, in relation to Articles 7, 8 and 40 of the TRIPS Agreement. These three provisions set out general principles and objectives of international intellectual property law, but they also recognise that intellectual property rights must be balanced against several other societal and economic interests, including the promotion of innovation, the protection of public health and the promotion of public interest.[33] Copyright is recognised as being part of the human rights regime in several international instruments,[34] including the Universal Declaration of Human Rights (UDHR).[35] Article 27(2) UDHR prescribes rights for 'moral and material interests resulting from any scientific, literary or artistic production'.

Can we argue that there cannot be a true and proper scope of copyright

---

31   T. Koskinen-Olsson and D. Gervais, 'Electronic Commerce and Copyright: A Key Role for WIPO', in *WIPO Advisory Committee on Management of Copyright and Related Rights in Global Information Networks*, Geneva: WIPO, 1999, Document No. ACMC/2/1.

32   This is very much like the American basis for copyright protection – see Article 1.8, US Constitution.

33   UNCTAD-ICTSD, *Resource Book on TRIPS and Development*, Cambridge University Press, chapters 6.6 and 6.7.

34   P. Drahos, 'The Universality of Intellectual Property Rights: Origins & Development', in *Intellectual Property and Human Rights*, Geneva: WIPO/OHCHR, 1998, 31.

35   UDHR, Article 27. Also see International Covenant on Economic, Social and Cultural Rights (ICESCR), Article 15; UNESCO Recommendation on the Status of Scientific Researchers 1974, Articles 35–7. The European Convention on Human Rights (ECHR), in contrast, has no equivalent provision in respect of intellectual property rights though courts have accepted that there is a muted basis for copyright in Article 1, 1st Protocol, ECHR, which promises peaceful enjoyment of 'possessions'.

unless the provisions rest largely on fundamental freedoms and rights? Both classical and modern rights theory states that the existence and exercise of some rights presupposes the existence of other rights. Rights of freedom, for example, should be accompanied by welfare rights, whereas the right to education aids the exercise of a right of freedom of speech. It has been further argued that the rights created through the enactment of intellectual property laws are instrumental rights, and such rights, including copyright, should serve the interests and needs that citizens identify through the language of human rights as being fundamental, for example access to health and access to education.

It may be that intellectual property rights could be pressed into service on behalf of human rights, and *vice versa*. This is, of course, converse to the current economic theory that market regulation dictates public interest being subordinate to private interest. But, in economic terms, the best climate for the production of knowledge goods is not only a market structure with legal protection but also a market structure which allows for the taking and borrowing of knowledge. The creation of intellectual property goods depends on fundamental human rights such as the freedom of expression, and the right to education.

Future intellectual property regimes and conventions could be revised to take into account the following concerns and needs:

- the current international and national copyright laws are not adequately addressing the needs of the education community;
- that the globalisation of intellectual property rights and the increasing width of copyright protection have caused concerns amongst the developing and poorer nations regarding access to knowledge resources and their educational needs;
- international copyright law should be interpreted and/or re-written to emphasise that copyright, as one fundamental human right, co-exists with other fundamental freedoms such as the right to access and share scientific and cultural benefits, and the right to freedom of expression.

The future for copyright reform should turn away from furthering the power of rights holders and turn towards furthering the complementarities of international copyright law and international human rights law. One means of achieving this nexus is to look at the area of development and intellectual property. This movement started in a small way with the WIPO Development Agenda, which was launched in 2004 and which propelled the WIPO to ensure that future intellectual property policy and laws took into account development policies. This, in part, is supported by the Millennium Development Goals which were agreed on in 2000 at the United Nations Millennium Summit. Of the eight goals, the one which is relevant in the area of education and copyright is the second goal which is to achieve universal primary education.

4. Changing mechanisms in copyright's ontology – Structure, reasoning and the fate of the public domain

Guido Westkamp

We must be systematic, but we should keep our systems open.
Alfred North Whitehead, *Modes of Thought*

1. INTRODUCTION

Prior to the advent of the information revolution and its perceived danger to the control over copyrighted works, copyright doctrine could rely on key terms shaping the exterior structure in the copyright infringement test. Such a test was firmly based on rather undiluted concepts of meaning with respect to the three segments that methodogically shaped copyright analysis: subsistence, infringement (by committing a restricted act) and (absence of) defences.

Today, the situation is different. Regional and international instruments, such as the Digital Millennium Copyright Act 2000 in the United States,[1] the WIPO Copyright Treaties 1996 and the EU directive on Copyright in the Information Society[2] expand the scope of copyright protection from a bundle of rights in the expression of a work towards an access and use right resembling industrial property rights. The changes will eventually command a novel evaluation based on a rigid categorical ontology. As will be shown, this elides the conventional test from an estimation allowing for a wide-ranging scrutiny of underlying principles into a test based on a few key terms. These changes impart an increasing role for ontology in copyright assessment. Ontologically, this appears as a step back from an analytical to a categorical ontology. As will be exposed, the crucial

---

[1]   The Digital Millennium Copyright Act 2000 (HR 2281), § 1201 (1) (A) provides that 'No person shall circumvent a technological measure that effectively controls access to a work protected under this title'.
[2]   Directive 29/2001/EC of the European Parliament and of the Council of 22 May 2001 on the Harmonisation of certain aspects of copyright and related rights in the information society. Official Journal L167, 22/06/2001 P. 0010–0019.

transformation lies in a shift from a customarily essential balancing-test evaluation, firmly rooted in copyright doctrine, towards an assessment based of a purely pragmatic approach and possibly repudiating the applicability, existence and importance of principles.

2. ONTOLOGY AND LEGAL REASONING

An assessment of these changes from an ontological perspective is useful. It can highlight that the supposed amendments to copyright law do more than simply complement existing rules to make them viable in a digital age. Ontology is the study of existence,[3] the theory of objects and their connections. The unfolding of ontology provides criteria for distinguishing various types of objects (concrete and abstract, existent and non-existent, real and ideal, independent and dependent) and their ties (relations, dependences and predication). As a method in law and legal interpretation, it is the key means in identifying meaning and connotation,[4] a technique to set apart meaning by devising legal categories enabling the unfolding and distinguishing of essential relations. As the study of existence the ontological method presupposes the existence of objects and categories.[5] The more abstract these terms are, the more emphasis is placed upon the detection of principles underlying black letter law rules. There exists a logical distinction between rules and principles. Rules exist according to an all or nothing principle. They are either valid – in which case the legal consequence will eventuate – or invalid, in which case they are useless.[6] Principles, on the contrary, may be identified only by moral contemplation.

The way in which ontology affects legal reasoning is reflected in the 'multi-layer approach',[7] the effect of which is to devise an ontology of struc-

---

[3]   David R. Koepsell, *The Ontology of Cyberspace – Law, Philosophy and the Future of Intellectual Property* (Chicago, 2000), p. 35; J. Dale, *Ontology (Central Problems of Philosophy)*, (Acumen Publishing, 2002), pp. 6 et seq.; Jean-Paul Sartre, *Being and Nothingness: A Phenomenological Essay on Ontology* (Washington Square, 1993); Herman Philipse, *Heidegger's Philosophy of Being* (Princeton, 1998); Gustav Bergmann, *New Foundations of Ontology* (Wisconsin, 1992); W.V. Quine, *Ontological Relativity* (Columbia, 1977); R. Gibson, Jr, *The Philosophy of W. V. Quine: An Expository Essay* (Florida, 1986).

[4]   Cf., for example, Armin Kaufmann, *Rechtsphilosophie*, 4th edn (Munich 1993), pp. 85, 90.

[5]   B. Smith, 'On Substances, Accidents and Universals: In Defence of a Constituent Ontology', http://wings.buffalo.edu/academic/department/philosophy/faculty/smith/articles/greensboro.html.

[6]   R. Dworkin, *The Model of Rules*, 35 (1967) *Univ. of Chicago Law Rev.* 14–46 (p. 26).

tures and interrelations between these layers.[8] The first layer, usually deemed to be the one bearing the absolute foundations of principle, is not present in the law itself. Its features are abstract and general principles, neither normative nor positive.[9] The second layer then includes the corpus of all legal norms, irrespective of their allocation to categories such as private or public. It does not comprise unchangeable principles as such yet sets forth those principles recognised as fundamental. The third layer finally constitutes the immediately applicable substantive law, the immediate substantive law as formulated by statute or precedent. The effect of this approach is that no rule can exist without principle, and that legal decisions cannot be reached by simple and exclusive deduction.[10] The effect is that an ontology of existence only ensues within the third stage.[11] Such a system has been described as dynamic.[12]

The distinction and function, the interplay of rules and principles, is highly perceptible in copyright law, dealing, in essence, with protection afforded to information.[13] The application of ontology in copyright law – and all other branches of Intellectual Property – creates many more problems than in real property, dealing with 'things' as ontologically accessible entities.[14] The application of ontological principles to copyright assessment is therefore potentially

---

[7] See F. Bydlinski, *Das bewegliche System im geltenden und kuenftigen Recht*, (Springer: Vienna, 1986) p. 36 (favouring the view of an open system of principles in legal interpretation). Some authors would take the view that a direct reference to principles can only be asserted in cases concerning no possible gaps in interpretation.

[8] Cf. A. Kaufmann, Gedanken zu einer ontologischen Grundlegung der juristischen Hermenuetik, Festschrift Coing, 1982, Vol. I, pp. 537 et seq. On the contrary view – ontology cannot exist in law as nothing precedes it but language – see N. Luhmann, *A Sociological Theory of Law (International Library of Sociology)*, (Routledge, 1985), pp. 45 ff. Expanding ontology from categories to relations reflects a development from Aristotelian approaches based on the things and categories to an analytical model. Cf. Walter Leszl, *Aristotle's Conception of Ontology* (Padova: Antenore, 1975).

[9] See W. Krawietz and K. Opalek (eds), *Sprache, Performanz und Ontologie des Rechts, Festgabe fuer Kazmierz Opalek* (Berlin, 1993).

[10] See Kaufmann, *Rechtsphilosophie*, p. 79; G. Radbruch, *Rechtsphilosophie*, R. Dreier (ed), 2nd edn (Heidelberg: Müller, 2003), p. 26.

[11] This reflects the idea that ontology in law is a three step test, including the stages of archaeology and direct ontology, see Koepsell, *The Ontology of Cyberspace*, p. 41.

[12] On the distinction between abstract and concrete terms see G.W.F. Hegel, *Legal Philosophy, Philosophy of Right* (Mineola, NY, 2005), §§ 41, 161, 164.

[13] In a wider sense, it is also trite that IP in general protects information. Ontology is, however, naturally easy for the question of subsistence of registered rights such as patents. See further Jean Nioclas Druey, *Information als Gegenstand des Rechts* (Zurich, 1997), p. 80.

[14] On attempts to define information see C.-F. von Weizsäcker, 'Sprache als Information', in Weizsäcker (ed.), *Die Einheit der Natur* (München, 1974), p. 51; M.

circular if it refers to the fact that it is deemed property. The key notions in both the UK copyright systems and civil law authors' right systems – such as the terms reproduction, public and, in particular, the notion of originality – are not easily definable as they entail a profound philosophical impact. If underlying principles are eradicated, the assessment necessarily leaves no scope for an ontological construction outside the ordinary meaning given by statute. For example, if a temporary or ephemeral copy is defined, a priori, as a reproduction in the legal sense,[15] a violation of property rights cannot be called into question.

3. MODERN COPYRIGHT EXPANSION

Copyright is dramatically changing in both substance and doctrine. The current changes are reflected in the discourse on whether copyright entails – or should entail – an access right. One effect will be an unrestricted control over communications and uses of the work in question, enriched by legal provisions favouring the protection of technological measures preventing access. In addition, the pressures, particularly in Europe, to approximate copyright laws have created norms echoing a lowest common denominator solution. The formulation of rights afforded to authors is expansive; yet a sound foundation and reflection of the underlying copyright philosophies is absent. Hence, any rule expanding exclusive rights will create different results, depending on whether it is applied in an author's right system, thus founded on principles aiming to protect the author's personality, or in copyright systems based on principles of investment and misappropriation of commercially exploitable values. This clash of standards appears to result in the most simplistic and all-embracing formulation of economic rights and standards.

The aim here is to take a look at these changes, primarily with respect to copyright theory, and to expose the structural mechanisms underlying it. These changes, in short, are designed to modify copyright from a restricted right in the expression of ideas and information in certain defined categories of works and

---

Heidegger, 'Der Weg zur Sprache', in Bayerische Akademie der Schönen Künste (ed.), *Die Sprache* (München, 1959); R. Capurro, 'Heidegger über Sprache und Information', in *Philosophisches Jahrbuch* 88 (1981) 32, pp. 333–43.

[15] See the approach taken by the EU Information Society Directive, Article 3 (1): 'Right of communication to the public of works and right of making available to the public other subject-matter

> 1. Member States shall provide authors with the exclusive right to authorise or prohibit any communication to the public of their works, by wire or wireless means, including the making available to the public of their works in such a way that members of the public may access them from a place and at a time individually chosen by them'.

an accompanying bundle of exclusive rights into a right to control or prevent access. Yet, an access right has never been used as a statutory term in copyright.[16] The methodology through which this shift is prompted is, rather, a subtle modification of meaning of key connotations embedded in the formulation of exclusive rights that, in turn, produces interpretative constraints on a more principled approach to copyright. The three main pillars are an expansion of the right to reproduce, now expressly incorporating the stance that even ephemeral copies are reproductions within the meaning of classic copyright doctrine as provided for by international instruments. Secondly, the inclusion of a new right to communicate to the public, including a right to make available works to the public at a time or place chosen by the user. And, thirdly, the introduction of protection for technological measures designed to protect copyrighted works.[17]

Recent instruments and legislative developments are heavily based upon ontological terms. Their starting point is to proclaim the proprietary nature of copyright and deduce, from there, the existence of an access right.[18] The pitfall is that the term 'property' in itself is not ontologically accessible but a creature of legal invention.[19] If an access right is advocated, this would a priori mean access not only to expression (in which property rights subsist) but also to infor-

---

[16]   See infra, pp. 102 ff., and Thomas Hoeren, 'Access Right as a Post-Modern Symbol of Copyright Deconstruction', ALAI Congress (New York, 2001). As an express legal term 'access' only appears in Article 3 (4) of the Conditional Access Directive; Mihaly Ficsor, 'Copyright for the Digital Era: The WIPO "Internet" Treaties', in *Columbia-VLA J.J. & The Arts* 21 (1997), 197; Pamuela Samuelson, 'The US Digital Agenda at WIPO', in: *Virginia Journal of International Art* 37 (1997), 369, 390 ff. Thomas Dreier, 'Copyright Digitized: Philosophical Impacts and Practical Implications for Information Exchange in Digital Networks', in WIPO Worldwide Symposium on the Future of Copyright and Neighbouring Rights, March 1993, 15 ff.; J. Ginsburg, 'Putting Cars on the "Information Superhighway"', in Bernt Hugenholtz (ed.), *The Future of Copyright in a Digital Environment* (The Hague, 1996), 189 ff.; J. Ginsburg, 'From Having Copies to Experiencing Works: The Development of an Access Right in U.S. Copyright Law', Columbia Law School Public Law & Legal Theory Working Paper Group, Paper No. 8, pp. 11–12 (2000), http//papers.ssrn.com/ paper.taf?abstract id=222493; J. Ginsburg, 'Copyright Legislation for the "Digital Millennium"', 23 [1999] *Col.-VLA J.L. & The Arts* 140, 146 .

[17]   See *Los Angeles Times v Free Republic*, Civ. No. 98-7840, 2000 US Dist Lexis 5669 (CD Cal. April 5, 2000), 67; *Universal City Studios, Inc. v Reimerdes*, 111 F Supp. 2d 346, 2000 US Dist Lexis 11949 (SDNY August 17, 2000).

[18]   Mihaly Ficsor, 'Copyright for the Digital Era: The WIPO "Internet" Treaties', in *Columbia-VLA J.J. & The Arts* 21 (1997), 197.

[19]   Even the theory of creating property by applying labour to mix goods cannot explain the scope of property but merely its existence. See John Locke, *Two Treatises of Government*, ed. Peter Laslett (Cambridge, 1988), § 27. ('. . . whenever we use our own effort to improve the natural world – the resulting products belong to us as well. Though the earth, and all inferior creatures, be common to all men, yet every man has a property

mation. The problem may perhaps be less rigorous with respect to identifiable categories (such as musical works)[20] but the distinction between information and expression becomes obstinate.

4. ONTOLOGY IN INTELLECTUAL PROPERTY AS ONTOLOGY OF RELATIONS

It can be ascertained that ontology in Intellectual Property is not merely one of categories but much more one of relations. 'Categorical' ontology in the Intellectual Property system rests on two chief elementary levels, mirroring the second and third layers reflecting the 'multilayer approach' in legal theory.

The immediate interpretational or statutory level, relates to the terminology within the statute and sets forth the key elements necessary to assess whether copyright infringement has occurred. The three stages can be identified as subsistence, exclusive right and (absence of) defences or limitations.[21] At each level, the analysis must distinguish the exact connotation of the language used in the statute. The second level, which may be deemed as underlying, consists of those features not recognisable initially from the text. This layer can be deemed the fundamental layer. It recognises the effects of copyright being restricted to only certain types of information. As will be seen, the effect of introducing a notion of a general use and access right at the stage of statutory interpretation is that courts will be significantly constrained in formulating methodical pathways to safeguard instances where traditional copyright assessment would have maintained the public domain – the novel ontology hidden in the terms 'use' and 'access' will foreclose arguments based on principle deriving from the second layer.

The process of correct ontological methodology in law is subject to a more complex discourse which cannot be presented here. Determining the correct approach is also known as the approach from first principles, that is to say developing and examining categories of legal objects (such as 'the work') with-

---

in his own person: this no body has any right to but himself. The labour of his body, and the work of his hands, we may say, are properly his. Whatsoever then he removes out of the state that nature hath provided, and left it in, he hath mixed his labour with, and joined to it something that is his own, and thereby makes it his property.')

20   A good example is the protection afforded to phonograms. Here, no further requirements exist apart from the fixation of sounds.

21   The view might as well be taken that only two systematic segments exist, as the intervention of statutorily defined limitations is strongly interwoven with the question of doing 'acts restricted by copyright'. There is an interesting hint to it in that this would involve the question as to whether defences can be contracted out by agreement or whether they reflect the basic right of receiving and imparting ideas and information.

out reference to existing legal categories.[22] This would include not merely the legal prerogatives associated with a particular term but also social, psychological and philosophical elements which shape its meaning.[23] This suggested approach adjudicated reflects a method which allows a commonsense distinction if and when these elements bear an identifiable meaning.[24]

In copyright law, ontology features in both the vertical process of identifying infringement and the process of identifying underlying principles. This process appears, in its systematic approach, very similar as between the copyright and authors' right systems.

However, one of the supposed pitfalls in the method of assessment is that the segments are not interrelated. Once the ingredients of one segment, i.e. subsistence, have been affirmed by the court, the question of infringement then is a simple test of identifying the violation of an exclusive right. In that sense, the statutory text does not require an assessment expressly based upon and designed to provide a balancing test between those features. From the wording of most copyright or authors' right statutes the impact of ontology remains, at best, diffuse.

The systematic, i.e. segmented, approach appears to be roughly equivalent as between copyright and authors' right systems. Any addition of the three main ingredients can eventually be added to the equation of copyright infringement. This, supposedly, incorporates two features which are quite striking. First, the segments are closed in themselves, that is to say the affirmation of copyright subsistence is not put under scrutiny when assessing infringement. Secondly, the impression such a segmented approach portrays is to propose the idea of a closed and absolute system of deductive reasoning. The conclusion reached within each singular segment (i.e. the finding that a work is protected by copyright) is disconnected from the ontological findings made in the previous segment. If X downloads a collation of sounds from a website and later uses these on his own website, the question as to subsistence denotes only whether the material is copyrighted. If it is, the question of infringement then turns on whether any of the restricted acts have been committed, and whether he can rely on any statutory limitation. In this case, violation of restricted acts may be both physical (storage in computer memory) and non-physical (rights as to public performance). Here, copyright assessment is self-referential. Whether it is a copyrightable work depends on whether it can ontologically be perceived as such. Whether an exclusive right has been violated, again, depends on whether the statutory elements within these segments alone can be interpreted as having

---

[22]   Cf. Koepsell, *The Ontology of Cyberspace*, pp. 34–5.
[23]   For instance, applied by Adolf Reinach, *The A Priori Foundation of the Civil Law*, Aletheia 3 (1983) 1–142, 83ff.
[24]   See, on law and ontology, ibid., pp. 91 ff.

been fulfilled. When added, this equates to copyright infringement. This, roughly, is the position taken with respect to modern copyright laws. At first glance, the only difference is a slight extension of particular aspects. In fact, as will be seen, the effect is a use right which negates the core underlying principles and forces copyright doctrine to incorporate perspectives from the second stage (i.e. the fundamental legal norms irrespective of its location in any legal discipline), most notably human rights issues and competition control aspects.

The premise that the copyright infringement case consists only of various unrelated layers is dangerous. It is close to denying the existence of underlying principles, best described as 'dichotomies' in Intellectual Property theory which can be accommodated as perhaps the second stage under the multilayer approach.[25]

The first such dichotomy is that between copyright and patents and other types of Industrial Property rights. The dichotomy is twofold. Copyright protects not against any use of the information, only against the taking of expression. In contrast, patent law is restricted to commercial uses.[26] This might be deemed to be the very foundation of the global Intellectual Property system as otherwise information itself would be protectable as such.

A subsequent dichotomy, now within the narrow ambit of copyright evaluation, is present in the idea/expression dichotomy,[27] seeking to exclude information and ideas, and to interleave an approximate demarcation line. The fact that such exclusionary methods exist is, again, closely interwoven with the first premise. Information needs to remain outside the scope of copyright protection as otherwise this would create impediments to the free flow of information and its legitimate use.[28]

Then, perhaps more noticeably in statutory rather than case law, copyright differentiates as between published and unpublished works.[29] This may well be perceived as a mere moral and exclusive right to prevent publication without any further significance for information exclusion. Yet, one of its underlying features is that the author has no further rights in the communication of the content after publication.[30] This implies that control over private communications cannot be

---

[25]　A good example is the extensive copyright protection afforded in *Whelan Associates v Jaslow Dental Lab. Inc.* [1987] FSR 1, 7; conversely, see *Computer Associates v Altai* [1927] USPQ 2d 1641; *John Richardson Computers v Flanders* [1993] FSR 497.

[26]　J. Reichman, 'Legal Hybrids between the Patent and Copyright Paradigms', [1994] 94 *Columbia Law Review* 2432.

[27]　Cf. A. Laddie, P. Prescott, and M. Vitoria, *The Modern law of Copyright and Designs* (3rd edn, London: Butterworths, 2003), pp. 31–3.

[28]　J. Litman, 'The Public Domain', [1990] 39 *Emory L.J.*, 965.

[29]　Cf. expressly the German Authors' Rights, Article 12 (2), providing that the author may control the first publication only.

exerted.[31] The fact that publication has occurred simultaneously denotes that the publication right, once exercised, evokes a public interest right in the communication of the information, ideas, schemes or principles contained or embodied in a work.

At the level of exclusive rights, a further dichotomy is present: published works may be the subject of any private communication. The common denominator for non-physical rights is that only the public performance according to certain acts implicitly defining commercial uses can be performed.[32] The reason is that otherwise not only the right to communicate information and ideas would be imperilled. The owner would also be enabled to exert control over communications as such. Hence, a one-to-one communication is *private*.[33] Interestingly, the patent/copyright dichotomy re-emerges. A monopoly in communication, albeit under commercial circumstances, is restricted to patent law.[34]

As to physical rights, the right to exercise control over reproduction is restricted to expression. Here, disparities between the systems are easily detectable. The question of copying poses perhaps the most intrinsic complexities when dealing with the proper scope of protection. Under the UK system, it refers to the taking of at least a substantial part[35] of a work.[36] Under authors' right systems, it means the taking of original expression, i.e. only parts which

---

[30]   W. van Canegem, 'Copyright, Communications and New Technologies' [1995] *Federal Law Review* 322.

[31]   Cf. *Jennings v Stephens* [1936] Ch. 469; *Performing Rights Society v Commonwealth Bank of Australia* [1992] IPR 157, 177; *Harms Ltd v Martans Club Ltd* [1927] 469, 473.

[32]   K. Garnett, G. Davies and G. Harbottle (eds), *Copinger and Skone James on Copyright*, 13th edn, 1999, No. 7-18.

[33]   Cf. *Canadian Admiral Corporation v Rediffusion Ltd* [1954] Ex. R. Can. 382. The judgment did not deal with the commercial impact here.

[34]   See, for example, Sec. 60 (5) (a) Patents Act 1977 (asserting that infringement is not effected by an act '. . . which is done privately and for purposes which are not commercial'); German Patent Act, Article 69.

[35]   See Copyright, Designs and Patents Act 1988, Sec. 16 (3).

[36]   One of the clear boundaries of the ontology used under the UK system is that once a work has been copied in its entirety, the systematic approaches offered by the extensive wording of the substantial parts test is redundant. The fact that a work has been copied as a whole does not, however, automatically denote worthiness of protection. The problem is significantly highlighted in the protection of structural works such as compilations. A compilation may consist of few or many elements. The decisive factor is then merely whether the whole has been taken or only parts. This dissociation is arbitrary as it equates everything that can be perceived as a work as a priori protected. For a different solution under the database directive's substantial parts test see G. Westkamp 'Protecting Databases under US and European Law: Methodical Approaches to the Protection of Investments Between Unfair Competition and Intellectual Property Concepts', 34 [2003] IIC.

when perceived in isolation from the work reflect the author's own intellectual creation.[37] Yet, as will be shown, the substantial parts test has sometimes been employed as a watershed in trying to achieve a balance.

Non-physical rights are restricted to public communications in certain defined categories of use. Unlike industrial property, copyright does not entail an express restriction on acts affecting commercial interests only, accomplished by referring to certain acts reaching the public, such as performances, broadcasts, cable programmes, re-transmission of broadcasts etc. However, even in assessing the connotation of the term 'public', the term itself is restricted to clear categories of certain commercial acts.[38] These acts imply that the public must be reached simultaneously.[39] This, in turn, is a cipher for commercial uses, simultaneously reflected in the description of commercial activities ranging from exhibitions to broadcasts.

5. HORIZONTAL ONTOLOGY: IDEAS, INFORMATION, EXPRESSION AND THE ONTOLOGY OF CATEGORIES

Copyright, of course, is restricted to the protection of *expression*. This is common to all copyright or authors' right systems as well as being the underly-

---

[37] Cf., for example, V. Loewenheim, in G. Schricker, *Urheberrecht*, 2nd edn (Munich, 1998), Article 16 annotation 11.

[38] Cf. German Authors' Right Act, Article 15:

'(1) The author shall have the exclusive right to exploit his work in material form; his right shall comprise in particular:

1. the right of reproduction (Article 16);
2. the right of distribution (Article 17);
3. the right of exhibition (Article 18).

(2) The author shall further have the exclusive right to communicate his work to the public in non-material form (right of communication to the public); his right shall comprise in particular:

1. the right of recitation, performance and presentation (Article 19);
2. the right of broadcasting (Article 20);
3. the right of communication by means of video or audio recordings (Article 21);
4. the right of communication of broadcasts (Article 22).

(3) The communication of a work shall be deemed public if it is intended for a plurality of persons, unless such persons form a clearly defined group and are connected by personal relationship with each other or with the organizer.'

[39] In that sense, see Kammergericht Berlin [2003] *Multimedia und Recht* 110. Despite the fact that the use of a cinematographic work – the movie *Paul und Paula* – on the Internet could not be subsumed under any of the non-physical acts enumerated in Articles 15 ff. of the German Authors' Right Act, the court applied the general provisions under Article 15 (1), 94 by way of analogy. The court saw a statutory gap diminishing the commercial value.

ing principle in international copyright law.[40] It is here that the problem of ontology commences. Despite the fact that there is no statutory and express exclusion of ideas and information from the concept of property, its existence is unadorned both when assessing the inherent exclusionary mechanisms within the statutes as well as the position of copyright within the Intellectual Property system.[41]

Within the level of statutory analysis, the idea/expression dichotomy exists on two *express* levels, subsistence and defences. In addition, the supposedly closed systems have developed other means of excluding elements which are deemed to be outside the system.

As to subsistence, the distinction between authors and copyright systems bears the most prominent disparities. If skill and labour – or investment – is advocated as the minimum standard for eligibility, the exclusion of information on the subsistence level is, in terms of statutory interpretation, naturally more complicated. Authors' right systems have devised a different technique of elimination, primarily by an assessment of the term 'personal intellectual creation'.[42]

This distinction with respect to originality, however, does not merely have consequences for the scope of categories to be protected. It certainly is not true to infer that the English system therefore simply safeguards more informational elements under the skill and labour approach than the continental systems do. The assessment of copyrightability does not end here.

Whereas, as will be shown, continental droit d'auteur systems can avoid an overspill of copyright protection by eliminating non-original works at the initial level of copyright subsistence, the UK skill and labour concept must rely on a strict description of subject matter in order to initially define what should be protected.[43] The effect is a strict assessment and mutual elimination of these categories, i.e. an approach much based on an ontological exercise. Interestingly, such ontology reaches its borders in cases where the ontological approach is difficult to apply. This can be observed in relation to 'modern' and technical works, i.e. structural rather than high authorship works. For example, UK law finds it extremely difficult to accommodate multimedia works into its system. These may be described as films, databases or compilations. Another example is the distinction between categories as either literary or artistic or musical. The

---

[40]   See, for example, Article 9 (1) TRIPS; on the Berne Convention, see S. Ricketson, *The Berne Convention: 1886–1986* (Oxford: Oxford University Press, 2005), p. 14.

[41]   See, on the question of 'property', B. Sherman and L. Bently, *The Making of Modern Intellectual Property Law* (Cambridge: Cambridge University Press), pp. 30 ff.

[42]   See, for example, Article 2 (2) of the German Authors' Right Act: 'Personal intellectual creations alone shall constitute works within the meaning of this Law'.

[43]   On the historical background underlying the shift from labour to object see Sherman and Bently, *The Making of Modern Intellectual Property Law*, pp. 173 ff.

fact that a compilation is described as a sub-category of a literary work therefore leads to the consequential dilemma of having to assess the 'information' as either on the grounds of its intellectual originality or its commercial value.

German law rests its assessment on the key term 'authorship', which is tightly interwoven with the term 'personal intellectual creation'. There is, consequentially, no strict categorisation according to certain classes of works. However, this appears to be rather a means of simplifying the evaluation as in most cases protectability may well be concluded by way of assumption. The approach, in general, is therefore much less based on ontology, yet the meaning of 'creation' is perceived in various different approaches. In this respect, ontology has led courts in earlier cases to come to a very simplistic assessment based upon categories. The dispute as to what constitutes a personal creation surrounds the broader discourse on the protectability of small change works such as pure data compilations. The same reasoning has also been put forward in the discussion relating to the protectability of computer programs. One such attempt has been the so-called above average formula. According to this, scientific or structural works (including software) need to reach a level of originality which represents a decisive distance from what the average creator would have created. The underlying idea is to exclude informational works, restricted to only the selection and arrangement of contents,[44] in particular with respect to scientific or technical works. There are various arguments underpinning the discourse. One of the more prominent stances is that, even if statutory elements may be present in terms of ontology, the necessity to uphold the public domain can eliminate protection as the case may be. Dogmatically this is deduced from the legitimate restrictions on the constitutional right to property, according to which property rights may be restricted and must be exercised in accordance with the public benefit.[45] The foundations of this principle can be explained in a dual way. Some argue that public domain considerations merely present an ever-present antinomy to the scope of protection, something rooted in the statute yet not expressly incorporated. Others would argue that technical or structural works would always be beneath what the term creation connotes.[46] In that sense, the public domain arguments elide individuality into a compensatory sentiment in order to let the unity of protection – in comparison to high authorship works – prevail. A different, yet related, argument would be that the necessity to keep informational works, even on a case by case basis, within the public domain needs to be

---

[44]   A. Troller, 'Urheberrecht und Ontologie', (1962) *UFITA* 11.
[45]   See, for example, Federal Court of Justice, *BGHZ* 116, 136, 146.
[46]   See M. Loeffler, 'Informationsfreiheit als Schranke des Urheberrechts', (1980) *Neue Juristische Wochenschrift* 201, 203; J. Ensthaler, *Gewerblicher Rechtsschutz und Urheberrecht*, 2nd edn (Springer: Berlin, 2002), pp. 21 ff.; Federal Court of Justice, *BGHZ* 73, 288 – Airport plans.

assessed by recourse to an overarching information freedom principle: only some preliminary sketching of what constitutes the public domain would devise a reliable method of subsequently finding the proper ambit of protection.[47] This would reduce protection for either pseudo-dogmatic reasons or by virtue of a simple balancing test.

If a structural work contains an element of method, such methods are not within the ambit of protection. There is, however, a perceived danger that such methods and processes come into the realm of protection via individual selection or arrangements. Likewise, scientific methods are excluded.[48] Despite the assertion of protectability, there is dogmatic exclusion by which the public domain is understood as a normative counterpart to copyright, which may override the property interests.[49] Protection is afforded to the representation of the methods or processes only. The application of these methods does not form part of copyright protection. The underlying reason is not merely one deduced from the information/expression dichotomy. Much more, there exists a second layer consideration, an inference from the copyright/patent dichotomy. If copyright were to protect information (including methods or processes), this would contradict the fact that such protection is restricted to patent law: here, the protection of information is reduced to a commercial situation, demands registration and is a use right.[50] In addition, it would also violate the public/private dichotomy with respect to the communication of such information, conferring an exclusive right only where the communication is public. Otherwise, copyright and patent would be inseparable, and copyright protection would easily override patent despite the obligation to register.

In conclusion, with respect to both systems, despite the seemingly segmented and ontological methods within the third layer ontology, it is clear that more fundamental principles play a significant role in finding the demarcation line between copyright protection and free public domain.

---

[47]   See, with respect to software protection, T. Hoeren, in P. Moehring and K. Nicolini, *Urheberrechtsgestz*, Commentary, 2nd edn (Munich, 2000), Article 69a Ann. 4.; E. Ulmer, *Urheber- und Verlagsrecht*, 3rd edn (Munich, 1985), p. 119; in the same sense, Federal Court of Justice (1985) *GRUR* 1041, 1044 – Debt clearance program.

[48]   Cf. also the exclusion of non-literal elements of a computer program in *Plains Cotton Coop. Ass. v Goodpasture Computer Services Inc.*, 807 F.2d 1256 (5th Cir. 1987).

[49]   Cf. Ulmer, *Urheber- und Verlagsrecht*, p. 123.

[50]   Cf. R. Rogge and G. Benkard, *Patentgesetz, Gebrauchsmustergesetz, Kommentar*, 9th edn (Munich, 1994), Article 9 Ann. 3.

6. VERTICAL ONTOLOGY: THE ONTOLOGY OF EXCLUSIVE RIGHTS

Vertically – with respect to exclusive rights – a comparison between both systems reveals that – despite its seemingly unequivocal language – ontology is relinquished in favour of a more balanced approach allowing public domain considerations to surface. In view of its all-embracing catalogue of protected works and its low threshold, the need to exclude certain informational items is to a great extent higher in UK law.

An interesting comparison between the German and UK approach can, first, be made with regard to the right of reproduction. Whereas under German law the taking of informational (non-literal) elements cannot constitute a reproduction per se,[51] the skill and labour threshold enables courts to find an interesting solution in cases of non-literal taking based on unfair competition principles. Admittedly, the jurisprudence on the substantial parts test is not entirely cohesive. However, what becomes apparent is that the taking of a substantial part refers to the quality of a work rather than its quantity. The term 'quality', here, embraces two meanings. First, it can denote personal authorship just as in authors' right systems. With respect to structural or informational works, some parallels can be observed that evoke the impression of some functional equivalence between the substantial parts test under UK law and the test based on creativity in the German system. It seems that the substantial parts test allows courts a wide margin to indirectly shape the boundaries of protection, albeit at a different systematic level. What constitutes a substantial part of the expression of a work then may be either assessed on the merits of creativity or, in cases of borderline technical or structural works, on the merits of protecting against acts of unfair taking. The substantial parts test thereby mirrors the second layer principle of investment as a fundamental aspect of UK copyright law. Courts have pointed out that the term 'substantial', at first glance referring to a mere evaluation of the work itself, has connotations much more reflecting the unfair competition acts of imitation or slavish reproduction. Hence, the question as to whether the defendant has taken a substantial part refers to whether he has appropriated not only the skill and labour (i.e. the typical 'reaping without sowing' test),[52] but that the commercial consequences and thereby the intention to enter into competition are the primary decisive factors. This shows that the copyright test is indeed not self-referential. Both underlying factors from the second level

---

[51]   That is, the elements taken must represent personal creation as such, see Ricketson, *The Berne Convention*, p. 35.

[52]   Cf. S. Ricketson, '"Reaping Without Sowing": Unfair Competition and Intellectual Property Rights in Anglo-Australian Law', [1984] *UNSW L.J.*, S. 1.

(protection primarily for investment) and the first layer (prevention of unfair competition) are introduced into the test.[53]

The second ontological exercise is the definition as to what constitutes 'the public' with respect to rights in certain acts of communication. The reason why this constitutes a requirement is that otherwise copyright would turn into a control tool *vis-à-vis* communications. This is reflected to some extent at the early stage of defining originality under authors' right systems. Under both systems, however, the usual definition is that the public is constituted of people not sharing a personal relationship.[54] In traditional copyright doctrine, the need to clearly define the term was only necessary in the case of non-simultaneous communications, such as hotel video transmissions or music used in automated telephone answering systems. Simultaneous communications were only within the ambit of copyright control once that act fell into one of the explicit rubrics of restricted acts in the communication of works. Most copyright statutes have opted for an enumeration of these, typically ranging from a small public (such as in the case of a theatre audience) to very large audiences, such as in the case of television broadcasts. At first glance, there appears to be no ontological relation between the description of these acts and the question as to whether they reach the public. However, by defining the act there is at least an assumption about the public and its size. Such an assumption makes recourse to an assessment of what constitutes the public almost redundant. The underlying rationale is that the relation between act and public is a cipher for typified commercial uses, which simultaneously reflects the fact that copyright does not embrace private communications. If this particular interrelation is eradicated, the proper definition of the 'public' becomes difficult, as is reflected in cases concerning the non-simultaneous reception of such communication. The reason is that now the commercial cipher is absent. If the term public is assessed merely on an isolated basis, courts will take the view that a repeated reception by different persons cannot constitute a public performance of that work, precisely because public means more than a person not interrelated with the sender. The right to participation is only violated once an act has been conducted which is intended to reap from the authors' work in commercial circumstances. The same is reflected in almost all cases dealing with non-simultaneous communications. Typically, courts have shied away from using the definition. The typical way of doing so is to deduce a commercial interest. This is precisely the reverse way from a strict ontological inquest into what the 'public' means. The underlying

---

53   There are, however, examples reflecting a purely ontological approach under a 'sterile' system, most notably the decision *Elanco Products v Mandops Ltd* [1979] FSR 46.

54   See, for example, the WIPO Glossary of Terms in Intellectual Property (Geneva, 1993).

reasons are inferred not from a defined term but from underlying principles, in line with the three step test under Article 9 (2) Berne Convention (BC). But the test itself has been subjected to criticism.

7. ACCESS RIGHT: CONSEQUENCES OF THIRD LAYER ONTOLOGY IN MODERN COPYRIGHT

The so-called third layer ontology, thus, will function in identifying the interrelations between the segments. The application of rules in each segment will shape the scope of protection alongside the demarcation lines imposed by the dichotomies discussed above. The pillars on which digital copyright rests call this system into question.

The formulation of the communication to the public right, which then includes the making available of works in an interactive manner, is likely to affect not only the general scope of control right over acts of communication, but will also modify and shift the judicial freedom of movement as far as the reliance on underlying principles is concerned. The first is one from a commercial situation, as previously implied in the interrelated acts, to an interpretation by status. Hence, each person sharing no personal relation with the sender will become the 'public'.[55] In addition, the right to publicly communicate will embrace all potential uses. Article 8 World Copyright Treaty (WCT), for instance, does not require an active act. The provision not only eradicates the commercial connotation that is present in cases relating to more specific acts of communication. It also eliminates the more subtle interrelationship between the traditional approach – a description of a specific act of communication on the one hand and the resulting ability to more accurately demarcate the boundaries between acts that are addressed to 'the public' and acts that will continue to remain 'private'. In doing so, the legislation removes any connotation of a commercial impact and renders the communication right an all-embracing right that allows right owners to legally control even one to one communications. The only decisive feature is the status of the person receiving the communication.

Even if a communication process does not reach the public, the newly formulated reproduction right may serve as a control mechanism. With regard to reproduction, the EU directive in particular takes the view that ephemeral and temporary copies are reproductions in the conventional sense. Some such copies which are an integral part of a technological process are exempt from the owners' control, yet this is subject to such copies not having any own economic

---

[55]   On this 'umbrella solution' see M. Ficsor, *The Law of Copyright and the Internet: The 1996 WIPO Treaties, their Interpretation and Implementation* (Oxford, 2001), No. 3-82.

significance. This is supposed to bring the exception in line with the three step test, i.e. to reserve to the author the right to fully participate in commercial uses. The reproduction right, hence, is supposed to cover all aspects of a digital use. Without such ephemeral copies, which simply speed up the communication process, the receptive use of the work would be impossible. The same is true of other copies, such as RAM-reproductions, occurring when a work is loaded to be eventually viewed on screen. The decision taken is one of pure ontology, as each technical copy is equated with a reproduction in the traditional sense. The effect, naturally, is to devise a control mechanism with respect to the entire use of the work, regardless of whether the purpose is taking of expression or reception of pure information. In contrast to the former method of adjudicating such communication within the copyright framework, there exist some significant deviations. In traditional copyright, the right to reproduce has the function of maintaining the authors' control for the first step in commercial uses. Such commercial use was perceived to subsist once a physical copy had been *manufactured*. The physical copy characteristically replaces the original, i.e. the process of communication may be channelled towards the copy rather than the original. In that sense, there was a significant distinction between the act of copying and communications.

The new right of reproduction, as formulated, can be employed for all types of digital uses. Thereby the dichotomy between non-physical and physical uses is sacrificed. The adaptation of the reproduction right hence reflects that communication processes embodying ephemeral copies can be controlled by employing either right, physical or not. The effect is that a non-physical use can be controlled through hypothetical copies. A communicative process thereby does not need to reach the public. The limitation to certain temporary copies does not deviate from this. The directive makes it clear that ephemeral and technically necessary copies may be employed once the 'use' has its own commercial significance. Such significance appears to exist in all instances in which a licence is absent. This significantly deviates from the traditional notion. In effect, the owner is given a right to control the active use.

Perhaps the most important pillar provides that it is a tort to circumvent anti-copying devices. There are several important issues. The primary reason for a separate protection against the circumvention does not resemble any copyright principle. In effect, it endangers these principles to be sacrificed in favour of an all embracing access right. It is plain to see that this would eradicate the possibility of applying any overriding principles because the legal protection of protecting technological protection measures may effortlessly be classified as a parallel and unrelated regime. Whereas it may still seem possible to exclude certain acts which have the purpose of gaining information by way of applying an overriding test (such as the expression/information dichotomy), such methodology will be inopportune. Committing the act of circumvention itself amounts to a tort not affiliated with any copyright principle.[56] These issues – i.e. access to information for the purpose of receptive communication – have not been dealt with at all during the evolution of the provision.[57] The discourse, for the most part, emphasised the relation between protection of anti-copying devices and statutory defences and limitations. This is an over-simplification. The statutory defences only act, as has been pointed out, as the last resort.[58]

The premise suggested by such a stance is firmly based on the traditional notion of categories. The misapprehension is that copyrighted works do not merely consist of expression but of information not subject to copyright protection.

The first issue refers to the question as to whether the circumvention of anti-copying amounts to copyright infringement. The question is highly important as, should circumvention constitute copyright infringement, such evaluation would automatically entail the assessment of fundamental principles. Despite still presenting access impediments, circumvention for the purpose of non-infringing acts would be legitimate. If not, protection would per se elide copyright into more than even a use right. The owner would hence be granted a control right over the information as well as the expression. In addition, this would eradicate both the substantial parts test as well as the applicability of statutory defences. On the other hand, it may well be argued that the act of circumvention requires a sound analysis as to whether copyright infringement was intended. The act of circumvention must affect a work that is protected by copyright. If copyright protection cannot be established, the prohibition on circumvention, as an element of copyright legislation, is necessarily inapplicable. From a dogmatic point of view, it would appear highly inconsistent if a different conclusion would be reached in cases where a TPM is removed in order to gain access to unprotected information that is part of perhaps a protected structure. As a matter of traditional copyright doctrine, there is no qualitative distinction between appropriating information from a work that is not protected and from a work that is protected only on the basis of some arrangement since in both cases the result is that copyright cannot be infringed. In both cases, the object of protection

---

[56]   In that sense, *Universal City Studios, Inc. v Reimerdes*, 111 F. Supp. 2d 346, 347 (SDNY, 2000) *(Reimerdes II)*. Shawn Reimerdes was one of the original defendants, but he settled with plaintiffs. Eric Corley, a.k.a. Emmanuel Goldstein, was the only individual defendant who appealed the injunction to the Second Circuit.

[57]   See, for example, *Felten v Recording Industry Association of Amer.*, No. 01-CV-2669 (D. New Jersey); *DVD Copy Control Association v Bunner*, 113 Cal. Rptr. 2nd 338 (Cal. Dist. Ct. App. 2001); *Universal City Studios, Inc. v Corley*, 273 F.3d 429 (2d Cir. 2001).

[58]   On the relationship and legal status of limitations see Lucie Guibault, *Copyright Limitations and Contracts* (Kluwer, 2002) (Information Law Series 9).

remains copyrightable expression. However, if it is accepted that through the TPM protection regime copyright embrace a positive 'right of access' not merely to expression but necessarily to ideas, information, methods and procedures as elements of that expression, then what remains is the sanctioning of the possession of information. If so, the traditional ontological layers in copyright laws, that used to provide courts with an arsenal of argumentative powers to strike the necessary balance, must become obsolete. From a systematic point of view, the emergence of notions of access and use cannot simply be constrained to digital uses but may well develop into fundamental components of copyright.

8.   CONCLUSION

In essence, the three pillars extend copyright protection as against access to information. Indeed, 'digital' copyright reform has arguably a much more drastic impact on the consistency of copyright doctrine than the concept of a mere adaptation of existing law to digital technology may initially suggest. It will systematically affect not only the stability and consistency of the intrinsic copyright system and its function as a means of both allocating rights whilst preserving the necessary level for an unconstrained flow of information; in addition, it may also dilute the underlying rationales of copyright protection, obscure the boundaries between copyright and patent law and thus pave the way towards a very perilous notion of information property. It may be anticipated that the impediments to the free flow of information ascertainable so far will redirect the social conflict at issue. Information freedom, whether the information is contained in copyrightable expression or not, is an issue not necessarily interwoven with copyright questions. As the monopoly granted now does not only cover expression but possession of information, the debate about the proper relationship between copyright and competition control will receive a hefty new impetus. In particular, this debate will fuel the arguments favouring the application of the essential facilities doctrine in cartel law.[59] The situation here is different as what amounts to a dominant position may no longer be the Intellectual Property right but the factual possession of information. Whereas competition law may be the route for activities geared against monopolies in information, human rights issues may also become important.

---

[59]   See, for example, *Radio Telefis Eireann v Commission*, (*Magill*), [1995] ECR 743; Commission Decision, *Magill TV Guide v ITP*, *BBC und RTE*, OJ EC 1989, No. L78, 3.

5. The structure of control – Communication systems and copyright law

John Cahir

1. INTRODUCTION

Since the emergence of the Internet as a popular communications platform copyright law has been central to public debates on the future shape and development of information policy. One often overlooked issue is the extent to which the *structure* of communication systems influences the ability of copyright owners to exercise control over their works. The aim of this chapter is to outline the relationship that exists between the structure of communication systems and the nature of rights conferred on copyright owners by copyright statutes. It will be argued that the Internet's unique communicative architecture does not fit within the conventional copyright paradigm, and that resort to novel exclusionary practices – 'digital rights management' (DRM) technology and clickwrap licences – reflects the inability of the copyright model to provide authors and creators with the desired level of protection in the online environment.

Viewed from their historical context it is clear that copyright laws were drafted with a particular model of mass communication system in mind: one with the media owner at the centre and a passive, receiving public at the end nodes. As the means of communicating information developed over the past 300 years, copyright law proved adept at subsuming the resulting communicative uses within its purview. Changes to copyright law may not always have been controversy free, yet in the end an acceptable compromise was invariably reached between the interested parties.[1] The advent of the Internet

---

[1]   J. Litman, *Digital Copyright* (New York: Prometheus Books, 2001) gives a historical account of the process of copyright law reform in the United States. The practice developed whereby the interested parties would first come to a compromise amongst themselves and present Congress with a draft legislative document, which was then enacted without much fuss.

as a popular means of communicating information has shaken the cosy process of copyright law reform. Copyright dependent industries regard the Internet simply as a novel means of exploiting protected works that should automatically be taken under the wing of existing exclusive rights or within newly formulated ones. Sceptics, on the other hand, view the changes as a way of locking up information in a manner that was inconceivable in the pre-Internet world and they call for maintaining the balance of interests accommodated within the existing copyright compact. Both viewpoints, it is submitted, fail to get to the heart of the matter. The structural nature of the Internet has brought us to an impasse: the publicly ordered 'top-down' copyright model is incapable of performing its exclusionary function in the Internet environment; private ordering via DRM technology and contractual licensing are the *only* effective mechanisms for exercising control in the Internet environment.

This chapter will explain why this impasse has been reached and will argue that critics who wish to replicate the traditional copyright regime in the online environment misunderstand the nature of private ordering.[2] There will be six remaining sections to the chapter. First, a brief account will be given of the communicative function of the exclusive rights conferred by copyright law. Secondly, the nature of property and contractual rights will be considered. Thirdly, the variables that determine the structure of communication systems will themselves be identified and the strategies for maintaining control across these different structures described. Fourthly, the Internet's communicative structure will be outlined. Fifthly, the emergence of novel exclusionary practices in the Internet environment will be described. Finally, some comments on how we should approach the challenges to traditional copyright law will be offered.

2.   THE RIGHT TO COMMUNICATE

This essay works on the premise that copyright laws are best viewed in terms of how they regulate communicative acts that may be made between individuals. Copyright is in essence the right to communicate certain types of information. The reason we today speak in terms of 'copying' and 'reproduction right' is because of the historically contingent relationship that exists between the physical act of copying a work and communicating it to other people. Most histories of copyright take the invention of the printing press in 1450[3] as their

---

    2   Some authors have argued for the implementation of user rights into electronic management systems – e.g. D. Burk and J. Cohen, 'Fair Use Infrastructure for Rights Management Systems' (2001) 15 Harvard J of L & Tech 41.
    3   See generally M. Rose, *Authors and Owners: The Invention of Copyright* (Cambridge, MA: Harvard University Press, 1993); J. Feather, *A History of British*

starting point. On its own the printing press cannot be classified as a communications technology: in order for printed books to be communicated a distribution and transportation network must also be in place. The copying function was however integral to the business of publishing books and the Statute of Anne 1710 accordingly granted the 'sole right and liberty of printing' books to the book's author or proprietor so that they could exercise control over the distribution of the work. Since then we have been labouring under the misconception that the act of 'copying' in itself possesses some trespassory significance. It does not. The eccentric who prints a thousand copies of a book in the privacy of his own home affects neither the author nor anyone else so long as he does not make them available for another person's benefit.

From its origins as a means of regulating the book trade copyright law grew to become the chief legal means of controlling the mass communication of cultural and other informational works. The mass communications industry, i.e. news, book and music publishing; film production and distribution; television and radio broadcasting etc., is premised on the ability of the content owner to exclusively control communication of a work. Without that exclusivity it is unlikely that a viable market in such works would emerge. Subject to some small qualifications,[4] the principal concern of rights conferred by section 16 of the Copyright Designs and Patents Act 1988 is, it is submitted, to ensure that the copyright owner has *an exclusive* in rem *right to communicate* informational objects.[5] Communication occurs when information is transmitted from a sender to a receiver, e.g. by sending an email. While the terms 'copy' and 'perform' may accurately describe acts that can be carried out in respect of protected works, the only reason why a person performs them is so that he/she can communicate a work to other people.

Printing (London: Routledge, 1988); L. Patterson, *Copyright in Historical Perspective* (Nashville: Vanderbilt University Press, 1968); and R. Bowker, *Copyright: Its History and its Law* (Boston: Houghton Mifflin Co., 1912).

[4] Information protected by copyright law can also have 'instrumental uses', some of which fall within the owner's exclusive domain. First, the reproduction right prohibits the incorporation of non-substantial parts of a protected work into a new work – *Designer's Guild v Russell Williams* [2001] FSR 11. Secondly, the adaptation of protected works is one of the exclusive rights conferred on the copyright owner under the Copyright Designs and Patents Act 1988, ss. 16(1)e and 21. Adaptive uses (e.g. translations) are normally instrumental in nature. Thirdly, under s. 17(3) copying of a two-dimensional artistic work into a three-dimensional form and vice versa is deemed an infringement of copyright.

[5] Section 16 of the 1988 Act lists the following exclusive rights: (a) to copy the work, (b) to issue copies of the work to the public, (c) to rent or lend the work to the public, (d) to perform, show or play the work in public, (e) to communicate the work to the public, (f) to make an adaptation of the work or to do any of the above in relation to an adaptation. Sections 22 to 27 deal with acts of secondary infringement in relation to infringing copies.

By conceiving the rights conferred by copyright law as a more general right to communicate, the dependency relationship that exists between copyright law and communication systems can be seen in a clearer light.[6] A communication system is an entity where connections are made amongst objects for the purpose of transmitting information.[7] For instance, television broadcasting consists of a broadcaster transmitting signals across the electromagnetic spectrum so that viewers in possession of television sets may receive them. Content owners obviously require that communication systems be in place so that their 'product' may reach a paying audience (or one that will consume advertisements). The most efficient and profitable way of achieving this objective is through *mass communication systems.*[8] Copyright law's principal economic function is therefore to vest legal authority in the content owner or his assigns to determine if and when communication takes place across a given communication system, i.e. it is the right to communicate.

3.   CONTROL: THE NATURE OF PROPERTY RIGHTS

Property and contract are the two bedrock legal institutions of market economies. The exclusive rights conferred on the author of a copyright work are, as a matter of positive law at least, a category of property right.[9] The essence of the analysis in the preceding section was that under copyright law, property rights = the right to communicate. Brief consideration will now be given to the normative character of property rights as applied to the objects of copyright protection.[10]

---

6   To some extent this re-conceptualisation of copyright has occurred with the passing of the Copyright Directive (Directive 2001/29/EC). Article 3 thereof establishes a general 'right of communication of works to the public'. This right will replace the existing broadcast and transmission by way of cable programme rights under UK law though will not impact on the sanctity of the reproduction right.

7   I. de Sola Pool (ed.) *Handbook of Communications* (Chicago: MacNally, 1973), chapter 1.

8   Umberto Eco defines 'mass communications' in industrialised societies as the 'channels of communication which make it possible to reach not determined but an indefinite circle of receivers in various sociological situations' (U. Eco, *A Theory of Semiotics* (Illinois: Indiana University Press, 1976), p. 13). Use of the term 'mass communications' in the remainder of this section can be taken to embody that meaning. See also S. Baran and D. Davis, *Mass Communication Theory: Foundations, Ferment and Future* (Belmont, CA: Wadsworth, 2002, 3rd edn); and D. McQuail, *Mass Communication Theory* (London: Sage, 1994, 3rd edn).

9   Section 1(1) of the Copyright, Designs and Patents Act 1988 declares that the rights conferred on authors by that Act are 'property rights'.

10   See generally S. Munzer, A *Theory of Property* (Cambridge: Cambridge

The standard approach to conceiving property rights in legal theory is the Hohfeld-Honoré treatment of property as a subclass of legal relations – the 'bundle of rights' thesis.[11] Hohfeldian analysis fragments private propery into a bundle of rights and correlative propositions (such as duties) that exist between persons in respect of their use of items of property. Hohfeld's analysis teaches us that property rights are a set of legal relationships that exist between human beings in respect of their use of a given resource. Property rights do not involve any relationship between the owner and the object, but rather between the owner and other citizens.

Hohfeld's other related concern was with the traditional concepts of rights *in rem* and rights *in personam*.[12] Property rights are a category of right *in rem*, i.e. they are a right that gives rise to duties in the world at large. The fact that I must not trespass on your land is not because of some negotiated agreement between us but rather because the law of property dictates that I may not. Contractual rights are a category of right *in personam*, i.e. they are personal rights that only give rise to legal obligations amongst the contracting parties. For instance if I contract with my neighbour to stay off my own land for a period of time, I owe a contractual obligation to him alone not to enter the land, though no law of trespass prevents me from so doing. The rights conferred by copyright law are archetypal rights *in rem*. Even persons not in a contractual relationship with the copyright owner are under a duty not to infringe the exclusive rights conferred on him by statue.

In rem copyright norms are however, unlike most other private property rights, a product of centralised public ordering.[13] While property rights with respect to tangible objects have existed since time immemorial, copyright and intellectual property rights more generally, only came into being in the aftermath of the Industrial Revolution. The expansion of copyright law has mirrored the growth of the regulatory state itself. The reason why copyright entails such a high level of public ordering is because the object of its protection – information

---

University Press, 1990); J. Waldron, *The Right to Private Property* (Oxford: Clarendon Press, 1988); and L. Becker, *Property Rights: Philosophical Foundations* (Boston: Routledge & Kegan Paul, 1977).

[11] W. Hohfeld, *Fundamental Legal Conceptions as Applied in Judicial Reasoning*, W.W. Cook (ed.) (Connecticut: Greenwood Press, 1978); A.M. Honoré, 'Ownership', in A. Guest (ed.), *Oxford Essays in Jurisprudence* (Oxford: Clarendon Press, 1961). Their approach is widely, though not universally accepted, e.g. J. Penner, *The Idea of Property in Law* (Oxford: Clarendon Press, 1997) argues that property rights can be conceived as a single 'duty of non-interference'.

[12] For a full account and criticism of Hohfeld's analysis of *in rem* and *in personam* rights, see J. Penner, 'The "Bundle of Rights" Picture of Property' (1996) 43 UCLA L Rev 711.

[13] On the normative character of rights in general see J. Raz, 'On the Nature of Rights' (1984) 93 *Mind* 194.

– is in a different ontological category from tangible things. Information has no physical or spatial form; it consists of symbolic-linguistic representations; it can have both abstract and concrete meaning; and, most importantly, it can be everywhere and anywhere at once. Even philosophers of information have great difficulty in explaining the exact nature of informational objects. It is not possible therefore to rely on obviousness of form and the exclusivity of possession, as one does with tangible things, if one wants to recognise and enforce a standardised exclusionary *in rem* right to informational objects.

In fact the only conceivable way to construct an informational property right is through exceptionally complex legislation that specifies, *inter alia*, the owner's identity (since more than one individual might claim the benefit of *in rem* duties); the subject matter of copyright protection (since not all informational objects qualify for protection); the term of protection (since copyright works can exist forever); and the extent of rights conferred (since to grant total control would be undesirable). The unprecedented role played by the legislature in framing this individual right justifies it being classified as a species of 'publicly ordered property right'. Furthermore, once legislation has secured its protection, countervailing individual rights (e.g. freedom of expression) and public interest claims (e.g. educational and library privileges) that copyright law implicates, must also be accommodated. The process of interest group claim and counterclaim for rights and privileges serves only to magnify the extent of public ordering in information markets.[14]

4. CONTROL: THE STRUCTURE OF COMMUNICATION SYSTEMS

In law and communication studies the popular approach for analysing control within communication systems is the 'layers' concept of Professor Benkler.[15] He divides communication systems into three layers – the physical infrastructure layer (i.e. the wires, spectrum etc. that actually carry information); the

---

[14]   This practice of individuals and interest groups petitioning the legislature for favourable treatment is known as 'rent-seeking behaviour' under public choice theory. See D. Farber and P.P. Frickey, *Law and Public Choice: A Critical Introduction* (Chicago: University of Chicago Press, 1991).

[15]   Y. Benkler, 'The Battle over the Institutional Ecosystem in the Digital Environment' (2001) 44 Communications of the ACM 84; Y. Benkler, 'From Consumers to Users: Shifting the Deeper Structure of Regulation Towards Sustainable Commons and User Access' (2000) 52 Federal Communications LJ 561; and Y. Benkler, 'Overcoming Agoraphobia: Building the Commons of the Digitally Networked Environment' (1998) 11 Harvard J of L & Tech 287. See also L. Lessig, *The Future of Ideas* (New York: Random House, 2001).

logical infrastructure layer (i.e. the protocols and software on which protocols run); and the content layer (i.e. the information that is transmitted within the communication system). Each of these layers, Benkler argues, may in principle be controlled (normally through private ownership) or be free (organised in a commons). One can assess the extent to which control is exercisable within a particular communication system by reference to the degree of control exercised over the individual layers. The 'layers' concept provides an extremely useful framework for analysing the degree of control that exists in a communication system, when one assumes that control is *a priori* possible. It does not, however, provide an explanation for the more fundamental issue of how and indeed if control can be effected within a communication system. Only by analysing the structure of the communication system itself can this preliminary matter be resolved. The structure more so than the ownership of individual layers is, it is submitted, the most important determinant in relation to the maintenance of control over communication.

Three variables determine, it is submitted, the structure of a mass communication system: (a) the number of persons with an ability to send information, (b) the number of persons with an ability to receive information, and (c) the ability of senders of information to 'broadcast' as opposed to 'narrowcast' their transmissions. 'Broadcast' refers to the simultaneous transmission of information from a single sender to many recipients, e.g. by television signal; 'narrowcast' refers to the transmission of information from a single sender to a single or few recipients, e.g. a facsimile. This important variable in communication structures is collectively referred to as 'reach'.

By combining these features Table 5.1 is submitted as a list of the different types of communication systems' structures that may arise.[16]

Table 5.1 illustrates that the hierarchical/decentralised nature of a communication system is determined by the presence or absence of a large number of people with the capacity to *send* information. The traditional mass communication systems all contain relatively few senders and many recipients – they are by definition hierarchically structured. This feature of communication systems is not because of some Orwellian design but is rather a consequence of both physical and economic limitations. First, the natural limits on using the electromagnetic spectrum mean that governments must ration access to it; only a few licensed radio and television broadcasters are therefore allowed to operate analogue signals. Secondly (and more importantly), the high fixed

---

[16]   This is not an exhaustive list of all possible structures; it is intended to represent only those that are most common in the modern communications environments. For instance the message contained in a petition signed by many people and sent to a politician is an example of a communication system consisting of many senders but only one recipient.

Table 5.1

Structure	Senders/recipients	Reach	Example
Hierarchical	Few senders, many recipients	Broadcast	Radio, television
Hierarchical	Few senders, many recipients	Narrowcast	Book and music publishing
Decentralised	Many senders, many recipients	Narrowcast	Email, telephone
Decentralised	Many senders, many recipients	Broadcast	World Wide Web

capital costs associated with establishing conventional means of communication (e.g. a printing press or satellite) have the effect of deterring most putative senders of information.

The systems 'reach' also places a limit on the number of persons likely to assume the role of sender. Thus a 'narrowcast' communication system like traditional book publishing requires an elaborate distribution network to be in place if a large number of recipients are to be reached. Each copy of a book must be packaged, transported and placed for sale; a radio signal need only be emitted once from its broadcasting source. Both hierarchical systems – broadcast and narrowcast – are nonetheless predicated on the likelihood that the average recipient will not himself be in a position to broadcast or redistribute the work in competition with the original sender. Modern culture, the mass media and indeed copyright law have been hugely influenced by the fact that conventional mass communication systems only permit a limited number of active senders; their economic model is after all dependent on there being a large consuming audience.

Decentralised communication systems in contrast are defined by the ability of most persons to play the role of *both* sender and recipient of information. The earliest examples of such systems are the postal, telegraph and telephone networks.[17] A more recent example is email. In respect of each there are generally an equal number of senders and recipients of messages. The great majority of communications that take place on these systems are two-way interactive exchanges, e.g. telephone conversations. The interactive nature of these communication systems is integral to both their functionality and popularity. A person would likely tire of email if he/she were not able to respond to messages in his/her inbox.

---

[17]   See T. Standage, *The Victorian Internet: The Remarkable Story of the Nineteenth Century's Online Pioneers* (New York: Walker Publishing, 1998).

The common trait of the decentralised communication systems cited in the above paragraph is that they are all 'narrowcast' technologies, i.e. they facilitate the transmission of content to a single person rather than a mass audience. Thus while we may all be senders within these systems, we are so in respect of only a limited range of recipients. A decentralised narrowcast communication system does not therefore have the potential to compete with hierarchical mass communication systems. The real challenge to hierarchical communication structures comes from a communication system that is both decentralised (i.e. containing many senders and recipients) and broadcast enabled. Certain applications of the Internet, as we will see, offer this potential.

Copyright laws fit seamlessly with hierarchical communication structures. The rights conferred by copyright law, as noted above, are property rights. They are a set of 'trespassorary rules'[18] that prevent non-owners from making unauthorised communications of protected works. In an environment where there are but few senders of information they operate as a convenient form of market regulation. The legitimate senders of information, motivated as they are by the desire to maximise their profits, have a common interest in preserving a stable market structure. Copyright laws enable them to achieve this goal and thereby overcome the temptation to enter collusive arrangements amongst themselves. In this environment, the pirate of copyright works is someone who clearly acts outside the pale. His actions are motivated not by the desire to communicate works to another person, but rather by the desire to acquire for himself a share of the market pie. He too is a profit-seeking actor and copyright laws enable legitimate market players to prevent him from undermining the market's stability. In summary, a hierarchical set of norms is an efficient means for ordering market transactions that occur within hierarchical communication systems.

Under conventional mass communication systems copyright laws had little direct impact on the average recipient of copyright works. He was generally in no position to communicate the work himself, therefore the fact that the copyright owner held the exclusive right to do so was of no concern to him. He was probably quite pleased to be able to receive the protected work in the first place. The copyright regime even grants certain limited privileges to him with respect to certain uses of protected works, e.g. the first sale doctrine and the fair dealing exceptions. These entitlements may advance some important interest unrelated to the copyright owner's economic interests but they in no way pose a threat to the market's overall integrity; they are therefore tolerated.

---

[18]   J. Harris, *Property and Justice* (Oxford: Clarendon Press, 1996) puts forward the idea that a property institution consists of two elements – the 'ownership spectrum' and 'trespassorary rules'.

Even the type of private copying of protected works that has become common as a result of developments in consumer reproduction technologies is manageable within the hierarchical framework. The consumer who makes a few extra copies of a music recording for his friends has no broadcast capability and cannot therefore seriously undermine the content owner's right to communicate to the consuming public.

The principal point being made in this section is that historically the hierarchical structure of mass communication systems was the principal means for exercising control in respect of works transmitted across them. Beyond setting the terms of reference by which this market operated, copyright's role was relatively modest. This publicly ordered model cannot however cope with the situation where the average consumer also has the capacity to communicate the work by broadcast means.

5.   THE INTERNET AS A COMMUNICATIONS SYSTEM

The above analysis of communication systems leads one naturally to consider the Internet. There is little doubt that the Internet is a unique communications system.[19] Castells summarises its potential as follows:[20]

> For all the science fiction ideology and commercial hype surrounding the emergence of the so called 'information superhighway,' we can hardly underestimate its significance. The potential integration of text, images and sounds in the same system, interacting from multiple points, in chosen time (real or delayed) along a global network, in conditions of affordable and open access, does fundamentally change the character of communication.

From the perspective of this chapter, the principal importance of the Internet is that it is a decentralised communication system consisting of many receivers and senders of information, all with potential broadcast capacity. Another feature of the Internet that is of significance to copyright law is its utilisation of digital technology so that text, computer code, images and sound converge into a single transmittable form.[21] This technological breakthrough has the

---

[19]   For a general history and user-friendly technical description of the Internet see J. Naughton, *A Brief History of the Internet: The Origins of the Internet* (London: Phoenix, 2000); and J. Abbate, *Inventing the Internet* (Cambridge, MA: MIT Press, 1999).

[20]   M. Castells, *The Information Age: Economy, Society and Culture* (London: Blackwell, 2000), Vol.1, p. 356.

[21]   Digitalisation refers to the conversion of analogue signals into sequences of ones and zeros which are then transmitted through a channel, e.g. telephone wire, and reconverted into an analogous form by a receiver – see Naughton, *supra* note 19, at

potential to undermine standard classifications of copyright works, e.g. literary versus musical works, though this is outside the scope of this chapter.

The Internet embodies what is known as the 'end-to end argument' of communications – the notion that the intelligence should reside at the end nodes of a communication system rather than at its core.[22] The end-to-end character varies according to which Internet application one is using. For instance, most people gain access to the World Wide Web through an Internet Service Provider (ISP); this 'client–server' relationship introduces a degree of hierarchy into the network. Notwithstanding, the 'specific application level functions'[23] that define the communicative functionality of the Internet still largely reside at the end nodes, i.e. individual computers. The Internet in all its forms therefore remains a predominately decentralised communications system.[24]

The two principal Internet applications – email and the World Wide Web – represent respectively the narrowcast and broadcast models of communication 'reach'. Email as a narrowcast decentralised communications system has a similar communicative architecture to the telephone, fax and telegraph. It differs in that it can be used to communicate all digital representations of information, i.e. text, sound, image and code, in great volume; furthermore it is free of time imposed constraints, i.e. it can be used for both instantaneous interactive communication and time delayed transmissions. The decentralised nature of email communication means that it is not naturally susceptible to control. It is therefore very difficult for an information owner to exercise his property rights over information that is sent via email. Once a recipient receives information he can easily send it on to others. The only effective way to ensure against this happening is to superimpose some technical device on

---

98–9 for a non-technical overview of digital communications. For an overarching and optimistic view of the revolutionary significance of digitalisation, see N. Negraponte, *Being Digital* (New York: Vintage, 1995) and his collection of articles for *Wired* magazine at http://web.media.mit.edu/~nicholas/Wired/.

[22] See D. Clark and M. Blumenthal, 'Rethinking the Design of the Internet: The End to End Argument vs The Brave New World' (Cambridge, MA: MIT, TRPC submission, August 2000). The end-to-end design principles of the Internet were first formally laid out in J. Saltzer, D. Reed and D. Clark, 'End-to-End Arguments in System Design' (1984) 2(4) ACM Transactions on Computer Systems 277.

[23] Clark and Blumenthal, *supra* note 22 at 1.

[24] Lessig, *supra* note 15, at chapter 10 argues that providers of broadband access to the Internet are undermining the 'end-to-end' principle of the Internet. The introduction of discriminating practices such as restrictions to the choice of ISP, Lessig argues amounts to a transfer of control to the broadband providers. These arguments undoubtedly have some force, however, the fact remains that dial-up and DSL connections are a ready and popular alternative to broadband and furthermore that some broadband providers have decided against using discriminatory practices.

the recipient's computer or within the information itself that disables the recipient's ability to resend the information. However, the fact that email is not broadcast enabled restricts the extent to which it can erode the copyright owner's control. Where the copyright owner himself retains control over the broadcast of information, the point-to-point transmission of information only partially subverts his position of dominance.

The World Wide Web as a widely used broadcast enabled, decentralised communication system is the first of its kind. All previous broadcast communication systems, such as radio and television, were hierarchically structured and therefore naturally susceptible to the exercise of control over information transmitted across them. One gains broadcast capacity on the Web simply by creating a Web page or by posting information on someone else's Web page. Once made available in this fashion information can in theory be received by everyone else in the world with access to the Web. The Web does, however, embody some degree of hierarchy as it consists to a large extent of client and server machines. The server can potentially exercise a controlling role over the client.[25] The *ne plus ultra* of decentralised communication systems are the peer-to-peer networks that are rapidly emerging as distinctive communicative applications in themselves. Napster was of course the first and most infamous of them, however a plethora have emerged in its wake.[26] The distinctive structural feature of these networks is that they reduce the ordinary sender's dependency on server machines. An average Internet user can therefore broadcast what information he wants across these networks without having to seek an intermediary's permission. The intelligence of these networks resides at each individual end node's computer, all of which have an equal capacity to function as a broadcaster as well as a recipient of information. It is not surprising therefore that they have spawned a sea of litigation from the entertainment industries.

6. EXERCISING CONTROL IN THE INTERNET ENVIRONMENT

The radical communicative nature of the Internet led early writers on the issue to predict that copyright laws would not survive in the new environment.[27]

---

[25]   ISPs are being increasingly viewed by business and legislators as a way of realising a degree of control over Internet communications. For instance Article 14 of the Electronic Commerce Directive (Directive 2000/31/EC) establishes a notice and take down procedure in respect of 'illegal information' hosted by ISPs.

[26]   The best known successors include Grokster, KaZaa and Morpheus (all of which run on Fast Track software).

[27]   J. Barlow, 'The Economy of Ideas: A Framework for Rethinking Patents and

The consensus has since gone full circle; most commentators[28] now agree that predictions of copyright's demise were premature and that information control on the digitally networked environment is, if anything, potentially more robust than on previous communication platforms. Cohen describes the emerging environment as follows:[29]

> The intellectual property regime that is emerging on the Internet will do three things: It will allow proprietary control over access to information. It will leverage that control to achieve an astonishingly broad range of restrictions on information use – not only by copyists and other free riders, but also by citizens, consumers, critics, and legitimate competitors. And, as a result, it will shape the ways in which online interaction is structured. To the extent that it cannot adapt traditional intellectual property law to these tasks, it will harness a serviceable collection of other legal doctrines, both new and old, to assist.

The task of redrawing the legal boundaries to capture information communicated via the Internet within copyright law's remit was, in retrospect, relatively easy to achieve. The WIPO Internet Treaties, 1996[30] confirmed that the general 'right to communicate to the public' was a property right of copyright owners; this was sufficient to capture both Web and peer-to-peer communications of copyright works. However, declaring the existence of new property rights does nothing to address the more fundamental issue of how one can exercise control over information that is communicated via a decentralised broadcast enabled communication system. For this a new strategy is required.

It is becoming clear that the method by which control will be achieved is

---

Copyrights in the Digital Age' (1994) 2.03 Wired proclaimed: 'Intellectual property law cannot be patched, retrofitted, or expanded to contain digitized expression any more than real estate law might be revised to cover the allocation of broadcasting spectrum (which, in fact, rather resembles what is being attempted here). We will need to develop an entirely new set of methods as befits this entirely new set of circumstances.' See also E. Dyson, 'Intellectual Value' (1995) 3.07 Wired.

28   E.g. Y. Benkler, 'Net Regulation: Taking Stock and Looking Forward' (2000) 71 U of Colorado LR 1203; J. Boyle, 'Cruel, Mean or Lavish?: Economic Analysis and Digital Intellectual Property' (2000) 53 Vanderbilt LR 2007; and J. Cohen, 'The Perfect Curve' (2000) 53 Vanderbilt LR 1799.

29   J. Cohen, 'Intellectual Property in the Information Economy' to be published in W. Lehr and L. Pupillo (eds), *Cyber Policy and Economics in an Information Age* (The Hague: Kluwer Law, 2003) – http://www.law.georgetown.edu/faculty/jec/ipandinfoeconomy.pdf.

30   The WIPO Copyright Treaty and the WIPO Performances and Phonograms Treaty both adopted on 20 December 1996. They have been implemented in Europe by the Directive on the Harmonisation of Certain Aspects of Copyright and Related Rights in the Information Society (Directive 2001/29/EC) and in the United States by the Digital Millennium Copyright Act, 1998.

through the establishment of a new legal compact *founded* on the use of DRM technology and contractual licences. The default rules of copyright law are suited to regulating a market with few active participants and many passive consumers; they are incapable of commanding obedience amongst a potentially universal network of sender/receivers. The establishment of a decentralised nexus of legal relationships through self-help technological protection measures and contract is the information owner's answer to the apparent collapse of the hierarchical model of traditional copyright law. The tactic is to fight decentralisation with private ordering.

DRM is a general term that refers to the practice of 'wrapping' digital content with encryption and access control technologies. By so doing the content owner is able to determine precisely the terms and conditions under which a user may access electronically available material. DRM may also entail the monitoring of user activity to ensure compliance with licence terms, and the use of technological measures to take remedial action in the event of a breach of a licence term. It is still a matter for debate as to the extent to which these technological control systems can or will be implemented. However, it seems highly likely that the large content industries will only make their material available under protection of some form of robust DRM.

Some commentators have argued that the method of controlling human behaviour through computer code (the aim of DRM) represents a *sui generis* source of norms that is distinct from those that arise as a result of rules of law.[31] Under the 'modalities of regulation' thesis, as it is known, law and computer codes are classified as distinct elements of some general set of nebulous control mechanisms. This analysis, while possessing some explanatory insights, should not be taken to be a radical reappraisal of the concept of law. There are many institutions in society other than law that have the effect of controlling individual behaviour, e.g. the family. To equate all of these as conceptually equivalent is however theoretically unsound. In societies where the 'rule of law' is said to govern, there must ultimately be some legal norm to validate actions or designs that have a coercive impact on other persons' behaviour. With traditional copyright law, statute law sanctioned the practice of exclusion. With privately ordered information markets in the Internet environment a combination of liberties consequent on owning DRM technology and binding contractual obligations serve the equivalent function.

To summarise, the Internet's applications – email, the Web and peer-to-peer networks – all embody to one degree or another a decentralised communications

---

[31]   The principal exponent of this thesis is L. Lessig, *Code and Other Laws of Cyberspace* (New York: Basic Books, 1999). See also A. Murray and C. Scott, 'Controlling the New Media: Hybrid Responses to New Forms of Power' (2002) 65 Modern L Rev 491 for a revised version of this thesis.

structure. The shift to a control regime founded on DRM technology and contract represents a natural response to collapse of the hierarchical copyright model.

7. CONCLUSIONS

This chapter has attempted to trace the transformation of copyright law's role from being a 'publicly ordered' form of market regulation to that of playing merely a supporting role for governance by technology and mass contract. Furthermore it is argued that these novel exclusionary practices are the only means for establishing viable information markets in a decentralised communications environment. Regrettably the discussion surrounding these changes has concentrated on the deleterious impact that they are alleged to have on fair dealing and other user privileges. 'Fair use' has become the rallying cry for people who oppose in principle the use by commercial information providers of DRM technology and shrinkwrap licences. All of a sudden traditional copyright law has been fêted as a paragon of democratic governance, and it is said to strike an objectively fair balance between private and public interests.

In truth traditional copyright law is no longer capable of achieving its exclusionary function; that being the case no attempt should be made to impose regulations simply so that the structure of copyright-ordered markets of traditional mass media are mimicked in the Internet environment. DRM technology and shrinkwrap licences are legitimate and plausible means for information and entertainment sectors to achieve exclusion, and hence profit from their works. They are, however, examples of private ordering, and should not therefore be subjected to the type of 'interest group' compromises that one normally associates with publicly ordered copyright law. We should in fact welcome their emergence: they offer a painless exit strategy from copyright dependency and the possibility of more efficient, less regulated, information markets.

6. Circumventing the idea/expression dichotomy: The use of copyright, technology and contract to deny access to ideas

Noam Shemtov

It is a trite law that copyright protects expressional works rather than the ideas that underlie such works. Ideas, albeit not in abstract but rather when harnessed to produce a useful and tangible result, may be protected via patent law. The rationales for lack of copyright protection for ideas are many and vary from public domain based arguments to economic efficiency based ones. The legal principle according to which copyright protects expressional aspects of a work rather than the ideas that underlie it is often referred to as the idea–expression dichotomy. Free circulation of ideas is considered vital for the fostering and dissemination of knowledge and information, which, in turn, is one of the fundamentals elements of an efficient and optimally productive society. From an economic efficiency prospective, the idea–expression dichotomy principle seeks to ensure that creators will not find themselves obliged to embark on the wasteful task of 'reinventing the wheel' each time they wish to create, but rather be able to build upon an accumulated pool of logical building blocks. It is important to point out that the concept of freely circulating ideas is irrespective of their originality or their novelty. The operation of the doctrine requires no objective assessment of the merits of an idea, as is the case under patent law.[1] Hence, copyright law is not at odds with the appropriation of ingenious and highly creative ideas. Appropriation of such ideas by other creators is seen as a desirable feature of a society that encourages the progress of knowledge and the dichotomy serves as a mechanism for preventing the monopolization of ideas under copyright law. However, while in theory there is almost unanimity as to the prominence of the principle of the idea–expression dichotomy (as well as to its significance), it is its application that proves most problematic.

---

[1] The requirement of novelty under patent law.

Notwithstanding the principle of free access to ideas under copyright law, the present legal position greatly restricts such access in the case of computer programs. Decompilation, which is the only effective method by which one may uncover ideas and concepts used in the development of a new computer program, is a highly regulated practice under our copyright regime. This chapter will argue that the traditional mechanisms built into copyright law for safeguarding free access and use of ideas as the building blocks of our culture are being circumvented by both legislators and software vendors, with the effect of by-passing these traditional protection mechanisms and enabling software vendors to control and monopolise ideas and concepts that underpin their proprietary computer programs.

To put the relevant issues in their proper context, section 1 of this chapter offers a brief overview of the case law and statutory development on the idea–expression dichotomy principle, in both the UK and US. Section 2 examines copyright doctrinal justifications, which support the idea–expression dichotomy principle. Section 3, aimed at the non-technical reader, describes the practice of reverse engineering of computer programs and highlights some key facts concerning decompilation. Section 4 of this chapter describes the conceptual anomaly concerning decompilation, which is a result of the current intellectual property regime. The anomaly is that on one hand ideas and concepts are expected to be open for public access, whilst on the other hand the current intellectual property regime greatly restricts the only method by which one may gain such access in the case of computer programs. In Section 5, the US Courts of Appeal decisions on legitimate decompilation will be reviewed. This chapter will establish that prior to the implementation of the Digital Millennium Copyright Act (DMCA) 1998, United States courts manifested a relaxed approach towards decompilation. Thus, decompilation was considered to be legitimate as long as it was done to uncover un-protectable ideas and concepts that underlined the computer program concerned. Section 6 will look at the effect that the introduction of anti-circumvention provisions have had on the scope of legitimate decompilation. This chapter will argue that the narrowing of the said legitimate scope was done without relevant public policy considerations being taken into account. Finally, Section 7 will examine the growing tendency of software vendors to prohibit or restrict decompilation by using restrictive contractual provisions to that effect in software licences. The effect of such restrictive contractual provisions on both EU and US copyright regimes will be assessed and the legal tools available to the public to combat the said contractual provisions will be analysed. This chapter will conclude with a grim picture of our public domain assets, being constantly under attack, shrinking, while the scope of exclusive rights granted under copyright law is ever-growing.

1.   IDEA–EXPRESSION DICHOTOMY: CASE LAW AND STATUTORY DEVELOPMENT

Case Law Development

The idea–expression doctrine emerged in the second half of the nineteenth century. Up until that point there was no real need for protection against the appropriation of ideas under copyright law. The application of copyright law, even in the case of expression rather than of ideas, was so limited that no risk of monopolisation of ideas existed. For example, early English copyright law gave authors the exclusive right to 'print, reprint or import' their works.[2] Thus, for example, literal translations of works were kept outside the ambit of authors' exclusive rights.[3] Early American copyright law followed the same path. Authors were given the exclusive right '. . . of printing, reprinting, publishing and vending' their works.[4] Under both jurisdictions, the fundamental rationale for the restrictive approach towards copyright protection was the recognition of the main goal of copyright law: the encouragement of new creative works and the recognition that derivative works, such as translations, may well be as important as the initial work. It is clear that as long as copyright law was so narrow in its application, no real need for a mechanism which prevented the monopolisation of ideas was present. It is with the ongoing expansion of the boundaries of copyright protection that the idea–expression dichotomy doctrine began to develop.

As aforementioned, as early as the nineteenth century, courts started to draw the line between ideas and expressions and to recognise that certain ideas could only be expressed in a limited number of ways and therefore their expression could not be protected under copyright law.[5] In one case, *Hollinrake v Truswell*,[6] an English Court of Appeal found that the plaintiff's 'Sleeve Chart' was in fact an apparatus or a mechanism, rather than a literary work. The 'Sleeve Chart' was used for the purpose of accurately measuring the inner part of a sleeve and incorporating, for that purpose, certain lines and figures printed on a piece of cardboard with the following words upon it: 'Top

---

2   The Statute of Anne c. 19 (1709).

3   For example, see *Burnett v Chetwood*, 2 Mer. 441, 35 Eng. Rep. 1008 (Ch. 1720).

4   Act of 31 May 1790, c. 15 S.1, 1 Stat. 124, 1st Cong., 2d Sess. For a similar American approach on literal translations see *Stowe v Thomas*, 23 Fed. Cas. 201 (CCED Pa. 1853).

5   This scenario later become known as the 'merger' doctrine under American copyright law; it is when an idea can only be expressed in a limited number of ways and is, therefore, merged with its expression rendering such expression un-protectable.

6   3 Ch. 420 (1894).

curve line; under curve line; under arm curves; measure round the thick part of the arm; measure round the thick part of the elbow; measure round the knuckles of the hand'. The fact that the 'Sleeve Chart' was a combination of words, curved lines and figures[7] did not lead the court to find that the work in question was a proper subject matter of copyright protection. Thus, the court refused to grant protection to a functional apparatus, irrespective of the fact that this apparatus was expressed in a manner usually found in literary works. It should be noted that the courts' reluctance to grant protection was not a result of the subject matter being a utilitarian functional work. Indeed, the court acknowledged that copyright protection is granted, as a matter of law, to utilitarian works and compilations, such as Post Office Directories, maps etc. In this case, however, protection was sought for an actual apparatus or a system. As the court puts it: 'Copyright, however, does not extend to ideas, or schemes, or systems, or methods; it is confined to their expression'.[8]

American courts faced with similar scenarios adopted a similar line of analysis. The development of the idea–expression dichotomy doctrine, as we know it today, is widely attributed to the Supreme Court decision in *Baker v Selden*.[9] Selden developed a system of bookkeeping by using forms also developed by him, which contained lines and columns explaining how the system was to be employed. Selden published his system in a book in which a textual explanation as to how to use the system and the forms was included. Baker published a book on its own, using the system developed by Selden, but the organisation of columns on his forms was different and different headings were used. Selden sued Baker for copyright infringement. There was no copying of the textual explanation in Selden's book and the parties agreed that the question before the court should be whether Selden's system constituted a copyrightable subject matter. Selden argued that he had copyright in the system since there was no way to use the system without using the ruled lines in his forms. Since the forms were a part of his book, in which he had copyright, it followed that he owned the copyright in the system. Justice Bradley, delivering the court's opinion, stated that: '. . . there is a clear distinction between the book, as such, and the art which it is intended to illustrate'. In describing Selden's ruled lines forms he stated: 'It is a mechanical device, by which a skilled person may accomplish certain results and avoid errors in book-keeping . . . Its ingenuity as a mechanical device may entitle it to entry at the Patent Office, but copyright is intended for authors, not inventors.' Justice Bradley concluded that: 'to give the author of the book an exclusive property in the art described therein, when no examination of its novelty has

---

7   These are the classic components of a literary work.
8   per Lindsey LJ.
9   101 US 99 (1879).

ever been officially made, would be a surprise and a fraud upon the public. That is the province of letters-patent not of copyright.'

The significance of *Baker v Selden* lies in its being the first judicial manifestation of both the idea–expression dichotomy and its close relative – the 'merger' doctrine.[10] Some scholars, as Professor Melville Nimmer has argued,[11] maintain that the underlying reason for the decision in *Baker v Selden* is that Selden's 'blank' forms were not copyrightable since they 'expressed' the system in such a way as to merge with it. Thus, there was no other way to describe the system and therefore the expression of the idea embodied in Selden's work was deemed to be non-copyrightable as the idea itself. It is suggested, however, that Nimmer misinterpreted Justice Bradley decision by reading into it too much of the merger argument. Reading *Baker v Selden*, it appears that the court was not at all concerned with the question of whether there was another way to 'express' the system. Admittedly, the court stated that where an idea may only be expressed in one way, that expression becomes necessary for using the idea and is therefore unprotectable. However, in the case before it the court simply found that the 'ruled lines' and 'headings', incorporated into the 'blank' forms, were not part of a description of the system,[12] but that they were in fact part of the system itself. Thus, the 'blank' forms were found to be non-protectable on the basis of being part of a system. On this view, it appears that even if Selden's bookkeeping system could have been employed using other sets of forms,[13] Selden's forms would still be non-copyrightable since they would still be a part of a system.

English courts continued throughout the second half of the nineteenth century as well as through the twentieth century to reiterate the idea–expression dichotomy doctrine as an axiom of copyright law and to implement it in relevant copyright cases. In *McCrum v Eisner*[14] Peterson J reiterated with approval Lindsey LJ's holding in *Hollinrake v Truswell* to the effect that copyright does not protects ideas but rather protects their expressions. Similarly, in *Harman v Osborne*[15] Justice Goff, as he then was, stated that it was a long-established principle of copyright law that 'there is no copyright in ideas or schemes or systems or methods – it is confined to their expression'.

Indeed, the idea–expression dichotomy has become one of the fundamental

---

10   Supra, note 5.
11   See Melville B. Nimmer and David Nimmer, *Nimmer On Copyright* (New York, M. Bender, 2006 [1963]) § 13.03 [F].
12   That is, part of the work's expression.
13   Thus, not giving rise to the 'merger' doctrine.
14   (1917), 87 LJCh 99 at p. 102.
15   [1967] 2 All ER 324, [1967] 1 WLR 723.

principles of English copyright law.[16] However, although every English court grappling with the subject has contended that the idea–expression dichotomy is a trite law and a well-established principle of copyright law, one may identify a growing tendency by the courts to decide such relevant cases by reference to the rule of originality rather than to the dichotomy principle. Hence, English courts have been collapsing the dichotomy principle into the rule on originality[17] rather than deciding cases on the dichotomy principle, which requires consideration of public policy matters.

Statutory Development

Admittedly, American courts have been more vigilant in preserving the dichotomy principle. Furthermore, the US legislature embedded the dichotomy principle, which originated from copyright case law, within the 1976 copyright legislation. At first, the Copyright Revision Bill that was brought before the US Senate Sub-Committee did not pay any heed to the idea–expression dichotomy.[18] That, however, was met with a strong resistance at the Senate Sub-Committee hearings stage, in particular by representatives of educational organisations, who argued that the broad language of the Bill could be interpreted as covering functional elements of computer programs.[19] As a result, the Sub-Committee had come up with the language of what we now know to be 17 USC § 102(b) on copyrightable subject matter, which makes it clear that copyright protection does not extend to ideas, procedures, processes, systems, methods of operation etc. In addition, the Sub-Committee added to the Committee Report its own explanatory comment on the objective

---

[16]   For other examples of English courts' application of the idea – expression dichotomy see *Poznanski v London Film Production, Ltd*, (1937), MacG. Cop. Cas. (1936–45) 107; *Rees v Melville*, (1914) MacG. Cop. Cas. (1911–16) 168; *Kenrick v Lawrence*, (1890) 25 QBD 99.

[17]   See, for example, *L.B. (Plastics) Limited v Swish Products Limited*, [1979] RPC 551; *Ibcos Computers v Barclays Mercantile*, [1994] FSR 275; *Designers Guild Ltd v Russell Williams (Textiles) Ltd*, [2001] 1 All ER 700.

[18]   Maybe not so surprisingly since the Bill was essentially put together by different interest groups with the blessing of the US copyright office; needless to say, in the case of the distinction between idea and expression, there was no interest group with the relevant vested interest represented in the laborious process of the drafting of the bill.

[19]   See Copyright Law Revision: Hearings on S. 597 Before the Subcomm. on Patents, Trademarks and Copyrights of the Senate Comm. on the Judiciary, 90th Cong., 1st Sess. (1967), at 196–200 (testimony of Arthur Miller, Ad Hoc Committee of Educ. Insts. and Orgs. on Copyright Law Revision); id. at 550 (testimony of Edison Montgomery, Interuniversity Communications Council); id. at 1058–9 (testimony of W. Brown Morton, Interuniversity Communications Council).

of 17 USC § 102(b), which was to 'make clear that the expression adopted by the programmer is the copyrightable element in a computer program, and that the actual processes or methods embodied in the program are not within the scope of the copyright law' (emphasis added).[20] Although the dichotomy never found its way into the British copyright Act, it does have direct statutory application in the UK, at least as far as computer programs are concerned. Recitals 13 and 14 of the Software Directive read as follows:

> [13] Whereas, for the avoidance of doubt, it has to be made clear that only the expression of a computer program is protected and that ideas and principles which underlie any element of a program, including those which underlie its interfaces, are not protected by copyright under this Directive;

> [14] Whereas, in accordance with this principle of copyright, to the extent that logic, algorithms and programming languages comprise ideas and principles those ideas and principles are not protected under this Directive.

Similarly, Article 1(2) of the Software Directive provides that ideas and principles which underlie any element of a computer program are not protected by copyright under the directive. Keeping in mind that the software directive is intended to create a harmonised European regime for copyright protection for computer programs and that it has direct application in the national laws of all member states, one may say that the dichotomy principle forms part of the statutory framework of copyright protection for computer programs all over the European Union.

On the international scene, the dichotomy principle plays a similar role. Article 9(2) of the Agreement on Trade-Related Aspects of Intellectual Property Rights (TRIPS) provides that copyright protection shall not extend to ideas, methods of operation and mathematical concepts.

In the light of the aforementioned global recognition of the dichotomy principle, both judicial and statutory, one may be excused for maintaining that market players within the software industry are entitled to use each other's ideas, for example, algorithms, data structure and overall software architecture, not to mention access to such ideas in the first place. The reality, however, could not be more different.

Prior, however, to examining the reason for the dichotomy principle's lack of effectiveness in the context of computer programs, it is first necessary to consider what objectives the dichotomy principle is designed to serve and what may be the possible justifications for its existence.

---

20   S. Rep. No. 983, 93d Cong., 2d Sess. 107 (1974). See US Copyright Office, (Draft) Second Supplementary Report of the Register of Copyrights on the General Revision of the US Copyright Law: 1975 Revision Bill 57-103 (1975), at 10.

2. JUSTIFICATIONS TO THE IDEA–EXPRESSION DICHOTOMY PRINCIPLE

Under the utilitarian theory, copyright protection is designed to maximise collective social welfare, by encouraging creation and dissemination of knowledge. Thus, ideally, protection should be set at an optimal level by striking a balance between providing sufficient incentives to create by granting exclusive rights, while at the same time conferring these works on the public as close as possible to an optimal level, both in quantity and quality terms. Admittedly, generally speaking the utilitarian theory underlies copyright law in common law systems and has no holding in copyright protection under civil law systems. Civil law systems traditionally justify copyright/author's right by reference to ethical considerations based on natural rights doctrines. Nevertheless, it is clear that at least in the case of computer programs, although being classified as literary works, civil law systems have in mind objectives other than respecting the natural rights of the author. It is sufficient to briefly examine French and German copyright laws with respect to issues such as the concept of originality and works made by employees for this to become apparent.[21] Both French and German laws take much more similar approaches to those taken under common law systems than the approaches taken in these jurisdictions regarding traditional copyrighted works with respect to what they consider to be functional or utilitarian works. Thus, it seems that civil law systems too recognise that copyright protection for utilitarian works such as computer programs is mainly justifiable on the basis of incentive related doctrines. If this is so, one may refer solely to utilitarian based concepts in trying to justify the global acknowledgement that the dichotomy principle enjoys. There are a number of detailed arguments supporting the dichotomy principle, the examination of which is beyond the scope of this chapter.[22] For our purposes, it is sufficient to conclude that most

---

[21]   On the issue of computer programs see: on the concept of originality: generally in the EU – Article 1(3) of the computer programs directive, in France – the Pachot judgment, Plen. sess. 7 March 1986: RIDA July 1986 at 136 and the Isermatic judgment, 1st Civ. Ch., 16 April 1991: Expertises (1991) at 194 and in Germany – decision BGH, CR 1991, 80 – Betriebssystem; on employees' rights: generally in Europe – Article 2(3) of the computer programs directive, in France – Article 45 of the French Statute of 3 July 1985 and in Germany – s. 69(b) of The Second Copyright Act Amending Law of 9 June 1993.

[22]   For some examples, see R.P. Adelstein and S.I. Peretz, 'The Competition of Technologies in Markets for Ideas: Copyright and Fair Use in Evolutionary Perspective', *International Review of Law and Economics* (1985); W.M. Landes and R.A. Posner, 'An Economic Analysis of Copyright Law', *Journal of Legal Studies* (1989), E. Mackaay, 'Economic Incentives in Markets for Information and Innovation',

of these arguments are based on economic efficiency considerations. Thus, monopolising ideas through copyright law and without the checks and balances built into patent law,[23] would almost certainly result in an under-producing society and a less than optimal level of collective social welfare.

3. DECOMPILATION

Reverse Engineering

The dichotomy principle supports free use of ideas and principles under copyright law. Thus, it provides that one may be able to appropriate another's creative endeavour and use it for one's own purposes, as long as the said endeavour remains within the realms of ideas and does not constitute an expression of such an idea. But when exactly does an idea cross this invisible line and become a protectable expression?

This question has troubled jurists for many decades and it seems that on this point no general guidelines may be formulated. As the great early twentieth century American Intellectual Property (IP) jurist, Judge Learned Hand, put it: '[n]obody has ever been able to fix that boundary, and nobody ever can'.[24] Fixing the boundary must therefore 'inevitably be ad-hoc'.[25] Thus, the question of whether one is infringing another's work by borrowing from that work would depend on how exactly one defines an idea. The main focus of this chapter is not, however, the legitimate or illegitimate appropriation of ideas. It is the initial access to ideas that this chapter is concerned with.

In expressional works such as novels and plays, initial access to the ideas and concepts employed in the creation of the original work is a non-issue. Every person who uses the work for its intended purpose, i.e. reading or viewing, is free to analyse the different components and the logical format that the author of such a work employed. This is one of the reasons why copyright law never required an author to disclose the essence of his work as a prior condition for granting protection.[26] Computer programs, however, present a totally different set of considerations. Most of the logic, ideas and concepts employed in the creation of computer programs are not evident from the face of the prod-

---

Harvard Journal for Law and Public Policy (1990), J.E. Cohen, 'Reverse Engineering and the Rise of Electronic Vigilantism: Intellectual Property Implications of "Lock-Out" Programs', *California Law Review* (1995).

 [23] That is, meritorious examination of the different elements of the work at stake, short term of protection and the requirement of sufficient disclosure.

 [24] *Nichols v Universal Pictures Corp.* 45 F.2d 119, at 121.

 [25] Ibid., at 121.

 [26] As inventors are required to provide enabling disclosure under patent law.

uct. Thus, in order to analyse a computer program, one has to go beneath its surface and to look into its internal parts. Such practice is often referred to as reverse engineering.

Reverse engineering may be defined as ' . . . the starting with a finished product and working backwards to analyze how the product operates or how it was made'.[27] The practice of reverse engineering has always had a significant role in assisting human scientific and industrial development. Throughout the history of mankind, people have continually disassembled nature-made and human-made artefacts in order to understand the ideas and concepts that underlie them. Thus, the practice of reverse engineering supports and promotes the idea–expression dichotomy principle. Moreover, the significance of reverse engineering holds true to an even larger extent in the case of the modern software industry. The incremental nature of software development inherently supports the practice whereby one may build upon the ideas of another in the development of a new software product.

However, notwithstanding the legal principle of idea–expression dichotomy, which supports free access to ideas and concepts, and notwithstanding the economic and societal benefits that reverse engineering may encourage, in practice the current copyright regime as well as recent contract law based practices employed by most software vendors enable those vendors to lock away certain intellectual spaces which are not the subject of any property right. It is only in the case of computer programs that the public is denied its otherwise unchallenged right to access ideas and concepts in freely circulating works. The main question this chapter attempts to answer is whether a prohibition on reverse engineering in the form of decompilation of computer programs, together with contractual restrictions against reverse engineering and decompilation, defeat the dichotomy principle and result in monopolisation of ideas and concepts in the software industry, while constituting an excessive reward for software proprietors.

The Need for Decompilation of Computer Programs

A person may wish to engage in the practice of reverse engineering of computer programs for two main reasons: (1) understanding the internal working of computer programs; (2) understanding performance failures of computer programs. Understanding the internal working of a computer program may have three primary objectives: (1) to produce a functional equivalent or better program (i.e. competition); (2) to produce a program that

---

27   *Secure Services Technology Inc. v Time & Space Processing*, 722 F.Supp. 1354, 1361 n.16 (E.D. Va. (1989)).

operates with the studied program (i.e. compatibility); (3) to analyse solutions adopted by the studied program for educative purposes.[28] Understanding performance failures of a computer program is done for diagnostic purposes whereby the programmer attempts to understand why it is that a program fails to perform.

Thus, the ability to 'pick' into a program's internal organs serves objectives which are central to the wellbeing of the software industry. But what practical methods are open to a programmer to employ while trying to understand the internal working of a computer program? Opponents of decompilation point out that there are three primary methods for understanding ideas and concepts which are embodied in a computer program: (1) reading the program documentation; (2) observing the program in operation; (3) disassembly and decompilation. Therefore, the argument goes, there is no necessity to practise decompilation, which is the only method involving reproduction of the program's code (i.e. copyright infringement), when it is possible to achieve the same objectives while engaging in non-infringing activities. However, this chapter argues that it is only the practice of decompilation which provides an effective means of accessing ideas and concepts embodied in a computer program.[29] As regards reading the program's documentation, although it may provide some useful information, it does not enable a programmer to discern anything more than the most basic elements underlying the studied program. For a start, the program's documentation is almost always incomplete, out of date and inaccurate compared to the actual software itself. In addition, the documentation is portraying a picture of what the software should have been like, rather than what the software actually is. Finally, the documentation is useless in the case of an attempt to understand why a program fails to perform. Observing the program in operation as a means of accessing ideas embodied in a computer program is, again, a bogus technical myth that needs to be confronted. It consists of no more than an educated guess as to how the program's coding is structured and it fails to ascertain information as fact. In addition, like reading the program's documentation, it is useless for revealing the precise cause of a program's failure.

That leaves us with the third and final method of reverse engineering a computer program: disassembly and decompilation of the program's code. Decompilation is a long and complex technical process. In a non-technical reader friendly language it may be described as ' . . . a species of reverse engineering that involves translating the object code into human-readable form, or

---

[28]   Which may be done with either commercial or non-commercial objectives in mind.

[29]   Supra, note 3. It should be noted that decompilation may be the most effective method for doing so, but this practice, too, provides only partial information.

"pseudo source code", largely through trial and error'.[30] It differs from traditional mechanical reverse engineering in that it involves prima facie infringement of copyright at two different levels: the creation of intermediary copies of the original program and the additional contribution of the reverse engineer, in combination with the original bits of the program, which may constitute a derivative work. There are a few myths that need to be refuted when assessing the nature of the practice of decompilation. First, decompilation of a computer program is a demanding, expensive and time consuming process. It is not a cheap and parasitical method for appropriating a computer program's secrets. Second, decompilation does not lay bare the program's inner secrets. As one technologist put it: 'the inner secrets of the program, the real crown jewels, are embodied in higher level abstraction materials, such as the source code commentary and specification. This never survives the process of being converted into object code'.[31] Finally, decompilation does not enable a programmer to determine the original design rationale. The reverse engineer can discern what the program is doing, but not the underlying reason as to why it does it the way it does. Some of the missing information may be supplemented by a tedious process of trial and error, accompanied by educated guesses based on the reverse engineer's competence and expertise.

Under these circumstances, one would accept that, surely, decompilation would be permitted under our Intellectual Property regime. After all, a right to decompilation merely enables access to ideas and concepts which underlie computer programs. It has nothing to do with wrongful appropriation of such ideas. Such appropriation is regulated by the 'substantial similarity' principle of copyright law in combination with the application of the idea–expression dichotomy rule. Surprisingly, this is not the case. Decompilation is a practice that is heavily regulated under our intellectual property law regime. In EU member states decompilation is permissible only for the limited purpose of achieving interoperability. In the US, although initially the scope for legitimate decompilation under the 'fair use' defence of section 107 of the Copyright Act[32] was greater, things have changed with the implementation of the DMCA[33] and the growing practice of inserting restrictive contractual provisions into software licences.

---

[30]   J. Litman, 'Copyright and Information Policy', *Law & Contemporary Problems* (Spring 1992) 185, 197–8.

[31]   Supra, note 3.

[32]   Both in *Sega Enterprises v Accolade, Inc*, 977 F.2d 1510 (9th Cir. 1993) and *Sony Computer Entertainment, Inc. v Connectix Corp.*, 203 F.3d 596 (9th Cir. 2000), cert., *Denied*, the court held that disassembly is fair use as a matter of law where it is necessary to gain access to the ideas contained within a copyrighted program.

[33]   Digital Millennium Copyright Act 1998.

The DMCA (at the very least) puts into question the ability of competing software developers to reverse engineer a program in order to gain access to its un-copyrighted ideas and concepts. With the enactment of the DMCA and the provisions concerning technological protection measures, the previous, more relaxed, position has been effectively changed.[34] The only thing required from a software proprietor to do in order to safeguard the ideas and concepts underling his program from being exposed through reverse engineering is to apply technological protection measures that effectively prevent reverse engineering. Circumventing these technological protection measures, unless done for the limited purpose of achieving interoperability, will result in infringement of the anti-circumvention provisions. In Europe, the position under the Software Directive has always been that reverse engineering is permitted only for the limited purpose of 'interoperability'.

4.   THE ANOMALY

Having the idea–expression dichotomy principle on the one hand and prohibitions and restrictions on decompilation on the other hand creates a legal anomaly. This anomaly may be better illustrated by way of a simple analogy with the world of real property. Let us assume, for example, that there is a country where private ownership of land is permissible and encouraged due to the government's recognition of the advantages of such a system over common management of land. Now, let us also assume that due to a policy based decision, the government enacts a law which prohibits private ownership over natural resources such as ports, river banks and roads[35] and requires that such resources should be kept open for the use of the public at large. On the basis of these given circumstances, it would not make any sense for the government to grant farmer X exclusive ownership over a plot of land which is adjacent, for example, to a natural port, so that the only way to access such a port would be by trespassing onto farmer X's private property. Such grant of exclusive ownership would give farmer X a de facto monopoly over a resource (i.e. a natural port) to which open access is considered to be essential for the efficient functioning of the market and therefore for general public welfare. A system that wishes to promote efficiency by ensuring that such essential resources are open to public use, must provide that such an exclusive grant of land is subject to some form of public 'right of way' which enables the public to access the

---

34   17 USC s. 1201(f).
35   For example, due to efficiency arguments related to the significance of such resources in the development of commerce, trade and thus its general contribution to public welfare.

aforementioned natural port, albeit with as minimal interference as possible with farmer X's exclusively owned land. This analogy reflects the anomaly present in the intellectual property laws concerned with the decompilation of computer programs. On the one hand, our intellectual property regime explicitly recognises the significance of ideas as building blocks of our society, and the role that allowing open access to ideas plays in promoting competitiveness and market efficiency. On the other hand, in the case of certain elements of a computer program's architecture, exclusive rights are granted under circumstances where ideas and concepts are essentially barred from public access due to a unique technological reality.

As discussed above, the position in the US was quite different until the implementation of the DMCA. In a series of decisions on the legitimacy of decompilation of computer programs, different US Courts of Appeal followed the rationale of the dichotomy principle to the letter.

5.   LEGITIMISING DECOMPILATION AS 'FAIR USE'

In *Atari Games Corp. v Nintendo of America Inc.*,[36] the Court of Appeal for the Federal Circuit had to determine, inter alia, whether reverse engineering for the purpose of uncovering ideas and concepts, involving intermediate reproductions, constituted copyright infringement. The court believed that it does not. The court stated that

> the author does not acquire exclusive rights to a literary work in its entirety . . . society is free to exploit facts, ideas, processes, or methods of operation in a copyrighted work. To protect processes or methods of operation, a creator must look to patent laws. An author cannot acquire patent-like protection by putting an idea, process, or method of operation in an unintelligible format and asserting copyright infringement against those who try to understand that idea, process, or method of operation.[37]

The court continued and expanded on what it believed to be the societal objective behind copyright law:

> The copyright holder has a property interest in preventing others from reaping the fruits of his labour, not in preventing the authors and thinkers of the future from making use of, or building upon, his advances. The process of creation is often an incremental one, and advances building on past developments are far more common than radical new concepts.[38]

---

[36]   975 F.2d 832.
[37]   Ibid., at 842.
[38]   Ibid., at 843.

Although the decision was concerned with reverse engineering for the purpose of achieving interoperability, it can clearly be seen that the court's decision is not limited to this scenario only. The court made it clear that it would not allow a software proprietor to lock away ideas and concepts that underpin their computer programs behind the technological reality of computer technology, since that would defeat one of the main purposes for which copyright protection is granted in the first place: the free-flow of ideas for the benefit of society at large.

In *Sega Enterprises Ltd v Accolade, Inc.*,[39] the Court of Appeal for the Ninth Circuit had to confront a similar scenario. Again, the case involved decompilation for the purpose of developing video games that interoperate with the plaintiff's game console. Again, the court's language was not limited to this particular scenario. The court stated that in establishing whether decompilation of copyrighted material amounts to fair use under section 107, the public policy underlying copyright legislation must be kept in mind. The court reminded itself that 'the immediate effect of our copyright law is to secure a fair return for an "author's" creative labour. But the ultimate aim is, by this incentive, to stimulate artistic creativity for the general public good'.[40] The court then observed that

> the fact that computer programs are distributed for public use in object code form often precludes public access to the ideas and functional concepts contained in those programs, and thus confers on the copyright owner a de facto monopoly over those ideas and functional concepts. That result defeats the fundamental purpose of the Copyright Act – to encourage the production of original works by protecting the expressive elements of those works while leaving the ideas, facts, and functional concepts in the public domain for others to build on.[41]

Thus, it is clear that in both cases the court felt that it would be wrong, on public policy grounds, to allow software proprietors to use the unique technological reality of the software world to deny access to and gain protection over what would be otherwise considered as un-protectable subject matter.

In *Sony Computer Entertainment v Connectix*, the Ninth Circuit was called, again, to decide on the issue of the legitimacy of decompilation and disassembly of computer program code found in a video game console in order to gain access to functional ideas hidden beneath the program's surface. In this case the court went one step further. Unlike the two aforementioned cases, this case did not involve decompilation of computer games software in order to

---

[39]   977 F.2d 1510.
[40]   Ibid., at 1527, quoting *Sony Corp.*, 464 US at 432 (quoting *Twentieth Century Music Corp. v Aiken,* 422 US 151, 156, 45 L. Ed. 2d 84, 95 S. Ct. 2040 (1975)).
[41]   Ibid., at 1527.

develop a console that would be compatible with these games; neither did it involve decompilation of console software in order to develop compatible computer games. The case rather concerned decompilation of console software in order to gain access to the functional ideas that underpin it for the purpose of developing a competing system, a console emulator. That console emulator was designed to be compatible with Sony video games. Moreover, not only did the defendant in this case disassemble Sony's code in order to study it, but he actually used that code in developing its own program. That fact was one of the reasons why the District Court found in favour of Sony. The District Court Judge distinguished the case from *Sega* and stated: 'They disassembled Sony's code not just to study the concepts. They actually used that code in the development of their product'. The Circuit Court of Appeal, however, found that distinction to be of little relevance, if any. According to the Circuit Court of Appeal, once it is acknowledged that the functional elements in question are not the subject matter of copyright protection, it is open to the public to use them as it sees fit, as long as the end product, in this case the console emulator software, is non-infringing. It is submitted that this approach encapsulates public policy considerations that underpin copyright protection. One should not be able to take advantage of the unique nature of computer technology in order to bar access to un-protectable elements of copyrighted works. As much as any competitor may examine and analyse ideas and concepts that are used in the creation of other, more traditional, types of copyright works, so should competitors in the software industry be entitled to do so. Holding otherwise may result in broadening the scope of subject matter of copyright protection to ideas, schemes and functional processes. This, in turn, may have negative repercussions on the software market. It should be recalled, at this stage, that a right of decompilation does not go as far as the court in Sony went. Decompilation is concerned with the right of access to ideas. The type of use one may choose to make of such ideas should be examined according to general copyright principles. The idea–expression dichotomy suggests that appropriation of such ideas may not amount to infringement. This, however, is outside the scope of this chapter. The author of this work is solely concerned with the right to access, view and study ideas and concepts that underpin computer programs.

On top of the unique technological reality that obscures a program's underlying ideas from the user,[42] software vendors have started to use deliberate technological measures designed to make the uncovering of such ideas even more difficult.

---

[42]   Hence, requiring decompilation in order to uncover such ideas.

6. THE APPLICATION OF TECHNOLOGICAL PROTECTION MEASURES

In Europe, the Information Society Directive provides that, except for limited instances, the directive shall not affect Community provisions relating to, inter alia, the legal protection of computer programs. Hence, the limited right of decompilation for the purpose of interoperability could not be overridden by the application of technological protection measures. Where a rightholder applies technological protection measures to that effect, circumvention of such measures should not result with infringement of the anti-circumvention provisions.

In the US the position is somewhat different. As we have seen, decompilation in order to gain access to unprotectable elements of a computer program was, in principle, permitted under the broad exception of 'fair use'. Such permissible decompilation was not necessarily limited to cases of interoperability. The introduction of the DMCA has effectively changed this position. Section 1201(f) authorises circumvention and the development of means for such circumvention for the sole purpose of identifying program elements necessary for achieving interoperability. Thus, although in principle prior to the DMCA decompilation may have been available for purposes other than interoperability, as long as it was done in order to gain access to un-protectable program elements, applying technological protection measures may have had the effect of limiting the ability of a competitor to decompile a computer program to scenarios of interoperability only. The legal position on decompilation for purposes other than achieving interoperability is, however, far from certain. Section 1201(c)(1) states that nothing in section 1201 affects rights, remedies, limitations or defenses to copyright infringement, including fair use. Hence, if one accepts that prior to the introduction of DMCA decompilation was permissible under the 'fair use' defence for a wider range of purposes than achieving interoperability, then according to section 1201(c)(1) such practices shall continue to be permissible. If, however, this was the intention of Congress, why did it find it necessary to stipulate explicitly that in the case of decompilation, circumvention of technological protection measures shall be permitted only for the sole purpose of achieving interoperability? These two seemingly contradictory provisions are difficult to reconcile. On the face of it, section 1201(c)(1) seems to suggest that nothing has changed and that the previously available scope of 'fair use' defence was not affected. Thus, circumventing technological protection measures in order to be engaged in 'fair use' practices should not amount to infringement. On the other hand, the fact that Congress stipulated an explicit and sole exception for circumvention of technological protection measures in the case of decompilation indicates a clear legislative intention to limit decompilation to the scenario of achieving interoperability only. It is suggested that in case of a conflict between the two provisions, the explicit legislative intention would prevail over the general provision, thus having the effect of bringing the US position into line with the European one.

On top of the said potential restriction concerning the practice of decompilation, market players in the software industry have been facing another, potentially more damaging, onslaught: the implementation of restrictive contractual provisions.

7.   THE APPLICATION OF RESTRICTIVE CONTRACTUAL PROVISIONS

Under most legal systems, once an article is sold the purchaser is entitled to do with it as he sees fit. Even in the case of intellectual property products, such as books, sound recording etc., the end user is entitled to use the particular copy as he wishes, so long as this use does not result in copyright infringement. In the case of computer programs, however, the situation is different. Software vendors have been claiming for some time now that their wares are licensed rather than being sold. This is designed to enable them to control, inter alia, the type of use the end user may wish to make. One of the activities that software vendors often seek to prevent, through the use of licensing terms, is decompilation. A detailed discussion of the different models of licences software vendors most commonly deploy is beyond the scope of this chapter.[43] It is sufficient to list the three models of licence that are most commonly used: shrinkwrap, clickwrap and browsewrap licences.

A Shrinkwrap licence is a licence in a tangible form where the customer is informed (by terms wrapped on the packaging in a transparent film and visible to the customer) that by opening the seal of the package he is accepting the terms of the licence.

A Clickwrap license is a type of licence that came into use when software vendors began distributing software by means other than disks, such as when the software is pre-installed on a computer for the user, or when the software is downloaded over the Internet. Upon downloading, installation or first use of the application, a window containing the terms of the licence opens for the user to read. The user is asked to click either 'I agree' or 'I do not agree'. If the user does not agree, the process is terminated. The clickwrap licence gives

---

[43]   For a detailed discussion on the different models of software contracts, see, M.A. Lemley, P.S. Menell, R.P. Merges and P. Samuelson, *Software and Internet Law*, 2nd edn (New York: Aspen, 2003).

rise to many factual questions as to whether the user had adequate notice of the licence terms and clearly assented to them. With respect to software downloads, the clickwrap terms are regularly displayed at the very start of the contract formation process, although often the terms are contained in a scrollable window that requires the user to scroll down to read all of the terms.

A Browsewrap licence is a licence that does not appear on the screen and the user is not compelled to accept or reject the terms as a condition for proceeding with further computer operations. Instead, a browsewrap agreement appears only as a hyperlink that is accessed by clicking on the link. It is optional, not required. This makes browsewrap agreements much more susceptible to challenge on the grounds of lack of reasonable notice and bona fide consent to the browsewrap terms.

There are numerous contract law based legal arguments against the enforcement of contractual terms in each of the aforementioned licence models. Some US courts have focused on the question of whether describing the transaction as a licence suffices for the transaction to be treated by the courts as such.[44] Other courts have preferred to focus on the contractual question of whether the licence terms were indeed incorporated into the transaction so that it could be said that the parties manifested their consent to the said terms. A detailed discussion of the aforementioned contractual dilemmas is beyond the scope of this chapter. Moreover, the outcome of such a discussion would greatly depend on contract law principles in the jurisdiction concerned. This chapter would rather focus on theoretical and doctrinal arguments in favour of disregarding contractual provisions which prohibit a lawful user from accessing the concepts and processes underlying computer programs.

First, it is important to note that the EU position regarding such contractual provisions is markedly different to the US position. Although limited in the first place, one may argue that at least the EU approach on the matter is consistent. Permitting decompilation of computer programs for the limited purpose of achieving interoperability, the Software Directive explicitly provides that any contractual provision to the contrary shall be void.[45] Thus, after identifying a policy based objective according to which decompilation is advantageous to the market only for the limited purpose of achieving interoperability, EU legislators were not prepared to let such an objective be overridden through the use of contractual provisions to the contrary. Hence, the use of restrictive contractual provisions has no effect on the legitimacy of decompilation within EU member states. In the US, however, the position is different.

---

44   For example, in *Microsoft Corp v DAK Indus*, 66 F.3d 1091 (9th Cir. 1995) the court stated that it is the economic realities of the transaction that would ultimately determine whether a transaction would be categorised as a licence rather than as a sale.

45   Software Directive, Recital 24.

There is no statutory provision rendering a contractual provision prohibiting a legitimate 'fair use' in general or a legitimate 'fair use' decompilation in particular, as void. Thus, prima facie, a software vendor may circumvent the 'fair use' protection a lawful user enjoys by inserting restrictive contractual provisions into the software licensing agreement. It therefore seems that in the case of restrictive contractual provisions, a user may be able to turn to three types of legal recourses for protection: general principles of contract law: usually arguing that he did not consent to the said contractual provisions within contract law meaning; competition law principles: arguing that the restrictive provisions infringe anti-trust principles; and copyright misuse doctrine. While neither contract law nor competition law principles require further introduction, the equitable doctrine of copyright misuse does.

In *Lasercomb America v Reynolds*[46] the Court of Appeal for the Fourth Circuit, explaining the nature of this equitable doctrine, stated: 'The question is not whether the copyright is being used in a manner violative of antitrust law (such as whether the licensing agreement is reasonable), but whether the copyright is being used in a manner violative of the public policy embodied in the grant of a copyright'. Thus, where a software vendor is using copyright in order to gain commercial advantages that go beyond the public policy rationale underlying copyright law, copyright misuse doctrine may come into play. The court further elaborated: 'The misuse arises in Lasercomb's attempt to use its copyright in a particular expression, the Interact software, to control competition in an area outside the copyright, i.e. the idea of computer assisted die manufacture, regardless of whether such conduct amounts to an antitrust violation'. Applying this rationale, it may be argued that any anti-decompilation contractual provision, which would otherwise amount to 'fair use', should be rendered unenforceable under the copyright misuse doctrine. After all, we have seen that free use and access to unprotectable ideas and concepts is one of the tenets of our copyright regime. Using copyright licensing terms in order to extend a vendor's monopoly to those program elements which lie outside the ambit of copyright protection should amount to copyright misuse. Unfortunately, however, no decision to that effect has been delivered by any US court to this date. The application of copyright misuse doctrine has been scarce and the use of restrictive contractual provisions by software vendors is continually growing.

---

[46]   911 F.2d 970 (4th Cir. 1990).

8.   CONCLUSIONS

As we have seen, decompilation is the only effective practice of reverse engineering in the case of computer programs. Reverse engineering is a practice whose value was often appreciated throughout history. In *Bonito Boats, Inc. v Thunder Craft Boats, Inc.,*[47] the United States Supreme Court examined the important societal benefit of reverse engineering, pointing out that 'reverse engineering of chemical and mechanical articles in the public domain often leads to significant advances in technology'. The Court further stressed that 'the competitive reality of reverse engineering may act as a spur to the inventor, creating an incentive to develop inventions that meet the rigorous requirements of patentability'.[48] It is therefore surprising to find that the constant push by software vendors to limit and restrict the legitimate scope of decompilation has been so successful and has met very little legislative and judicial resistance. After all, computer programs' internal architecture or algorithms are a type of a system or a process;[49] they are a set of steps or phases designed to bring about a requisite result. As we have seen, both US and UK copyright laws acknowledge that systems and processes should lie outside the scope of copyright protectable subject matter. Why is it then that a competitor is not allowed to view software architecture for competitive or research purposes? What public policy based reason might exist to justify the retention of ideas and concepts that underlie a computer program as a trade secret, when a patent proprietor, who is required to satisfy a strict set of requirements, enjoys an exclusive right for a period of only 20 years, and must provide a full disclosure of the ideas and concepts that make his invention work? This chapter suggests that whatever these reasons may be, they have nothing to do with a coherent legal theory justification, nor do they have any market efficiency and public policy justification.

---

[47]   489 US 141.

[48]   On the economic importance of reverse engineering see also Lawrence D. Graham and Richard O. Zerbe, Jr., 'Economically Efficient Treatment of Computer Software: Reverse Engineering, Protection, and Disclosure', 22 *Rutgers Computer and Technology Law Journal* 61, 125 (1996), arguing that Microsoft software development process was slow with regard to its early DOS software partially because of absence of competition, and suggesting that a more relaxed reverse engineering policy might have encouraged Microsoft to innovate at a faster pace.

[49]   It resembles an industrial manufacturing process rather than any traditional copyright creative platform.

7. The pharmaceutical industry, the evolution of patent law and the public interest: A brief history

Graham Dutfield

The manufacture of synthetic medicinal agents, artificial perfumes, sweetening materials, antitoxines, nutritives, and photographic developers are all outgrowths of the coal-tar industry, and in great part still remain attached to the colour works where they originated. Of these subsidiary industries the most important is the manufacture of synthetic medicinal preparations, which has already attained to large proportions, and bids fair to revolutionise medical science.

Arthur G. Green, FIC, FCS, 1901[1]

This chapter traces the historical development of the modern pharmaceutical industry and shows how the development of this industry and of patent law were tightly linked. As the chapter indicates, patent regulation has never been solely an economic issue or just a technical matter. Politics and international relations are essential elements as well. The way that the industry has helped to shape the development of patent law requires us to consider the extent to which the public interest has been accommodated.

1. THE SCIENTIFIC FOUNDATIONS OF THE MODERN PHARMACEUTICAL INDUSTRY

The nineteenth century experienced some major pharmacological break-throughs, especially in the extraction and purification of the active principles of plant-based drugs. Pharmacists and doctors were able to sell and administer powerful alkaloid substances such as morphine, codeine, quinine and cocaine whose purity, strength and dosage could at last be regulated (Porter 1997:333–4). There is little doubt that such advances made the use of traditional natural product remedies appear unscientific, unless they were exploited as sources of active compounds rather than as drugs themselves.

---

[1]   Green 1915[1901]:190.

Consequently, 'since the late 1800s, when specific agents were isolated and characterized, the need for standardization and synthesis of natural substances favoured the development of the drug industry' (Duffin 1999:107).

Modern pharmaceutical science is inherently multidisciplinary. Apart from synthetic organic chemistry, it is based on pharmacology, physiology, immunology, bacteriology and fermentation science, among other life science disciplines. While scientists and institutions from various countries contributed to the development of these new fields of enquiry, the modern pharmaceutical industry was invented in late nineteenth-century Germany. Bayer and Hoechst were the most prominent pioneering firms. In hindsight, there are very good reasons why the industry emerged in Germany and is, to some extent at least, an offshoot of dyestuff research and development.

The application of synthetic chemistry to drug discovery began to bear fruit from the late nineteenth century, and the dyestuff firms were at the forefront, along with a small number of longer established pharmacy firms. Arguably, Bayer became the world's first pharmaceutical company when, in 1888, it placed on the market an anti-pyretic drug that it sold as Phenactin. 'For the first time, a drug had been conceived, developed, tested, and marketed, all by a private company. It marked the creation of the modern drug industry, the marriage of science and business that has transformed this century, making huge profits even as it saves lives' (Mann and Plummer 1991:23).

By the outbreak of the First World War, Bayer and other German firms had developed a range of pharmaceutical products based on advanced research carried out in-house and in universities and hospitals. To give an early example, in 1874 at St Mary's Hospital in London, a therapeutic compound developed by a team led by Frederick Pierce turned out to be 'one of the first drugs ever produced by modifying a natural molecule' (Stone and Darlington 2000:93). Two decades later, Bayer adopted this new chemical and subsequently marketed it under the brand name 'Heroin'. But without doubt, the most famous (as opposed to notorious) drug produced in these early years of the pharmaceutical industry was Bayer's Aspirin.

Another hugely significant advance around the turn of the century was Salvarsan. This arsenical compound, synthesized by Paul Ehrlich, was discovered by him and his colleagues to be effective against syphilis, and patented in 1909 by Hoechst. In fact, most of the early chemotherapeutic drugs came out of the laboratories of the German dyestuff companies or of academic chemists who had connections with these firms.

Advances in bacteriology and immunology associated with Pasteur, Koch and Ehrlich also catalysed the emergence of the modern pharmaceutical industry. Pasteur and Koch showed that many illnesses were caused by invasive bacteria, identified the microbes causing several of the major diseases, and produced a number of highly effective vaccines. Discovering the role of white blood cells in destroying disease-causing bacteria inspired the idea of using biological agents to fight disease. This, and the realization made in 1888 by two of Pasteur's students that it was not necessarily the bacterial cells but the toxins they produced which caused disease, led eventually to the discovery and industrial production of penicillin and the antibiotics (Bynum 1994:160). These are substances produced by fungi or bacteria which inhibit or destroy other bacteria yet cause no harm to humans. This huge advance for pharmaceutical science and, as it turned out, for the pharmaceutical industry, was nonetheless somewhat slow in coming, not taking place until the 1940s.

The insight that blood serum also contained anti-bacterial agents inspired another scientific approach to pharmaceutical research and development. The bacteriologist Paul Ehrlich, impressed by the specificity of coal tar dye staining applied to human and animal tissue, investigated the chemical structures of various dyes (Porter 1997:450). His aim was to discover synthetic versions of natural antibodies. Eventually this strategy led to the twentieth-century chemotherapeutic revolution whose origins by many accounts lie in the sulphonamide drugs, first discovered in 1935.

Patent law may originally have had something to do with this orientation towards synthetic chemistry. In Germany, among the court decisions from 1888 to 1890 which expanded the scope of patentability in chemistry was one which to some extent circumvented the pharmaceutical exception in applying these changes to medicines as long as they were chemically synthesized substances (Wimmer 1998:287–8). These changes probably encouraged German and Swiss dyestuff firms (which were dependent on the German market) to move into pharmaceuticals and to manufacture synthetic rather than natural products.

From the 1940s to the 1960s, though, many of the most important new drugs were based on the discovery of substances found in nature, such as microorganisms and hormones. This situation favoured companies whose expertise lay in natural product research and fermentation science. Since many of these companies were American or British, these two countries became relatively more innovative than the German, Swiss and French firms whose scientific and technological traditions were more on the side of synthetic chemistry. By the mid-1960s, it was becoming apparent that the balance of industrial power was shifting from the chemical-pharmaceutical giants like Bayer, Hoechst, Du Pont and ICI to those firms whose background was related more closely to the biological sciences (Thomas 1994:478). Most recently, the new biotechnologies are pushing pharmaceutical research and development ever closer to biology and away from chemistry (though chemistry continues to be the source of much of the scientific and legal discourse).

Patent law turned out not to be an insurmountable obstacle to the protection and exclusive commercialization of such products. In most legal jurisdictions the mere discovery of a compound found in nature does not constitute a patentable invention. But in time, the courts in several countries determined that isolated and purified natural substances could be patented, as could partially and completely synthetic versions.[2]

Nowadays, the situation is somewhat confusing. To many in the pharmaceutical industry, natural product research is quite unappealing, being slow and expensive (ten Kate and Laird 1999:56), especially when the therapeutic effect involves the interaction of a complex of chemicals acting together. Drug discovery is generally considered to be a laboratory-based activity carried out by skilled technicians employing advanced methods such as combinatorial chemistry allowing for the generation of huge numbers of new compounds. Rather than seek new chemicals existing in nature, companies often prefer to build up and screen huge 'libraries of synthetic compounds from basic inorganic and petroleum-based chemicals' (ibid.:50).

One can only be impressed at the ability of chemists to construct completely novel molecules, that they have created 10 million since the birth of synthetic chemistry, and that pharmaceutical companies can now synthesize 25 000 varieties of a single molecule (Bensaude-Vincent and Stengers 1996:254–5). It is plausible that combinatorial chemistry and the new biotechnologies will herald a new era in which rational drug design is *the* method of discovering new therapeutic compounds and old-fashioned serendipity is no longer necessary.

Even so, the pharmaceutical industry is still surprisingly dependent on natural products and even on the traditional knowledge of rural communities, including those inhabiting isolated parts of the globe such as the Amazon (Plotkin 2000). University of Illinois pharmacologist, Norman Farnsworth, found that 119 plant-based compounds were used in medicine worldwide in 1988, of which 74 per cent had the same or related uses as the medicinal plants from which they were derived (Farnsworth 1988). In the same paper he also indicated that 25 per cent of the total sales value of drugs sold in OECD countries as a whole was constituted by products containing at least one plant-derived ingredient. Using these findings, an economic study estimated that the total market value of plant-based medicines sold in OECD countries in 1990 was US$61 billion (Principe 1998:44–5). A more up-to-date estimate for the USA is that, from 1989 to 1995, 60 per cent of new anti-cancer and anti-infective drugs were of 'natural origin', meaning that they were either 'original

---

2   In 1884, the Commissioner of the United States Patent Office (see *Cochrane v Badische Anilin & Soda Fabrik* (1884), 111 US 293 Commissioner's Decisions 230) denied a patent for synthetic alizarin because it was a copy of what existed in nature and therefore lacked novelty. But over time, patent offices and courts began to allow such patents as long as the claims did not extend to the chemical in its natural state.

natural products, products derived semisynthetically from natural products, or synthetic products based on natural product models' (Cragg et al. 1997:52).

Moreover, it continues to be difficult for therapeutic molecules to be designed and manufactured from scratch without using existing chemical structures as initial leads. Even the new combinatorial chemistry techniques need to work on existing lead structures to generate their compound libraries, and some of these will originate from natural sources (ten Kate and Laird 1999:50, 57). This difficulty in developing completely new substances explains why the first biopharmaceuticals were not novel proteins but naturally occurring ones like insulin and human growth hormone that were produced in transgenic microorganisms.

2. DRUG DISCOVERY IN THE TWENTIETH CENTURY: A BRIEF SURVEY

Considering the tremendous advances in organic chemistry during the nineteenth and early twentieth centuries, and the establishment of microbiology as a scientific discipline, it may seem strange that the therapeutic revolution was so long in coming. Until the Second World War, the number of new chemical entities was small, the research-based pharmaceutical industry hardly existed, especially outside Germany, and most of the drugs available would be considered primitive by today's doctors, pharmacists and patients. According to the medical journalist James Le Fanu (1999:206):

> The newly qualified doctor setting up practice in the 1930s had a dozen or so proven remedies with which to treat the multiplicity of different diseases he encountered every day: aspirin for rheumatic fever, digoxin for heart failure, the hormones thyroxine and insulin for an underactive thyroid and diabetes respectively, salvarsan for syphilis, bromides for those who needed a sedative, barbiturates for epilepsy, and morphine for pain. Thirty years later, when the same doctor would have been approaching retirement, those dozen remedies had grown to over 2,000.

This lack of early success probably had much to do with the basic lack of understanding about cell function. This meant that discovering compounds affecting the functioning of target cells was of necessity heavily dependent on serendipity (Le Fanu 1999:209). Once cell function was better understood, researchers became less dependent on good fortune. Be that as it may, good luck continues often to be an essential condition for success.

Our intention is not to provide an exhaustive account of drug discovery over the course of the twentieth century. Rather, we focus on what are generally considered to be among the most significant breakthroughs. The three therapeutic revolutions are chosen for a number of reasons and not just because they resulted in the saving of millions of lives and the improvement of the lives of many others suffering from non-fatal chronic illnesses. Each of them involved the development of not just one but many successful and profitable drugs. They also played a major role in fostering the growth and transformation of the pharmaceutical industry. Not only did the industry begin to generate huge profits, but success and the likelihood of further success encouraged drug companies to invest increasingly large sums of money in the discovery and development of more drugs. In short, these three revolutions provided the conditions for the emergence of today's research-based pharmaceutical industry.

The sulphonamide revolution was founded on the working hypothesis first formulated by Paul Ehrlich, that the ability of dye chemicals to stain microbes and tissues selectively might enable them to affect the metabolism of disease-causing microbes without damaging or killing friendly ones and tissues. The story begins in the late 1920s, when Gerhard Domagk, a senior researcher at I.G. Farbenindustrie, which was formed in 1925 by the merger of the main German chemical firms, decided to follow Ehrlich's example by testing his company's dyes for therapeutic effects. In 1932, he discovered that an azo dye given the name of Prontosil Red inhibited streptococcal infections in mice, and in 1935 he published the results of his experiments. The dye turned out to produce a bacteriostatic effect, which is to say that it did not kill bacteria outright, but prevented them from reproducing. Domagk's company subsequently played a major role in the sulphonamide revolution, and his achievement was recognized with a Nobel Prize.

The first country after Germany where commercial and scientific activity in this area took place was France. Roussel Laboratories in that country had the advantage of being able to copy I.G. Farben's French patent on Prontosil Red. This was because French patent law at the time allowed it to be protected as a dye but not as a medicine (Sneader 1985:287). Subsequent research at the Pasteur Institute in Paris led to the discovery of a more effective substance, called sulphanilamide. This chemical was actually the active part of the prontosil compound, released into the body as the dye was metabolized. It worked by inhibiting the multiplication of bacteria, thereby helping the immune system to eradicate them (Weatherall 1990:150). Since sulphanilamide had been synthesized three decades earlier and described in a publication, it was unpatentable.

Soon after, a British company called May and Baker developed a related drug called M&B 693 that was more effective against streptococci as well as other organisms including pneumococci, and was also less toxic (Sneader 1985:288). Other similar substances were subsequently synthesized and found also to have therapeutic effects against a range of infectious diseases, including leprosy. These became known collectively as the sulphonamides, or sulpha drugs (Weatherall 1990:152). Achilladelis notes that 'the companies that rushed to ride the [sulphonamide] bandwagon, and did so successfully, were predominantly chemical companies with strong R&D expertise in dyestuffs: Ciba, Geigy, Sandoz, Hoffman LaRoche, as well as ICI, American Cyanamid, Rhône-Poulenc/May and Baker' (Achilladelis 1993:285). Merck and Sharp and Dohme (which merged in 1953), which were also involved, were among the few exceptions to this rule (ibid.:286).

The sulpha drugs were undoubtedly a tremendous boon for the many patients who might otherwise have lost their lives. They also contributed to future drug discovery. Research into the mode of action of sulphanilamide led to the formulation of a new working hypothesis that guided scientists in their design of new drugs for specific microbial targets, competitive antagonism. The idea is that certain chemicals play a vital role in metabolic processes that are specific to particular species of microbe. The possibility arises that structurally related chemicals can be designed which 'trick' the target microbe into taking them up and using them in place of the real substance. But since they do not perform the same role, the process cannot take place, and the microbe is weakened or destroyed (Weatherall 1990:152–4). Adoption of this principle led to the development of several important drugs. These include para-amino salicylic acid (PAS), a treatment for tuberculosis discovered in 1946 by the Danish doctor, Jorgen Lehmann; azathioprine, an immuno-suppressive drug developed in a US lab of Burroughs Wellcome by George Hitchings and Gertrude Elion; and the beta-blockers, such as propronalol, that were pioneered in the 1960s by James Black, then at ICI. A decade later, Black was responsible for another triumph of rational drug design, the anti-ulcerant cimetidine. Under the brand name of Tagamet, this drug generated massive revenues for Smith, Kline and French, where he was employed at the time.

Unfortunately, there was at least one tragic incident. In 1937, 76 people in the USA lost their lives after taking the highly toxic Elixir of Sulphanilamide. The government responded by introducing regulations requiring that drugs be tested for safety before they could be sold to the public (Mann 1999:35). These measures were subsequently adopted elsewhere. Allowing drugs to be sold without safety testing is of course unthinkable now.

The discovery of penicillin is often, though not perhaps correctly (since earlier claims exist), traced to 1928, when Alexander Fleming found a mould displaying antibacterial properties in his laboratory at St Mary's Hospital in London. Little progress was made for a decade. This changed when Howard Florey and Ernst Chain at Oxford University decided to study penicillin, and, with the help of Norman Heatley and the financial assistance of the Rockefeller Foundation, produced enough for a very small-scale clinical trial that proved its effectiveness. With the Second World War under way, the urgent need to scale up production was manifest, but companies like ICI,

Burroughs Wellcome and Boots, while interested, were unable or unwilling to invest in the development of new technologies to mass-produce penicillin. This may have been because the Medical Research Council, which had also funded the Oxford team's research, believed it would be unethical to file patents. Without the possibility of market exclusivity, the companies might have been less willing to invest large sums of money in research (ibid.:51). But this is unlikely to be the whole story. A recent history of Glaxo reveals that the company made efforts to contact Florey expressing interest in penicillin, but he did not reply to the two letters sent to him. To the author of this history, 'these events contrasted with Florey's later assertion that he had contacted several British pharmaceutical manufacturers without success' (Jones 2001:64). In fact, at least three British companies – ICI, Glaxo and Kemball-Bishop – produced increasing quantities of penicillin from the early 1940s using surface fermentation. But neither the existing technologies, nor minor improvements to them, were sufficient for mass production on anything like the scale achieved soon after in the USA.

   Whatever the exact truth, Florey felt he had no alternative but to go to the USA if he wanted production levels to meet the high wartime demand. Heatley, who accompanied Florey to the USA, and scientists at the US Department of Agriculture (USDA) discovered that corn-steep liquor was an excellent medium for culturing penicillin and managed to increase production considerably. Subsequently four US pharmaceutical companies – Merck, Pfizer, Lederle and Squibb – became involved in penicillin research. Pfizer's patented deep fermentation technology turned out to be especially productive and generated tremendous profits for the company. By 1944, 19 US companies were producing penicillin, with five of them producing 88 per cent of the total (Temin 1979:435). In time the market became less concentrated as more companies entered it and the price fell.

   Penicillin was no one-off. Various types of penicillin and semi-synthetic analogues came on the market during the following decades, including those effective against resistant strains of disease-causing microbes like staphylococcus. And while its discovery was accidental, penicillin inspired scientists to search for other microorganisms producing substances that are toxic for other microbes but harmless to humans. The result was the discovery and development of such antibiotics as streptomycin (1943), cephalosporin (1945), and tetracycline (1953). Many of the antibiotics came from the soil, but there were a range of sources including a chicken's throat (streptomycin), a sewage outlet (cephalosporin), and monkey dung (fusidic acid) (Le Fanu 1999:13). It was largely out of the investment of profits from the antibiotics revolution into research and development that today's research-based pharmaceutical industry emerged, especially in the USA and Britain.

   While not usually considered to be as significant in the commercial sense as the antibiotics, the development of the anti-inflammatory steroid drugs was hugely important for the pharmaceutical industry. Like the antibiotics, the cortico-steroids are naturally occurring substances whose seemingly miraculous therapeutic effects could not have been predicted by pharmaceutical chemists. Nonetheless, their discovery was not purely accidental either. In 1948, Philip Hensch at the Mayo Clinic in Rochester, Minnesota decided to experiment by treating a rheumatoid arthritis sufferer with a synthetic version of a secretion from the adrenal gland that had been sent to the hospital by the Merck company. This compound, later known as cortisone, resulted in rapid improvements to the condition of the patient and to several others during the following months.

Why did Hensch decide to try this particular compound? First, he had already observed that the condition of rheumatoid arthritis sufferers improved when they were pregnant or had jaundice. In fact, other afflictions such as hay fever and asthma also went into remission under these conditions. This led him to speculate that a hormone might be responsible. Second, he was fortunate enough to work at the same establishment as Edward Kendall, who had been studying the adrenal hormones. Kendall had isolated some of the adrenal hormones, including one named Compound E. With the war under way and rumours that the Germans had found a way to enable their pilots to fly at extraordinarily high altitudes through injections of an adrenal hormone, the US Air Force began a research programme and encouraged firms and laboratories already involved in this area to intensify their work. But it was not until 1948 that Merck managed to produce enough Compound E to test on a patient. This was no mean achievement. At that time 'it took the slaughter of forty head of cattle to treat one patient for one day by a process with forty-two chemical steps' (Werth 1994:202).

Although cortisone turned out to have some unpleasant side-effects, the drug and the derivatives subsequently developed (collectively known as the steroids) had a major impact since they successfully treated a tremendous range of hitherto untreatable diseases that were not obviously related and whose causes were hardly understood. Among others, these include Hodgkin's disease, cerebral oedema, glandular fever, septic shock and male infertility (Le Fanu 1999:25).

Other important breakthroughs, such as the beta-blockers, took place during the post-Second World War period. But from the 1970s the number of new drugs placed on the market began to decline. According to one study, between 1969 and 1989 the number of new chemical entities launched per year on the world market fell from over 90 to under 40 (CIPA 1998). And increasingly the 'new' chemical entities are so-called 'me-too' drugs, which are not significant improvements upon existing treatments (Le Fanu 1999:246). This was recognized early on by the pharmaceutical industry. In a study published in 1973, the authors were told by several industry representatives 'that the end of the first chemotherapeutic revolution is almost in sight' (Taylor and Silberston 1973:365). The situation has reached the stage where 65 per cent of 'new' drugs approved by the Food and Drug Administration for sale in the USA from 1989 to 2000 contained active ingredients found in existing products. Of these newly approved drugs, 54 per cent 'differed from the marketed product in dosage form, route of administration, or were combined with another active ingredient', while 11 per cent 'were identical to products already available on the US market' (Hunt 2002:3).

There are two possible explanations for this situation. First, the pharmaceutical industry had to deal with increasingly stringent safety regulations. Partly in response to the thalidomide tragedy, drugs had to be rigorously tested for safety and effectiveness before they could be sold. These regulations were introduced at about the same time as the number of new drugs declined, which suggests the possibility of a connection. This is plausible considering that compliance substantially raised the cost of research and development. In the United Kingdom, for example, 'by 1978 the "development time" for each new drug had increased to around 10 years, while the "development costs" had escalated from £5 million in the 1960s to £25 million in the mid-1970s to a staggering £150 million by the 1990s' (Le Fanu 1999:247). Moreover, while such testing was undoubtedly a good thing, it is possible that several drugs that could have provided substantial benefits for patients in spite of their side-effects were weeded out that ought not to have been. Walter Sneader, a medical historian, has suggested that if current safety standards had been applied to aspirin and paracetamol, they might well not have been approved (1985:87).[3]

Second, it is possible to argue that, as long as disease processes are not well understood and researchers must depend to a large extent on serendipity, even the prepared mind must eventually contend with the law of diminishing returns (Le Fanu 1999:237). And, while rational drug design has had some major successes (such as the beta-blockers), its promise is far from being realized as yet. It almost goes without saying that the pharmaceutical industry is keen to accentuate the first of the two explanations.

While important drugs, including treatments for HIV/AIDS, continue to be developed and manufactured, it is a fact of economic life that the most profitable medicines are not necessarily the ones that save the most human lives or even that save any lives at all. This was recognized even by the industry from

---

[3]   Carl Djerassi, the renowned steroid chemist, points out that (2001:282–3) aspirin causes birth defects in various animals but only rarely in humans. Since new drugs must now be tested on animals, most companies would likely have dropped aspirin as a potential drug candidate.

at least as far back as the 1950s. Henry Gadsden, a head of Merck shortly after it had merged with Sharp and Dohme, told his researchers in a meeting that 'there are more well people than sick people. We should make products for people who are well' (quoted in Werth 1994:131). Examples of such products he mentioned – to the disgust of the scientists present – included a quick-tanning formula and a treatment for straightening hair. Since that time vast sums of money have been spent on a range of 'lifestyle drugs' which may admittedly improve the quality of peoples' lives but are not exactly lifesavers.

3. THE GROWTH OF THE RESEARCH-BASED PHARMACEUTICAL INDUSTRIES IN THE TWENTIETH CENTURY

Nowadays, the pharmaceutical industry is usually considered to consist of the research-based companies, which are responsible for the development and sale of new prescription drugs, and the generic drug companies, which sell drugs that are not patent protected, usually because the patents protecting the product have expired. This distinction is not universally accepted. For one thing, some research-based companies have generic subsidiaries, and, for another, it is just as plausible to divide the industry into producers of brand-name (that is, trade mark-protected) drugs and producers of generics. This alternative classification of drug companies has some merit given the importance of brand names, and also that governments often fund a great deal of basic pharmaceutical research, especially that of the USA, which benefits the industry as a whole. In other words, the state often pays government agencies and universities to carry out much of the research that the 'research-based' sector would otherwise have to do itself or perhaps even never would. Some companies are reluctant to admit this and even claim the credit for research they benefited from but did not themselves undertake. For example, Bristol-Myers Squibb played down the significant role of the US government in discovering and developing Taxol, and in bearing nearly all of the costs of doing so (Goodman and Walsh 2001). It is also true that companies claiming to be research and development-based often market under-licence products developed by other companies. During 2001, for example, GlaxoSmithKline in-licensed 10 products discovered and developed elsewhere. The managing director of one of the larger Indian drug companies explained to the author that in his view most of the conceptual breakthroughs that form the basis for the development of innovative medicines are achieved by university- and public sector-based scientists and not in corporate research and development labs. He also considers that many research-based companies nowadays produce mostly 'me-too' drugs, which do not achieve significant therapeutic advances. We will see more about this in the next section. But suffice to say, at this point, that, while such criticisms may go too far, they are not without merit.

What we can say is that, over the last 120 years, new therapeutic chemical substances have been discovered and developed in the laboratories of universities, government research institutions and companies in several countries. However, when investigating the origins of the most significant pharmaceutical products, it becomes apparent that firms from four countries have made an especially large contribution. German companies played a pioneering role, and their example was followed in very quick time by their Swiss counterparts, which interestingly also tended to be dyestuff manufacturers. The US industry was also quite an early developer, while the British drug companies took a long time to commit themselves to pharmaceutical research and development but ultimately became highly successful.

For these reasons the present account focuses on the pharmaceutical industries of these four countries, tracing some of the major commercial and business developments that have taken place in each of them over the last century. It finishes by describing the state of the pharmaceutical industry at the beginning of the twenty-first century.

3.1   Germany: Early Dominance, Continued Success

The first ever pharmaceutical products were developed in-house or by chemists based in German universities and licensed to companies, most of which were primarily dyestuff firms. Several reasons may be given to explain why these companies decided to move into drug development and were successful in doing so. First, there was good reason to believe that the research strategies they had adopted and the mass production capabilities they had acquired could be harnessed to drug discovery. Second, the same equipment they used for dyestuff production could also be used for drug production. Third, they soon realized that pharmaceutical compounds could be developed from analogous or even identical raw materials (Stolz and Schwaiberger 1987:195). Investigating Paul Ehrlich's hypothesis that some dyestuffs have properties allowing them to treat infective agents but without harming human tissue, it seemed feasible to carry out research aimed at discovering dual-use substances to dye clothes and heal the sick (Bynum 1994:167; Porter 1997:450). Fourth, as their dyes became increasingly profitable, large funds became available to plough back into research and development. In short, since pharmaceutical research and development could be carried out with the same research strategies, technologies and equipment (Wengenroth 1997:144), drug development was a commercially attractive and feasible proposition.

Even before the turn of the twentieth century, Hoechst, Bayer, AGFA and the main Swiss dyestuff firms were producing pharmaceuticals. And until well into the century virtually all the important new chemotherapeutic drugs were developed by German firms. This was despite the fact that most were still primarily dyestuff producers that treated drugs as no more than a promising sideline. These included Hoechst's Antipyrin (1883), Pyramidon (1896), Novocain (1905) and Salvarsan (1909), Bayer's Phenactin (1888), Sulfonal and Aspirin (both 1889), and Kalle's Antifebrin (1886). Antifebrin is interesting because it was probably the first drug to be marketed under its brand name in competition with generic versions. This business strategy was adopted because processes to manufacture the substance were well-known and therefore unpatentable. It succeeded because so many physicians accepted the brand name rather than the chemical term of acetanilid even though Kalle charged a higher price than its competitors (Mann and Plummer 1991:22–3). Another important drug, E. Merck's Veronal (1903), was an exception because its producer was not a dyestuff firm but had begun as a pharmacist shop and subsequently became a bulk producer of alkaloids. In common with another former pharmacy business, Schering, E. Merck's US branch separated and eventually became a major research-based pharmaceutical corporation that outgrew its parent by some considerable distance. In Merck's case the separation took place after the First World War. The Schering split followed the Second World War.

As mentioned earlier, the main German chemical companies merged in 1925 to form I.G. Farbenindustrie, which immediately became a dominant player in various types of chemical product, including pharmaceuticals. At the end of the Second World War, I.G. Farben was broken up and Hoechst and Bayer were revived as separate companies. For much of the second half of the century, both were among the world's biggest pharmaceutical companies. However, in 1999, Hoechst merged with Rhône-Poulenc to form a new company, Aventis.

3.2 Switzerland: A Successful Follower

The Swiss pharmaceutical industry, like its German counterpart, benefited from early advances in synthetic chemistry. Three of the four most successful companies during the twentieth century – Sandoz, Ciba and Geigy – began as dyestuff manufacturers. In 1895, Sandoz was the first of these companies to graduate to pharmaceuticals when it began producing Antipyrin, originally developed by Hoechst. In 1917, the company established a pharmaceutical research laboratory. Five years after Sandoz, Ciba moved into pharmaceuticals, developing two products, Vioform (an antiseptic) and Salen (for rheumatism). Geigy set up its pharmaceutical research department in 1938, and 11 years later marketed its first major drug, an anti-rheumatic called Butazolidin. Other important drugs that came out of the Geigy labs after the Second World

War included Tofranil (a psychotropic drug), Hygrotone (for high blood pressure), and Tegretol (for epilepsy). In 1970, Ciba and Geigy merged to form Ciba-Geigy, although the 'Geigy' part of the name was dropped 22 years later. Finally, 'Ciba' and 'Sandoz' effectively disappeared when the two companies merged in 1996 to form Novartis.

The other Swiss pharmaceutical giant of the twentieth century, Hoffman LaRoche, is different in that it was founded in 1896 specifically to produce pharmaceuticals. Before the First World War, Roche produced several successful products, including Aidin (a thyroid preparation), Airol (an antiseptic), and Sirolin (a cough syrup) and Digalen (a purified digitalis preparation), both of which were marketed for six decades. During the inter-war period, Roche distinguished itself by its development of synthetic vitamin products and analgesics. After the Second World War, Roche became one of the world's biggest drug companies, largely on the strength of its successful development of a series of tranquillizers of the benzodiazepine class of chemicals, most notably Librium, Mogadon and Valium.

3.3   The United States: Towards Global Leadership

While the German and Swiss drug discovery approaches were based on synthetic organic chemistry, the North American and British strategy was initially geared towards extraction and purification of natural products (Achilladelis 1993:283). The German and Swiss firms were the most successful up to the mid-1930s, but, from the Second World War onwards, the US industry began to dominate. And, from the 1970s, several British pharmaceutical firms also joined the ranks of the world's most innovative and commercially successful.

The impetus for early growth of the US pharmaceutical industry came from such factors as the growing population, the availability of chemists and medical scientists trained in American and German universities, and the close links between university scientists and companies (Liebenau 1984:339). In addition, drug regulation introduced in 1902, which required a government laboratory to monitor the production of new drugs for safety, increased competition and encouraged innovation and growth. 'The Act made possible a new means of competition: competition based upon the quality of laboratory facilities that the company could provide and the stringency of the standards which they could meet. It also implied that the leading producers could benefit by extremely tough standards which would be difficult for smaller companies to equal' (ibid.:341). Company laboratories no longer 'used simply to standardise basic products or to fiddle with new combinations of drugs, but rather they were now in the business of setting standards, meeting the requirements of the regulators, and producing as many novel products as they were capable of doing which would distinguish their product lines from those of their competitors' (ibid.:341).

After the USA joined the First World War in 1917, the government decided the country needed to become self-sufficient in the production of drugs. At the time, many important drugs (as well as dyes and other chemicals) in high demand were made only by German companies. When the war ended in November 1918, the Alien Property Custodian was established under the Trading with the Enemy Act to confiscate and sell off the German-owned patents. The 4767 chemical patents, which included drugs such as Novocain and Salvarsan, were sold to the Chemical Foundation, which represented the US chemicals sector, for only US$266 400 and then licensed to companies (Greenberg 1926:23; Roe 1943:702). Even though it turned out that many of these patents did not fully disclose the inventions claimed (see below), the US industry benefited to some extent, albeit less than was hoped for. For example, Sterling Drug was transformed by its acquisition of Bayer's US properties, including aspirin. At least as important as the transfer of these patents, the war resulted in the loss by some German companies of their US branches (such as Merck). Perhaps the most important outcome of the crisis created by the war was that the US government (as did the British government) finally decided to follow Germany in adopting industry policies specifically geared to promoting the development of their domestic chemical (including pharmaceutical) industries (Steen 1995).

Even before the antibiotics and cortico-steroids eras, American companies began to achieve some good results from their research. A few pioneering firms such as Abbott Laboratories, Parke Davis and Co., and E.R. Squibb began from the 1920s to invest profitably in research in such areas as vitamins and hormones (Chandler 1990:164). Eli Lilly became the first commercial producer of insulin, which had been discovered by University of Toronto scientists (see below).

However, it was not until the Second World War that the US pharmaceutical industry became committed to any great extent to in-house research and development (Mowery and Rosenberg 1998:96; Noble 1977:118). The stimulus for this was the desperate need for anti-infectives to treat injured combatants. But it would be incorrect to suggest that research and development was purely in-house. On the contrary, then and up to the present time, the US industry benefited tremendously from collaborations with universities where biomedical research programmes were reaching very high standards, and also from the tremendous expansion in government spending on such research which continues to be substantial. Between 1950 and 1965, the biomedical research budget of the National Institutes of Health (NIH) 'grew by no less than 18 per cent per year in real terms, and by 1965, the federal government accounted for almost two thirds of all spending on biomedical research'

(Mowery and Rosenberg 1998:96). Although the federal government share of biomedical research and development declined thereafter, it still made up a substantial 39 per cent of the ($30 billion) total in 1993, compared to 50 per cent for industry-funded research and development (ibid.:97). The US pharmaceutical industry did not advance rapidly because the firms had outstanding expertise in synthetic chemistry, as did their German rivals, but because their expertise in natural product research and also in chemical engineering enabled them to scale up production of fermentation-based products to unprecedented levels (ibid.:95–6). So while the sulphonamide revolution was a European one, the antibiotics revolution was largely American (even though the initial breakthroughs took place in Britain), as indeed was the biotechnology revolution which, as we will find later, 'represented a fundamental discontinuity in the nature of pharmaceutical research, a transition from the realm of chemistry to that of biology' (ibid.:99).

The discovery of the antibiotics created opportunities for the pharmaceutical industry, but also presented difficulties. The problem was that product life cycles were likely to be quite short, owing to the fact that anti-infectives such as antibiotics were bound to induce resistance after a certain period. But while this situation placed a lot of competitive pressure on firms, the potential for attaining high rewards from successful research and development was very great.

It has been estimated that, from 1942 to 1986, 31 natural and semi-synthetic antibacterials were developed that could be classed as radical innovations in the sense of being 'innovations based on different scientific principles, technology or materials which have replaced or competed successfully with existing products and processes, and gave rise to a swarm of incremental innovations' (Achilladelis 1993:281–2). Of these (mostly antibiotic) products, 26 were developed or co-developed by US firms. Seven were developed or co-developed by British firms, two each by German and Swiss firms, and one each by Danish and Japanese companies.

3.4   The United Kingdom: A Slow Starter that Caught Up

The British pharmaceutical industry developed into a successful research and development-based one much later than that of the USA. The country's early advances in synthetic chemistry did not, unlike the German case, lead to the development of new drugs. It cannot at all have helped that companies during the early twentieth century generally employed very few chemists. And, given the positive influence of drug safety regulations in the USA, the fact that they were virtually non-existent in Britain until as late as 1922, when the Dangerous Drugs Act was passed, to be followed in 1933 by the Pharmacy and Poisons Act (Slinn 1995:172), was likely also to have hindered the development of a world-class pharmaceuticals sector.

In the main, the British pharmaceutical industry in the pre-First World War era consisted of rather conservative small and medium-sized family firms. Most of these companies extracted drug ingredients from imported plants and minerals for wholesalers, pharmacists and physicians (ibid.:169–70). Some of them also prepared their own proprietary remedies from these ingredients. Often, these companies were originally retailers that had later on moved into manufacturing. Examples include Boots and Allen and Hanburys.[4] Other firms, like May and Baker, began as manufacturing chemists before becoming retailers.

Burroughs Wellcome, formed in 1880 by two American pharmacists who had emigrated to Britain, was an exception to the rule that the industry had little interest in research and development. Sir Henry Wellcome's 'introduction of a research and development laboratory was a direct effort to adopt methods which his American colleagues had originally brought across the Atlantic from Germany' (Liebenau 1984:336). The Wellcome Chemical Research Laboratories, set up in 1896, played an important role 'as providers of qualified and experienced research scientists to other companies, including Boots, Glaxo, and May and Baker' (Slinn 1995:174). This firm also introduced the tablet form of drug manufacture and delivery which had been pioneered in both Germany and the USA (ibid.:184).

In spite of its relative backwardness in pharmaceuticals, Britain enjoyed a trade surplus on the eve of the First World War. In 1913 drug imports were worth £2 million, whereas exports were valued as £2.4 million (ibid.:174–5). Even so, the outbreak of the war made plain to the government how dependent the country had become on German dyestuffs and drugs, and how the patent system seemed to reinforce such dependence.

The drug whose unavailability caused most concern was Salvarsan. Unfortunately, it was extremely difficult to manufacture in a form safe enough to administer to patients. The Board of Trade authorized Burroughs Wellcome, Poulenc Frères and May and Baker to manufacture the drug, which, once produced, needed to be tested for impurities. This was carried out by the recently founded Medical Research Committee (later renamed the Medical Research Council). Another important drug whose supply was interrupted was Bayer's Aspirin, which was protected by several patents covering the substance itself, its intermediates, and the design of the manufacturing plant, and also by the company's trade mark (Fairley 1978:139). As with Salvarsan, these patents did not provide all the information needed to mass-produce the product. Realizing this, the government offered a prize of £20 000 to the first person in Britain or the Commonwealth to develop a feasible manufacturing

---

4   This company was acquired by Glaxo in 1958.

process. The winner was George Nicholas, a chemist from Melbourne, Australia, who called his product 'Aspro'. The lessons of the war were not lost on the government or industry. For one thing, the government took a more mercantilist approach to strategic industries. The 1921 Safeguarding of Industries Act imposed import tariffs on certain goods, including fine chemicals (Abraham 2002:233; Owen 1999:363). And, for another, the industry began to make efforts to improve its research and development capabilities. Two companies that increased their involvement in pharmaceutical research during the inter-war period and became highly successful decades later were Beecham and Glaxo. Beecham's Powders, a proprietary aspirin-based cold remedy launched in 1926, was a popular product for decades. Glaxo began life as a department of a company called Joseph Nathan that manufactured a dried milk product named 'Glaxo'. In 1924, the company negotiated a licence to extract vitamin D from fish oil using (and improving upon) a process patented by Columbia University. Glaxo Department subsequently produced a range of vitamin products and other dietary supplements, and was turned into a private limited company in 1935.

Nevertheless, the British pharmaceutical industry continued to consist during the inter-war period of small and medium-sized firms that were solely producers of drugs. In contrast, the chemical industry of the time in the UK and Germany was undergoing a radical consolidation phase that resulted in the creation of two very large firms, Imperial Chemical Industries (ICI) and I.G. Farben. The former, formed in 1926, initially had little interest in drugs, while I.G. Farben, created in 1925 out of Bayer, BASF, Hoechst and five other companies, was from the start a major developer and exporter of drugs.

Not surprisingly, then, the industry's progress was steady but unspectacular. But in the late 1930s, May and Baker, by that time owned by the French firm Rhône-Poulenc, became one of the first British pharmaceutical companies to develop an internationally important new product, M&B 693, and from the end of the Second World War the British pharmaceutical industry began to take off. Nonetheless, in the early 1960s, the major British firms like Glaxo, Beecham, ICI (which had only set up its pharmaceuticals division in 1942) and Wellcome were still minor players globally. In fact, some of the UK-based subsidiaries of US firms had higher sales in the UK market (Jones 2001:163). A decade later, the 10 largest pharmaceutical companies were exclusively American, Swiss and German, with the three biggest companies being Roche, Merck and Hoechst. Glaxo, the biggest British company, was only sixteenth. While the USA was the largest producer of pharmaceuticals, West Germany was the biggest exporter (ibid.:174).

When the antibiotics revolution first got under way, British companies seeking to produce these new kinds of drug had little choice but to license the patented deep fermentation processes developed by US companies like Merck and Squibb. Despite the resentment this situation aroused, it did not appear to hold back the British licensee firms, especially Glaxo. In fact, they went on to discover and manufacture a wave of profitable natural and semi-synthetic penicillins and antibiotics. These not only generated large returns, but also financed, and justified, increased investment in research and development. The most financially successful and innovative British companies during the antibiotics revolution were Glaxo and Beecham. From the 1950s, Glaxo increased its focus on prescription drugs, and not just penicillins and antibiotics, but also the cortico-steroids. By increasing its product portfolio through in-house research and development, mergers and acquisitions,[5] and its decision to market its products in North America and Europe, Glaxo gradually became a major transnational research-based pharmaceutical company.

From 1959, Beecham became very successful at developing semi-synthetic penicillins, starting that year with phenethicillin (marketed under the name Broxil), and following up, most notably, with ampicillin (Penbritin) and amoxycillin (Amoxil). Thanks to these and other successes, the company's pharmaceutical sales increased nearly 16-fold between 1960 and 1970.

From the early 1970s, the international competitiveness of the British pharmaceutical industry began to increase, and by the 1980s this was becoming very apparent. In 1982, Glaxo, the largest British firm (based on its turnover of prescription drugs), was still at only number 20 in the world league table, way behind the big three, which were then Hoechst, Bayer and Merck (ibid.:163). But by the late 1980s, the British pharmaceutical sector's share of the world market was second only to that of the USA, with Glaxo also reaching second place in sales (Thomas 1994:454).

The 1990s saw continued success for the British pharmaceutical industry, but also some major changes. Concerned that the patent protection of its most successful product, Zantac, was nearing the end of its life, Glaxo took over Wellcome in 1995. In January 2000, Glaxo merged with SmithKline Beecham – itself the result of a 1989 merger between Beecham and SmithKline Beckman – to form what would become the world's largest pharmaceutical company, GlaxoSmithKline, with a 7 per cent share of the global prescription drug market and a research and development budget of £2.4 billion (Jones 2001:442). In 1993, a new pharmaceutical company, Zeneca, was created that comprised the pharmaceutical activities of ICI. In 1999, Zeneca merged with the Swedish company, Astra, to form AstraZeneca, which then also became one of the world's largest pharmaceutical corporations thanks to the world's best-selling prescription drug, the anti-ulcerant Losec.

---

[5]   Involving such companies as Allen and Hanburys (1958), Evans (1960), and British Drug Houses (1968).

4. THE PRESENT-DAY GLOBAL PHARMACEUTICAL INDUSTRY

While the science and technology of pharmaceutical research and development have been transformed over the last hundred years, there are marked continuities in terms of the identities of the major producer countries and of the businesses involved. Today's pharmaceutical industry is dominated by transnational corporations almost entirely from the USA and western Europe, especially the UK, Switzerland and Germany. Neither Japan nor the newly industrializing economies have any large 'top 10' transnational drug firms. And of the top 20 corporations by sales and global market share in 2000, only one was not from the USA or western Europe.

The dominance of the US pharmaceutical industry, which, as we have seen, was an early developer (albeit after Germany) has been long-standing, though its peak period of dominance was the middle of the twentieth century. From 1941 to 1963, 60 per cent of new drugs were discovered in the USA, about 8 per cent originated in Switzerland, 6 per cent in Germany and 5 per cent in Britain (Slinn 1995:181). From 1975 to 1994, US firms were still the most innovative but relatively less so. The British industry had become the second most innovative in terms of the numbers of new drugs being placed on the market. Clearly, those countries that were among the first to establish pharmaceutical industries continue to be among those with the biggest and most scientifically advanced firms. And most of these firms were established during the early years of the industry in the nineteenth or early twentieth centuries.

However, this picture of continuity may be deceptive. The last decade of the twentieth century saw a tremendous change in the industry with several mergers and acquisitions involving most of the biggest companies, and result-ing in some very large corporations indeed whose nationalities are not always so obvious as they were before (see Table 7.1). This situation is a consequence of a decline in the quantity – and allegedly also the quality – of new chemical entities reaching the market. Many of those that do closely resemble existing ones in terms of their chemical structures and therapeutic effects, are disparagingly referred to by some commentators as 'me-too drugs'. Consequently, the global market for pharmaceuticals has become extremely competitive albeit also highly concentrated at the level of therapeutic groups. The most vulnerable companies are those which have become excessively dependent on one or two highly profitable drugs nearing the end of their patent lives, but lack the security of having a large portfolio of potential best-sellers in the pipeline. As the twentieth century came to an end, famous names like Wellcome, Beechams, Ciba, Geigy, Hoechst and Rhône-Poulenc disappeared from the list of big names in the pharmaceutical industry.

Table 7.1   Mergers and acquisitions in pharmaceuticals, 1989–2000

Year	Companies involved (nationality)
1989	Dow (US)/Marion (US)
	Bristol-Myers (US)/Squibb (US)
	SmithKline (US)/Beecham (UK)
1990	Rhône-Poulenc (France)/Rorer (US)
	Roche (Swiss)/Genentech (US)
1994	SmithKline Beecham (US/UK)/Sterling Health (US)
	BASF (Germany)/Boots (UK)
	American Home Products (US)/American Cyanamid (US)
	Elf Sanofi (France)/Sterling Drug (US)
	Roche (Swiss)/Syntex (US)
1995	Glaxo (UK)/Wellcome (UK)
	Hoechst (German)/Marion Merrell Dow (US)
	Pharmacia (Swedish)/Upjohn (US)
	Rhône-Poulenc (French)/Fisons (UK)
1996	Ciba-Geigy (Swiss)/Sandoz (Swiss) = Novartis
1997	Roche (Swiss)/Boehringer Mannheim (Germany)
1999	Hoechst (Germany)/Rhône-Poulenc (France) = Aventis
	Astra (Swedish)/Zeneca (UK)
2000	Glaxo Wellcome (UK)/SmithKline Beecham (UK/US)
	Pfizer (US)/Warner-Lambert (US)

Source: Owen (1999:382).

5.   PHARMACEUTICAL PATENT LAW IN THE TWENTIETH CENTURY: EVOLUTION AND BUSINESS STRATEGY

5.1   The Importance of Patents

Pharmaceutical companies need to make increasingly large research and development investments not only to discover new products but especially to secure government authorization to sell them. According to the Tufts Center for the Study of Drug Development (2001), the average cost of developing a new drug in the USA rose from US$54 million in 1979 (at 1976 dollars), to $231 million in 1991 (at 1987 dollars), and as much as $802 million in 2001. While such statistics are welcomed by the industry for their propaganda value, the methodologies used to produce these estimates are problematical to those who believe the figures are unrealistically high.[6] For example, a civil society organization called Public Citizen (2001) has calculated that the total for 1991 should be only about $110 million. Pharmaceutical Research and Manufacturers of America (PhRMA) took this alternative study seriously enough to commission the accountancy firm Ernst and Young to produce a response.

Wherever the truth lies, there is no doubt that many (though by no means all) of the new drugs entering the market cost a great deal of money to develop. Owing to past tragedies, especially thalidomide, new drugs in the industrialized countries must now undergo extensive clinical trials to demonstrate safety. These are hugely expensive in both time and money. Since patents have to be filed at the drug discovery phase prior to the development period, by the time the product reaches the market the patent may well have less than half of its 20-year term left to run. Consequently, 'new drugs must be sold worldwide, since no company can fully exploit a patented product, recouping its research and development costs solely in its own home market, even in the two largest national markets, the USA and Japan' (Slinn 1995:168).

Patents are extremely important for pharmaceutical companies. Monopoly protection of a commercially successful drug provides huge returns that more than make up for the required investment in discovery and development. Several surveys (for example, Levin et al. 1987; Mansfield 1986; Taylor and Silberston 1973) indicate that pharmaceuticals are one of the few industrial sectors in which patents are effective means of capturing returns from research and development. This effectiveness is enhanced by the ways – sometimes highly questionable – in which these companies use the patent system. It is important in this context to understand that drugs are not usually protected by single patents whose expiry allows anybody to produce the drug. As Correa explains (2001a:11),

> Only a few (several dozen) 'new chemical entities' . . . are developed and patented each year. Nonetheless, thousands of patents are granted annually in this sector. This paradox can be explained by the enormous capacity that the sector's major firms have built up not only for developing authentic inventions, but also for taking out patents on secondary, occasionally trivial developments, in order to extend their monopoly over a product or process, beyond that allowed by the original patent.

Thus, pharmaceutical companies use patents (and also trade marks) strategically in order to restrict competition, in some cases for several years beyond the 20-year patent duration. 'Evergreening' or 'line extensions' are terms used

---

6   For example, see the critiques of the Center's studies by Public Citizen (http://www.citizen.org).

to refer to the use of IP rights in order to extend the monopoly or at least the market dominance of a drug beyond the life of the original patent protecting it. We can get an idea of how much is at stake when we consider that 'drugs with annual sales of some $45 billion are set to go off patent between 2001 and 2005' (Reuters 2001a). It should not be surprising, then, that drug companies will try to stretch out their exclusive rights over blockbuster drugs for as long as possible, especially when they are heavily dependent on a small number of such highly profitable products (or even just one). For example, firms might seek to obtain patents on new delivery methods for the drug, on reduced dosage regimens, or on new versions of the active compound or combinations that are more effective or that produce fewer side-effects than the original substance. Another tactic that may be possible, in the case of those drugs that, when metabolized by the body, are transformed into another substance which directly causes the therapeutic effect, is to patent also this latter chemical.[7][8] Doubtless, companies other than the owner of the patent protecting the original substance will also seek to acquire such patents. But in many cases these firms will prefer to license their patents to the first company, since the latter already enjoys the monopoly position and is therefore better placed to make commercial use of them. In addition, pharmaceutical companies, like those in other industries, use patents for a range of strategic purposes such as creating broad zones of exclusion around their inventions, preventing other companies

---

[7] In one early case (in 1964), Colgate-Palmolive successfully appealed against the initial rejection of patent claims directed to a metabolite with antidepressant properties that formed in the body of people administered a closely related substance that was already patented (see Rollins 1983). But such strategies can fail (or at least only partially succeed). For example, Merrell Dow sought to extend its monopoly on an antihistamine drug called terfenadine by arguing that, since the patented metabolite could not be produced without taking the drug, the monopoly should expire only upon expiry of the metabolite patent. Courts in the USA and Germany both upheld Merrell Dow's metabolite patents in those countries but held that supplying terfenadine would not be an infringing act. In Britain, Merrell Dow's infringement claims were also dismissed on the grounds that the metabolite was not new. On appeal, the House of Lord not only upheld the lower court's decision but essentially invalidated the patent. See *Merrell Dow v HN Norton* (1996), *Intellectual Property Reports* 33:1–14; Grubb (1999:212–13).

[8] Correa (2001b:11–12) provides a list of patenting targets chosen by companies to extend their monopolies on drugs. These include polymorphs (crystalline forms of the active compound); pharmaceutical forms (that is, new ways of administering the active compound); selective inventions (elements selected from a group that were not specifically named in earlier patents claiming the group); analogy processes; combinations of known products; optical isomers; active metabolites; prodrugs (inactive compounds that produce active metabolites when introduced into the body); new salts of known substances; variants of existing manufacturing processes; and new uses for old products.

from exploiting their own patents, and enhancing bargaining positions in cross-licensing deals (Granstrand 1999:218–22; Rivette and Klein 2000).

Generally, such practices are legal. But other practices may not be, such as setting up price-fixing cartels with other patent-holding firms. They may also collude with generic producers, for example by paying them to drop their legal challenges to vulnerable patents or to agree to delay selling their own versions of drugs after the product patent has expired. For example, Bayer came to an agreement in 1997 with a generic company called Barr Pharmaceuticals. By this deal, Barr agreed to drop its legal challenge to Bayer's patent on its commercially successful antibiotic, Cipro (ciprofloxacin). In exchange, Bayer agreed to pay Barr around US$28 million a year until 2003, when the patent on Cipro is due to expire. Two other companies are also alleged to have been paid by Bayer not to challenge its patent (Reuters 2001b; USA Today 2001). In 2001, Abbott Laboratories was accused of paying generic firms to delay the commercialization of generic versions of Hytrin, a commercially successful treatment for hypertension and enlarged prostate (Austin 2001).

Companies also use trade mark law to extend their market power beyond the patented drug's expiry date.[9] Patented drugs are usually marketed under their brand name rather than the generic name. Since generic producers cannot use this name, it is often very difficult for them to promote their alternative product effectively. Therefore, physicians may continue to prescribe the branded product even if it is more expensive than the generic version. In fact, in many countries, physicians may not even know that alternatives exist. In the case of known compounds whose therapeutic properties were discovered several years after their discovery, this form of protection may, in the absence of product patent protection, be the most effective one available.[10]

A good example is an anti-cancer substance derived from the Pacific Yew (Taxus brevifolia). The compound in question was first isolated in 1966 by Monroe Wall, who was working at the Research Triangle Institute in North Carolina. The following year he gave it the name 'taxol'. In 1971, Wall and his colleague Mansukh Wani published the results of their work including their elucidation of taxol's chemical structure (Goodman and Walsh 2001:56–7). In 1991, the US National Cancer Institute (NCI) signed a research and development agreement with Bristol-Myers Squibb. According to the contract, Bristol-Myers Squibb (B-MS) was given access to the NCI's clinical trial data, and authorized to develop taxol as a commercial product, subject to the approval of the government's Food and Drug Administration (FDA). As it

---

[9]   As the American Pharmaceutical Association mentioned in its 1919 report, this is not a new practice (see pp. 136–7 below).
[10]   Although the manufacturer may have patents on, for example, production processes and formulations, and these may still provide quite substantial protection.

turned out, since much of the research and development had already been carried out by the NCI, this approval was granted as early as December of the following year (just four months after the application was submitted). Inexplicably, despite the existence of more than 600 published articles using the name 'taxol' to refer to the compound, the US Patent and Trademark Office accepted the company's application to register 'taxol' as a trade mark. 'Thereafter, all references to taxol would be required to carry the registered sign, hence taxol became Taxol®' (ibid.:169–70). Subsequently, the company succeeded in registering the name in over 50 countries, and actively defended its newly acquired rights to a word it had had nothing to do with coining or applying to the substance in question. This action by the company, which essentially privatized a word that had been coined over 25 years earlier and had become common currency among scientists, was condemned by *Nature*, the prestigious science magazine, which was then warned by the company's lawyers that it must use the word only in association with the product sold by Bristol-Myers Squibb (see *Nature* 1995:370). By 2000, taxol was generating over US$1.5 billion in annual sales (B-MS 2001).

In addition, trade mark law in certain countries can be used to protect the colour and form of the capsules. And to make the legal minefield even more treacherous for generic firms, the original producer of a drug may try to assert copyright over the printed information accompanying the product. According to Frederick Abbott of Florida State University, 'despite the apparent over-reaching in arguing that "take two tablets every four hours" is the subject of copyright protection, the pharmaceutical manufacturers do not hesitate to delay the introduction of generic drugs with litigation over this question' (2002:41).

In restricting price competition, the benefits of such tactics for the original producers can be substantial. There again, the recent wave of mergers and acquisitions, a phenomenon linked to the loss of revenues faced by some companies owing to the expiry of patents protecting particularly lucrative products, shows that 'evergreening' has its limits as a business strategy. It may be a panacea for a weak product pipeline, but it is certainly not a cure. In response to this situation, pharmaceutical firms and business associations actively seek to influence government intellectual property and health regulation. In doing so, they often find themselves competing over the relevant regulatory spaces with health and consumer lobby groups that can compensate for their lack of economic strength by effective organization and the moral force of their arguments.

One approach frequently used by the corporate sector is propagandizing. This may take such forms as advice, gentle persuasion, veiled or overt threats, and the publication (for example on their websites or in newspaper advertisements) of statistics that are selected and interpreted in order to back up whatever their demands are. In addition to producing their own propaganda literature, pharmaceutical business associations sometimes fund research in order to provide 'objective' evidence demonstrating the legitimacy of their claims. When it suits their interests they portray their business as a dynamic and innovative one that provides, not just advanced healthcare, but jobs and a huge positive contribution to the trade balance. But they may also try to convey the impression that they are suffering from unfriendly regulations and being unfairly victimized by uninformed activists with a hostile agenda. Pharmaceutical corporations and business associations often find it expedient to instil in governments and policymakers certain impressions about the position of the national industry in the global market 'league table' to back their demands for a regulatory environment most conducive to the pursuit of profit. They may seek to show how strong this position is or they may argue that it is declining. Whichever the case, the regulatory environment is sure to be one of the main causes.

According to PhRMA (1998), of the 152 major new drugs launched between 1975 and 1994, 45 per cent came from the USA, 14 per cent originated in Britain, and 9 per cent in Switzerland. The figure for the USA is lower than the immediate post-Second World War period, but there is no suggestion of any decline in either of PhRMA's 1998 or 1999 reports. Instead, PhRMA (1999:10) praises the government for its relatively laissez-faire regulatory framework:

> It is no accident that the US leads the world in pharmaceutical research and development and that US companies have developed the lion's share of the important drugs of the past few decades. That's because, in contrast to the rest of the world, the US has a relatively free market for pharmaceuticals – one that rewards risk with at least the possibility of commensurate profit.

The European Federation of Pharmaceutical Industries and Associations (EFPIA) is less positive about Europe's prospects. Taking the total of new chemical and biological entities (NCEs and NBEs) placed on the market between 1975 and 1994 (numbering about a thousand), EFPIA's figures show that the share provided by US and Japanese firms has increased, while Europe's share, which has been higher than the others throughout this period, has declined steadily, from 65 per cent of the total between 1960 and 1965, to 60 per cent from 1975 to 1979, falling to only 36 per cent between 1990 and 1994. EFPIA seeks to demonstrate how important the pharmaceutical industry is to the European economy (which is undoubtedly true) while arguing that it is suffering from competition from the USA and Japan, where the regulatory environment is, apparently, more innovation-friendly. On the other hand, without explicitly mentioning the US government's continuing substantial financial commitment to biomedical research and development, EFPIA pointedly contrasts the USA with Europe where 'pharmaceutical R&D is funded almost entirely out of pharmaceutical companies' own earnings' (EFPIA 1998:22).

While both PhRMA and EFPIA claim to be opposed to state intervention in the market,[11] they fully support it when it comes to intellectual property regulation, since they do not consider this to be state intervention at all – which is bad – but the best way to support innovation, which of course makes it good. These organizations also link their patent-related demands to the interests of patients. According to EFPIA (1999), 'without the limited period of exclusivity conferred by a patent on a product most new cures would not be created'. EFPIA also warns that failure to remove the TRIPS provision on exhaustion of IP rights will, among other things, 'create potential health risks'. And PhRMA (1998:79) claims that 'without patent protection, it is highly unlikely that a company would be rewarded for its invention – or, more importantly, that patients would receive many new medicines'.

5.2 The United States

Knowing more about the development of the American pharmaceutical industry, one can readily understand that the companies' picture of an ideal patent regime would look very different over time. So in the early days when the industry was relatively backward compared to foreign competitors and producing few if any original products, its interests lay in a patent system offering fairly weak protection and containing public interest provisions such as working requirements and compulsory licensing. As it became more innovative, it preferred a system allowing the new types of product to be protected while opposing public interest or antitrust measures to weaken protection. Once the cost of doing research increased and the number of new products began to decline, one would expect the industry to seek privileges such as extended protection terms and to become more adept and aggressive in using IP systems strategically. Finally, as the industry became an important producer for international markets, one could predict that it would favour strong levels of patent protection around the world.

Those are our expectations. But were these assumed preferences ones that the companies actually held? And how successful was the US pharmaceutical industry in influencing patent law and policy anyway?

It is important first to be aware that the patent system has not always been

---

[11] Especially price controls to limit national healthcare budgets. Both EFPIA and PhRMA claim that pharmaceuticals contribute a relatively small percentage of total expenditure so that lower prices cannot compensate for the reduced incentive to innovate. Even if this is true, the overwhelming majority of people in the world cannot rely on state support but must pay their own medical bills.

popular. During the 1920s and 1930s, there was a strong mood of distrust towards big business. The antitrust movement was especially powerful during the Roosevelt administration, which took power in 1933. The patent system did not escape the critical scrutiny of the 'trust-busters', and Congress heard numerous condemnations of patents and calls for the rights to be rolled back such as through compulsory licensing, especially during the 1938–41 hearings to the Temporary National Economic Committee, which the administration and Congress had jointly convened (Owens 1991). But this movement went into decline when the USA entered the war in 1941. Recognition by the politicians that big business commitment to technological innovation was so important not only for the country's economic advancement but also for winning the war probably had much to do with this. So the Committee's recommendation for compulsory licensing was rejected in 1945 by the President Roosevelt-appointed National Patent Planning Commission. Given the Commission's inclusion of representatives of large corporations like General Electric and General Motors, this outcome was probably inevitable anyway. Nonetheless, these businesses did not always get their way in the courts, where anti-patent sentiments were very common during the 1950s and beyond. Yet despite the hostility directed at patents from time to time, the US patent system has at almost all times been more supportive of the interests of owners than have those of Europe. The USA has never required patents to be domestically worked, and compulsory licensing has been kept outside the patent system itself but left to competition and antitrust regulators to impose whenever this is deemed necessary.

Consequently, whenever a given industrial sector prefers weak protection levels (by the standards of the time), it has to campaign for a lowering of the standards rather than for a maintenance of the status quo. This is of course likely to encounter the opposition of more successful and economically important sectors. In fact, the US pharmaceutical industry did favour weakening protection in the early twentieth century. They justified this on the grounds that they were victims of unfair competition from abroad. In 1919, the American Pharmaceutical Association (APA), an organization founded in 1852 to represent pharmacists, publicly denounced the 'unfair monopolies on medicinal chemicals and dyes' held by German companies that they accused of abusing the US patent and trade mark systems. The Association alleged that they were doing this in two ways (APA 1919:77–9).

The first was to deliberately miss out important information when disclosing their inventions to the Patent Office. Consequently, they could not be copied by others even after the patent (or patents) protecting the chemical product or process had expired. Given that British companies were making similar complaints at this time, the Association's concerns were probably legitimate. One of the more extreme cases was the famous Haber-Bosch nitrogen fixation process, which was protected by several US patents owned by BASF. It took many years of effort and millions of dollars in research expenditure for scientists to replicate it even after the patents had been expropriated by the government during the First World War. According to one account 'the Badische Company had effectively bulwarked this discovery with strong, broad patents which detailed meticulously the apparatus, temperatures, and pressures, but cleverly avoided particulars as to the catalysts employed or their preparation. This last information was the core of the process so far as its practical operation was concerned.'[12]

The second way, which is common today and is not usually considered any more to be wrong, was to secure indefinite control over trade marks covering the names of drugs. This was very beneficial to companies seeking to maintain as far as possible their monopoly control over drugs after the patents protecting them had expired. Such control of the name, in the rather bitter words of F.C. Stewart, Director of the Scientific Department of H.K. Mulford Company and Chairman of the Committee on Patents and Trademarks of the American Pharmaceutical Association, 'practically enable[d] the commercial introducer to convert the entire educational machinery of the medical and pharmaceutical professions into a great advertising bureau for exploiting the sick room' (Stewart 1919:75).

The Association advocated changes to the law allowing only chemical processes to be patented. If product protection continued to be permitted, the law should provide for compulsory licensing. With respect to trade marks on drug names, protection should expire at the same time as the patent. This is certainly not a position that the US pharmaceutical industry would hold today! It is interesting to note that the Association took a strictly utilitarian line on IP rights:

> It should be understood that the patent and trademark laws, like all other laws, are primarily designed to benefit the public at large and only secondarily to benefit the individual . . . There are some who assume that the object of the Patent Law is to protect inventors in their so-called natural right to the exclusive manufacture and sale of their inventions and the object of the Trademark Law is to protect and foster monopolies. Nothing is further from the truth. The objects of the Patent and Trademark Laws are altruistic and not egoistic.

It may be worth mentioning that such a view is quite common among generic producers and firms in today's developing countries that fear competition from wealthier and more technologically advanced foreign companies better able to take advantage of IP protection.

---

12   Haynes (1945), quoted in Mowery and Rosenberg (1998:74).

The Association failed to achieve reforms to the patent and trade mark laws. It cannot have helped their cause that the changes they proposed conflicted with the interests of businesses in other sectors that had benefited greatly from the existing standards of protection and whose desire for reform was limited to improving their efficiency. It is interesting to speculate whether the changes they wanted to see would have been made if the USA had not decided to take part in the war and then to expropriate the 4500 German-owned US chemical patents. As we will see, the British patent law *was* changed at this time to prohibit the patenting of chemical substances.

As the US pharmaceutical industry began to develop its own products, its interests did become rather different. Since its first products were not, as in Germany and Switzerland, synthetic chemicals but were of natural origin, the question arose of whether these could be protected. The product of nature doctrine, which was formulated in the previous century, set certain limits on the extent to which natural substances and life forms could be protected. Nevertheless, as the US pharmaceutical industry increased its ability to develop new products, the Patent Office was often quite flexible in its application of the doctrine to the extent of allowing purified or isolated natural products to be protected. In addition, the courts sometimes interpreted the law in ways that favoured owners in cases where the bounds of patentability relating to new kinds of product were unclear and needed to be demarcated.

A good example is a 1911 case relating to two patents issued in 1903 and 1904 for a glandular extractive product in the form of a purified form of adrenaline, and for this compound in a solution with salt and a preservative. Parke Davis and Co., which was accused by H.K. Mulford and Co. of infringing its patents, defended itself on a number of grounds, one of which was that the inventions were mere products of nature and that this made the patents invalid. The judge, ruling in favour of Mulford, held that 'Takamine [the inventor] was the first to make it available for any use by removing it from the other gland-tissue in which it was found, and, while it is of course possible logically to call this a purification of the principle, it became for every practical purpose a new thing commercially and therapeutically'.[13] [14]

Merges and Nelson have used this case to argue, with justification, that the practice of claiming, not just a method of producing a purified natural substance but the end-product as well, can result in patents that are unnecessarily broad: 'The adrenaline patent would be infringed by the use of a radi-

---

[13]   *Parke Davis and Co. v H.K. Mulford and Co.*, 189 Fed. 95 (SDNY 1911), affirmed, 196 Fed. 496 (2nd Cir. 1912).
[14]   Controversially, Parke Davis registered 'adrenaline' as a trade mark in the United States. Consequently, the natural substance is referred to as epinephrine in that country.

cally different, and better, process for making the same natural product unless the characteristics of the product were judged substantially different. Yet the argument is not convincing that what the original inventor invented was the product, in addition to her particular process for making it' (Merges and Nelson 1990:67).

However, court decisions sometimes frustrated the interests of those seeking to expand protection to cover new subject matters. In 1939, the Court of Customs and Patent Appeals upheld a US Patent Office rejection of claims relating to vitamin C isolated from lemon juice.[15] The main basis for the ruling was that, while the two inventors had been first to isolate vitamin C crystals from lemon juice, they had not been first to isolate vitamin C from *any* source. There again, this was not exactly a subject matter issue, since it did not preclude the patenting of vitamins that had not previously been isolated.

Proof of this came a decade later. In December 1947, scientists at Merck isolated a cobalt-containing substance called cyanocobalamin from a microorganism called Streptomyces griseus, the source also of the antibiotic streptomycin (see below).[16] This substance, which was useful in treating pernicious anaemia, was christened vitamin B_{12} by the scientists who had isolated it, and was patented by the company. The substance was protected by two US patents: 2 563 794 ('Vitamin B-12'), which was issued in 1951, and 2 703 302 ('Vitamin B-12 active composition and process of preparing same'), which was issued in 1955. Although the product claims of the latter patent were invalidated by a district court in 1957, they were reinstated on appeal. Both patents were the subject of another court case in 1967. The court upheld the first patent entirely, stating: 'The patentees of the '794 patent have given to the world, for the first time, a medicine that can be used successfully in treating all patients suffering with pernicious anemia, a medicine that is subject to accurate standardization, and avoids the unfavorable reactions of the earlier liver extracts. It did not exist in nature in the form in which the patentees produced it, and nothing in the prior art either suggested or anticipated it.'[17]

Although five of the 12 claims in the second patent were invalidated, the principle that a 'composition of matter' consisting of a purified form of a natural product could be patented subject to passing the tests of non-obviousness and utility was not called into question.

Two early pharmaceutical breakthroughs that also turned out to be patentable despite their being new types of subject were insulin and the antibiotic streptomycin. These are interesting cases, not least because the companies

---

[15]   In *re King and Waugh* (1939), *United States Patent Quarterly* 43:400–02.
[16]   In doing so, Merck beat Glaxo by five months.
[17]   *Merck and Co., Inc. v Chase Chemical Company et al.* (1967), *United States Patent Quarterly* 155:152.

involved were heavily dependent on their collaborations with universities where the initial discoveries had been made, and in consequence found it expedient not to jeopardize their reputation by asserting their rights in the aggressive way that subsequently became the norm in the industry.

In 1923[18] and 1924,[19] two US patents for isolated and purified insulin and the extractive process were granted and assigned to the University of Toronto. The inventors of the earlier invention were Frederick Banting (who became a Nobel laureate that year) and three colleagues from the university, while the inventor named in the second patent was a scientist employed by the Eli Lilly company. The reason for the assignment of the latter patent to Toronto was that the two had come up with an agreement whereby Eli Lilly would enjoy temporary monopoly rights in the US market for insulin. In exchange, they would collaborate to further develop insulin and scale up production, and pool patent rights from any follow-up inventions. Although the patent pooling deal only applied to non-US patents, Toronto persuaded Eli Lilly to assign the patent to the university. One reason the company agreed to this was that Washington University had come up with a similar invention which made the patent's validity questionable (Bliss 1982: 139, 180–1). This suggests a hard-nosed commercial motivation that one does not normally associate with universities, at least not of that era.[20] But while the university's dealings with Eli Lilly were undoubtedly very shrewd, its motivation was public-spirited. Toronto's intention was to prevent any company from holding a secure and long-term monopoly position in the US. As for Canada, the university granted production rights to Connaught Medical Research Laboratories, which it had established in 1914 to carry out medical research and the not-for-profit production and distribution of health products to the Canadian public.[21] Banting and his colleagues gave up the rights to their British and Canadian patents to the university in exchange

---

[18]   US patent number 1 469 994 ('Extract obtainable from the mammalian pancreas or from the related glands in fishes, useful in the treatment of diabetes mellitus, and a method of preparing it'). The inventors named in the patent were Frederick Banting, Charles Best and James Collip.

[19]   US patent number 1 520 673 ('Purified antidiabetic product and method of making it'). The named inventor was George Walden.

[20]   Nonetheless, the IP and commercialization policies of some universities attracted controversy even in those days. Perhaps most controversially, the University of Wisconsin gained considerable royalties from the 1920s onwards thanks to the assertiveness of the Wisconsin Alumni Research Foundation, which was set up to maximize the university's income from its patents (some of which were health-related). The university and the foundation encountered heavy criticism over several decades from those who felt that universities should not be associated with such behaviour (see Weiner 1989:95–9).

[21]   The university sold Connaught in 1972. In 1999, it became the Connaught Campus of Pasteur Aventis, the vaccines division of Aventis.

for a nominal sum of one dollar each, with no royalties (Fishbein 1937:899). From 1922, Connaught worked closely with scientists at Eli Lilly to purify insulin and increase production. Thanks to its control of the insulin patents, the university was able to force companies licensed to manufacture insulin to send their batches to the university's Insulin Committee for assessment of quality and approval for sale. The patents also enabled it to fulfil its public service role by ploughing back revenue from the patents into further research, including support for a paediatric research foundation.[22]

In 1948, Merck was granted a patent for crystalline salts of the antibiotic, streptomycin, and for a process for preparing them. Streptomycin, the second antibiotic to come onto the market after penicillin and the first drug to be effective against tuberculosis, was discovered by Selman Waksman of Rutgers University, who had received financial support for his research from Merck. In exchange for royalties to the university, Waksman agreed to assign to the company any patents arising from his research. At that stage there was no certainty that his discoveries would turn out to be patentable anyway. In the event, they were. Although streptomycin was a natural product that could hardly have been invented by the Merck scientist named in the patent, it was claimed to the satisfaction of the examiner that 'for the first time, streptomycin is available in a form which not only has valuable therapeutic properties but also can be produced, distributed, and administered in a practicable way'.[23] Subsequently, Waksman managed to persuade Merck, concerned perhaps not to be seen to be exploiting what had recently become a state university, to transfer ownership of all patents to the Rutgers Research and Endowment Foundation so that production could be licensed to as many manufacturers as possible. Not surprisingly, while the university earned millions of dollars, the price of streptomycin fell during the following decade as competition increased and production methods improved (Sneader 1985:325; Temin 1979:436). From 1946 to 1950 alone, it dropped seventy-fold (Weatherall 1990:181).

Subsequently, the regulatory environment changed in ways that made the drug firms more determined to keep price levels high by preventing competitors from entering the market for their drugs. Most of the reforms were introduced after the war and had to do with safety and efficacy testing, but an important early change came in with the 1938 Food, Drug and Cosmetic Act,

---

[22] See: C.J. Rutty (2000), 'Dr Robert Davies Defries (1889–1975): "Canada's Mr Public Health"' (http://www.healthheritageresearch.com/Defries-biopaper.html); 'Discovery of Insulin' website (http://www.discoveryofinsulin.com/Experiments.htm). Also: Fishbein (1937:893).

[23] See US patent number 2 446 102 ('Complex salts of streptomycin and process for preparing the same').

which divided drugs into over-the-counter drugs and prescription (or 'ethical') drugs. The latter could only be sold with a doctor's prescription. While prescription drug sales promotion was aimed at the doctors, the actual buyers were wholesalers, pharmacies and hospitals. Doctors generally had no particular reason to treat price as a factor in determining which drugs to prescribe. Therefore, the demand for drugs was more price-inelastic than it would have been if the buyers and the prescribers were the same people (Steele 1962:139–43; Temin 1979:434–5). The streptomycin patent was in itself an important new regulatory development since it clarified to the industry that the new antibiotics were patentable despite being 'products of nature' (Steele 1962:136; Temin 1979:436).

In spite of all this, as companies began to discover and market increasing numbers of effective but very similar antibiotics, there was a very real threat of price-reducing competition. This actually happened in the case of both penicillin and streptomycin. In the USA, the price per dose of penicillin fell from $20 during the Second World War (when the government purchased all penicillin produced) to $1 in 1946, and to 10 cents in 1949. Between 1948 and 1955, the price of streptomycin plunged from $20 per gram to only 15 cents (Achilladelis 1993:287).

The companies responded in three ways (ibid.:288). First, they adopted strategic IP policies. For example, they protected their drugs by a combination of patents and trade marks, and asserted their rights aggressively in the courts. Ironically, the German companies who pioneered this tactic earlier in the century had been condemned for doing so by the American firms of the time. Second, those companies that developed new drugs but did not market their own products (such as Merck and Pfizer) set up large sales teams or acquired or merged with companies that already had them. Third, they sought to keep competitors out and prices high for as long as their patents remained in force. Three options were available to them that could under certain circumstances be adopted simultaneously. One way was to restrict patent licensing.[24] Among the first companies to adopt this tactic in a collective way were the five that cornered the market in broad spectrum antibiotics. The synthetic steroid producers followed their example from the late 1950s (Temin 1979:442). Companies that continued to license their patents to all-comers often found it unprofitable to do so. This was the experience of Ciba, with its plant-derived

---

[24]   Licensing nonetheless had its uses as it does today. For example, it may have been useful to patent-holding companies unable to meet a large international demand for a product. In addition, licensee companies may be better equipped than the patent holders to market the product. And small companies discovering a new chemical entity but lacking the funds to cover the research, development and marketing may have had no alternative. Such is the case for many present-day dedicated biotechnology firms.

drug reserpine (Serpasil),[25] and with isoniazid, a tuberculosis treatment that had been developed independently by Hoffman LaRoche and Squibb (Frost 1963:97). The second option was to license patents using highly restrictive provisions that, for example, prevented licensees from supplying foreign markets, and required them to purchase the intermediate chemicals from the licensors, or that retained the rights of licensors to follow-on innovations by licensees. The third option was to cooperate in certain ways with competitors selling similar products, for example by sharing patents and fixing prices.

One of the most controversial instances of the use of patents to support anti-competitive behaviour by the industry took place during the 1950s when five companies formed an international antibiotics cartel. The story begins with the introduction of the broad spectrum antibiotics, whose chemical structures were unknown when they first came to market, but turned out often to be extremely similar to each other. The earliest of these products were Lederle's Aureomycin (introduced in 1948), Parke Davis' Chloromycetin (1949), and Pfizer's Terramycin (1950). The similarity of these products stimulated intense competition which was reflected not just in increased marketing and advertising expenditures but also in a determination to elucidate the chemical structures of these drugs and to develop portfolios of related compounds. Pfizer's research proved the close affinity of Aureomycin and Terramycin and resulted in a very similar but more effective new substance, which was the first ever semi-synthetic antibiotic. This was patented and given the name 'tetracycline'. Lederle also discovered tetracycline by the same method and filed patent applications. Subsequently, Bristol and Hayden Chemical Corporation came up with tetracycline by another method and also applied for patents. Pfizer's and Bristol's patents were granted in 1955 after being initially rejected (Sneader 1985:327).

The other companies' patent applications failed. However, it was extremely doubtful that either patent should really have been awarded and the companies themselves were apparently fully aware that they were vulnerable to legal challenge (Braithwaite 1984:184–5). But by agreeing to recognize Pfizer's patent and to limit competition, a group of five companies – Pfizer, Cyanamid (Lederle's parent company), Bristol, Squibb and Upjohn – cornered the tetracycline market and managed to ensure that the price of their closely related products remained high and almost equal for about a decade. According to John Braithwaite, the situation suggested that the patent was providing 'a cover for conspiratorial behaviour to partition a market which in the absence

---

[25]   It is possible that Ciba's decision to license reserpine came about because it was uncertain about the validity of its patent, since the compound was the isolated active principle of an Indian medicinal plant used for centuries in traditional medicine (Steele 1962:159).

of the patent would have been clearly illegal' (ibid.:184). The prices began to decline from the early 1960s during the US Senate's investigation of anti-competitive behaviour by the pharmaceutical industry, and afterwards when a generic drug producer, McKesson and Robbins, entered the market and stayed there by convincing Pfizer that it was willing to face a patent infringement suit with confidence that the court would find in its favour. Although the government failed – despite its determined efforts – to prove that the companies had violated antitrust law or had defrauded the Patent Office, they had to pay hundreds of millions of dollars in legal settlements. Nonetheless, the profits the five companies made not just in the USA but worldwide through their control of tetracycline were enormous, and helped turn them into major pharmaceutical corporations (ibid.:176; Temin 1979:441). One can only speculate about how many people's lives might have been saved if prices had been allowed to fall earlier.

Unsurprisingly, such behaviour provoked a backlash. Politicians responded by subjecting the industry to very close scrutiny. From 1959 to 1962, the Senate Subcommittee on Antitrust and Monopoly, under the chairmanship of Senator Estes Kefauver, carried out an inquiry into the pharmaceutical industry. After three years of hearings, the subcommittee concluded that the drug companies were charging too much for their drugs and making excessive profits. Through patenting and branding, Kefauver and the subcommittee believed, they were free to charge as much as they liked, and were using this freedom to excess. Yet many of these companies were spending more money on sales promotion than on research. Moreover, many seemed more interested in developing modified versions of existing drugs than in trying to achieve genuine therapeutic advances. The subcommittee believed that the patent system encouraged such 'inventing-around' owing to the fact that chemical substances were protectable, and not just processes (Kefauver 1966:29–99).

Some of the subcommittee's findings were subsequently discredited, such as the claim that countries without patents produced a higher quantity of therapeutically advanced drugs than those with patents. In fact, the breakdown of important drugs (as listed by the subcommittee) that were discovered by countries allowing product patents, only process patents, and no patents at all for drugs, was 94:82:0 respectively (Cooper 1966:160). Nonetheless, the subcommittee made a strong case that many companies had indeed been indulging in profiteering and anti-competitive behaviour with the help of the patent system, and that the public was ill-served by such practices. Even so, attempts to introduce legislation to drastically weaken patent rights failed, and the industry managed to get away with its profits intact, albeit with a tarnished reputation.

Two decades later, the pharmaceutical industry became the focus of further legislative activity, this time successful, in the form of the 1984 Drug Price Competition and Patent Term Restoration Act (usually referred to as 'the

Hatch-Waxman Act'). Powerful as the research-based sector was, and experienced as it was in lobbying members of Congress, it finally had an effective competitor on Capitol Hill in the form of the generic manufacturers. These latter firms' IP-related interests were of course quite different and they had become sufficiently well-organized to ensure that any legislation affecting them would not stunt their growth.

For the research-based firms, the Act allowed patent term extensions of up to five years to compensate for the restriction on the effective protection term because of the time needed to acquire the FDA's marketing approval. There was of course some justification for this. It was taking increasingly long periods of time for the FDA to approve new chemical entities for sale, and this was reducing the effective period of market exclusivity. But the fact that the agrochemical industry, whose products also took a great deal of time and expense to get approved for sale, was unable to acquire a similar privilege is a testament to the political influence of the pharmaceutical companies.

As for the generic firms, the Act meant that they would only need to file a so-called Abbreviated New Drug Application (ANDA) with the FDA, rather than go through extensive clinical trials to demonstrate the safety and efficacy of their version of the soon to go off-patent drug. This meant that approval could take as little as three months. Second, the legislation incorporated the so-called 'Bolar exemption', which meant that certain acts performed before the expiry date of the patent that would normally infringe it were allowed as long as they were related to seeking FDA approval and did not constitute commercial use. The Bolar exemption was named after a court case involving Hoffman LaRoche and a generic producer called Bolar, and has been incorporated into the patent laws of several other countries.

Alfred Engelberg, formerly of the Generic Pharmaceutical Industrial Association (GPIA), describes the legislative process which led to the Act as 'a congressionally supervised negotiation between the generic and brand-name pharmaceutical industries in which the parties were compelled to reach a compromise by the legislature' (1999:390). In this negotiation the respective sections of the industry were represented by the Pharmaceutical Manufacturers Association (PMA, now PhRMA) and the GPIA. According to Engelberg, the Act did not advance the interests of either side of the pharmaceutical industry, or of the public (ibid.:392): 'patent-term extensions and the Bolar exemption are self-cancelling provisions, which, taken together, have no effect on the length of the exclusive marketing period of most drugs. The patent certification procedures are being abused by both sides and produce no public benefit that would not otherwise occur.' When we consider that as many as 19 per cent of prescription drugs sold in the USA that year were generics, it was no surprise that the generics sector had become more influential and that the research-based firms in consequence had to compromise. Since then, the competition facing companies whose drugs have just gone off patent has increased considerably despite their increasingly creative evergreening strategies. By 1996, thanks in large part to the Hatch-Waxman Act, the generics sector of the industry had increased its share to 43 per cent (Engelberg 1999).

Significantly, the effective patent life of drugs seems again to be lengthening. The Tufts Center for the Study of Drug Development reported in 2000 that average clinical development times had shortened from over seven years in the early 1990s to less than five years, while average FDA approval times had shortened from around three years to about one (Kaitin 2000). Moreover, the same decade saw a marked increase in the number of new drug applications subsequently approved for sale by the FDA. According to Jennifer Washburn, writing in *The American Prospect* (2001), 'whereas in the early 1990s the FDA approved 60 per cent of the industry's applications for new products, by the end of the decade 80 per cent were getting approved'. If such trends continue, the extension provided by the Hatch-Waxman Act may soon no longer be necessary. In this case, though, we can expect determined efforts from the industry to block its removal.

Despite the assertiveness of the generics sector and their rather different interests, the self-styled research-based firms are as influential as ever in the corridors of power. Their interests are represented by an army of Washington-based lobbyists, and they are generous donors to the electoral campaigns of parties and politicians. However, there is a growing number of pressure groups that seek to counter this influence. In spite of their relative lack of financial muscle, some of these groups carry out very impressive research and include some sophisticated and effective activists, such as the Consumer Project on Technology and Public Citizen.

5.3   The United Kingdom

Like the US system, the British patent system at the start of the twentieth century provided owners with stronger rights by the standards of the day. But, as will soon become clear, the historical development of the two systems took quite divergent courses so that for much of the century they varied quite widely, and offered quite different levels of protection for pharmaceutical inventions. Interest group politics provides at least part of the explanation.

As was explained earlier, the British pharmaceutical industry was a slow developer, and its economic importance prior to the First World War was thus quite small. Neither was it particularly innovative, so it had little use for the patent system. When it came to patent reform, while elements within the much larger chemical industry were very vocal and gained the ears of policymakers and politicians, the drug manufacturers had very little to say. Probably the most vocal and effective of these elements was a German-born industrial chemist and businessman, Ivan Levinstein.

The first legislative development in patent law that had a direct bearing on the interests of the pharmaceutical industry took place in 1919 with the passage of an amendment to the 1907 Patents and Designs Act. As a consequence of wartime shortages of important products, the political establishment was ready to adopt a more mercantilist and defensive attitude towards strategic industries. The legislation reflected this attitude very strongly.

The 1919 Act to amend the Patents and Designs Acts brought British patent law further into line with the law in most of Europe in that, while it extended the duration of patents from 14 to 16 years for the benefit of inventors who had been prevented from working their patents by the war, it singled out chemicals, foods and medicines for weakened protection. Patent protection was available only for those chemical substances produced by the particular process or processes claimed in the application. According to the Act, 'in the case of inventions relating to substances prepared or produced by chemical processes or intended for food and medicine, the specification shall not include claims for the substance itself, except when prepared or produced by the special methods or processes of manufacture described and claimed or by their obvious chemical equivalents'.

In effect, then, the achievement of secure product protection required applicants to anticipate all possible ways of manufacturing the chemical. The main purpose of these measures was to make it easier for British firms to circumvent the patent monopolies of the German dyestuff firms while acquiring their own (process) patents into the bargain. But the law did not make it too easy for them either. In infringement cases concerning new chemicals protected by a patented process, the burden of proof was on the party whose manufacture of the chemical was alleged to infringe the patent.

Another measure affecting holders of patents for inventions 'intended for or capable of being used for the preparation or production of food or medicine' was that applicants for a licence could acquire one from the comptroller general (the head of the Patent Office). In settling the terms of the licence including royalty payments, the comptroller was required to take into account 'the desirability of making the food or medicine available to the public at the lowest possible price consistent with giving to the inventor due reward for the research leading to the invention'.

Clearly, the dyestuff industry was not the sole concern. The wartime shortage of drugs was obviously another factor in the wording of this section of the legislation. However, the government's interest was not primarily to increase the international competitiveness of the British pharmaceutical industry but to ensure greater self-sufficiency and create a level playing field for the country, bearing in mind that neither Germany, France nor Switzerland allowed chemical products to be protected except through the patenting of manufacturing processes.

It must be said that the pharmaceutical industry was not very influential in government or Parliament at that time. In fact, the industry did not even have a trade association to represent its interests until as late as 1929, when the Wholesale Druggists Trade Association (renamed the Association of the British Pharmaceutical Industry in 1948) was founded 'to advance the interests of its members through improved organisation especially regarding departmental or parliamentary legislation affecting the drug trade' (Abraham 2002:232). Evidently, the government did not need to be persuaded by the industry that the measures it introduced were necessary for the country.

In 1930, the Board of Trade set up a committee under the chairmanship of Sir Charles Sargant to advise the government on possible reforms to the patents and designs law and on practices of the Patent Office (UK Board of Trade 1931). In all, 53 individuals gave evidence, including five from the Chartered Institute of Patent Agents, three from the British Medical Association, two from the Medical Research Council, and two from Joseph Nathan and Co. Nonetheless, the interests of the chemical industry were still given far more attention than those of the much smaller pharmaceutical industry. This may not have concerned the drug companies too much, though, as both sectors were primarily concerned to prevent foreign companies from using the patent system to dominate the domestic market. As it was, no substantial changes were made to the patent system during the inter-war era, which was a period of consolidation and gradual progress for the pharmaceutical industry.

The lessons learned from the Second World War were quite different from those of the First World War. In 1918, the British pharmaceutical industry barely existed. In 1945, this was hardly the case. And in the years that followed, exports of various types of product including pharmaceuticals played an important role in Britain's post-war economy recovery (Abraham 2002:238). Moreover, the new Labour government was extremely concerned about public health, including the availability of drugs, and was willing to take radical measures. In 1946, the National Health Service Act was passed, leading two years later to the establishment of the NHS.

The NHS formed a key plank in the construction of the welfare state, extending free medical care – including prescription drugs – to the whole population. This had two effects, of which one was favourable to the industry, and the other much less so (though on balance the creation of the NHS was beneficial for the drug manufacturers). First, it vastly expanded the market for drugs. Second, the government essentially because a monopsonist, that is to say a sole buyer. In addition to its obvious interest in controlling expenditure, it thus had a very strong bargaining position *vis-à-vis* the industry.

The 1949 Patents Act took on board the recommendations of the Swan Committee, whose report was published two years earlier. Regarding the bar on the patenting of substances 'produced by chemical processes or intended for food or medicine', the committee's report had the following to say:

> It has been strongly urged that this limitation on the claiming of new substances should be removed as not being in accordance with modern technical developments. It has been argued that the real invention lies in the discovery of a new substance, with new and useful properties, and that the process of manufacture often involves little novelty in itself. Many valuable new substances are produced by synthesising a large number of possible compounds by known methods and then determining which of the new substances have useful properties. It has also been pointed out that the limitation imposed by this sub-section has little practical value, and that it merely encourages the drafting of a specification to cover all conceivable methods of manufacture, so that, in effect, it is the substance itself and not the process of manufacture which is protected by the patent. (UK Board of Trade 1947)

Impressed with these arguments for removing the bar on complete product protection[26] in respect of chemicals, the committee faced a choice. The first was to allow such protection for chemicals whether or not they were intended for food or medicine. The second, which it preferred, was to maintain the bar on protection of substances intended for food or medicine except by a specified process but to allow full protection of other chemicals. For the sake of legal certainty, the committee recommended the first course of action, and this was implemented by the government in the 1949 Act. But it recommended retaining the 1919 provision on acquiring licences from the comptroller in the case of foods and medicines. This measure was maintained under Section 41 of the new legislation.

The new legislation contained two other interesting provisions. The first, another committee recommendation, was that any application may be refused that 'claims as an invention a substance capable of being used as food or medicine which is a mixture of known ingredients possessing only the aggregate of the known properties of the ingredients, or that it claims as an invention a process producing such a substance by mere admixture'. In other words, mere recipes and mixtures lacking synergistic effects creating unforeseen new properties were unpatentable (Satchell 1970:187–8). The second was that claims to a new substance were to be 'construed as not extending to that substance when found in nature'. A patent examiner writing in 1970 had the following to say about this provision:

---

[26]   Complete protection in the sense that it included all possible methods of manufacture.

> This raises the question whether the person who first discloses the chemical consti-
> tution of a substance which is known in nature, for example, an alkaloid or an
> enzyme, and prepares it by a synthetic method, should be allowed to claim the
> synthetic product, notwithstanding that it is indistinguishable from the natural prod-
> uct. So far we have not been called upon to decide this question. Where an appli-
> cant has discovered for the first time the chemical constitution of such a compound
> and has disclosed at least one method by which it may be synthesized, a claim to
> the compound defined by its chemical constitution might be allowed under British
> law. (ibid.:180)

Universal healthcare provision is of course expensive, which is why successive governments were concerned to keep drug prices at reasonable levels. Yet,
these same governments generally accepted the desirability of allowing drug
companies to patent their inventions and of respecting patent rights unless
there were very good reasons not to. As things turned out, it was not always
easy to meet the needs of patients and deal with budgetary constraints without
intruding on patent monopolies.

In 1961, the government decided to confront the broad spectrum antibiotics
cartel by authorizing the NHS Hospital Services to purchase imported (mostly
Italian) generic versions of several of these drugs whose patents were still in
force. This action saved the NHS £4 million. Generic producers were encouraged by this and began to apply for compulsory licences. Consequently, 50
Section 41 applications were submitted to the comptroller during the 1960s.
Before 1960, no applications at all had been submitted. However, of the 50
applications only four were allowed, most of the rest being withdrawn. This
situation was due to the difficult legal procedures that applicants needed to
comply with. Even so, the very possibility of compulsory licences probably
encouraged the patent-holding firms to be more cooperative about prices than
they would otherwise have been.

Pfizer was not at all happy with this situation and decided to make a stand
by taking the Ministry (now Department) of Health to court for infringing its
patent on tetracycline. In 1965, the House of Lords decided that the Ministry
was acting within the provisions of the 1949 Act that permitted use – but not
sale – of inventions by 'services of the Crown' subject to payment of royalties
to the patentee. Although the decision did not allow the General Medical and
Pharmaceutical Services, through which 80 per cent of NHS-provided drugs
were consumed, to do the same thing, 'the pharmaceutical companies were
aghast at what they felt to be abrogation by the State of the fundamental principle of patent rights. Prophecies were made that the British industry would
wind up its drug research and become totally dependent on foreign developments' (Taylor and Silberston 1973:237).

As it turned out, such prophesies were unjustified. This was so despite the
fact that worse was to follow for the industry. In 1967, the Sainsbury

Committee, set up to investigate the relationship between the pharmaceutical industry and the NHS, published a report which recommended that the General Medical and Pharmaceutical Services also be treated as a service of the Crown with authority to acquire generic versions of patent-protected drugs (UK Ministry of Health 1967). The government was initially reluctant to implement this, owing no doubt to pressure from the industry. But the provision was incorporated through an opposition amendment into the 1968 Health Services and Public Health Act (Hancher 1990:321).

On the other hand, Section 41 compulsory licences were abolished as recommended by another committee established by the Board of Trade to examine the patent system and the patent law ('the Banks Committee'), whose report was presented to Parliament in 1970 (UK Board of Trade 1970). The government of the time was reluctant to act upon the recommendation, but in 1977 another government did so through legislation incorporating the European Patent Convention into UK law. Its decision to do so was part of a negotiation with the industry in which the latter agreed to cooperate on the introduction of advertising regulations (Hancher 1990:323).

Nowadays, the government identifies the economic health of the nation with that of the pharmaceutical industry. This is understandable given that it is one of the country's most innovative and successful in terms of export performance. But the government continues to have an interest in ensuring that the drugs it purchases on behalf of the public provide value for money. Thanks to the NHS, the prices of drugs and their relationship with the patent system is not a highly charged political issue as it is in the USA and many developing countries. The final report of the Pharmaceutical Industry Competitiveness Task Force, which consisted of representatives from government and industry in equal number, and was published in 2001, had little if anything to say about the UK patent system (UK Department of Health 2001). In contrast, the industry was very eager to ensure that the government took heed of its IP interests at the international and European Community levels. It seems clear from the report that the government was extremely sympathetic to these interests.

5.4 Continental Europe

The patent laws of France, Germany, Switzerland and other western European countries have evolved along somewhat different paths. Even so, one can make two fairly reliable generalizations. First, most of these countries did not allow pharmaceutical substances to be patented as such for most of the twentieth century. Only the processes for manufacturing them could be. Second, this situation changed from around 1960, so that by the early 1990s virtually all of them provided product protection for pharmaceuticals.

One might suppose that pharmaceutical industry lobbying was behind the changed situation. In fact, this was not always the case. For example, the change to the German patent system allowing full product protection of pharmaceutical substances was introduced in January 1968 with the entry into force of an Interim Law that removed the following text from the German patent law: 'excluded from patentability are: ... (2) inventions relating to foods, luxury provisions, and drugs, as well as substances produced by chemical processes to the extent that they do not relate to a particular process for the production of these articles'. The main purpose of the measure was to facilitate the work of the German Patent Office and the Federal Patent Court. Companies had effectively overcome the bar on patenting chemical substances by acquiring multiple patents covering all conceivable manufacturing processes. Partly in consequence of this, the Patent Office had a massive backlog of unexamined patent applications that it was anxious to clear (Nastelski 1972:268). Another reason to enact the change was to harmonize German law with the emerging new European standards being established by the 1963 Convention on the Unification of Certain Points of Substantive Law on Patents for Invention. In addition, policymakers no longer saw any particular need to maintain the bar on product protection for chemicals. Long gone were the days when such a bar was deemed necessary to protect the industry from foreign competition.

On the other hand, the 1978 overturning of the bar on patents for pharmaceuticals in Italy was a direct result of corporate activism. More than 10 companies acting together challenged the constitutionality of the bar in the Constitutional Court. The court concurred with the companies, on two grounds. The first was that the bar unfairly discriminated against pharmaceutical entrepreneurs and inventors employed in the sector, since they had no legal entitlement to compensation for their inventions. The second was that the Italian Republic had a constitutional obligation to protect and encourage scientific research.

Nonetheless, the 1963 Convention and the European Patent Convention were crucial forces for harmonization of European patent law in the area, among others, of pharmaceutical inventions. Once the texts of these treaties had been agreed, countries had little alternative but to fall into line.

But why did it take so long for many European countries to allow product patents for pharmaceuticals? It is important first to be aware that many countries have for public policy reasons excluded or restricted pharmaceutical products from patentability, and that even in western Europe (though never in the USA) this situation persisted in many countries for most of the twentieth century. The main scientific explanation for the removal of the exclusion in western European countries during the mid-to-late twentieth century lies in the changing research strategies pursued by the modern pharmaceutical industry from the post-Second World War period owing largely to the difficulty in coming up with new substances. Moreover, the research and development costs per product rose considerably. It is frequently claimed that an average of 10 000 substances will need to be tested to come up with a new therapeutic product, and a drug will not go on the market until it has been subjected to pharmacological and toxicological tests and extensive clinical trials. Given the increasing scarcity of new chemical entities (NCEs) entering the market, companies have more to lose from failing to prevent competitors from copying them or inventing around them to develop similar me-too products. This situation is likely to affect both the research strategies of firms and their IP interests. The commercial promise of product innovation increases, while process innovation becomes less interesting. And when it comes to IP, strong and broad patent protection becomes more important than ever.

The industry's demands for stronger and broader protection bore fruit in 1992, when the European Council adopted a Regulation requiring European Union countries to provide monopoly rights for medicinal products beyond the life of the basic patents protecting them, to make up for the time taken to secure marketing authorization (Bently and Sherman 2001:551). These rights are known as supplementary protection certificates (SPCs). Applications by a patent holder for an SPC must be made to the national patent offices within six months of receiving marketing authorization for the drug in question in that country. EFPIA and the major European drug companies lobbied hard for these rights on the grounds that such privileges were available to their American and Japanese competitors in their domestic markets. But the industry did not completely get its own way. As a result of campaigning by patient and consumer groups and generic producers, the maximum possible extension period was just five years (Cornish 1999:159; NCC 1991:47). This was somewhat shorter than EFPIA's original demand for an effective patent life of 20 years.

6.   CONCLUSIONS

Like other types of business, the pharmaceutical industry seeks to maximize its profits. As a major user of the patent system, the industry in the developed world understandably seeks to influence intellectual property policymaking. This chapter has shown that this is nothing new. But while, in the past, the outcome of their efforts was a weakening of rights, nowadays the research-based or branded companies among them consistently lobby for ever stronger rights. Given the economic importance of the industry in countries like the US, the UK, Germany and Switzerland and the support they get from the patent practitioner community in persuading policymakers that stronger rights are good for the country, it is hardly surprising that they are so often successful. Consequently, if we compare today's patent systems of North America and

Europe with those of a hundred years ago and follow the trends during the intervening years, we find that the legal rights available to pharmaceutical inventors have never been stronger or more secure in all of these countries than they are today.

On the basis of what we have learned so far, let us try to answer four very important questions. First, how did pharmaceutical corporations use patent law and other IP rights to maximize returns from their research and development investments through the market-place? Second, what did corporations do when they found patent systems to be inadequate in furthering their interests? Third, how successful were their attempts to change patent systems? Fourth, can it be concluded that patent law stimulated scientific and technological advancement and thereby resulted in more cures than there would have been without patents?

Taking the first question, pharmaceutical companies used patents and other IP rights, especially trade marks, in various ways and for different purposes. Using IP rights strategically to exclude competitors from markets in particular drugs, or classes of drugs, was pioneered by German businesses and has become increasingly sophisticated over the years. The evergreening tactics described in this chapter provide some good examples. While the overall goal of such behaviour has always been to maximize profits, the specific aims of using IP rights include those of recouping and profiting from huge and growing research and development investments, differentiating one company's products from similar ones produced by a rival, and of maintaining high price levels for as long as possible by preventing generic producers from entering the market. The use of IP rights and licences to cartelize the supply of broad spectrum antibiotics is a good example of how a number of objectives were achieved, though profit maximization was of course the primary one.

Pharmaceutical businesses are never completely satisfied with the levels of protection available, at least not for long. Companies tending to favour increased levels of protection are those which are innovative or that invest large sums of money in the attempt to be so, and those that may have little to show for their present research expenditures but at least have some products developed earlier that continue to generate large revenues. Companies that are not in the business of being innovative, such as generic producers, are happier with weaker IP systems. In countries where a firm's innovation level is typical of the industry as a whole, it is likely to collaborate politically with other companies, perhaps through a business association, to persuade the government to reform IP rights so that they better meet their needs. This may result in increased or decreased levels of protection. But as levels of innovation increase across the industries, preferences for stronger levels of protection arise and may well prove to be irresistible. The history of the European and North American pharmaceutical industries as recounted here bears this out.

One should not go too far and assume that IP reform is necessarily imposed by a particular group of powerful firms – in this case brand-name or research-based pharmaceuticals. For one thing, legislation is sometimes based in part on negotiations between different business groupings, as with the 1984 Hatch-Waxman Act in the USA. In other cases, regulators act on their own initiative, as when the bar on pharmaceutical product patents was lifted in Germany in 1968. Also, attempts by the industry to reform patent systems do not always succeed. For example, they may fail to convince policymakers that the economic stakes are high enough for the national economy to justify the cost of reform. Or perhaps the proposed changes would hurt wealthier or more influential industries. This is what happened to the US pharmaceutical industry just after the First World War when it sought unsuccessfully to weaken the patent system.

The most difficult question to answer is the last one. We cannot turn the clock back and re-run past centuries without a patent system and then compare the number of life-saving and enhancing remedies, not to speak of the number of jobs and the various other economic benefits of profitable industries, that have arisen with those that a patent-free world would have created. But there is circumstantial evidence that, on balance, patents were probably a positive force for pharmaceutical innovation even with their obvious drawbacks, such as their tactical deployment to build excessively broad and long-lasting monopolies.

But all of this rather misses the point. The key issue facing policymakers today is not whether or not to have a patent system, but how to design a patent system that meets certain objectives, among which are to improve the health of the population while establishing or maintaining an innovative and wealth-generating pharmaceutical industry. Patents definitely have a role to play. But how to design an optimal patent system that meets both of these objectives effectively is extremely difficult. Does history help? To a certain extent it does. It cautions against a one-size-fits-all approach of the kind that the TRIPS Agreement arguably represents. It also demonstrates how important it is for policymakers to base their patent reform decisions on an understanding of developments in science and technology and their implications for intellectual property regulation, *and* on the need to listen to the views of as many different interests as possible, *especially* the biggest and most important of all interest groups: the general public.

REFERENCES

Abbott, F.M. (2002), 'The TRIPS Agreement, access to medicines, and the WTO Doha Ministerial Conference', *Journal of World Intellectual Property*, **5**(1), 15–52.

Abraham, J. (2002), 'The political economy of medicines regulation in Europe', in H. Lawton-Smith (ed.), *The Regulation of Science and Technology*, Basingstoke: Palgrave.

Achilladelis, B. (1993), 'The dynamics of technological innovation: the sector of antibacterial medicines', *Research Policy*, **22**, 279–308.

American Pharmaceutical Association (1919), 'Report of the Committee on Patents and Trademarks of the American Pharmaceutical Association, August 1919', *Journal of the Patent Office Society*, **2**(1), 76–82.

Austin, M. (2001), 'Colo. AG sues 3 firms over drug', *Denver Post* 28 September.

Bensaude-Vincent, B., and I. Stengers (1996), *A History of Chemistry*, Cambridge and London: Harvard University Press.

Bently, L. and B. Sherman (2001), *Intellectual Property Law*, Oxford: Oxford University Press.

Bliss, M. (1982), *The Discovery of Insulin*, Toronto: McLelland and Stewart.

Braithwaite, J. (1984), *Corporate Crime in the Pharmaceutical Industry*, London: Routledge and Kegan Paul.

Bristol-Myers Squibb (2001), *Annual Report*, 2000.

Bynum, W.E. (1994), *Science and the Practice of Medicine in the Nineteenth Century*, Cambridge: Cambridge University Press.

Chandler Jr., A.D. (1990), *Scale and Scope: The Dynamics of Industrial Capitalism*, Cambridge and London: Belknap Press.

Chartered Institute of Patent Agents (CIPA) (1998), 'Briefing paper – patenting in the pharmaceutical industry – Supplementary Protection Certificates', London: CIPA.

Cooper, M.H. (1966), *Prices and Profits in the Pharmaceutical Industry*, Oxford and London: Pergamon Press.

Cornish, W.r. (1999), *Intellectual Property: Patents, Copyright, Trade Marks and Allied Rights* (fourth edition), London: Sweet and Maxwell.

Correa, C.M. (2001a), *Trends in Drug Patenting: Case Studies*, Buenos Aires: Corregidor.

Correa, C.M. (2001b), 'Public health and patent legislation in developing countries', *Tulane Journal of Technology and Intellectual Property*, **3**: 1–53.

Cragg, G.M., D.J. Newman, and K.M. Sander (1997), 'Natural products in drug discovery and development', *Journal of Natural Products*, **60**(1): 52–60.

Djerassi, C. (2001), *The Man's Pill: Reflections on the 50th Birthday of the Pill*, Oxford: Oxford University Press.

Duffin, J. (1999), *History of Medicine: A Scandalously Short Introduction*, Toronto: University of Toronto Press.

European Federation of Pharmaceutical Industries and Associations (EFPIA) (1998), *The Pharmaceutical Industry in Figures. 1998 Edition*, Brussels: EFPIA.

Engelberg, A.B. (1999), 'Special patent provisions for pharmaceuticals: have they outlived their usefulness? A political, legislative and legal history of US law and observations for the future', *IDEA The Journal of Law and Technology*, **39**(3), 389–425.

Fairley, P. (1978), *The Conquest of Pain*, London: Michael Joseph.

Farnsworth, N. (1988), 'Screening plants for new medicines', in E.O. Wilson (ed.), *BioDiversity*, Washington DC: National Academy Press.

Fishbein, M. (1937), 'Are patents on medicinal discoveries and on foods in the public interest?', *Journal of the Patent Office Society*, **19**(12), 891–904.

Frost, G.E. (1963), 'The case against drug patent compulsory licensing', *The Patent, Trademark and Copyright Journal of Research and Education*, **7**(1), 84–102.

Goodman, J., and V. Walsh (2001), *The Story of Taxol: Nature and Politics in the Pursuit of an Anti-cancer Drug*, Cambridge: Cambridge University Press.

Granstrand, O. (1999), *The Economics and Management of Intellectual Property: Towards Intellectual Capitalism*, Cheltenham, UK and Northampton, MA, USA: Edward Elgar.

Green, A.G. (1915[1901]), 'The relative progress of the coal-tar colour industry in England and Germany during the past fifteen years', in W.M. Gardner (ed.), *The British Coal-Tar Industry: Its Origin, Development and Decline*, London: Williams and Norgate.

Greenberg, A.S. (1926), 'The lesson of the Germany-owned US chemical patents', *Journal of the Patent Office Society*, **9**(1), 19–35.

Grubb, P.W. (1999), *Patents for Chemicals, Pharmaceuticals and Biotechnology*, Oxford: Clarendon Press.

Hancher, L. (1990), *Regulating for Competition: Government, Law, and the Pharmaceutical Industry in the United Kingdom and France*, Oxford: Clarendon Press.

Haynes, W. (1945), *American Chemical Industry. Volume 2, The World War Period: 1912–22*, New York: Van Nostrand.

Hunt, M. (2002), *Changing Patterns of Pharmaceutical Innovation*, Washington DC: National Institute of Health Care Management Research and Educational Foundation.

Jones, E. (2001), *The Business of Medicine: The Extraordinary History of Glaxo, a Baby Food Producer, Which Became One of the World's Most Successful Pharmaceutical Companies*, London: Profile Books.

Kaitin, K.I. (2000), 'Don't turn back the clock on drug regulatory reform', Boston: Tufts Center for the Study of Drug Development.

Kefauver, E., with the assistance of I. Till (1966), *In a Few Hands: Monopoly Power in America*, Harmondsworth: Penguin Books.

Le Fanu, J. (1999), *The Rise and Fall of Modern Medicine*, London: Little, Brown and Co.

Levin, R.C., A.K. Klevorick, R.R. Nelson, and S.G. Winter (1987), 'Appropriating the returns from industrial research and development', *Brookings Papers on Economic Activity*, 783–820.

Liebenau, J. (1984), 'Industrial R&D in pharmaceutical firms in the twentieth century', *Business History*, **26**(3), 329–46.

Mann, J. (1999), *The Elusive Magic Bullet: The Search for the Perfect Drug*, Oxford: Oxford University Press.

Mann, C.C., and M.L. Plummer (1991), *The Aspirin Wars: Money, Medicine, and 100 Years of Rampant Competition*, Cambridge: Harvard Business School Publications.

Mansfield, E. (1986), 'Patents and innovation: an empirical study', *Management Science*, **32**(2), 173–81.

Merges, R.P., and R.R. Nelson (1990), 'On the complex economics of patent scope', *Columbia Law Review*, **90**, 839–916.

Mowery, D.C., and N. Rosenberg (1998), *Paths of Innovation: Technological Change in 20th Century America*, Cambridge: Cambridge University Press.

Nastelski, K. (1972), 'Product protection for chemical inventions in Germany', *International Review of Industrial Property and Copyright Law*, **3**(3), 267–94.

National Consumer Council (NCC) (1991), *Intellectual Property: The Consumer View of Patents, Copyright, Trade Marks and Allied Rights* (International Trade and the Consumer Working paper No. 6), London: NCC.

Nature (1995), 'Names for hijacking' (editorial), **373**, 370

Noble, D.F. (1977), *America by Design: Science, Technology, and the Rise of Corporate Capitalism*, New York: Alfred A. Knopf.

Owen, G. (1999), *From Empire to Europe: The Decline and Revival of British Industry Since the Second World War*, London: HarperCollins.

Owens, L. (1991), 'Patents, the "frontiers" of American invention, and the Monopoly Committee of 1939: anatomy of a discourse', *Technology and Culture*, **32**(4), 1076–93.

Pharmaceutical Research and Manufacturers of America (PhRMA) (1998), *Industry Profile. 1998 Edition*, Washington: PhRMA.

Pharmaceutical Research and Manufacturers of America (PhRMA) (1999), *Annual Report 1999–2000*, Washington: PhRMA.

Plotkin, M.J. (2000), *Medicine Quest: In Search of Nature's Healing Secrets*, New York: Viking Penguin Porter 1997.

Principe, P. (1998), 'Economics and medicinal plants', in T.R. Tomlinson and O. Olayiwola Akerele (eds), *Medicinal Plants: Their Role in Health and Biodiversity*, Philadelphia: University of Pennsylvania Press.

Public Citizen (2001), *Rx R&D Myths: The Case Against the Drug Industry's 'R&D Scare Card'*, Washington DC: Public Citizen.

Reuters (2001a), 'AstraZeneca holds off rivals as US patent on world's top drug dies', 6 October (http://www.economictimes.com/today/06worl11.htm).

Reuters (2001b), 'Bayer says US Cipro patent "beyond doubt"', 26 October (http://biz.yahoo.com/rf/011026/l26516703_1.html).

Rivette, K.G., and D. Kline (2000), 'Discovering new value in intellectual property', *Harvard Business Review* (January–February), 54–66.

Roe, J.E. (1943), 'War measures, the Alien Property Custodian and patents', *Journal of the Patent Office Society*, **25**(10), 692–728.

Rollins, A.D. (1983), 'Novelty of metabolic product', *Journal of the Patent Office Society*, **65**(7), 403–7.

Satchell, R.D. (1970), 'Chemical product patent practice in the United Kingdom', *International Review of Industrial Property and Copyright Law*, **1**(2), 179–89.

Slinn, J. (1995), 'Research and development in the UK pharmaceutical industry from the nineteenth century to the 1960s', in R. Porter and M. Teich (eds), *Drugs and Narcotics in History*, Cambridge: Cambridge University Press.

Sneader, W. (1985), *Drug Discovery: The Evolution of Modern Medicines*, Chichester, New York, Brisbane, Toronto, Singapore: John Wiley and Sons.

Steele, H. (1962), 'Monopoly and competition in the ethical drugs market', *Journal of Law and Economics*, **5**, 131–64.

Steen, K. (1995), 'Confiscated commerce: American importers of German organic chemicals, 1914–1929', *History and Technology*, **12**, 261–84.

Stewart, F.C. (1919), 'Letter to M.H. Coulston, President of the Patent Office Society', *Journal of the Patent Office Society*, **2**(1), 73–5.

Stolz, R., and R. Schwaiberger (1987), 'The correlation between dye chemistry and pharmacy in creating the modern chemotherapy', *History and Technology*, **3**, 193–203.

Stone, T., and G. Darlington (2000), *Pills, Potions and Poisons: How Drugs Work*, Oxford: Oxford University Press.

Taylor, C.T., and Z.A. Silberston (1973), *The Economic Impact of the Patent System: The British Experience*, Cambridge: Cambridge University Press.

Temin, P. (1979), 'Technology, regulation, and market structure in the modern pharmaceutical industry', *The Bell Journal of Economics*, **10**, 429–46.

ten Kate, K. and S.A. Laird (1999), *The Commercial Use of Biodiversity: Access to Genetic Resources and Benefit Sharing*, London: Earthscan.

Thomas, L.G. (1994), 'Implicit industrial policy: the triumph of Britain and the failure of France in global pharmaceuticals', *Industrial and Corporate Change*, **3**(2), 451–89.

Tufts Center for the Study of Drug Development (2001), 'Backgrounder: a methodology for counting costs for pharmaceutical R&D', Boston: Tufts Center for the Study of Drug Development.

United Kingdom Board of Trade (1931), *Report of the Departmental Commission on the Patents and Designs Acts and Practice of the Patent Office ('The Sargant Committee')*, London: HMSO.

United Kingdom Board of Trade (1947), *Patents and Design Acts. Final Report of the Departmental Committee ('The Swan Committee')*, London: HMSO.

United Kingdom Board of Trade (1970), *The British Patent System: Report of the Committee to Examine the Patent System and Patent Law ('The Banks Committee')*, London: HMSO.

United Kingdom Department of Health (2001), *Pharmaceutical Industry Competitiveness Task Force. Final Report – March 2001*, London: Department of Health.

United Kingdom Ministry of Health (1967), *Report of the Committee of Enquiry into the Relationship of the Pharmaceutical Industry with the National Health Service, 1954–1967 ('The Sainsbury Committee')*, London: HMSO.

USA Today (2001), 'Cipro saga exposes how drugmakers protect profits', 29 October: 14A.

Washburn, J. (2001), 'Undue influence', *The American Prospect*, **12**(14).

Weatherall, M. (1990), *In Search of a Cure: A History of Pharmaceutical Discovery*, Oxford: Oxford University Press.

Weiner, C. (1989), 'Patenting and academic research: historical case studies', in V. Weil and J.W. Snapper (eds), *Owning Scientific and Technical Information*, New Brunswick and London: Rutgers University Press.

Wengenroth, U. (1997), 'Germany: competition abroad – cooperation at home, 1870–1900', in A.D. Chandler, F. Amatori and T. .Hikino (eds), *Big Business and the Wealth of Nations*, Cambridge: Cambridge University Press.

Werth, B. (1994), *The Billion-dollar Molecule: One Company's Quest for the Perfect Drug*, New York: Touchstone.

Wimmer, W. (1998), 'Innovation in the German pharmaceutical industry, 1880 to 1920', in E. Homburg, A.S. Travis and H.G. Schröter, *The Chemical Industry in Europe, 1850–1914: Industrial Growth, Pollution, and Professionalization*, Dordrecht and Norwell: Kluwer Academic.

8. Seabirds, series and sonar: Claiming registered rights

Alison Firth*

INTRODUCTION

The registration of industrial property rights provides notice to the world at large of the existence and extent of exclusive rights. Third parties can search the registers, so clarity and proper elaboration serve the public interest. This underlies the classical 'fence post' or 'peripheral' approach to patent drafting and interpretation found in the common law world. Traditionally this leads to a hierarchy of precise claims, but a given system of registered rights may allow only a single claim, to one embodiment of a creation.[1] Tootal has argued[2] persuasively that a European utility model should indeed be restricted to one claim, strictly construed. However, the registered proprietors themselves hope to enjoy a long period of undisturbed exclusivity over large and small inventions, marks, designs and plant varieties. In a changing world, some flexibility of interpretation may be necessary to achieve this, hence the 'central claiming' of inventions traditionally favoured in Germany and Japan. Achieving a proper balance between right-holders and third parties is an issue for all forms of intellectual property right but registered rights are interesting in that the scope of protection is publicly declared by the right-holder. To assist them in this task, most industrial property systems permit multiple claiming and also make allowance for inexact infringements. This chapter looks briefly

---

*   This chapter was first presented as a paper at the SPTL/SLS annual conference at Oxford in September 2003. Warm thanks to colleagues at Queen Mary, to members of the SLS Intellectual Property subject section, to Paul Cole and to Tariq Baloch for helpful comments and suggestions; all errors and infelicities remain my own.
   [1]   In the Malaysian Patents Act of 1983, as amended by the Patents (Amendment) Act 1993, Schedule 2 modifies patent provisions for the case of 'utility innovations' (s 17A). Section 28 is amended to refer to 'the claim' in the context of a utility innovation certificate. For a Malaysian author's perspective on utility models, see Lim, 'The long march – utility model protection for minor inventions' (1993) March MIP 37.
   [2]   Tootal, 'Second tier protection' [1994] EIPR 511.

at these issues and their interaction and considers the possibility that the natural tendency of an applicant to claim rights with the broadest possible scope may result in their enjoying narrow protection – 'more is less'.

MULTIPLE CLAIMS AND SERIES REGISTRATIONS

Examples of multiple claiming in patents abound: the patent application included by way of illustration in Professor Bainbridge's book on intellectual property[3] runs to 39 claims,[4] all for a relatively simple mechanical device to impart an enticing froth to canned beer. Weston, Kaminski and Agarwal[5] assert that more than 95% of all patents have multiple claims.[6]

For trade marks there are two considerations – representation of the protected mark and the specification of goods or services for which the mark is to be used and protected. It is possible to register the same mark for a number of different products, in the same or different product classes.[7] The advantages and problems of broad specifications of goods or services in trade

---

[3]   Bainbridge, *Intellectual Property*, 6th edition, pp 338–47.

[4]   Nineteen product claims, 19 method or process claims and one product-by-process claim. Note that, in the light of the House of Lords' decision in *Kirin-Amgen Inc. and others v Hoechst Marion Roussel Ltd and others* [2004] UKHL 46, ruling against the novelty of a product-by-process claim, the UK Patent Office no longer accepts such claims unless a means of defining a new and inventive product. See Examination Guidelines for Patent Applications relating to Biotechnological Inventions in the UK Patent Office (May 2005) at para. 14, available at http://www.patent.gov.uk/patent/p-decisionmaking/p-law/p-law-manual/p-law-manual-biotech.htm.

[5]   Weston, Kaminski and Agarwal, 'The future of the doctrine of equivalents' (1998) 26 AIPLA QJ 277 at 283n17.

[6]   The US Patent and Trademark Office is more generous in allowing multiple independent claims than the European patent offices, which generally require a single main claim for each class of invention, eg product or process, upon which all others depend. See Manual of Patent Practice in the UK Patent Office, 5th edition with revisions, available at http://www.patent.gov.uk/patent/p-decisionmaking/p-law/p-law-manual/p-law-manual-practice.htm. By contrast, before the US Office, hierarchies of dependent claims can make a US patent application very expensive, because of the way that fees are calculated; for USPTO patent filing fee structure, see http://www.uspto.gov/web/offices/ac/qs/ope/fee20030101.htm#patapp.

[7]   The 2002 version of the Nice classification assigns goods and services to 45 different categories or classes. It facilitates searching and other aspects of trade mark administration. The UK Patent Office web site has posted an interesting and useful note on recent changes to the classification system and also on common mistakes as to classification, which is ultimately a question for the Registrar: Trade Marks Act 1994, s 34.

mark registrations are interesting, but not the subject of this chapter.[8] Product specifications may be 'pruned', during the registration process or afterwards,[9] whereas a mark cannot be altered to any significant extent once an application to register has been filed.[10]

Some trade marks are unique and unchanging, but others may need to be used in different versions. Can the 'essence' or 'personality'[11] of such marks be captured in a single registration, or should the proprietor be required/allowed to declare the variants? Section 41(1)(c) of the UK Trade Marks Act 1994 provides for the registration of a series of related marks on a single application and the UK Patent Office has issued an amended Practice Notice[12] on the subject. Registration of marks in a series has two major advantages for the proprietor. Firstly, only one registration need be achieved and renewed, with consequent saving of fees. Secondly, the registration may be kept valid by using[13] any one of the variants. Indeed, a slightly different version of the mark may be used because section 46(2) allows use in a form differing in elements which do not alter the distinctive character of the mark. This also applies to marks registered singly.

The US Federal trade mark registration system[14] does not permit more than one mark to be the subject of a single application; consequently there are guidelines for the consolidation of 'companion applications' by the same person for the same or similar marks.[15] UK trade mark law used to have a system of 'association' of trade marks, whereby identical or closely resem-

---

[8]   See, eg, Wilkinson, 'Broad Trade Mark Specifications' [2002] EIPR 227, in which the author surveys what can be done to do to 'stop the nonsense' of overbroad product specifications, using challenges based on non-use, bad faith, or public policy. See also UK Trade Mark Registry's Practice Amendment Notices (PAN) 8/02 'Classification: Examination of wide specifications and objections under Section 3(6) of the Act' which may be consulted on the Patent Office web site at http://www.patent.gov.uk/tmmanual-chap2-classi.pdf.

[9]   Trade Marks Act 1994, ss 39(1), 45(1), 46(5), 47(5) in the UK.

[10]   Trade Marks Act 1994, s 39(2).

[11]   For the protection of personal and other images, see Mitchiner, 'Intellectual Property in Image: a mere inconvenience?' [2003] IPQ 163 and citations.

[12]   Practice Amendment Notice PAN 1/03, now incorporated in Chapter 3, section 34 of the Manual of Trade Mark Practice, available at http://www.patent.gov.uk/tmmanual-chap3-exam.pdf.

[13]   On the question of proper use of a trade mark, see Maniatis, 'Aspects of trade mark use and misuse' in Dawson and Firth (eds), *Trade Mark Retrospective*, Vol 7, *Perspectives on Intellectual Property*, p. 229; Phillips and Simon (eds), *Trade Mark Use* (2005).

[14]   15 USC §1051(a), (b), and 15 USC §§1126(d) and (e) govern representations of the mark in actual-use and intent-to-use filings, domestic and foreign.

[15]   USPTO Examination Guide 1-01, which can be consulted at http://www.uspto.gov/web/offices/tac/notices/guide1-01.htm.

bling marks could be assigned only as a group, thus keeping them in common ownership.[16] This occasionally caused problems in the event of insolvency,[17] but an advantage of association was that use of one associated mark could be deemed use of another,[18] thus protecting the group from revocation on the grounds of non-use. This system was abolished by the repeal of the Trade Marks Act 1938.[19]

The UK is a member of the Madrid Protocol for the international registration of marks.[20] Registration under the Protocol is based upon a home application. As there is no provision under the Madrid system for registering a series of marks, where the home application is a filing in the UK to register a series of marks, the applicant will have to choose one of the series for international registration. To register the whole series internationally will require a series of separate Madrid applications.[21]

The Community Trade Mark Regulation[22] does not cater for series of marks either, but the Community Design Regulation[23] envisages multiple design applications:[24] except for ornamental designs, the different embodiments must be intended for application to products falling within the same class under the International Classification for Industrial Designs.[25] This is proving useful for sets – tea-sets, cutlery and the like. Recital 25 suggests that multiple registration is intended for designs in sectors where many ephemeral designs are generated but only a few enjoy a significant commercial life. Article 37(4) provides that each design in such a multiple registration may be

---

[16]   Trade Marks Act 1938 s 23.
[17]   Hull 'Intellectual property problems arising in insolvency and receivership' [1992] JIBL 323.
[18]   Trade Marks Act 1938, s 30(1).
[19]   Trade Marks Act 1994, s 106(2) and Sched 5.
[20]   Protocol relating to the Madrid Agreement concerning the international registration on marks (Madrid, 28 June 1989); see http://www.wipo.int/madrid/en/index.html. The USA has also acceded to the Protocol. See http://www.uspto.gov/web/trademarks/madrid/madridindex.htm for links to the Madrid Protocol Implementation Act and other useful information.
[21]   UK Patent Office's Trade Marks Registry Work Manual, ch 10 (January 2003) which may be consulted on the UK Patent Office web site at http://www.patent.gov.uk/tm/reference/workman/chapt10/index.htm.
[22]   Council Regulation (EC) No 40/94 as amended by Reg 3288/94. Proposed changes to the Community Trade Mark Regulation relate to division of registrations as between different goods and services but not as between marks, see http://www.patent.gov.uk/policy/policy-issues/policy-issues-trademarks/policy-issues-trademarks-trademarkseuro.htm.
[23]   Council Regulation (EC) No 6/2002 of 12 December 2001 on Community designs [2000] OJ L3/1.
[24]   Art 37.
[25]   Locarno, 8 October 1968.

dealt with separately – published, surrendered, assigned, licensed and so forth. This seems bizarre where the designs form the different elements of a set, but makes more sense for ornamental designs which might be applied to a multitude of products, or a handful of successful designs amongst a bevy of failures. Izquierdo Peris has pointed out that a separate application for invalidity must be filed, along with fee, for each design in a multiple application.[26]

US design patents may have only a single claim,[27] but an applicant may file 'modified forms' – depicting different embodiments of a single design concept.

WHERE THERE IS MULTIPLE CLAIMING, MUST THERE BE UNITY OF CREATION?

This is certainly the case for 'modified forms' shown in a US design patent.[28] Article 82 of the European Patent Convention states that a patent application shall relate to one invention only or to a group of inventions so linked as to form a single inventive concept. This is usually a matter for the patent examiners, who will assess whether the subject matter of all the claim shares features characteristic of the core invention. Since the European Patent Office prefers a 'problem-solution' approach to inventive step,[29] it is not surprising that a patent application will be seen to have unity if the claims all provide solutions to the same technical problem. If an application is found to contain more than one inventive concept, the applicant may ask to divide it[30] into parallel applications for the different inventions.[31]

Likewise, all trade marks registered as a series under the UK rules must show a very close family resemblance: the Registrar must be satisfied that the marks constitute a series, defined in section 41(2) of the Act as 'a number of trade marks which resemble each other as to their material particulars and differ only as to matters of a non-distinctive character not substantially affect-

---

[26]   Izquierdo Peris, 'Registered community design: first two-year balance from an insider's perspective' [2006] EIPR 146.
[27]   37 CFR § 1.153; see http://www.uspto.gov/web/offices/pac/design/index. html#types.
[28]   Which must share a single design concept with the basic design patent: USPTO Guide to Filing a Design Patent Application: Types of Designs and Modified Forms, available at http://www.uspto.gov/web/offices/pac/design/toc.html#types.
[29]   T01/80 *BAYER/carbonless copying* OJEPO 7/1981, 206; [1982] RPC 321 EPO Guidelines C-IV, 9.8.
[30]   Hence 'divisional application'.
[31]   See EPC r. 25(1), r 46, EPO Guidelines C-IV, 9.1 and A-IV, 1; each may enjoy the priority date of the original application.

ing the identity of the trade mark'. Groom and others[32] suggest that a series application might be used where the proprietor wishes to register a plain word together with a stylised version, a mark which could be written as one word, hyphenated, or two words or a mark consisting of a distinctive word together with non-distinctive suffixes. The UK Patent Office's Practice Amendment notice 1/03 lists a number of other types of trade mark series, including: Character marks (the same cartoon character, in slightly different stances), Geographical marks (where the location of (say) a restaurant is added to a distinctive root), Domain names (same name but different suffixes), Colour marks, and so forth.

The required nexus between marks in a series was considered in Logica's TM,[33] where the applicant sought to register 308 marks as a single series; the name Logica on its own together with 307 'dot' combinations having domain name suffixes. In hearing the applicant's appeal from the UK Registry's refusal of the application, the Appointed Person outlined the history of series registrations from their inception as a means to enable proprietors to secure protection for label marks abroad[34] and noted that the Madrid System for the International Registration of Marks, of which the UK is a member, does not recognise series registrations. She analysed section 41(2) as having a positive aspect – requiring the trade marks for which series registration is sought to resemble each other in their material particulars – and two negative aspects – any difference in the trade marks must not comprise matter, which when considered:

(a) as a separate element of the trade mark would be regarded as having distinctive character; and
(b) in the context of the trade mark as a whole, substantially affects the identity of the trade mark.

As to the last requirement, Professor Annand adopted Jacob J's observation in *Neutrogena Corporation v Golden Limited*:[35]

---

[32] Groom, Abnett, Pennant and Spencer, *UK Trade Marks Act 1994: A Practical Guide* (1994), pp. 31–2.

[33] An appeal to the Appointed Person, Prof Ruth Annand, BL O/068/03 which can be consulted at http://www.patent.gov.uk/tm/t-decisionmaing/t-challenge/t-challenge-decision-results/006803.pdf. See, also, *Digeo Broadband Inc's Trade Mark Application* [2004] RPC 32, refusing a series of 308 marks, mostly domain names, based on the root DIGEO.

[34] Report of the Herschell Committee, 1888, C-5350, Minutes of Evidence, paras 1113, 1116–21, and 2051– 2.

[35] [1996] RPC 473, at 488–9, relating to the identical phrase in s 30(1) of the Trade Marks Act 1938; see also PELICAN TM [1978] RPC 424 to which Mr James of the Registry referred.

'Not substantially affecting its identity' means what it says . . . an alteration which affects the way a mark is or may be pronounced, or its visual impact or the idea conveyed by the mark cannot satisfy the test.

Applying this to the Logica application, Professor Annand dismissed the appeal.

This decision suggests a high test of 'unity' for series trade mark registrations in the UK, and, by analogy, a sparing exercise of section 46(2).[36] As with patents, if the marks in a series application are held to be insufficiently similar, the application may be divided into two or more separate applications.[37] In Logica, division of the application into the word mark on the one hand and a series of 307 domain names on the other would not have altered the outcome. In Digeo, Geoffrey Hobbs QC, sitting as the Appointed Person, noted that for section 41(2)

A relatively high degree of homogeneity is required in order to ensure that the marks included in the application can be treated as uniformly eligible or uniformly ineligible for protection by registration. The wording of s.41(2) establishes that there must and can only be iteration of the material particulars of a trade mark with variations of a non-distinctive character not substantially affecting the identity of the trade mark thus reiterated. Each of the marks in question should be considered as a whole, from the perspective of the average consumer of the goods or services concerned, when assessing whether they form a series of the kind contemplated by the Act.[38]

And that, furthermore,

Section 41(2) permits less variation between marks than s.46(2) of the Act (Art.10(2)(a) of the Directive; Art.15(2)(a) of the CTMR). Variations can be treated as inconsequential under the latter provisions if they 'do not alter the distinctive character of the mark' for which protection is claimed, but must also have no substantial effect on 'the identity of the trade mark' in order to be acceptable under s.41(2). This reinforces the point that marks can be distinctively similar without necessarily satisfying the statutory requirements for registration as a series.[39]

Curiously, the provision for multiple registration of Community designs does not have a requirement of conceptual unity apart from the same-class requirement for non-ornamentation designs under Article 37(4). Many of the classes under the Locarno Agreement are broad,[40] thus there is, as Musker states, 'no

---

[36]   See above, between n8 and n9.
[37]   Trade Marks Act 1994, s 41(a).
[38]   *Digeo Broadband Inc's Trade Mark Application* [2004] RPC 32 at para. 3.
[39]   At para. 4.
[40]   For example, class 11 'articles of adornment', class 12 'means of transport or

requirement that the designs should be similar, or applied to articles to be used together'.[41] He recommends that textile or wallpaper designs be identified as ornamentation designs for broadest protection.

INEXACT INFRINGEMENT

Most systems of registered and unregistered intellectual property rights confer exclusive rights not only over exact replicas of the rights owners' products, works, or processes, but also extend the exclusive rights to close approximations. UK copyright is infringed if a copyist reproduces a substantial part of a copyright work.[42] A trade mark on the US federal register is infringed by the unauthorised use of a 'colorable imitation' as well as a precise counterfeit.[43] A Community plant variety right may be infringed by the propagation of related varieties as well as the protected variety.[44] The harmonised registered design laws of EC Member States must adhere to the principle of Article 9 of Directive 98/71/EC on the legal protection of designs by including in the scope of protection of a registered design 'any design which does not produce on the informed user a different overall expression'.

Infringement of patents granted by the European Patent Office at present is a national matter[45] but national courts must have regard to the Protocol to Article 69 EPC,[46] which states that assessment of patent infringement should find a middle way between strict literal interpretation of the claims and wide interpretation using the claims only as guidelines, such that there is 'a fair protection for the patentee [combined] with a reasonable degree of certainty for third parties'.

---

hoisting', class 21 'games, toys, tents and sports goods'. The Office for Harmonisation in the Internal Market, the institution responsible for registration of Community designs, has devised an updated 'Eurolocarno' classification scheme: http://oami.eu.int/en/design/eurolocarno.htm.

[41] Musker, *Community Design Law* (2002) para. 2-211.

[42] Copyright, Designs & Patents Act 1988, s 16(3)(a); *Designers Guild v Williams* [2001] FSR 113.

[43] 'Lanham Act', 15 USCA §1114(1); for the European test of 'global appreciation' in comparing non-identical marks, see *Sabel v Puma* [1997] ECR I-6191; [1998] 1 CMLR 445; [1998] ETMR 1; [1998] RPC 199 (ECJ).

[44] Reg 2100/94, Art 13(5).

[45] The European Patent Office grants a bundle of national patents in Contracting States designated by the applicant.

[46] Protocol on the Interpretation of Article 69 of the Convention, adopted at the Munich Diplomatic Conference for the setting up of a European System for the Grant of Patents on 5 October 1973, text available at http://www.european-patent-office.org/legal/epc/e/ar69.html#A69.

DOES MULTIPLE CLAIMING INCREASE CERTAINTY FOR THIRD PARTIES AND/OR PROTECTION FOR THE PROPRIETOR?

Spelling out the extent of exclusive rights is consistent with the concept of notice to third parties, who may reduce the risk of litigation by searching the registers before manufacturing or marketing a new product. As with the small print of contracts, however, there comes a point where 'more is less'. The perceived burden of a large mass of undigested information may be evident in the proposals to cease searching for earlier trade marks at the Office for Harmonisation in the Internal Market (OHIM).[47] In the context of pre-franchise disclosure,[48] the French legislator came up with the concept of 'sincere information', a disclosure that is informative but not over-laden. When the courts attempt to achieve a balance between right-holders and others, we might expect over-elaborate claiming to result in a reduction rather than an increase in scope of protection and certainty for the proprietor. To test this hypothesis we could look for instances where the courts afford reduced or no protection to a proprietor with highly elaborated claims, perhaps in a patent or a family of registered marks. There are at least two examples of this in UK jurisprudence, the case of the sonar patent and the case of the seabird trade marks.

SONAR

Submarine Signal Co v Henry Hughes & Son[49] was a patent infringement action. The claim in issue, held valid and infringed at first instance,

---

[47]   At present OHIM, the European Community trade mark office, instigates searches for earlier marks similar to an applicant's. These are subcontracted to private licensees and the UK Patent Office: see http://oami.eu.int/pdf/mark/licencees.pdf. France, Germany, Italy, Cyprus, Estonia, Latvia, Lithuania, Malta and Slovenia do not take part in the search system. OHIM do not refuse marks on 'relative grounds' (conflict with earlier marks); this is left to opposition. For UK proposals see the UK Patent Office consultation at http://www.patent.gov.uk/about/about-consult/about-formal/about-formal-current/consult-relativegrounds.htm, Consultation: Relative grounds for refusal – the way forward. The UK Office's preferred model is to search and notify the applicant only. See Isaacs, 'Should the United Kingdom adopt a European system for the registration of trade marks?' [2006] EIPR 71.

[48]   The so-called 'Loi Doubin' – Law no 89-1008 of 31 December 1989 relating to the development of commercial and craft enterprises and to the improvement of their economic, juridical and social environment (author's translation).

[49]   (1932) 49 RPC 149. I am grateful to one of my postgraduate students, for bringing this case to my attention; it is quoted in successive editions of *Terrell on the Law of Patents*.

described echo-location technology that was recognised as important by the court:[50]

> 11. Means for measuring by the aid of sound waves, in which an electric oscillator is adapted to be intermittently excited by the aid of a rotating contact device and the echo is received by the oscillator (or by an independent receiving transmitter) intermittently connected to an indicating or recording instrument through part of the said rotating contact device, which is provided with movable contact brushes the displacement of which measures the time interval between the sound emission and the reception of its echo.

Although Submarine Signal was decided in 1931, the judges' approach to infringement, both at first instance and on appeal, has many echoes of the modern approach. Firstly, it was recognised that effect must be given to a single, valid claim.[51] Secondly, the 'purposive' approach to claim construction[52] was foreshadowed: 'I cannot therefore hold that we are to look at the last few lines of Claim 11 without bearing in mind the purpose of the claim as a whole . . .'[53] Thirdly, claim 11, being meritorious in other respects, could be given a 'benevolent construction'.[54] By contrast, *Terrell on the Law of Patents*[55] cites Sedley LJ's rejection of benevolence in SmithKline Beecham Plc's (Paroxetine Anhydrate) patent.[56] It is submitted that 'benevolent construction' as actually applied in Submarine Signal – the court took considerable trouble to discern the meaning of 'electric oscillator' – did not exceed the Protocol requirement[57] of 'fair protection for the patentee'. Fourthly, the court considered evidence as to meaning of technical terms. Fifthly, claim 11 was construed in the light of the specification as a whole[58] and, lastly, in a manner respecting 'a reasonable degree of certainty for third parties':

---

50   (1932) 49 RPC 149 at 169, Lord Hanworth, MR; the patent was dated 1914, giving plenty of time for this to become apparent by the time of trial.

51   (1932) 49 RPC 149 at 170, Lord Hanworth, MR.

52   As recommended in *Catnic Components Ltd v Hill & Smith Ltd* [1982] RPC 183 by Lord Diplock at 243 and discussed inter alia in *Kirin-Amgen Inc v Transkaryotic Therapies Inc* (no. 2) [2004] UKHL 46; [2005] RPC 9 and *Glaverbel SA v British Coal*, [1995] RPC 255 at 268–70.

53   (1932) 49 RPC 149 at 171, Lord Hanworth, MR.

54   (1932) 49 RPC 149 at 174, Lord Hanworth, MR.

55   15th edition, 2000, at 6-101, but remarking that 'all canons of construction are in the end guides, and an over-rigid application of any of them is not appropriate. *Brugger v Medic-Aid* [1996] RPC 635 at 642.'

56   [2003] RPC 49 at para. 103; sub nom *BASF AG v SmithKline Beecham Plc* [2003] EWCA Civ 872.

57   See n. 46 above.

58   (1932) 49 RPC 149 at 173, Lord Hanworth, MR; see now Art 69(1) EPC.

It is the duty of the patentee to indicate clearly to the public what is the field which he circumscribes to himself. He must warn the public as to the territory on which they are not to trespass . . .[59]

Construing the claim in the light of the whole specification, the Court of Appeal was clearly propelled to a narrow construction by the patent's claim structure, and perhaps by the fact that many of the early claims were so broad as to be invalid. Romer LJ had this to say:[60]

At the present time, when the claims at the end of a specification commonly run into double figures, there is in truth very little scope for the operation of the doctrine of mechanical equivalency.

He went on to opine that the defendant's mechanical sound emitter, consisting of a hammer, spring and trigger, was not an 'electrical oscillator' within the meaning of claim 11 (more general but invalid claims had used the phrase 'sound emitter').

Although this is a case decided under an earlier Patents Act,[61] it is submitted that the inverse relationship it suggested between elaboration of claims and breadth of construction may still obtain today. Against this view, Paul Cole[62] might argue that even the best-informed and best-prepared patent agent should claim everything in combination with everything else in the hope that one of the claims turns out to be of the right scope. I am grateful to Paul Cole for a quotation from President Lincoln's inaugural address[63] to fellow-citizens of the United States of America: 'No foresight can anticipate nor any document of reasonable length contain express provisions for all possible questions'.

SEABIRDS

United Biscuits (UK) Ltd v Asda Stores Ltd[64] involved a dispute over chocolate biscuits. United Biscuits and its predecessors in title had for many years sold chocolate sandwich biscuits under the name PENGUIN, in black lettering on red and yellow packaging with at least one depiction of the seabird. They also made extensive use of the 'stuttering' slogan 'P . . P . . P . . . Pick up a . . .

---

59   (1932) 49 RPC 149 at 172, Lord Hanworth, MR.
60   (1932) 49 RPC 149 at 175–6.
61   The Patents Act 1907 as amended by the Patents and Designs Act 1919.
62   Cole 'Effective specification drafting – a case study based on the windsurfer patent' [2003] CIPAJ 482 and private communication.
63   Monday, 4 March 1861.
64   [1997] RPC 513; Benjamin, *'Penguin v Puffin'* [1997] EIPR 484.

Penguin'. Four styles of penguin device had been used at various times, with naturalistic and cartoon versions. United Biscuits had several 'penguin' registrations for biscuits: the slogan, the word Penguin *per se*, the word together with a realistic side view of a penguin, baby and adult penguins in rubber boots and cartoon penguins wearing chefs' hats.[65] The marks had been associated under the Trade Marks Act 1938, but this status had lapsed in 1995 when the 1938 Act was repealed. Asda re-launched their 'Take a Break'[66] biscuit as Puffin. Red packaging showed a cartoon seabird holding a baton and wearing a baseball hat. Asda's design brief had been to create a 'brand beater' using 'cues' to the Penguin brand. Wisely, perhaps, Asda had dropped initial plans to use yellow along with red for the packaging and to give their puffin a paper crown. At launch, they exhorted their customers to 'Pick up a Puffin' but quickly stopped after protest from United Biscuits. A witness for Asda later admitted that their puffin had 'parodied' the United Biscuits penguins.

United Biscuits sued for infringement of their registered trade marks and in passing off. Asda counter-claimed for revocation of the pictorial marks, on the ground of non-use under section 46(1) of the Trade Marks Act 1994. The counter-claim was successful; in the learned judge's view, none had been used since 1988 in an identical form, or in a form differing only in elements which did not alter the distinctive character of the mark. Recent representations used by United Biscuits showed a penguin with skis and a penguin on skates wearing a scarf. The word Puffin was held insufficiently close to Penguin to infringe the word registration, so all claims to trade mark infringement failed except in relation to use of the slogan 'Pick up a Puffin'. However, the combination of features on the Puffin packaging – name, lettering, dark seabird device – amounted to a misrepresentation that Puffin and Penguin biscuits were in some way connected, probably that they were made by the same manufacturer. Since Penguin enjoyed substantial goodwill and United Biscuits had satisfied the court as to damage,[67] the claim in passing off succeeded.

The seabird case supports the proposition that 'more is less' when it comes to registering trade marks. A witness for Asda accepted in cross-examination that the 'cue' they wanted to use was that of a seabird, covering the name and depiction. Robert Walker J, whilst quoting this exchange in his judgment, clearly regarded the differences between the marks used and registered by

---

65   The 'chef' registrations were apparently series marks: [1997] RPC 513 at 520.
66   A name somewhat reminiscent of the rival biscuit Kit-Kat's 'HAVE A BREAK . . .' slogan.; see [1993] RPC 217; *Nestlé SA's Trade Mark Application (Have a Break)* [2004] FSR 2 CA; *Société des Produits Nestlé SA v Mars UK Ltd* [2006] FSR 2; [2005] ETMR 96; [2005] 3 CMLR 12 (ECJ).
67   Although damage was hard to quantify. United Biscuits did not seek an interim injunction but pursued their case to a speedy trial.

United Biscuits as going to the distinctive character of the respective marks. Thus we have a very distinctive trade mark concept, that of a black and white seabird, apparently imperilled by registration of an over-specific range of variants.

IS CANON RELEVANT?

It is intriguing to consider the seabird case in the light of subsequent authority. Where a mark is weakly distinctive it might be necessary to register and rely upon very specific representations. But where a mark is more distinctive, intrinsically or perhaps as a result of long use, one might expect a single registration to cover many variants and for matters of detail to go less and less to the distinctive character of a mark. Robert Walker J implicitly held that United Biscuits' Penguin imagery was particularly distinctive. The learned judge commented that there was 'a good deal of authority for the proposition that long use of a particularly distinctive get-up does (without creating a monopoly) place on a new competitor (minded to use a similar get-up) a special obligation to avoid confusion'.[68]

In *Canon KK v Metro-Goldwyn-Mayer Inc*,[69] the European Court of Justice held that distinctiveness and reputation should be taken into account when assessing infringement rights, in this case the range of goods which could be regarded as similar to those for which the mark was registered. It is submitted that a similar approach could be used for the purpose of deciding whether use of a resembling mark by the proprietor satisfies section 46(2) of the 1994 Act.[70]

Paradoxically, where a mark is so well-known that customers enjoy almost perfect recollection, there may be little danger of confusion where a variant is used.[71] Since the question of confusion is an issue of fact,[72] this view may remain tenable[73] post-Sabel. However, even with a potential household name, over-elaborate 'claiming' of the mark should be avoided, since it would only serve to emphasise that the mark is not readily confused with similar versions.

---

[68]   [1997] RPC 513 at 524.
[69]   Case C-39/97. [1998] ECR I-5507; [1999] ETMR 1; [1999] FSR 332; [1999] RPC.
[70]   And Art 10(2)(b) of trade marks harmonisation directive, 89/104/EEC.
[71]   Kitchin et al, eds, *Kerly's Law of Trade Marks and Trade Names* (2001, 13th edition) at para. 8-24, n18 refer on this issue to *Smith Hayden* (1946) 63 RPC 97 at 102; *Ana Laboratories* (1951) 69 RPC 146.
[72]   *Marca Mode v Adidas* [2000] All ER (EC) 694; [2000] ECR I-4861; [2000] ETMR 723.
[73]   Kitchin et al, *Kerly's Law of Trade Marks and Trade Names* at para. 8-24, n18.

CONCLUSION AND APPLICATION TO COMMUNITY DESIGNS?

The problems to third parties and to patentees of over-broad claims have been eloquently debated in the literature on biotechnology patents and plant varieties.[74] In any field the degree of detail with which an applicant for registered rights should delineate 'the field which he circumscribes to himself' is a delicate matter – and an important part of the patent and trade mark attorney's art.[75] It is tempting to devise an exhaustive sequence of claims or to register every imaginable variant of a mark or design in an attempt to maximise protection for the client. However, the sonar and seabird cases indicate that this approach, taken too far, can be counter-productive for the proprietor. Will this principle of 'more is less' also apply to the Community Registered design, with its lack of a unity requirement? Over-enthusiastic depiction of variants will increase fees,[76] but may also influence a court's decision as to whether an alleged infringement falls within the scope of a registration. Article 10 of Regulation 6/2002 reads:

1. The scope of protection conferred by a Community deign shall include any design which does not produce on the informed user a different overall impression.
2. In assessing the scope of protection, the degree of freedom of the designer in developing his design shall be taken into consideration.

Including some variants may assist the court in 'getting its eye in' to design freedom in the relevant area, but too many may lead the court to a narrow view on scope of protection, so that a competitor whose design does not correspond closely to one of the multiple designs may escape infringement.

---

[74] Wibbelmann, 'Broad claims: a nuisance?' [1997] EIPR 515; Roberts, 'EPO: patents – breadth of claim' [1998] EIPR N18; Funder, 'Rethinking patents for plant innovation' [1999] EIPR 551.

[75] See reprinted a classic article on drafting by EWE Micklethwaite, 'Brushing up our drafting' at [2003] CIPAJ 320 and 379; Cole, 'Effective specification drafting – a case study based on the windsurfer patent' [2003] CIPAJ 482.

[76] Although there is no limit to the number of designs in a multiple application, extra fees are payable for additional designs: *Commission Regulation (EC) n°2245/2002 of 21 October 2002 implementing Council Regulation (EC)No 6/2002 on Community designs*, Art 6(1)(c); Commission Regulation (EC) no 2246/2002 of 16 December 2002 on the fees payable . . . in respect of the registration of community designs.

THE PROBLEM OF REPEATED INSUBSTANTIAL TAKINGS

In the Seabirds case, Asda's Puffin packaging echoed a number of different aspects of Penguin – the use of a black and white seabird, the puffin's stance, its cartoon appearance, the colour scheme. Robert Walker J, correctly it is submitted, declined to take any of this into account when he considered whether the registered word mark was infringed.[77] Even if the pictorial registrations had been held valid, it might have been difficult to regard the Puffin get-up as infringing any given one of them. Likewise, a patent infringement must embody all the features of at least one claim.[78] In the absence of this, someone who 'mixes and matches' may escape infringement, although arguably engaging in unfair copying. This difficulty is not, however, limited to registered rights. In *Electronic Techniques (Anglia) Limited v Critchley Components Limited*,[79] Laddie J described as 'problematic' the question whether reproducing small parts of copyright works on a regular basis could amount to substantial copying, even though the individual takings were insubstantial. It did not fall to Laddie J to rule on this issue, but rather to conclude that the case was not suitable for summary judgment. A similar question arose in the 1990s when 'sampling' of recorded musical performances came into vogue.[80]

In United Biscuits, the passing off claim enabled Robert Walker J to provide a remedy for this form of unfair competition. Lahore has analysed the problem of unfair copying;[81] Horton and Robertson have questioned whether it is desirable for the UK to have a generalised law against unfair competition.[82] However, to date, only owners of database rights[83] and goodwill can

---

[77]   However, extraneous matter may be relevant in passing off or in infringement under s 10(3), as in *Pfizer Ltd v Eurofood Link (UK) Ltd* [2001] FSR 3.

[78]   Of which no element may be 'vitiated in its entirety', according to US law: *Warner-Jenkinson Co v Hilton David Chemical Co* 117 S.Ct. 1040, 41 USPQ 2d (BNA) (1997).

[79]   [1997] FSR 401 Ch D.

[80]   Tackaberry, 'The digital sound sampler' [1990] Ent LR 87.

[81]   Lahore, 'The Herchel Smith lecture 1992: intellectual property rights and unfair copying' [1992] EIPR 428.

[82]   Robertson and Horton 'Does the United Kingdom need an unfair competition law?' [1995] EIPR 568.

[83]   Directive 96/9/EC Art 7(5); implemented by *The Copyright and Rights in Databases Regulations 1997*, SI 1997 No 3032. Database right was considered in *British Horseracing Board Ltd v William Hill Organisation Ltd* (C203/02) [2004] ECR I-10415 (ECJ) and *British Horseracing Board Ltd v William Hill Organisation Ltd* [2005] EWCA Civ 863; [2005] ECDR 28 (CA (Civ Div)). See, also, Westkamp

obtain redress in the UK for systematic but insubstantial takings. This may be contrasted with the position in other EU Member States.[84] Although harmonisation of unfair competition laws in the EU has been mooted,[85] it remains to be achieved, except as between business and consumer.[86]

'Protecting databases under US and European law – methodical approaches to the protection of investments between unfair competition and intellectual property concepts' (2003) 34 IIC 7; Derclaye, 'The Court of Justice interprets the database sui generis right for the first time' [2005] EL Rev 420; Sampson and Penny, 'British Horseracing Board – an examination of recent case law arising from the ECJ database decision' [2006] Ent LR 39.

[84] For example, under the German Act against unfair competition of 1909, the 'systematic and deliberate imitation of another's achievements' was recognised as an actionable form of unfair competition; see Steckler, 'Unfair trade practices under German law: "Slavish imitation" of commercial and industrial activities' [1996] EIPR 390; Henning-Bodewig 'International protection against unfair competition' (1999) 30 IIC 166; Kamperman Sanders, *Unfair Competition Law* (1997); Schricker, 'Twenty-five years of protection against unfair competition' (1995) 26 IIC 782; WIPO, 'Protection against unfair competition – analysis of the present world situation', publ no 725(E). Germany has enacted a new law against unfair competition, Gesetz gegen den unlauteren Wettbewerb (UWG), BGBl. I 2004, 1414 of 3 July 2004.

[85] Henning-Bodewig and Schricker, 'New initiatives for the harmonization of unfair competition law in Europe' [2002] EIPR 271; Kirkbride, 'The law of unfair competition: is there an EC approach?' [2000] Comp Law 230.

[86] Directive 2005/29/EC of 11 May 2005 concerning unfair business-to-consumer commercial practices in the internal market [2005] OJ L149/22.

9. Post sale effects of a trade mark: Conceptual necessity or a gift to trade mark proprietors?

Spyros Maniatis

1. INTRODUCTION

Arsenal's adventure before the law courts introduced the concept of 'post sale effects' of a trade mark into European registered trade mark law and potentially into the common law tort of passing off. In the United States, following an initial period of uncertainty, post sale confusion now falls within the mainstream of trade mark law.

Ultimately, confusion is a correlation of the answers provided to three questions: 'who' is confused, 'when', and 'as to what'? The post sale effect is directly relevant to the question of 'when'. It might also influence 'who' and 'as to what' must be confused. It is argued that in Europe the acknowledgment of post sale effects into infringement considerations should not change the rationale for protection.

2. POST SALE EFFECTS IN THE USA

The relevant case law shows that post sale confusion has been applied at the boundaries of traditional trade mark law. According to Tichane,[1] it has contributed in the protection of product features and design falling outside the scope of copyright and patents and in cases where the 'reverse passing off' doctrine had to be fortified. It has also played a part in business reputation and counterfeit cases.

Viennetta,[2] an English case that exemplifies Tichane's thesis, brings together a number of issues, linked with the function of the shape of an ice

---

[1] See D.M. Tichane, 'The Maturing Doctrine of Post-Sales Confusion', [1995] 85 TMR 399, who provides an excellent review and analysis.
[2] *Société de Produits Nestle SA v Unilever plc* [2002] EWHC 2709.

cream dessert: use of multiple signs; seeking trade mark protection for the configuration of the product on its own; post sale effects; and, the balance between registrability and scope of protection. Jacob J stressed that the decisive trade mark – rather than design – registrability criterion is whether the sign denotes the origin of the marked product. Viennetta's shape denoted Walls' Viennetta, the product of a particular manufacturer, but in order to establish trade mark distinctiveness Walls had to prove that consumers trusted the shape on its own to identify the dessert. Otherwise, registration would be the result of a trick, the exploitation of the combined use and effect of a word mark with the shape of the product in order to claim, at a later stage, that the shape on its own functions as a trade mark and deserves registration, even though it has neither been nor intended to be used on its own to designate origin. 'Now [the proprietor] is in a position to stop other parties, using their own word trade marks, from selling the product, even though no-one is deceived or misled'.[3] For shapes it 'must be proved that consumers regard the shape alone as a badge of trade origin in the sense that they would rely upon that shape alone as an indication of trade origin, particularly to buy the goods'.[4] In practice, for most product configuration marks evidence of distinctiveness acquired through use should be required.[5] He illustrated the issue of the post sale effect of the shape on its own by the example of a dinner party where Viennetta is served outside its box. Walls would have to establish that someone being served a slice of Viennetta would in any way rely upon the shape to do anything. The mere supposition that the product is Viennetta would not suffice.

---

   ³   Ibid, par. 32.

   ⁴   Ibid, par. 34. For a comparison with the USA see *Loonen v Deitsch*, 189 F. 487 (CCDNY 1911): '. . . in principle, there is no possible ground for refusing to recognize any number of trademarks which are really such. That is to say, if a man can show that the public has in fact come to recognize six marks each as separately indicating his manufacture, even though they are used together, it should be no concern of the court to interfere. The hypothesis presupposes that the public does interpret the marks each as indicating origin or manufacture, and that is simply a question of fact, though it might be a very hard thing to prove, especially if the marks were all put near together on the article. If a man uses four or five marks together, it may be, therefore, doubtful whether as a matter of fact any single one had ever got to mean his goods, but the trouble is merely one of fact, and there is no reason that I can see, why if that fact exists, the court would take from him the means he has created of identifying his wares. . . . Certainly if the public has solved that difficulty of more than one mark, the court becomes officious in forbidding the maker from continuing to use what the public already understands.'

   ⁵   In Linde [2004] ECR I-36161 the ECJ has accepted that in practice it may be more difficult to establish distinctiveness in relation to a product shape than a word or figurative mark; in these cases evidence of acquired distinctiveness would be required.

3.   POST SALE CONFUSION IN THE USA

In the USA the touchstone for classic passing off and trade mark infringement, discounting dilution, is 'likelihood of confusion' that means 'probable' rather than 'possible' confusion[6] or 'call to mind'.[7] Its scope has been broadened in 1962, when the infringement provision was amended to cover use which was 'likely to cause confusion, or to cause mistake or to deceive', striking out the words 'of purchasers as to the source of origin of such goods or services'; and, in 1989, when use which 'is likely to cause confusion, or to cause mistake, or to deceive as to the affiliation, connection, or association' became infringing use.

In parallel, courts have been widening confusion's catchment area. In respect of type courts have acted against both 'forward' – customers perceive the later user's goods as goods of the earlier user – and 'reverse' – customers perceive the earlier user's goods as goods of the later user – confusion. As to the target of confusion some courts have ruled that confusion of investors[8] or ultimate users[9] might be relevant. Also, the relevant public can be wider than the class of actual or potential purchasers and include persons who have no intention of purchasing the product, a gift recipient or someone who simply views the contested marked product.[10] This willingness to expand the audi-

---

   [6]   The statement of the Supreme Court in *American Steel Foundries v Robertson* 46 S. Ct. 160 that under 'the facts, we are of opinion that it does not appear that the use of the word as a trade-mark upon the goods of the plaintiff will probably confuse or deceive the public, to the injury of the defendant or of any other corporation' is often quoted as the authority behind this limitation.
   [7]   In principle, something more than 'call to mind' would be required. In *re Ferrero*, 178 USPQ 167 (CCPA 1973), the traffic light example was used: when one sees amber, red or green comes to mind but there is no confusion between amber and red or amber and green.
   [8]   In *Morningside Group Ltd v Morningside Capital Group, LLC*, 51 USPQ 2d 1183 (2nd Cir. 1999) it was held that investors can be confused regarding the affiliation between two companies.
   [9]   In *re Artic Electronics Co.*, 220 USPQ 836 (TTAB 1983) likelihood of confusion was established between MARS used on coin operated arcade video games and MARS used on change making machines. The purchasers of the machines would not be confused; however, the end users would be likely to be confused. This likelihood could function as an incentive for the sophisticated purchasers of the machines to buy the product.
   [10]   See for example *Rolex Watch USA, Inc. v Canner* 1 USPQ 2d 1117 (SD Fla. 1986) and *United States v Hon* 14 USPQ 2d 1959 (2nd Cir. 1990), cert. denied, 111 S. Ct. 789 (1991). However, in cases where the product is very specialised courts are reluctant to take into account confusion of the public at large, see *Dorr Oliver, Inc. v Fluid-Quip, Inc.*, 39 USPQ 2d 1990 (7th Cir. 1996), where look-alike corn milling equipment was found in the defendant's manufacturing plant is a typical such example.

ence of the mark that is relevant in an infringement case is also linked with the time and place of confusion. Confusion before, after, or away from the point of sale often does not involve actual purchasers.[11]

Pre sale confusion involves products where confusion is resolved before the actual sale: where, for example, purchasers are confused at the point of choosing, but later, at the point of the actual sale or delivery,[12] they become disabused from their confusion but decide to stay with their original mistaken choice.[13] This led to the development of the 'initial interest confusion' doctrine.[14]

The original lineage of post sale confusion can be found in cases involving prestigious marks and/or the get-up of a product. In *Mastercrafters Clock & Radio Co. v Vacheron Constantin – Le Coultre Watches*[15] a copy of Vacheron Constantin's Atmos clock was sold by Mastercrafters. The court considered that some sort of actionable conspiracy existed between Mastercrafters and its customers: they would buy the cheaper clock for the purpose of acquiring the kudos gained by displaying what their guests would mistakenly regard as a prestigious article. Similar considerations dominate where a product is sold to customers who are alerted to the fact that the product is a copy of a prestigious item but are encouraged to buy it as a gift for potentially unsuspecting recipients.[16] In *Ferrari S.p.A. Esercizio Fabriche Automobili E Corse v Roberts*[17]

Those touring the plant could be confused but they were considered to be outside the much narrower relevant public of professional buyers.

[11] Sceptical courts combined the two elements and declined to find infringement; see, *Nike, Inc. v 'Just Did It' Enterprises* 28 USPQ 2d 1385 where it was noted that consumer confusion at the point of sale is more relevant than public confusion at viewing them from afar.

[12] *Lindy Pen Co. v Bic Pen Corp*, 230 USPQ 791 (9th Cir. 1986) shows how consumers can be 'trapped' into their initial confused choice; it considered an over-the-telephone order for pens where there was evidence of traditional confusion as to source. At the point of delivery a diligent customer would realise that the pens delivered were not the pens supposedly ordered but might, nevertheless, decide not to bother to return them at that late stage.

[13] *McNeil – PPC v Guardian Drug Co*, 45 USPQ 2d 1437 (ED Mich. 1997).

[14] See *Mobil Oil Corp. v Pegasus Petroleum Corp*, 2 USPQ 2d 1677 (2nd Cir. 1987) where it was held that cold calls to oil traders from Pegasus Petroleum could be attributed by their receivers to Mobil, the owners of a pictorial trade mark incorporating a flying horse. This constituted infringement despite the fact that traders were sophisticated and would not be confused when getting into an agreement. The doctrine has been ingrained in internet cases, see for example *Eli Lilly and Co. v Natural Answers, Inc.* 56 USPQ 2d 1942 (7th Cir. 2000) for PROZAC and HERBROZAC.

[15] 105 USPQ 160 (2nd Cir. 1955).

[16] *T & T Mfg. Co. v A. T. Cross Co*, 197 USPQ 763 (DRI 1978), cert. denied 202 USPQ 320 (1979).

[17] 20 USPQ 2d 1001 (6th Cir. 1991); see also *Rolls Royce Motors Ltd. v A & A Fiberglass, Inc.* 193 USPQ 35 (ND Ga. 1977).

the buyers of a high-priced replica car kit of the discontinued – and much more expensive – Ferrari Daytona were sophisticated car enthusiasts, not likely to be confused as to the actual source of the product. However, there were two types of potential harm: a prospective buyer of the replica kit might perceive it as sponsored, approved, or licensed by Ferrari; and, third parties might confuse the replica with the original and Ferrari's reputation could suffer despite the absence of confusion at the point of sale.

The visibility of the sign at the point of sale or following the sale can be critical. In *Smithkline Beckman Corp. v Pennex Products Co.*[18] a court rejected an attempt to protect the colour orange for a non-prescription aspirin-based product sold in opaque packaging. Confusion would be more likely if the packaging were transparent. Arguments based on post sale confusion were tenuous. Confusion of prospective customers is more likely when the contentious sign remains visible post sale and, in particular, during use of the product. In *Levi Strauss & Co. v Blue Bell, Inc.*,[19] the defendant's projecting label, which remained constantly visible following the sale, was likely to cause confusion among prospective purchasers with an imperfect recollection of the Levi Strauss's mark. The argument that confusion was unlikely because the trousers were clearly labelled at the point of sale with a paper billboard was rejected because it would be removed after the sale and would have no effect when the trousers were worn. The projecting label on the other hand would function as a permanent identifier and advertisement. In the same vein, conflicting messages between labels and packaging are unlikely to assist a defendant who has copied a product.[20]

4. PASSING OFF – THE CLASSIC APPROACH

The starting point in passing off is the misrepresentation that leads to confusion.

> In the common case the court must be satisfied that the defendant's conduct is calculated ['calculated' in the sense of being the reasonably foreseeable consequence. Fraud is not required.] to pass off other goods as those of the claimant, or, at least, to produce such confusion in the minds of probable customers or purchasers or other persons with whom the claimant has business relations . . . as would be

---

[18] 225 USPQ 963.

[19] 228 USPQ 346 (9th Cir. 1985). See also *Lois Sportswear, USA, Inc. v Levi Strauss & Co.* 228 USPQ 648 (SDNY 1985), aff'd, 230 USPQ 831 (2nd Cir. 1986).

[20] *Polo Fashions, Inc. v Craftex, Inc.* 2 USPQ 2d 1444 (4th Cir. 1987); *Reebok International, Ltd v Sung Hwa International Corp.* 12 USPQ 2d 1808 (1st Cir. 1989); *Payless Shoesource, Inc. v Reebok Int'l, Ltd*, 27 USPQ 2d 1516 (Fed. Cir. 1993).

likely to lead to the other goods being bought and sold for his. . . . This is the foundation of the action.[21]

The definition of the relevant public as the 'purchasers or probable purchasers of goods of the kind in question'[22] restricts the scope of the tort; the wider public is relevant only in the case of mass consumption products. Further, it is required that a substantial number of the relevant class must be confused. According to Lord Oliver, the question is whether '. . . is it, on a balance of probabilities, likely that . . . a substantial number of the relevant class will be misled into purchasing the defendant's [product] in the belief that it is the respondent's'.[23] The same passage, according to the authors of Kerly, is an indication that 'post-sale confusion can really only be relevant in passing off if the confusion persists through and results in a second/subsequent purchase'.[24]

Bostick Ltd v Sellotape G.B. Ltd[25] offers the classic 'post sale' passing off scenario. Both parties were marketing a blue re-usable adhesive tack. Blu-Tack had been on the market since 1972. Blue had been chosen because there were no blue foods at the time and children would not eat the tack.[26] Bostick stayed with the colour; it wanted its customers to associate 'a blue coloured re-useable adhesive product with [the] company'.[27] SelloTak was put on the market in 1992. Sellotape had been using blue on the packaging of a range of products since 1937. Both, like all other coloured – some blue – tacks, were sold in non-transparent packaging, similar in terms of shape, size, and functionality, but wholly different in external appearance, without any evidence of confusion. Bostick claimed that consumers would see SelloTak as a product supplied by Bostick or manufactured under licence, or that once SelloTak's

---

[21]   *Kerly's Law of Trade Marks and Trade Names* (14th edn.) (London, Sweet and Maxwell, 2005), par. 15.192.
[22]   Per Viscount Maugham, in *Saville Perfumery v June Perfect* (1941) 58 RPC 147 at 176.
[23]   Jif [1990] RPC 341 at 407.
[24]   Kerly, par. 15.192.
[25]   [1994] RPC 556.
[26]   In a way the colour was functional. For an example of a colour signifying that the product is edible and thus functional and outside the scope of trade mark protection see *William R. Warner & Co. v Eli Lilly & Co.* 265 US 526, 68 L. Ed. 1161, 44 S. Ct. 615 (1924), where chocolate was used as an ingredient (for a quinine medicinal preparation) for three functional purposes: to give the preparation a distinctive colour, to make it agreeable to the palate, and to serve as a suspending medium. The combination did not merely serve the incidental use of identifying the respondent's preparation. Other marketers should be allowed to manufacture and market an exactly similar preparation containing chocolate and, through its colour, notify the public to that effect.
[27]   Kerly, p. 557.

packaging was discarded, Bostick's reputation would be under constant risk because of the products' similarity. The assertion, though, that many purchasers of Blu-Tack were discarding the packaging at home was not substantiated. At the point of sale, there was no likelihood of confusion because of the opaque distinctive packaging of the two products. Also, there was no evidence that the colour on its own, without the name, functioned as a distinguishing sign. Post sale confusion remained improbable and would, in any case, be immaterial, because by then the sale had already been made.

Nevertheless, passing off could still be established if 'on returning to a shop to purchase some more re-useable adhesive putty, there is any likelihood of the consumer selecting SelloTak in the belief, because of his recollection of its blue colour, that it is Blu-Tack . . . If . . . he remembers that what he (or others) had been using was a product called SelloTak and that, like Blu-Tack, SelloTak is blue, is it conceivable that on making his purchase of re-useable adhesive putty, although he deliberately selects SelloTak and therefore, although he knows that what he is purchasing is not called Blu-Tack he nevertheless makes his purchase believing that what he is purchasing either is the plaintiff's Blu-Tack or is in some way associated with it?'[28] Such a possibility was exceedingly unlikely and would not justify the interlocutory injunctive relief sought by the plaintiff.

The variation in *Sodastream Ltd. v Thorn Cascade Co. Ltd*[29] was that the relationship with the customer was ongoing. The plaintiffs marketed refillable carbon dioxide cylinders to be used in home carbonating machines. Customers returned empty, in exchange for full, cylinders to retailers, paying only once the price for the cylinder as such. Retailers sent the cylinders for refilling back to the plaintiffs. The cylinders, in their majority, were grey and bore the 'Sodastream' trade mark and a label indicating that they had been filled by the plaintiffs that dominated the market. The defendants, once associated with the plaintiffs, produced a home carbonating machine under their own name using identical gas with that destined for the plaintiff's machine. Their cylinders were also identical in terms of shape and function but had a different colour and label. The conflict arose when the defendants made known their intention to refill any cylinders of the plaintiffs that reached them, superimposing their own name and trade mark. Whitford J had refused to grant an interlocutory injunction. However, the Court of Appeal found that it could be argued that the

---

[28]   At 563–4. Three witnesses, provided with SelloTak and Blu-Tack packets, thought that the SelloTak contents were Blu-Tack based on colour and texture. The evidence was not considered helpful in principle because it did not elucidate the mental processes a purchaser goes through in selecting the defendant's product at the point of sale.

[29]   [1982] RPC 459.

colour grey was a distinguishing sign and confusion was likely. The balance of convenience favoured the plaintiffs, who were only seeking to prevent the defendants from doing something that they had not yet commenced. The fact that the defendants attached labels to their own cylinders to distinguish them from the plaintiffs' at the point of sale was not enough since there was evidence that consumers did not read the labels or that, even if they did, they thought that the cylinders had been refilled by the defendant under licence.

5.   CONFUSION IN EUROPE

The ECJ's justification of registered trade mark protection has been based on their function as indicators of origin. In Rudolf Dassler Sport[30] it interpreted 'likelihood of confusion . . ., which includes the likelihood of association' as incorporated in Article 4(1)(b) of the Trade Mark Directive[31] and held that 'likelihood of association' is not an alternative to 'likelihood of confusion' but only serves to define its scope; confusion must be considered globally, taking into account all the factors that are relevant to the particular circumstances. In *Canon Kabushiki Kaisha v Metro-Goldwyn-Mayer Inc.*[32] the Court added that confusion exists where the public perceives the goods or services as originating from the same undertaking or from economically linked undertakings. In *Marca Mode CV v Adidas AG & Adidas Benelux BV*[33] it held that reputation is one of the factors co-determining confusion, but this did not imply a presumption of confusion resulting from association. A positive finding of likelihood of confusion is required. The Court has consistently rejected the position that any type of association between the two signs would assure trade mark protection, even when the earlier mark has a reputation; in that case protection could be afforded under Article 4(4)(a) where confusion is irrelevant but additional requirements must be satisfied.[34]

To determine likelihood of confusion the Court is looking at the case from the perspective of the average consumer of the relevant goods or services who normally perceives a mark as a whole and does not proceed to analyse it in its various details[35] and does not always have the opportunity to see the two

---

[30]   [1997] ECR I-6191.
[31]   Council Directive 89/104/EEC, 1988 OJ (L40) 1.
[32]   [1998] ECR I-5507.
[33]   [2000] ECR I-4861.
[34]   Article 4(4)(a) – mirrored by Article 5(2) covering infringement. See Davidoff and Adidas II.
[35]   *Sabel BV v Puma AG, Rudolf Dassler Sport* [1997] ECR I-6191.

marks side by side but has to rely on an imperfect recollection of one of the two marks when confronted by the other and whose attention is likely to vary according to the category of goods or services in question.[36] The average consumer is presumed to be reasonably well-informed, observant, and circumspect.[37] As to the audience of a trade mark that determines distinctiveness the Court has chosen the average consumer of the same type of product in the territory where protection is sought. Depending on the features of the product, the perception of those in the trade who deal commercially with the product might also be taken into account.[38] The view of potential competitors (e.g. chambers of commerce) should be sought when determining the distinctiveness of some types of marks, for instance geographical terms.[39]

The Court has limited the scope of infringement in cases under Articles 6 and 7 where the trade mark was not used as an indication of origin. A trader of lawfully marketed products could not be prevented from using the trade mark in advertising provided that the condition of the goods has not been impaired and use does not imply a commercial connection with the trade mark proprietor.[40] However, it added that the allure, the prestigious image, and the aura of luxury surrounding some trade marks must be taken into account, together with the product's actual physical condition, to decide whether the condition of the goods has been impaired. Further, it held that rights are limited if the marks are used by a third party to indicate the intended purpose of a product or service.[41]

Most importantly regarding the pre sale effects of a trade mark, the ECJ held in *Hölterhoff v Freiesleben*[42] that a proprietor cannot rely on the exclusive right where a third party, in the course of commercial negotiations, reveals that it has produced the product in question, uses the trade mark solely to denote the particular characteristics of the product it is offering for sale, and the trade mark is not being perceived as a sign indicating origin.

---

[36] *Lloyd Schuhfabrik Meyer & Co GmbH v Klijsen Handel BV* [1999] ECR I-3819.
[37] Gut Springenheide and Tusky [1998] ECR I-4657.
[38] *Bjørnekulla Fruktindustrier AB v Procordia Food AB* (judgment of 29 April 2004).
[39] Windsurfing Chiemsee, [1999] ECR I-2799.
[40] *Parfums Christian Dior SA & Parfums Christian Dior BV v Evora BV* [1997] ECR I-6013.
[41] *BMW AG & BMW Nederland BV v Deenik* [1999] E.C.R. I-905.
[42] [2002] ECR I-04187.

6. POST SALE EFFECTS IN *ARSENAL*

Arsenal involved the sale of unofficial football merchandise products; at the point of sale a sign informed prospective customers about their unauthorised nature. There was insufficient evidence of deception and damage and the action in passing off failed. Laddie J linked the absence of evidence of confusion with the function of the unauthorised signs: they did not indicate trade origin. Accordingly he sought clarifications from the ECJ as to whether (i) use that does not indicate trade origin, and at the same time does not fall within the scope of Article 6(1) of the Directive, constitutes an infringement and (ii) use that could be perceived as a badge of support, loyalty or affiliation constitutes use indicating trade origin.[43]

Advocate General Colomer, having noted that merchandising has become a lifeline for clubs, stated that the Directive allows the proprietor to prevent only use whose purpose is to distinguish the goods or services to which the sign relates from those of other undertakings; this included use leading to misleading indications as to origin, provenance, quality or reputation. He supported that use expressing support, loyalty, or affiliation to the club signified a connection between the goods and the football club because it influenced the consumer to buy the product. Critical in his reasoning was the commercial exploitation of the sign. Clubs register their signs in order to exploit them and should be entitled to object to third parties exploiting identical signs; the signs have become their intangible property.[44]

The ECJ accepted that the unauthorised use constituted use in the course of trade. The position of the trade mark proprietor and the function of a trade mark were pivotal in the Court's analysis. Protection was conferred in order to enable trade mark proprietors to protect their specific interests; in other words, according to the Court, to ensure that the trade mark fulfils its functions. This meant that a proprietor may not prohibit use of even an identical sign for identical goods if that use cannot affect its interests as proprietor of the mark, having regard to its functions. The signs, according to the ECJ, were used in such a way as to create the impression of a material link in the course of trade between the unauthorised goods and the club.

The presence of the notice at the point of sale made no difference because, even if those who were aware of it would not be confused, there was a possibility that others who came across the goods after their sale and away from the stall might perceive the signs as designating the club as the undertaking from which the goods originated. From a consumer's perspective, the guarantee that

---

43   [2001] RPC 46.
44   [2002] ECR I-10273.

all goods bearing the same trade mark are manufactured or supplied under the control of a single undertaking that is responsible for their quality would be impaired.[45]

Back to the High Court Laddie J considered that the ECJ had held that where the respondent's use is not intended by him, or understood by the public, to be a designation of origin, there can be no infringement because such use does not prejudice the essential function of the registered mark. The ECJ had gone on to assert that, in the circumstances of the case, the claimant should succeed; this was a finding of fact rather than law. The ECJ had exceeded its jurisdiction by disagreeing with his own findings of fact. Applying the law as interpreted by the ECJ, he concluded that there was no trade mark infringement.[46]

At the Court of Appeal,[47] Aldous LJ stated that Laddie J was entitled to disregard ECJ's conclusions to the extent that they were based upon an inconsistent with his judgment factual background. However the ruling upon interpretation was binding. Looking at the judgment as a whole, he summarised the position of the ECJ:

> registration of a trade mark gave to the proprietor a property right . . . The relevant consideration was whether the use complained about was likely to damage that property right or, as the ECJ put it, is likely to affect or jeopardise the guarantee of origin which constitutes the essential function of the mark. That did not depend on whether the use complained of was trade mark use.[48]

The ECJ looked at the interest of the proprietor, and considered whether that interest is liable to be affected, and not at the type of the allegedly infringing use. The

> consideration is whether the third party's use affects or is likely to affect the functions of the trade mark. An instance of where that will occur is given, namely where a competitor wishes to take unfair advantage of the reputation of the trade mark by selling products illegally bearing the mark. That would happen whether or not the third party's use was trade mark use or whether there was confusion.[49]

According to his interpretation the ECJ had relied on whether the right given by registration is likely to be affected by a third party's use rather than whether Mr Reed's use was such that it would be perceived by some customers or users as a designation of origin.

---

[45]   Ibid.
[46]   [2002] EWHC 2695.
[47]   [2003] EWCA Civ. 696.
[48]   Par. 33.
[49]   Par. 37.

He concurred with the ECJ that in the circumstances use by Mr Reed was liable to jeopardise the guarantee of origin function of the trade mark.

> The trade marks, when applied to the goods, were purchased and worn as badges of support, loyalty and affiliation to Arsenal, but that did not mean that the use by a third party would not be liable to jeopardise the functions of the trade marks, namely the ability to guarantee origin. To the contrary, the wider and more extensive the use, the less likely the trade marks would be able to perform their function.[50]

Aldous LJ also considered Arsenal's claim regarding passing off despite the fact that Arsenal had not challenged the dismissal of its claim by Laddie J. According to *Bollinger v Costa Brave Wine*,[51] he noted, the traditional form of passing off is no longer definitive of its ambit:

> If I may say so without impertinence I agree entirely with the decision in the Spanish Champagne case – but as I see it [it] uncovered a piece of common law or equity which had till then escaped notice – for in such a case there is not, in any ordinary sense, any representation that the goods of the defendant are the goods of the plaintiffs, and evidence that no-one has been confused or deceived in that way is quite beside the mark. In truth the decision went beyond the well-trodden paths of passing-off into the unmapped area of 'unfair trading' or 'unlawful competition'.[52]

7. CONCLUDING REMARKS

Until *Arsenal*, the ECJ's approach to classic infringement has been measured and circumspect. The concepts of 'who' and 'as to what' must be confused have been clearly developed and described; the foundation is that the primary protectable function of a trade mark is that of an indicator of origin. In *Arsenal* the Court had the opportunity to consider the post sale effects of a trade mark and indicated that they should be taken into account. Further, it is reminded that the Court also reiterated that trade marks are protected as indicators of origin.

It is submitted that the essence of the judgment is the combination of these two affirmative positions rather than the adoption of an interpretive approach based on the interests of the proprietor. It is supported that *Arsenal*, within the wider jurisprudential context set by the Court, is telling us that post sale confusion matters when it affects the function of a trade mark as an indicator of origin in the mind of the relevant reasonable consumer.

---

50   Note that according to the judge the emphasis is on the trade mark rather than the product to which the trade mark is applied.
51   [1960] RPC 16 and [1961] RPC 116.
52   Citing Cross J. in *Vine Products v Mackenzie & Co Ltd* [1967] FSR 402, at 427.

Perhaps a positive statement on post sale confusion coupled with a restatement on the scope of infringement provisions could have resulted in a conceptually clearer judgment that would not allow misconstructions. But it is because of the position and the role of the ECJ in the overall judicial process that the judgment failed to elaborate further on the nature and extent of post sale effects.

The law on trade marks in Europe is relatively recent; the interests of trade mark proprietors have been taken into account in its drafting and are reflected by the infringement provisions that balance them with the interests of consumers and competitors. In addition the ECJ has consistently chosen the function of a trade mark as the catalyst that reflects this balance. Accordingly, the combination between the actual legislative provision and a trade mark's protectable function should be the starting interpretive position rather than a one-sided reference to the interest the provision is supposed to protect.[53]

As to the future of post sale effects in passing off, a contemporary with the *Arsenal* judgment must be mentioned. In *Rugby Football Union v Cotton Traders Ltd*[54] Lloyd J demonstrated the balancing fluidity in the relationship between what is protected and the way it is protected. Following *Arsenal*, which dealt with how a mark is protected, he decided that the red rose appearing on the shirts of the English Rugby team between 1920 and 1998 was not perceived by members of the public as a mark of trade origin, but as a national emblem or symbol, associated with the English rugby team, and thus fell outside the scope of both registered trade mark law and passing off.

---

[53]   See *R. v Johnstone* [2003] UKHL 28 HL, in particular par. 13 and pars 16–17.
[54]   [2002] EWHC 467 (Ch) Ch D.

PART II

Intellectual property and international trade

10. Intellectual property rights as strategic weapon: Domestic and international trade considerations

Gary Lea

INTRODUCTION

In the past, some Intellectual Property (IP) academics, most definitely including this author, were often guilty of ignoring uses and abuses of Intellectual Property Rights (IPRs) in the marketplace; they could tell you about subject matter, thresholds of protection and the like – perhaps even discuss supraliminal issues in antitrust, contract or human rights – but they were often blissfully unaware of what commerce and industry was up to with these rights on a day-to-day basis once they got hold of them. This situation has changed considerably over the last decade but the process of enlightenment is as yet incomplete.

In August 2002, a Workshop was held by the Centre for Competition and Consumer Policy at the Australian National University, Canberra Australia; I had the great good fortune to attend this meeting and to listen to a paper called 'When Means Become Ends: Considering the Impact of Patent Strategy on Innovation' by Stuart Macdonald of the Management School at the University of Sheffield. The managerial practices and philosophies that Macdonald's paper revealed filled in many gaps for me and this chapter, accordingly, refers closely to it whilst, it is hoped, providing some additional food for thought from the lawyer's perspective.

Much of what is said in this chapter relates to patents but, as we will see, it is clear that many of the factors affecting the growth, perhaps over-growth, of IPRs are at work in the allied fields of trade mark and copyright law.

THE FACT OF GROWTH

First of all, it is an incontrovertible fact that, if we treat IPRs as virtual three dimensional objects, they have grown enormously in size over the last quarter of a century. Let us assign our three dimensions as follows:

- Width = SUM (the scope of subject matter covered – the threshold for acquisition of protection)
- Height = SUM (the range and number of infringing acts + the remedies/penalties for infringement – any legal limitations/exceptions)
- Length = Term

Now let us now consider a single, simple example: copyright protection for a literary work under UK law in 1980 (i.e. under the Copyright Act 1956 as amended) and as it is likely to be by the time of publication of this article (i.e. under the Copyright, Designs and Patents Act 1988 as amended to incorporate the provisions of Directive 2001/29/EC).

Whilst growth here is clear, admittedly not all IPRs fall so neatly into this framework: what about the indefinite duration of registered trade marks, for example? True, it is difficult to place a length value here because of the possibility of continuing renewals of registrations but, in this case, we may validly substitute intelligent discussion of the greater ease with which renewals are now achieved compared to 1980: on a global scale, we can look at such matters as the spread of multi-class applications and registrations with, in many cases, lower renewal fees than their single class counterparts and the diminishment of 'proof of use' requirements.

The consequence of growth is also clear: in relation to any use of any material embodying IPRs, there is now, in effect, a commercially oriented 'presumption of guilt' in relation to infringement.

THE RATCHET EFFECT AND RELATED ISSUES

How has IPR growth and the creation of the presumption of guilt happened? This is because of a fairly straightforward 'ratchet' effect which has been in operation, albeit at varying speeds and starting points in time depending on the IPR and jurisdiction in question, since at least the late 1970s, namely:

- actual or potential commercial rightholders will litigate or otherwise act within the IP system in order to push the outer boundaries of protection as far as they can be pushed;
- if a limitation develops through legislative, judicial or administrative acts/omissions and is maintained such that it forms a serious and continuing impediment to the rightholder's commercial interests then they will lobby legislators until it is removed.

In the context of the ratchet, Dexter Brooks of the Coca-Cola Company gives

Table 10.1   Illustrative copyright changes

Year	1980	2003
Subject matter	Questionable whether computer programs or databases included (s2)	Computer programs and databases expressly included (ss3 + 3A)
Threshold	'Skill, labour, judgment' originality test plus qualifying link (ss1 + 2)	Arguably raised originality test for C/P and D/B (but no difference in reality) and much extended range of qualifying links (ss3 + 153 et seq.)
Infringing acts	Reproduction in any material form, publishing, performing in public, broadcasting, causing transmission to diffusion service subscribers, adapting, doing any of the first five in relation to an adaptation (s2)	Reproduction in any form (temporary or permanent, material or immaterial), issuing copies to the public, renting or lending to the public, performing in public, communicating to the public, adapting [extended], doing any of the first five in relation to an adaptation (s16)
Remedies	Civil remedies = damages (incl. additional damages) or account of profits, injunctions, conversion damages (ss17 + 18) whilst criminal penalties = offences only triable in summary proceedings (short terms of imprisonment, low fines) and possible only against a person knowingly commercially importing/dealing in infringing copies (s21)	Civil remedies = damages (incl. additional damages) or account of profits, injunctions. Conversion damages removed but express powers for orders for delivery up or application of self-help seizure of infringing copies (ss96, 99 + 100) whilst criminal provisions now extended to cover knowingly making or possessing articles specifically designed for making copies of a particular work ('plates' or equivalent) and certain public performances. Many offences now triable on indictment with penalties of up to 10 years in prison and/or and unlimited fine (s107)
Limitations/ exceptions	Four relatively broad sets of permitted acts at ss6, 7, 41, 42	Approximately 35 much more restricted permitted acts between ss29–76 (especially in relation to C/P, D/B) with access controls through technological measures now taking priority over the same
Duration	Subject to various special exceptions, 50 years from death of the author	Subject to various special exceptions, 70 years from death of the author

an interesting example;[1] writing about the impact of trade mark and related law on the operations of the company in the mid 1990s, he cited three cases which he felt were significant in the US in the shape of *Two Pesos v Taco Cabana* 112 S. Ct. 2753 (1992), *Qualitex v Jacobson* 13 F 3d 1297 (9th Cir., 1993) and *White v Samsung* 989 F 2d 1512 (9th Cir., 1993). These cases – on trade dress, colour marks and commercial rights in personality respectively – were legally significant at the time because of their massive expansion of protection but Brooks's reaction here was interesting: he was more concerned that it was unlikely that such decisions would have been given in favour *outside* the US (the view of the bottle as 'mostly empty').

An innocent abroad might ask where democratic accountability and the balancing of societal stakeholdings – in short, the public interest – fits into all of the above. Commercial rightholders will, quite naturally, argue that the public interest is best served by such changes as allow economic growth and development; and there is some truth in this. Whilst it is wildly unfashionable to acknowledge it, we must always remember that commercial rightholders pay tax and provide employment to people who, in turn, pay tax on their employment income. Although much battered by recent events, shares in commercial rightholders also provide further economic opportunities; as Thomas Schumacher, head of Walt Disney Theatrical Productions, pithily put it in a recent interview:

> The other complaint I get is 'Oh, you make so much money'. Well, we're a publicly held company. When we're doing well, that's a teacher's pension fund in Cleveland, that's the grandmother who bought 500 shares for her grandchildren and it's their college fund. We're not just filling up some weird chamber of gold.[2]

These comments have to be taken seriously because, unless Communist notions of central planning suddenly regain popularity or, alternatively, Radical Green dreams of zero economic growth or even dismantling 'the technocracy' gain serious ground, we have to operate within the realities of present day corporate capitalism as we find them. However, all that having been said, 'right in one thing does not mean right in all': if one accepts that economic growth in a free or mixed-market economy is what is important and what is at stake here, then we *must* accept that there is – and will continue to be – something *prima facie* very odd indeed about using monopolies and quasi-monopolies to support it when most economists insist that, in the absence of special justification, monopolies deter the very competition in the marketplace that will provide that self-same growth.

---

[1]   'The global approach to building strong trademarks' in Cottier, Widmer, and Schindler (eds), *Strategic Issues of Industrial Property Management in a Globalizing Economy*, Hart, Oxford, 1999 at pp. 9 et seq.

[2]   Spencer, 'The Mouse takes centre stage', *Daily Telegraph* (13/03/03), p. 25.

Now, the special justification arguments for legally enforceable IPRs are well-worn – classical incentive theory, risk/reward theory and all the other usual suspects[3] – and I shall not insult the reader by reiterating them here. However, it is interesting that comparatively little *empirical* research has been done into the fundamental point as to whether IPRs cater for innovation and creativity at all. All too often, therefore, IP academics, again including the present culprit, are guilty of trading assertions without any supporting evidence and, indeed, two phenomena suggest to me that perhaps legal protection for IPRs is not as fundamental as we might like to think: the fact that 'TV format rights' are licensed and traded with little or no direct IPR protection and the fact that software producers in the GNU/Linux field do not rely on IPRs to appropriate value on their investment.[4] There is also much more room to investigate the point that, even if not directly harmful in themselves, IPRs often simply provide camouflage for lazy, anti-competitive behaviour.

Finally, even if we *do* assume that IPRs are 'useful' and 'acceptable', this does not deal with the argument that it is possible to have too much of a good thing, i.e. that it is possible to over-extend IPR protection in such a way that it actually creates a drag effect on innovation and creativity. The problem is that development in the arts and sciences is, essentially, accretive: there is no such thing as absolute originality for a copyright work, no such thing as absolute novelty for an invention.[5] When this point is recast in more easily economically modelled notions of production and dissemination of information, it means that those things, such as (over-)strong IPRs, which restrict circulation of information in the arts or sciences at present will reduce production of such information in the future. The threat of ever-lowering innovation, ever-lowering creativity; these, then, are the real concerns with the remorseless click, click, click of our little ratchet. Let us see, then, what Macdonald has to say about all of this.

THE OPENING SALVO

In the case of patents, the threat to innovation through over-protection is much wider and deeper than most lawyers and economists would care to admit. First, Macdonald argues, we often tend to assume a relationship – simple and

---

[3] For an excellent overview, see Drahos, *Intellectual Property*, Dartmouth, Aldershot, 1999, pp. 5–63

[4] Vaalimaaki, 'Strategic use of IPRs in the digital economy – the case of software markets' (2002) at www.hiit.fi/de/hamilton.pdf.

[5] Scotchmer, 'Standing on the shoulders of giants: cumulative research and the patent law', 5 *J. Econ. Pers.* (1991), pp. 29 et seq.

linear – which goes 'patents encourage invention encourage innovation' before reminding us that for most industries, patent-related activities represent less than 5% of overall R&D spending and, therefore, an even smaller proportion of total 'innovation cost';[6] there are obvious exceptions to this, such as pharmaceuticals, but, as Macdonald rightly notes, the patent system casts protection over all to meet the needs of the few. Indeed, instead of the situation 25 years ago where there were strong limitations on patenting of pharmaceutical products under the laws of many jurisdictions, virtually all now treat such patents neutrally and some, such as the US and the EU, now provide *additional* protection along the length axis (at the point at which normal patent terms would expire) in order to compensate for lost time in regulatory approval processes.[7]

Macdonald is openly hostile to the notion that one can equate the number of patents granted with the rate of innovation; to him, a statement by Thomas Cueni of Interpharma,[8] that 'there is a clear and established link between patent protection and the rate of innovation . . .' is simply and plainly wrong. Here, ironically, the lawyers have supplied just the ammunition that Macdonald needs to make his case ironclad by tracing the greater ease of obtaining patent protection over the last 20 years – thanks partly to a lowering of examination standards[9] – and the greater 'size' of the resultant rights in accordance with rule of ratchet and the virtual three dimensional object analogy discussed above. The classic example of this, of course, is the rise of the patent for the software related invention (SRI): starting from a position in the early 1980s where it was very difficult to obtain protection because of an implied (US) or express (EPC) subject matter bar, the combined impact of determined corporate filing programmes, overworked examiners without any financial/administrative reasons to say 'no' and increasingly sympathetic senior patent office administrators has made it virtually inevitable that such applications will proceed provided that they meet all the other requirements for patentability and the claims are presented in the proper form.[10]

In any case, the fundamental point here is that 'more does not equal better',

---

[6]   Macdonald (2002) at p. 3.

[7]   I.e. either term extension or supplementary protection certificate (SPC) substitution.

[8]   'Industrial property protection – lifeline for the pharmaceutical industry' in Cottier et al., *Strategic Issues of Industrial Property Management* at p. 15.

[9]   This now seems provable on the balance of probabilities – see survey work in Merges, 'Patent standards and procedures' (2002) at http://www.ftc.gov/opp/intellect/020228robertpmerges.pdf.

[10]   For a somewhat jaded view of this, see Lea, 'The Revolution that never was' (2000) at http://wwwlaw.murdoch.edu.au/dtlj/2000/vol2_1/lea_abstract.html.

i.e. innovation can only be truly measured qualitatively and is a rather nebulous thing at best: as Macdonald notes, so-called 'product innovation' in Japanese industry during the 1970s and early 1980s involved virtually no invention or patenting at all.[11] If we put this the other way round in the more familiar form, 'innovators enjoy no inherent market advantage', numerous examples spring to mind; the Xerox Star personal computer, the de Havilland Comet jet aeroplane and the EMI CAT scanner are all mentioned by Teece in this context.[12] All of this taken together suggests that, in reality, there are massive *discontinuities* between patents, invention and innovation.

One point worth emphasising is that it is not just legislators and administrators, especially state/regional IP offices, that have contributed to this but the judiciary as well: it is an observable fact that, starting with the creation of the Court of Appeals for the Federal Circuit in the US in 1982 and its following landmark judgment in *Polaroid v Kodak* (which resulted in the closure of a global instant camera business and the award of nearly $1 billion in damages), courts worldwide have been less inclined to look at patents as barely tolerable monopolies and more as valuable property to be protected against predation by third parties; in short they have developed a 'pro patent attitude'. Since the mid 1990s, this trend has been reinforced by two developments in particular: the entry into force of the IP enforcement provisions in TRIPs and the fact that so many jurisdictions, following in the wake of the US, have instituted and/or developed courts of special jurisdiction, i.e. which deal mainly or totally with patents and related matters; even a cursory knowledge of human psychology suggests that judges in such courts will ever be unlikely to limit or deny their special jurisdiction.

SIZE DOES MATTER

One point raised by Macdonald *en passant* is that the patent system does not suit all sizes of commercial entity such that small- to medium-sized enterprises (SMEs) are actually disadvantaged by it.[13] The most obvious disadvantages for SMEs we can chart in terms of simple things like filing, examination or renewal fees for pursuing their own applications but we also need to consider such factors as:

---

[11]   Macdonald (2002) at p. 5.
[12]   D. Teece, *Managing Intellectual Capital*, Oxford University Press, Oxford, 2000 at pp. 92 et seq.
[13]   Macdonald (2002) at p. 2.

- lack of experience/resources in licensing and other exploitation strategies;
- lack of experience/resources in undertaking or contracting for patent 'watching' services;
- the fear, uncertainty and doubt generated by the above in terms of worrying about possible infringements.

These things in themselves are problematic but consider these things now in the context of the commonplace existence of patent portfolios: most large companies will enjoy many patents over a wider area than their small firm counterparts, culminating with the giants like IBM which, in 1996, held in excess of 30,000 worldwide with as many applications again in train.[14] Where a patent portfolio exists, even on the very unlikely assumption that an SME has the means to challenge a shaky patent in it, it will be much less likely to challenge because of the risks of being hit by something else in the package later on; this increases the pressure to license or settle litigation by licensing and, in such situations, the notion of equality of bargaining power becomes laughable.

Since its forced introduction under a 1956 antitrust Consent Decree, IBM, in fairness to it, has become very much committed to the concept of open licensing whereby all-comers, even competitors, may come to it and seek licences on fair, reasonable and non-discriminatory terms;[15] this, however, may mean little in reality because of the almost 'black hole'-like forces its patent portfolio exerts on others simply by virtue of its size and existence. Moreover, IBM gains much easier access to technology which it needs – by its own admission, it is unlikely that any one company will own all pieces of a technology – and this gives it an automatic head start there, too.

THAT WOULD BE A MANAGEMENT MATTER

Macdonald notes that, until the 1980s, patents were, generally, the province of legal and scientific specialists operating in private firms or IP departments of large companies as small remote backwaters. However, with the rise of patents as a corporate asset during the 1980s, it was only a matter of time before business schools and their MBA graduates became interested in the topic.[16] By the mid 1990s, we had seen the rise of Knowledge Management (KM) and

---

[14]   T. Cottier and P. Widmer, 'Industrial property management in a multinational corporation' in Cottier et al., *Strategic Issues of Industrial Property Management* at p. 88.

[15]   D. Teece, *Managing Intellectual Capital* at p. 201 et seq.

[16]   Macdonald (2002) at p. 10

Intellectual Capital Management (ICM) and the removal of the control of IP management and strategy from its old box and right into management processes and structures. Patents suddenly acquired a new importance inside companies – as both a means and a measure of control – and also a trendy new set of purely functionalist clothes. Sullivan, one of the fathers of ICM, bluntly stated[17] that patents were intended to provide:

- protection from competition;
- complementary protection;
- design freedom and litigation avoidance;
- bases for alliances.

This trend has continued, however, until those patent attorneys and other IP specialists who have migrated into management now often direct R&D and other strategies to the point that patents, and not innovation, are what Macdonald memorably describes as 'the business of the business'. The term 'migration' above was used advisedly: many legal and accounting divisions connected with IPR protection are now treated as corporate profit centres in their own right.[18] The logical end to all this, in IPR terms, is the full availability of patents for business methods, now perfectly possible in the US and following fast behind within the EPC system (despite official protest to the contrary[19]) provided claims are in the right form; this matter goes much beyond the more problematic issues in the area of 'e-commerce patents'.

The other side to this is that litigation strategy is now also much more closely tied to business requirements: whether to play hardball or softball, whether to corral a prospective defendant towards a licensing settlement are all matters which will be considered rather than just the plain question of whether infringement has occurred. The rise of IPR insurance, too, has played a part in this process, especially in those circumstances where the insurers have the ability to take over claims or subrogate.

STACKING AND LAYERING

Perhaps one of the biggest problems that many IP academics have is their continuing tendency to revert to considering IPRs in isolation, pigeonholed

---

[17] *Value-driven Intellectual Capital*, Wiley, Chichester, 2000 at pp. 140 et seq.
[18] E.g. Lucent Technologies, Texas Instruments.
[19] Starting in 2000 and including Notice from the European Patent Office dated 26 March 2002 concerning business methods (2002) at http://www.european-patent-office.org/news/info/2002_03_25_e.htm.

according to type, jurisdiction and subject matter. However, IP managers are quite conversant with 'stacking and layering' techniques, that is to say the notion of dealing with multiple blocks of multiple right types simultaneously, often across many jurisdictions; there is, as Macdonald says, more to this than just good old patent pooling.

This phenomenon may go some way towards explaining the TV programme formats issue above, i.e. although there is no core 'format right', licences covering use of copyright material, trade secrets, etc. can provide enough combinatorial coverage for the system to work. It also explains the rise of meta-categories of IPRs, categories recognised not as strictly legal categories but certainly as terms of commercial art; in this context, consider the IPR component of franchise deals or the COKE 'brand' which, according to Brooks,[20] comprises not only the trade secret soft beverage formula(e) but also:

- registered trade marks (COCA COLA, COKE and others) in various classes;
- unregistered trade marks, trade dress and allied rights;
- goodwill and reputation relating to the above.

This list could extend to various copyrights and neighbouring rights relating to advertising and labelling and patents for various products and processes ancillary to the production and distribution of the beverage in question but Brooks gives a classic example of stacking under US law: the granting of a US patent in 1915 for the contour bottle and the granting of a trade mark registration for the same in 1977.

Again, to be fair, 'stacking and layering' has not always been some Machiavellian scheme but often, in the past, represented a genuine attempt to overcome over-harsh limitations on protection in a given jurisdiction. However, in the case of pharmaceutical companies working during the 1980s in the UK, a country with a very good IPR protection track record, it becomes less easy to explain why it was necessary to 'supplement' patent protection by attempting to force an expansion of trade mark law to cover tablet shapes and colours[21] or to use copyright in instruction leaflets to slow down the creation of generic alternatives.

In the past, IP managers had to play a waiting game of sorts: although developments on expanding protection in relation to a particular type of IP in one jurisdiction could be going quite well, it did not follow that this was the

---

20   Copttier et al., *Strategic Issues of Industrial Property Management* at pp. 4 et seq.

21   *John Wyeth & Bro. Ltd.'s Coloured Tablet Trade Mark* [1988] RPC 243.

case in others. Strictly speaking, this is still true in that an IP manager always has to accept that the most they can get might not be as much as they would like; today, though, TRIPs provides a working, very high-level baseline and trade representatives can always push for higher protection in the bilateral agreements which are still frequently made.[22]

FEAR, UNCERTAINTY AND DOUBT IN THE GLOBAL CONTEXT

Cynics may argue that much of the problem is the extent to which governments are 'in hock' to big business generally; but again, we have to accept the realities of this situation – of course, given their economic importance, governments, parliaments and similar public bodies have to work closely with commercial rightholders and, of course, those rightholders are among the few organisations that have the time and manpower to lobby effectively. The point, though, is that there is nothing new or, indeed, hidden in this – no great conspiracy – which leads me to suggest that perhaps the single biggest factor is the extent to which states and regions *fear and despise one another*, at least in connection with trade and economic development.

In the mid 1980s, the US was extremely worried by its lack of competitiveness: high-cost workers and inefficient practices were driving manufacturing overseas and so, as Macdonald rightly observes, the drive towards the pro-patent culture allowed protection of strategic US high technology interests and '. . . provided [albeit spurious] reassurance that all was well'.[23] The relationship between the subsequent recovery, patenting, invention and innovation is, of course, still open to dispute but what is clear is the reaction of other countries and blocs.

In 1999, the EU institutions took receipt of a report from the European Technology Assessment Network (ETAN), an expert body which noted developments in the US[24] before going on to say that, in order to maintain its own economic and trade position, the EU would have to provide a similarly favourable regime.

---

22 E.g. the US–Vietnam Bilateral Trade Agreement 2000.
23 Macdonald (2002) at p. 7.
24 Chapter 2.2, ETAN Final Report (1999) at http://www.cordis.lu/etan/src/document.htm.

CONCLUSION

With his references to patents as neo-totemic indicators of success for governments and companies, his savage attacks on seemingly innocent IP portfolio
management techniques and his stout arguments that patents are becoming an
end rather than a means in their guise as a business in themselves, Macdonald
paints a bleak and savage picture of IPRs. Ultimately, though, I am not sure
that we should, or indeed, can treat this as a call to the barricades, but more as
the need to wake up IP academics to the reality of 'IPRworld'.

11. Intellectual property law and political transformation: Post-socialist reform in Central and Eastern Europe

Mira Sundara Rajan

1. INTRODUCTION

Intellectual property rights have a number of implications for the transition to democracy in post-socialist countries. Over the past decade of intensive law reform efforts, however, the relationship between intellectual property and political change in Central and Eastern Europe has not received the attention it deserves. Rather, reform has been dominated by international demands for the implementation of intellectual property standards that reflect the practices of economically advanced countries. The standards of North American and Western European countries are embodied in the TRIPs Agreement, the most powerful legal instrument in the history of international copyright relations. Despite its coercive character, which is generally acknowledged throughout the world,[1] the TRIPs Agreement offers the overwhelmingly strong incentive of full participation in the international trade regime to less-developed countries. Transitional countries, like developing countries, have uniformly chosen to pursue membership.

Most ex-socialist countries aspire to join the European Union. Unlike other 'developing' intellectual property jurisdictions, transitional countries therefore face the additional challenge of meeting the requirements for IP regulation in the European 'internal market'. The EU is a member of the World Trade Organisation (WTO), and a signatory to TRIPs. While it necessarily shares many features of the TRIPs regime, however, the EU has approached international copyright regulation by attempting to anticipate and supersede developments at the WTO, often leading to sophisticated copyright rules in the Harmonisation Directives that effectively surpass TRIPs standards. An example

---

[1] For example, see the discussion in RC Dreyfuss and AF Lowenfeld, 'Two Achievements of the Uruguay Round: Putting TRIPs and Dispute Settlement Together' (1997) Va J Intl L 275, 301–2.

lies in the area of copyright term, where the EU duration of life of the author and 70 years after his death surpasses the WTO norm.[2]

With the prospect of EU membership becoming a reality for a number of post-socialist countries on 1 May 2004, it is a particularly appropriate moment to re-examine the progress of intellectual property law reform in the Central and East European region. In fact, the post-socialist experience of intellectual property rights has been mixed. The current situation in the region is quite diverse, ranging from the relative modernisation of countries like Poland and the Czech Republic, to the chaos of the Russian Federation. However, intellectual property law is far from settled in most transitional countries, with even the countries slated for the 1 May accession process continuing to have special concerns in this area.

The post-socialist experience, to date, suggests that ex-socialist countries have distinctive and deeply rooted needs in relation to intellectual property. In some instances, international levels of protection may well correspond to domestic requirements. Often, however, a conflict arises between the domestic needs of transitional countries, on the one hand, and the requirements of the international copyright regime, on the other. In these circumstances, the implementation of Western-style intellectual property standards may not be compatible with their underlying needs. Rather, the adoption of international standards may actually undermine development and democratisation in the region.

Special policy concerns related to intellectual property law in a 'transitional' environment arise in at least three distinct ways, involving the role of 'intellectual property' in the process of democratisation; the status of culture after socialism; and the problem of technological backwardness. In some respects, these problems are unique to the political circumstances of the post-socialist world. In other ways, however, related problems also arise in non-Western and less economically developed jurisdictions throughout the world.

First, the variety of creative and innovative activity that is designated by the term, 'intellectual property', is an especially important resource for post-socialist countries. Intellectual property represents human potential, which, in many cases, was unable either to express or to realise itself under socialist rule. Since the collapse of socialism, post-socialist countries have experienced an intense need for the products of intellectual activity, creative and innovative work that will help their societies to progress towards greater openness and prosperity. At the same time, the transitional need for creation and innovation

---

[2]   This situation has led to controversy in the United States, where attempts to extend copyright to match the EU term have met with free speech objections based on the American Constitution: see *Eldred v Ashcroft* 123 SCt 769, 789 (15 Jan 2003).

is deeper and more complex than the issue of access to knowledge. Transitional countries also need to revive the ability of their people to engage in creative activities, after a long period of time when creativity was strongly discouraged, either actively or implicitly, by state policy.

Intellectual property rights therefore have a dual significance for transitional countries. They must not impede the public from having adequate access to new works, but they must also provide an effective system, in traditional copyright parlance, of 'incentives to create'. Considered closely, the question of incentives is surprisingly complex: not only does it signify the provision of economic incentives, but it also encompasses larger issues, such as adequate legal protection for one's personal rights, and protection from state persecution of personal expression, or disadvantageous official exploitation of works or inventions.

Secondly, transitional countries must also deal with the problem of cultural reconstruction. In socialist countries, culture endured a long period of oppression. In some countries, cultural oppression simply meant the neglect of pre-existing culture; in others, it involved the active and systematic modification, mutilation, or destruction of culturally important works, accompanied by the simultaneous quest to destroy the reputations, personalities, and even physical existence of creative authors. Post-socialist governments must therefore address the problem of restoring rights and reputations to the works and authors of the past. This process is one of ongoing historical discovery and revision, and is likely to continue for many years.

In addition to cultural issues, access to knowledge and technology that are internationally current is a third, crucial objective for transitional countries. By bringing their copyright laws into line with the TRIPs Agreement, transitional countries hope that they will be able to assure themselves of access to current technologies, particularly those that originate in the United States and Western Europe. While their need for technology is especially intense, however, their ability to pay for the rights to use new technologies is limited.

It is apparent that intellectual property policy in transitional countries must satisfy unusually complex demands. A successful approach to law reform in the region will be correspondingly difficult to achieve. Indeed, many of the shortcomings of the past decade of reform reflect the absence of a larger perspective on the full range of issues involved. However, it is certain that the achievement of lasting legal change in post-socialist countries will depend on a change of orientation in the future.

An approach to intellectual property rights that addresses transitional concerns will require a fundamental shift in the conceptual framework behind reform. Law reform should not be driven exclusively, or primarily, by the requirements of international copyright standards, especially as expressed in the commercially driven model of copyright law in the TRIPs Agreement.

Rather, it should address the special needs of ex-socialist countries. This chapter suggests that intellectual property reform in transitional countries should be informed by a development-oriented perspective. Transitional countries may be called 'developing' in at least three senses: economically, culturally, and politically. Each of these aspects of the development problem is coloured by the peculiar circumstances of historic transformation in Central and Eastern Europe.

First, in dealing with intellectual property issues, transitional countries should be understood as areas that are, in economic terms, 'developing'. The circumstances of many transitional countries closely resemble the difficult situation of intellectual property law in the developing world. By recognising that many of the problems of transitional countries are tied to economic and technological lags, it becomes clearly apparent that intellectual property law must fulfil different policy objectives in these countries than those of the industrialised world.

Secondly, transitional countries are involved in a transformation in their approach to knowledge, information, and culture. In effect, they are in the process of moving out of an oppressive regime restricting the circulation of information in society, in both legal and practical terms, to a 'free' environment for knowledge. This transformation in the social role of knowledge may be understood as a fundamental cultural shift. Intellectual property rights, which are essentially concerned with the circulation of knowledge throughout society, are implicated in this transition. Indeed, it is likely that intellectual property rights will have an active role in facilitating the post-socialist movement into a new 'information regime'.

Thirdly, and finally, the conceptual discussion in this chapter introduces the idea that the values inherent in copyright law can make a positive contribution to political change. The structure and content of copyright law in these countries should therefore reflect the role of copyright principles in supporting democratisation.

A conceptual approach to law reform that is driven by the ideal of development will make intellectual property law more responsive to the special needs of transitional countries, both in the short-term period of transition, and in the long-term maintenance of social stability. It also presents the possibility of a new way of looking at intellectual property rights themselves.

The abuse of creative freedom in socialist regimes has led to an especially strong awareness in post-socialist societies of the need to protect creativity. The concepts of intellectual property protection arising out of the post-socialist legacy of cultural oppression are therefore likely to differ substantially from current international trends. However, the relevance of post-socialist approaches will not be limited to the transitional experience. Rather, they can make an important contribution to international copyright law, which, in recent years, has become increasingly dominated by commercial priorities, and is experiencing a renewed, though largely unacknowledged, need for humanitarian values.

2. TRANSITION AND DEVELOPMENT

New intellectual property standards in post-socialist countries have been adopted from international models, often with little analysis of the potential implications of these foreign provisions for societies in transition. As William Butler comments:

> [I]t must be elementary comparative law that no one attempts to transplant whole-sale one legal culture into another; that one works in the language of the recipient legal system; that one has a thorough command of the recipient legal system. As regards the former Soviet Union this is rarely the case, to the considerable disadvantage of everyone concerned. Law reform assistance to this day remains substantially uncoordinated, underfunded, and rendered by individuals and institutions who are not adequately equipped to deliver the product which is required.[3]

The primary objective of intellectual property reform in transitional countries has been to bring national intellectual property legislation into facial conformity with international requirements, particularly as these are expressed in the TRIPs Agreement.[4] Reform has also been concerned with ensuring adequate 'enforcement measures' for these provisions, mainly in the form of coercive and punitive measures rather than preventive ones. However, it is increasingly apparent that intellectual property rights have a larger role to play in the process of post-socialist transition. Intellectual property rights are a key element in the transformation of post-socialist 'information regimes', and in the democratisation of political values related to culture and expression. How should policy-makers attempt to harness the potential for development in intellectual property rights?[5]

---

3   WE Butler, 'Foreign Legal Assistance in the CIS: Lessons from the Early Years' in G Ginsburgs, DD Barry and WB Simons (eds), *The Revival of Private Law in Central Eastern Europe: Essays in Honor of FJM Feldbrugge* (Kluwer Law International, The Hague, 1996) 499, 509.
4   Through the Harmonisation Directives, the European Union has also been an important influence on intellectual property reform: for example, the impact of the Copyright Harmonisation Directives on Russian copyright law is discussed in detail by M Elst, 'The Interaction of European Community and Russian Copyright Law: A Matter of Partnership and Cooperation' (1996) 22:30 Rev Cent & E Eur L 267, 285–324. Elst, 276–85 also discusses the influence of an Agreement on Partnership and Cooperation between the EU and Russia on Russian copyright.
5   Interestingly, the Communists adopted a 'social engineering' approach to law

In fact, intellectual property law in Eastern Europe must satisfy two competing and potentially conflicting kinds of demands: those arising out of domestic policy objectives, and those flowing from international requirements.[6] As in every legal system, intellectual property rights in post-socialist countries will favour certain kinds of interests at the expense of others; achieving the appropriate balance of rights is one of the important tasks of policy-makers. However, the reality of the post-authoritarian transition means that the appropriate balance of rights in the transitional environment is almost certain to differ fundamentally from the equilibrium accepted in Western jurisdictions. Since socialist governments relied on ideology as the primary means of maintaining political power, the rights of authors and 'users' of intellectual property were balanced, not only against one another, but against the overpowering political interests of the state in controlling and manipulating information – often wielding it against those who produced or created it.[7]

At the same time, intellectual property law must accommodate the reality of a deficient economic and social legacy in the wake of socialist rule. In economic terms, the developmental level of post-socialist countries is significantly behind that of the West; the role of intellectual property rights in societies where economic growth is urgently needed must be determined. Here, too, the types of intellectual property protection and the balance among different kinds of intellectual property rights may be quite different from norms that are accepted in the West.

In this tension between domestic and international priorities, transitional countries closely resemble developing countries.[8] Like developing countries,

---

which could be a problem for policy-makers now, as they may be reluctant to adopt an obviously similar posture. For a discussion of 'parental law' in Soviet legal theory, see A Schmidt, 'Soviet Civil Law As Legal History: A Chapter or a Footnote?' in Ginsburgs et al. (n 5) 45, 49–50, 57–62.

[6]   This point is raised in relation to developing countries by EW Ploman and LC Hamilton, *Copyright: Intellectual Property in the Information Age* (Routledge & Kegan Paul, London, 1980) 29. Writing in 1980, Ploman and Hamilton did not assign the same importance to this distinction in socialist countries. However, their discussion of socialist legal systems may suffer from certain unavoidable limitations. Prior to Gorbachev's ascension to power in the Soviet Union in 1985, it was difficult for outsiders to assess the extent of economic collapse in the republics. With hindsight, it seems highly appropriate to consider the similarities between the challenges facing socialist systems and those in developing countries.

[7]   The complex relationship between Bolshevik 'power' and 'culture' in the early years of Soviet government is discussed by S Fitzpatrick, *The Cultural Front: Power and Culture in Revolutionary Russia* (Cornell University Press, Ithaca, 1992) 1–15. See also G Hosking, *A History of the Soviet Union 1971–1991* Final Edition (Fontana Press, London, 1992) 170, 179.

[8]   For a discussion of this situation in developing countries, see Ploman and Hamilton (n 6) 29–30.

the societies of transitional countries suffer from a number of historical disadvantages. While the problems of developing countries tend to be viewed primarily through an economic lens, the subtleties of development issues in transitional countries are more readily apparent.[9] Most developing countries must endure a daily struggle in meeting basic needs, such as feeding their populations. In most ex-socialist countries, impoverishment is less extreme, and economic problems can often be traced directly to the political mismanagement of socialist leaders.[10] Development problems in ex-socialist countries are recognised, above all, as a matter of political modernisation.

Intellectual property law is among the most powerful legal instruments dealing with information, knowledge, and culture. As such, it must fulfil objectives of information and cultural policy at the domestic level. At the very least, it should not impede the implementation of domestic policies. However, intellectual property laws must also meet the demands of the international harmonisation and standardisation of intellectual property rights, in order to enable active participation in economic and technological advances in the international arena. One of the most highly publicised aspects of the new international openness in transitional countries is the need to implement internationally viable intellectual property standards to help them attract foreign investment.[11]

The special needs of developing jurisdictions in relation to intellectual property require a sensitive legal treatment. In particular, development issues call for the achievement of an effective equilibrium between rights of control

---

[9]   The connection between economics and politics in developing countries is also controversial and poorly understood. One aspect of the pioneering work of an Indian economist, Amartya Sen, is his emphasis on the positive relationship between democracy and development – for example, he points out that democratic government has helped India to manage economic crises more effectively. For an introduction to Sen's comprehensive approach to development, see A Sen, 'Radical Needs and Moderate Reforms' in A Sen and J Drèze (eds), *Indian Development: Selected Regional Perspectives* (Oxford University Press, Delhi, 1997) 1–32.

[10]   This distinction is useful in distinguishing post-socialist from developing countries, but slightly artificial: the poverty of developing countries, especially those that are large and rich in human and natural resources, is often due to political mismanagement, as well.

[11]   For example, see SP Boylan 'United States–Poland Economic Treaty: A Blueprint for Intellectual Property Reform in Eastern Europe and the Developing World?' (1990) 6 Fla J Intl L 101, 113–17. The biased outlook of Boylan's analysis should be noted: although he draws a connection between the economic situations of post-socialist and developing countries, in his view, the transitional countries are victims of political oppression and, therefore, deserving of special intellectual property measures, whereas 'nations in the so-called developing world' implicitly are not. To date, it is not yet known whether higher intellectual property standards have in fact encouraged greater foreign investment.

and rights of access, domestic policy objectives and international standardisation, and, ultimately, intellectual property rights and other legally protected interests. These conflicts have historically been at the root of tensions between developing and industrialised countries over the appropriate international treatment of intellectual property rights.[12] Developing countries have accorded great importance to rights of access, and they have sought structural flexibility in the application of intellectual property rights. In different ways, they have also raised concerns about the impact of intellectual property protection on human rights and culture.[13]

Now, transitional countries find themselves confronting similar questions about the nature of a workable equilibrium among diverse rights and interests within their post-socialist and democratising societies. The virtual absence of empirical research on the relationship between intellectual property rights and development complicates this inquiry.[14] At the same time, the need for a suitable conceptual approach to intellectual property rights in the context of political and economic development is an inescapable reality of post-socialist reform.

The problem of intellectual property in developing societies is concisely expressed by N'dene N'diaye of Senegal:

> [L]e problème qui se posa . . . [aux pays en voie de développement après l'indépendance des puissances coloniales] fut celui de savoir s'ils devaient trouver à la base des droits de l'homme la même notion d'homme et si les exigences du développement se concilient avec la pleine application, en général, des droits que tous affir-

---

[12]   For example, the debate between developing and industrialised countries over the appropriate treatment of intellectual property rights in the developing world came to a head in the 1967 Stockholm revision conference of the Berne Convention. The way in which these issues were played out in the Stockholm Protocol on special provisions for developing countries is discussed in detail by S Ricketson, *The Berne Convention for the Protection of Literary and Artistic Works: 1886–1986* (Kluwer, Centre for Commercial Law Studies, Queen Mary College, London, 1987) paras 11.16–11.48.

[13]   For example, see N N'diaye, 'Influence du droit d'auteur sur le développement de la culture dans les pays en voie de développement' (1975) 86 RIDA 59; TS Krishnamurti, 'Copyright – Another View' (1968) 15:3 Bull Copyrt Soc'y USA 217; and C Masouyé 'Décolonisation, indépendance et droit d'auteur' (1962) 36 RIDA 85. Not surprisingly, these writers all have distinctive views on the nature of human rights and culture, as well.

[14]   This point is implicit in Henderson's discussion of patent rights and developing countries: see E Henderson, 'TRIPs and the Third World: the Example of Pharmaceutical Patents in India' [1997] 11 EIPR 651, 654–7. See also AS Oddi, 'The International Patent System and Third World Development: Reality or Myth' (1987) 5 Duke LJ 831. One of the few empirical studies on intellectual property rights in developing countries might be RT Rapp and RP Rozek 'Benefits and Costs of IP Protection in Developing Countries' (1990) 24:5 J World Trade L 75.

ment solennellement dans leur constitution – et en particulier ceux relatifs à la propriété . . . Les pays en voie de développement sont ainsi souvent contraints de n'accorder la priorité qu'aux entreprises visant à réaliser le développement de la société. Ce faisant, pour établir l'ordre et assurer le développement, d'aucuns relèguent au second plan la liberté et la justice, singulièrement la liberté dans l'acte de création et la justice dans la rémunération de l'auteur . . .[15]

It is clear that the relevance of N'diaye's argument is not restricted to the countries traditionally thought of as 'developing' over the past half-century; it applies equally to the 'transitional' countries of today. The resemblances between them suggest that transitional countries can benefit from a comparison of their experiences with intellectual property law and reform in developing countries.

3. INTELLECTUAL PROPERTY LAW IN TRANSITION: A NEW INFORMATION REGIME

The transitional reality of post-socialist countries may be understood as a kind of cultural transformation. In particular, this process of cultural development involves a new social status for knowledge, information, and heritage in all its forms. Cultural change in ex-socialist countries is closely bound to a radically shifting legal culture, as well, and the prospect of a cultural transition must also be considered in this sense.

3.1 Law in Transition

Intellectual property law in Central and Eastern Europe reflects the general disarray of law after socialism. Law reform has assumed a central role in enabling the transition out of socialism to occur smoothly. At the same time, the character of law has been altered fundamentally by the peculiarities of the transitional environment. Time, the 'fourth dimension', is a factor that transforms the ordinary significance of legal rules. Reform of intellectual property rights is conditioned by these unique historical circumstances. New law in this field, whether it originates with legislators, judges, or international conventions, must strive to meet the special requirements of historic social change.[16]

---

[15] N'diaye (n 13) 69.

[16] It is interesting to note that, in Russia, international conventions to which Russia is a party are automatically integrated into Russian law and, in case of incompatibility, may even take precedence over Russian provisions: see CL Broadbent and AM McMillian, 'Russia and the World Trade Organization: Will TRIPs Be a Stumbling Block to Accession?' (1998) 8 Duke J Comp & Intl L 519, 534.

Over the past decade, post-socialist law reform has focused intensely on the present political moment. It has developed largely as a response to over-whelming political crises – the collapse of governments and ideologies, and the dissolution of an empire. As reform enters a more stable period, it is apparent that legal modernisation involves somewhat neglected considerations of historical continuity.

In a unique study on the phenomena of post-authoritarian legal change, Ruti Teitel emphasises that the shape of new laws in post-authoritarian societies necessarily reflects the circumstances of oppression in the past.[17] New laws are a response to the character of the old political regime; inevitably, they aim at rectifying the abuses of authoritarian rule.

Once we understand the extent to which law reform is conditioned by the circumstances of authoritarianism, the reasons for law's special importance in post-socialist countries become clear. In Western history, changes of regime have most often been accomplished by violent overthrow, with the discrediting of the old regime and its structures, and the dispossession and destruction of its leaders, ensuring a clean and permanent break with the past.[18] In contrast, the contemporary, 'velvet revolutions' of Central and Eastern Europe have been less clear-cut. Although the authoritarian past has been repudiated, its legacy remains a deep and ever-present undercurrent in post-socialist developments.[19]

While law in post-socialist societies must come to terms with an authoritarian past, it must also project forwards, into an increasingly free and open future. Here, too, the post-socialist understanding of law's functions must be distinguished from typical perceptions of the law in stable, democratic societies. Of course, law in democracies is policy-driven in a variety of ways. However, the problem of developing policy for a future that aspires to depart fundamentally from historical tradition, and a long-established economic and social order, brings a peculiar intensity to post-authoritarian legal reform.[20] In

---

[17]   For example, see Teitel (n 17) 4–6.

[18]   The point is also noted by Teitel (n 17) 204, and is central to her discussion.

[19]   The resurgence of Communist political parties and politicians in certain formerly socialist countries can perhaps be traced to this unresolved situation. The phenomenon is noted in 'The left is back – in the centre' in *The Economist*, 27 Sep 2001, and 'A new misery curtain' in *The Economist*, 31 May 2001.

[20]   The different experiences of the transition among different countries is partly a reflection of different cultural traditions. For example, a number of Central European countries, such as Poland and the Czech Republic, appear to have experienced less trauma and relatively greater success in achieving stability. See H Izdebski, 'General Survey of Developments in Eastern Europe in the Field of Law' in Ginsburgs et al (n 3) 3, and P Karel, 'Political, Economic, and Legal Aspects of the Association of the Czech Republic with the European Union' (1997) 23:3 Rev Cent & E Eur L 205, 207–8 on the liberal past of the Czechs.

this context, the very act of developing new law is premised on a belief in the transformative power of the law. New laws become part of the process of transforming society into a new shape, one based on new political values and newly acknowledged social needs.

The dilemma of situating law reform in its appropriate historical context is captured by Ruti Teitel:

> Law is caught between the past and the future, between backward-looking and forward-looking, between retrospective and prospective. . . . Transitions imply paradigm shifts in the conception of justice; thus, law's function is deeply and inherently paradoxical. In its ordinary social function, law provides order and stability, but in extraordinary periods of political upheaval, law maintains order, even as it enables transformation. Accordingly, in transition, the ordinary intuitions and predicates about law simply do not apply. In dynamic periods of political flux, legal responses generate a sui generis paradigm of transformative law.[21]

However, Teitel's characterisation of the unusually dynamic quality of law in transitional countries as paradoxical seems incomplete. Teitel emphasises that the apparent contradiction between stability and transformation occurs because law in transitional countries has come to signify change, rather than maintaining its traditional association with stability and continuity. However, the transitional problem has an additional dimension: it arises because the role of law in socialist societies was fundamentally different from its role in democratic societies. The oppressiveness of socialist regimes when it came to political and social freedoms did not occur in a legal vacuum. Rather, oppression occurred within a legal framework; law was an accepted tool of political power, available for use by the state and its agents against potential enemies. For example, Katharina Pistor identifies the need 'to overcome the crudely instrumental use of law by the state and to rid the legal system of direct political influence'.[22]

In contrast, democratic societies are defined by the concept of law-limited power, whether in relation to private individuals, corporate entities, or the state. Law in post-socialist societies is itself in need of rehabilitation, and this is the fundamental difficulty confronting legal reform in virtually every field – the restoration of substance, values, and credibility to the law. Law in these peculiar circumstances becomes closely allied with moral values.[23] Law

---

[21] Teitel (n 17) 6.

[22] K Pistor, 'Supply and Demand for Law and Russia' (1999) 8:4 E Eur Const Rev 105, 106.

[23] Teitel's discussion traces the path of an earlier debate between legal theorists HLA Hart and Lon Fuller about the legality of Nazi law. She argues that the problem does not involve 'essential, universal attributes of the rule of law', but 'is particular to the transitional context'. See Teitel (n 17) 15.

reform in the post-authoritarian context is infused with a normative character that ultimately aspires to the moral transformation of civil society.[24] The role of law and legality in the transition period is likely to have a lasting impact on traditional conceptions of the law. The new concepts of law that are generated by the historical movement out of authoritarianism and into a more democratic pattern of society will extend their reach well beyond the transition period, and are likely to affect both transitional countries and law in the international arena. In effect, the historical phenomena of the transition will transform law in their own right, leading to new legal models that should become a permanent feature of post-authoritarian legal culture around the world. From this perspective, the transition represents an exciting opportunity for creative thinking about the law.

3.2   A New Information Regime

The transition is a unique environment for intellectual property rights. Intellectual property law, too, is caught within the temporal continuum that affects law as a whole in the transitional environment. In the case of Russia, intellectual property rights are influenced both by the Soviet past, and by a more remote, tsarist legacy. At the same time, the current Russian administration confronts the task of crafting intellectual property policies that will facilitate the development of a fundamentally different future in Russia.

The 'transitional' difficulty facing intellectual property rights in Russia is the movement away from a certain kind of authoritarian government based on ideological control – where the manipulation of knowledge, information, and culture was the chief means of maintaining political power and legitimacy[25] – to a society based on ideals of intellectual and expressive freedom, and ideological diversity. The legal framework for controlling these intangibles may be understood as an 'information regime'. The movement out of an authoritarian system of information management is an important part of the transition process. Russia's new information regime must aspire to compatibility with democratic institutions and values.[26]

---

[24]   Ironically, a certain conceptual continuity with Marx's view of progressive historical development through socialism is worth noting.

[25]   Hosking (n 7) 408.

[26]   The recent standoff between the Russian government and Chechnyan rebels who held theatre-goers hostage in Moscow illustrates the culture of restrictiveness that continues to be characteristic of Russia's approach to information. Russian troops eventually stormed the theatre to release the hostages. Before they entered the theatre, however, they released a gas into the environment that was supposed to sedate the hostage-takers. In the event, a number of the hostages died from the effects of the gas. The Russian government greatly complicated matters by refusing to tell doctors caring

Intellectual property law is an increasingly prominent feature of information policy. New intellectual property laws will have to respond to concerns about the protection of intellectual freedom, the encouragement of creativity and innovation among long-oppressed populations, and appropriate limitations on the power of the state to control information and knowledge – problems which may not be in evidence to the same extent in other jurisdictions. For example, modern copyright provides for the strong protection of individual rights of authorship, in both their proprietary and personal dimensions, in a way that was not possible, for ideological and practical reasons, within the Soviet legal system.[27] In dealing with the legacy of intellectual property under Soviet rule, Russia's reformers must strive for a sense of historical coherence. Post-Communist law may depart fundamentally from the legal norms of the Soviet era, but it must also respond creatively to the problems and failures of that era. By confronting these issues of information policy, intellectual property law can make a valuable contribution to legal modernisation.

The post-socialist treatment of intellectual property rights should attempt this project on two levels. First, intellectual property law in the transition should aim to ensure that information is protected from manipulation and abuse, particularly by the state, but also, by private entities and individuals against one another.[28] Specific concerns from the past that intellectual property law should address are rights of privacy, access to information, protection for broadcasting and communications media, and the rehabilitation of creative authors and intellectuals who suffered censure in the authoritarian period. Copyright law has a role to play in all of these areas, especially in relation to the individual rights of authors.

Secondly, revised intellectual property laws should reflect the aspirations of post-socialist societies for the future, and ensure that the information policies

---

for the hostages what kind of gas they had used. The information was finally released after several days, following intense pressure from the international community. The incident is described in 'What is fentanyl?' 31 October 2002, BBC News Online: <http://news.bbc.co.uk/1/hi/health/2380661.stm>.

[27] See Ploman and Hamilton (n 6) 123; they observe, '[f]ollowing the socialist doctrine, an author's right is not regarded as the equivalent of private property'. The adaptation of copyright to the political conditions of Soviet life is also examined by MA Newcity, *Copyright Law in the Soviet Union* (Praeger, New York, 1978) 17–31. Interestingly, Soviet law did recognise a right of remuneration for creative work; Newcity argues that, after amendments permitting the alienation of material rights in 1973, the Soviet provision 'suggests a substantive right of ownership akin to that enjoyed by copyright proprietors in the West'. Newcity 83.

[28] For example, in Russia, information needs to be protected from corporate abuse and organised crime. The realities of business and crime in today's Russia are described in 'States within the state' and 'Russia: A reconditioned model' in *The Economist*, Survey on Russia, 19 Jul 2001.

of post-socialist governments help to further political, social, and economic development. The new laws must demonstrate their practical effectiveness in building an appropriate framework for liberalisation, but they must also seek to recover the moral stature that was compromised by the degraded legal practices of authoritarian states. Indeed, the importance of restoring moral authority to intellectual property rights should not be underestimated. Rights for creators can have a moral and ethical force in the post-authoritarian context that may not be immediately apparent in countries where the large-scale repression of creativity is unknown.

4. AUTHORS' RIGHTS AND DEMOCRATISATION

Intellectual property rights are involved in the transition from a restrictive and highly politicised information regime under authoritarian rule to a democratically informed treatment of knowledge in the transition period. How can copyright law help to build a democratic approach to knowledge in post-socialist societies?

Copyright law has long been viewed as a highly specialised and technical area of the law. This is due in large part to its close association with creative and innovative work, and the technologies supporting its development and dissemination. However, the technical aspects of intellectual property rights should not obscure their role in expressing social values, especially those related to creativity. The failure of post-socialist law reform to recognise and explore the values built into Western-style intellectual property protection is a serious shortcoming of the reform effort. In particular, reform should consider the possible impact of these values on democratisation, the ultimate expression of political development in the region.

Through the dissemination of values about creative expression, copyright law can make a positive contribution to democracy, in both conceptual and practical terms. Certain aspects of copyright values are highly relevant to post-socialist reform. By providing incentives for creation, copyright seeks to promote individual creativity and, depending on the nature of the creation, entrepreneurship.[29] Copyright seeks to protect the individual rights of authors in their creative expression, emphasising the importance of the creative works themselves. Implicit in copyright is also a basic desire to protect the human rights of authors, reflected in the protection of both authors' economic and personal rights through copyright law.[30]

---

[29]   For a thought-provoking discussion of the policy objectives that copyright is traditionally supposed to accomplish, see Ploman and Hamilton (n 6) 22–30.

[30]   The humanistic element underlying copyright is reflected in the inclusion of

Post-socialist reform of copyright law has been approached primarily as a matter of economic policy. The close connection between copyright, international trade, and foreign investment has largely determined the shape of the new copyright provisions.[31] At the same time, the relationship between copyright and democratisation in Eastern Europe has not been explored in any depth. A more careful consideration of this relationship is important for understanding the extent to which intellectual property rights may be implicated in political development. A democratically aware approach to intellectual property rights may improve their uncertain status in post-socialist societies. The development of the TRIPs Agreement has recently led some scholars to consider the implications of increasingly powerful intellectual property rights for political change. One school of thought argues that copyright is by its very nature an expression of democratic values. On this view, the adoption of the copyright norms in TRIPs by diverse countries around the world inevitably signifies a liberalising trend. As Marci Hamilton argues:

> It is no accident that intellectual property norms are spreading worldwide at the same time that totalitarian regimes are falling. A people must value individual achievement and believe in the appropriateness of change and originality if it is going to concede to and adopt a Western-style intellectual property regime. Indeed, there is an intimate link between respect for individual human rights and respect for a copyright system that values and promotes individual human creative achievement . . . The encoded message within TRIPS is that change, creativity, and originality are positive goods.[32]

The connection that Hamilton draws between copyright and the social value of individual creativity is appealing. However, she goes on to argue that TRIPs, which imposes strict and rigid protections for intellectual property rights on member countries, is a form of 'freedom imperialism'.[33] This choice of expression is unfortunate: in its application to developing countries who are struggling to bring their intellectual property regimes into line with TRIPs requirements, it seems patronising and devoid of nuance. Indeed, the argument that TRIPs will bring about greater liberalisation and freedom in relation to

---

authors' rights in international instruments of human rights law. For example, see the Universal Declaration of Human Rights (adopted 10 December 1948 UNGA Res 217 A(III)), Art 27, and the International Covenant on Economic, Social and Cultural Rights (adopted 16 December 1966, entered into force 3 January 1976) 993 UNTS 3, Art 15.

[31]   Boylan (n 11) 116–17 emphasises the issue of foreign investment.

[32]   MA Hamilton, 'The TRIPS Agreement: Imperialistic, Outdated, and Overprotective' in AD Moore (ed), *Intellectual Property: Moral, Legal, and International Dilemmas* (Rowman & Littlefield, Lanham, 1997) 243, 245, 247.

[33]   Hamilton (n 32) 243.

knowledge through coercion – by the imposition of its Western-style, advanced norms on other legal systems – is disturbing, and possibly even dangerous.

Hamilton's proposition is subject to two powerful criticisms. First, the TRIPs Agreement adopts a stance of unprecedented protectionism towards those who control knowledge, while the consequences of increased intellectual property protection for public access to knowledge, information, and technology remain unclear.[34] Secondly, the standards in TRIPs do not reflect any meaningful international consensus on intellectual property rights. TRIPs provisions were not finalised through international debate and compromise. They signify, above all, the internationalisation of Western copyright norms.[35] As a result, the character of the TRIPs Agreement has widely been viewed as coercive and potentially damaging to non-Western interests.[36]

In an interesting series of articles, Neil Weinstock Netanel argues that copyright may indeed support democratic values. However, he points out that this democratic potential cannot be secured simply by the adoption of TRIPs norms. Rather, the realisation of the democratic values inherent in copyright will depend on achieving the appropriate balance of rights between the authors and 'users' of copyright works. He observes:

> [C]opyright law serves fundamentally to underwrite a democratic culture: By according creators of original expression a set of exclusive rights to market their literary and artistic works, copyright fosters the dissemination of knowledge, supports a pluralist, nonstate communications media, and highlights the value of individual contributions to public discourse. In this view, copyright's constitutive, democratic purpose is both the primary rationale for according authors proprietary rights in original expression and the proper standard for delimiting those rights. Copyright holder rights should be sufficiently robust to support copyright's democracy-enhancing functions, but not so broad and unbending as to chill expressive diversity and hinder the exchange of information and ideas.[37]

---

[34]   For example, the Anglo-American distinction between authorship and ownership of copyright can create problems. Where works are created in situations of employment, the employer rather than the employee may control its use. In industrial society, the employer and owner of the work will often be a representative of corporate power. The weak position of the creator in these situations is noted by Ploman and Hamilton (n 6) 27; they also trace the historical roots of the distinction (ibid., 16–17).

[35]   The lack of involvement of developing countries in the TRIPs negotiations, and their relative inability to resist membership in the agreement for economic reasons, are noted by Dreyfuss and Lowenfeld (n 1) 301–2.

[36]   For example, see BS Chimni 'Towards Technological Wastelands: A Critique of the Dunkel Text on TRIPs' in KRG Nair and A Kumar (eds), *Intellectual Property Rights* (UDCCS Seminar Papers Series No 1, Allied Publishers, New Delhi, 1994) 91, 100–1.

[37]   NW Netanel, 'Asserting Copyright's Democratic Principles in the Global Arena' (1998) 51 Vand L Rev 217, 220.

In particular, Netanel emphasises:

> The notion that upward harmonization under TRIPs will contribute to global democracy is seriously misguided. Copyright's constitutive value for democratic development depends heavily on local circumstances. Indeed, copyright may sometimes impede democratization unless substantial limits are placed on copyright holder rights. Asserting copyright's democratic principles in the global arena would entail a far more nuanced approach than TRIPS's apparent insistence on maximalist global copyright protection.[38]

Realising the democratic potential of copyright will depend, not only on the achievement of an appropriate balance between rights of control and rights of access to knowledge, but also, on balancing different kinds of rights within copyright. Post-socialist reform needs to weigh commercial and non-commercial interests, individual and non-individualistic creation, private and public concerns, personal and state power. Copyright laws that support democratisation may eventually prove to be somewhat broader in scope than currently accepted, international models of the law.

If a single value can be said to be most characteristic of copyright law, it is almost certainly the protection of free and individual creative expression.[39] It is interesting to consider that creative expression, despite its historic associations with patronage and elitism, can be a deeply democratic phenomenon. In modern societies, creative expression at its best is diverse, suspicious of convention, and, even in the face of physical danger, stoically independent.[40] If democracy means ideological diversity and the aspiration towards free thought and judgement, the right to creative expression must be given its due as an essential feature of modern democratic life.

In the context of Western society, where modern copyright first developed, creativity has come to be valued primarily in commercial terms. The commercial benefit of creative work ultimately accrues to the owner of the copyright, whether or not he is one and the same person as the author. However, moral

---

[38] Netanel (n 37) 222.

[39] The underlying value of individuality is especially emphasised by current scholarship that traces the development of modern copyright concepts to the rise of Western European Romanticism. For example, see M Woodmansee 'The Genius and the Copyright: Economic and Legal Conditions of the Emergence of the "Author"' (1984) 17 Eighteenth-Century Studies 425.

[40] There are many moving examples of creative authors and artists who have resisted persecution, as there were in Communist regimes and in countries dominated by colonial rule. One example is Nigerian writer and activist Ken Saro-Wiwa, whose death at the hands of a corrupt Nigerian government in 1995 led to an international outcry. See 'Symbolic funeral for Saro-Wiwa' 25 Apr 2000, BBC News online: <http://news.bbc.co.uk/hi/english/world/africa/newsid_725000/725009.stm>.

rights can only be exercised by the author, whether or not he is the owner of copyright. Through moral rights doctrine, copyright law also achieves a non-commercial, purely legal method of valuing creativity. It may even protect the non-commercial aspects of creative expression at the cost of economic losses to persons other than the author.[41] It is important to recognise that copyright has historically developed as an instrument of both commercial and cultural policy; it reflects a certain understanding of culture and a particular means of recognising and protecting its value.[42]

The idea of authorship, and its protection through copyright and moral rights, has a number of legal consequences. It assures the social status of the creative arts; it allows authors to earn a livelihood from their work; it creates incentives for at least certain kinds of creative activity, and supports cultural industries such as publishing, broadcasting, translation, and film. By protecting authorship, copyright potentially supports democratic institutions and values. However, its success in doing so depends on our understanding of copyright's content, the status of copyright within the hierarchy of domestic laws, and the development of a viable balance between international and domestic standards. Realising the contribution of copyright to democratisation in post-socialist societies is a matter of considering and reconciling diverse interests and issues among individuals, communities, the public, and the state. In the absence of policy-minded investigation, it is unlikely that post-socialist reforms will succeed in achieving this delicate balance.

---

[41]   Indeed, it is important to note that moral rights, which protect authors' personal interests in their work, may have serious economic implications. This is one of the main reasons why common-law countries, which have traditionally preferred to leave authors' personal interests to the more informal mechanisms of tort law, have been reluctant to adopt moral rights legislation. The United States is a case in point: a powerful film industry lobby blocked the adoption of comprehensive moral rights legislation when the US joined the Berne Convention in 1989. For a discussion of the ambiguous American position on moral rights, see D Nimmer, 'Conventional Copyright: A Morality Play' (1992) 3 Ent L Rev 94. Moral rights issues in Britain are considered in a similar light by WR Cornish, 'Moral Rights under the 1988 Act' (1989) 11:12 EIPR 449, 449.

[42]   A different balance between the commercial and cultural aspects of copyright is achieved in different legal systems, though they invariably coexist. For example, moral rights have traditionally been emphasised in the civil-law systems of continental Europe, to the extent that they may be said to provide a conceptual foundation for copyright protection in these countries. To some extent, this is reflected even in the terminology for copyright – *droit d'auteur* in France, and *Urheberrecht* in Germany. See T Dreier 'Authorship and New Technologies from the Viewpoints of Civil Law Traditions' (1995) 26:6 IIC 989, 991–3, who points to the close connection between moral rights and authorship, especially in France.

5. CONCLUSION

It would be difficult to exaggerate the complexity and scope of law reform in post-socialist countries. Intellectual property law is an integral part of this comprehensive process of reform. Information, knowledge, and expression of all kinds were infused with a special significance in the authoritarian regimes of the region, where political domination was intimately connected with the manipulation of ideas. Intellectual property rights after socialism should reflect the democratisation of knowledge in these newly democratic and developing societies.

Copyright law is among the most important means of regulating expression in modern societies. Its main purpose is commercial; but, especially through the protection of moral rights, copyright also transcends commercial concerns and becomes deeply implicated in culture and human rights. Copyright has a special contribution to make to legal modernisation and democratisation, by offering much-needed support to the ideals of creative expression and authorship. However, the realisation of this potential will depend on a sophisticated, well-informed, and long-term commitment to navigating the challenges of law reform in the largely uncharted waters of the transition.

12. Lessons from negotiating an amendment to the TRIPS Agreement: Compulsory licensing and access to medicines

Duncan Matthews*

INTRODUCTION

The announcement, on 6 December 2005, that the World Trade Organisation (WTO) Members had reached agreement on a permanent amendment to the Agreement on Trade Related Aspects of Intellectual Property Rights (the TRIPS Agreement) to allow WTO Members to issue compulsory licences to export generic versions of patented medicines to countries with insufficient or no manufacturing capacity in the pharmaceutical sector, marked the latest phase in a long process of negotiations on access to medicines that began with the Doha Declaration on the TRIPS Agreement and Public Health of 14 November 2001[1] and also included the 30 August 2003 WTO Decision on the Implementation of Paragraph 6 of the Doha Declaration on the TRIPS Agreement and Public Health.[2] The agreement of 6 December 2005 on the

* Reader, Intellectual Property Research Institute, Centre for Commercial Law Studies, Queen Mary, University of London. Sections of this chapter draw on the following articles by the author: Matthews, D. (2004) 'WTO Decision on Implementation of Paragraph 6 of the Doha Declaration on the TRIPS Agreement and Public Health: A Solution to the Access to Essential Medicines Problem?', *Journal of International Economic Law*, 7(1): 73-106; Matthews, D. (2006) 'From the 30 August 2003 WTO Decision to the 6 December 2005 Agreement on an Amendment to TRIPS: Improving Access to Medicines in Developing Countries?', *Intellectual Property Quarterly*, 2: 91–130.

[1]   *Declaration on the TRIPS Agreement and Public Health*, WT/MIN(01)DEC/2, 20 November 2001, available at: http://www.wto.org/english/thewto_e/minist_e/min01_e/mindecl_trips_e.htm.

[2]   *Implementation of Paragraph 6 of the Doha Declaration on the TRIPS Agreement and Public Health – Decision of 30 August 2003*, WT/L/540, 1 September 2003, available at: http://www.wto.org/english/tratop_e/trips_e/implem_para6_e.htm.

first ever amendment to the TRIPS Agreement will now be circulated to WTO Members for formal adoption. A deadline of 1 December 2007 has been set for WTO Members to accept the permanent amendment and, for the amendment to be put into effect, at least two thirds of WTO Members must formally adopt it.

This chapter reviews negotiations leading to this unprecedented agreement on an amendment to TRIPS and suggests that there are strong similarities, but also important differences, between these negotiations and the earlier multilateral trade talks that resulted in the original text of the TRIPS Agreement.

COMPULSORY LICENSING, ACCESS TO MEDICINES AND THE TRIPS AGREEMENT

Negotiations leading to an agreement to amend TRIPS centred on Article 31 of the TRIPS Agreement, which concerns the use of compulsory licences. A compulsory licence is a licence granted by the competent national authority to allow a third party to manufacture a patented product without the authorisation of the right holder. In the context of the TRIPS Agreement and public health, compulsory licensing may be used to address the issue of access to patented medicines by allowing WTO Member countries to produce generic drugs that are more affordable than patented proprietary medicines. Article 31 sets out conditions that must be satisfied before a compulsory licence can be awarded.[3] These conditions include, under Article 31(b), a requirement that a reasonable period of time is allowed to negotiate a licence with the right holder on the basis of reasonable commercial terms, but this requirement of prior negotiation and adequate remuneration[4] can be waived in the event of a national emergency or other circumstances of extreme urgency. So, on the face of it, compulsory licences could be granted by a developing country without prior negotiation with the holder of rights to key pharmaceutical patents in the case of a public health crisis of epidemic proportions.

However, under Article 31(f), generic drugs produced under a compulsory licence must be 'predominantly' for domestic use.[5] This has the practical

---

[3] For a negotiating history of Article 31 of the TRIPS Agreement see Gold, E.R. and Lam, D.K. (2003) 'Balancing Trade in Patents: Public Non-Commercial Use and Compulsory Licensing', *Journal of International Economic Law*, 6, 1: 5–31.

[4] For a theoretical and empirical analysis of royalties set under compulsory licences see Scherer, F.M. and Watal, J. (2002) 'Post-TRIPS Options for Access to Patented Medicines in Developing Nations', *Journal of International Economic Law*, 5: 913.

[5] For a discussion of the meaning of 'predominantly' within the context of

effect of preventing exports of generic drugs to countries that do not have significant pharmaceutical industries themselves.[6] Only about a dozen developing countries, among them China, India, Brazil, Argentina and South Africa, have the level of manufacturing capacity capable of producing significant quantities of off-patent generic drugs. For countries with insufficient manufacturing capacity, the only realistic sourcing mechanism is importation. In the past, developing countries were able to buy generic drugs from a few producers in countries such as India, but they have been unable to do so since 1 January 2005, when transitional arrangements under Article 65(4) of the TRIPS Agreement expired and provisions under Article 27(1) requiring patent rights to be enjoyable without discrimination as to place of invention, field of technology and whether products are imported or locally produced, were extended to all except a few least-developed nations.

ORIGINS OF THE ACCESS TO MEDICINES DEBATE AT THE WTO

The potential impact of the TRIPS Agreement on access to affordable medicines was brought sharply into focus in March 2001, when 39 global pharmaceutical companies, represented by the Pharmaceutical Manufacturers Association of South Africa, objected to provisions of the South African Medicines Act that gave the Health Minister the power to grant compulsory licences for patented pharmaceutical products when public health was at stake. The legal action threatened by the Pharmaceutical Manufacturers Association of South Africa concerned Article 10 of the South African Medicines and Related Substances Control Amendment Act 1997, which added Section 15c to the 1965 Medicines and Related Substances Control Act, in doing so allowing the Health Minister to abrogate patents, issue compulsory licences and allow parallel imports of pharmaceutical products in order to increase availability and lower the cost of medicines.[7]

The Pharmaceutical Manufacturers Association of South Africa claimed that these powers lacked the detailed provisions required by Article 31 of the TRIPS Agreement, particularly the requirement that compulsory licensing be granted only on a non-exclusive and non-assignable basis, with the possibility

---

Article 31(f), see Abbott, F.M. (2001) 'The TRIPS Agreement, Access to Medicines and the WTO Doha Ministerial Conference', *Quaker United Nations Office – Geneva, Occasional Paper 7*, at 26.

    [6]   Ibid. at 13.

    [7]   Ostergard, R.L. (1999) 'The Political Economy of the South Africa-United States Patent Dispute', *Journal of World Intellectual Property*, 2, 6: 875–88 at 875.

of judicial review and with adequate remuneration for the patent holder.[8] The case proved particularly emotive because access to anti-retroviral drugs for the treatment of HIV/AIDS, such as AZT (Zidovudine), was constrained in South Africa by the prohibitively high price of those medicines. The Pharmaceutical Manufacturers Association of South Africa ultimately abandoned the threat of court action in the face of intense public pressure and the prospect of former South African President Nelson Mandela taking the witness stand to testify against them. But by then the case had brought the access to medicines and public health debate to the fore on a global scale.

THE DOHA DECLARATION ON THE TRIPS AGREEMENT AND PUBLIC HEALTH

In response to concerns about higher prices for patented drugs and the problems created by the requirement that compulsory licences issued in accordance with Article 31 should be predominantly for domestic use, at the Fourth Ministerial Conference in Doha, 9–14 November 2001, WTO Members adopted a Declaration on the TRIPS Agreement and Public Health.[9] The Doha Declaration recognised the gravity of the public health problems afflicting many developing and least-developed countries, especially those resulting from HIV/AIDS, tuberculosis, malaria and other epidemics. It stressed the need for the TRIPS Agreement to be part of a wider national and international action to address these problems. It reaffirmed that the TRIPS Agreement does not and should not prevent measures to protect public health and affirmed that the TRIPS Agreement should be interpreted and implemented in a manner supportive of WTO Members' right to protect public health and, in particular, to promote access to medicines for all.

The Declaration recognised the flexibilities contained in the TRIPS Agreement with respect to the right to grant compulsory licences and the freedom to determine the grounds upon which such licences are granted; the right of each Member to determine what constitutes a 'national emergency' or other circumstances of extreme emergency, it being understood that public health crises can represent a national emergency or other circumstances of extreme emergency; and the effect of provisions of the TRIPS Agreement that allow each Member freedom to establish its own regime for exhaustion of intellectual property rights. Crucially, in recognition of the fact that the compulsory

---

[8]   Wooldridge, F. (2000) 'Affordable Medicines – TRIPS and United States Policies', *Intellectual Property Quarterly*, 4, 1: 103–11 at 108.

[9]   *Declaration on the TRIPS Agreement and Public Health*, above, n 1.

licensing provisions of the TRIPS Agreement are of little practical use to countries with little or no pharmaceutical manufacturing capabilities, Paragraph 6 of the Doha Declaration then went on to explicitly recognise that WTO Members with insufficient or no manufacturing capacities in the pharmaceutical sector could face difficulties in making effective use of compulsory licensing under the TRIPS Agreement and set a deadline of the end of 2002 to find an expeditious solution to this problem. Overall, then, the text of the Doha Declaration was interpretive in nature, designed to assist with the imprecise provisions of Article 31 of the TRIPS Agreement.[10]

The Paragraph 6 Negotiations

In an attempt to resolve the issues identified in Paragraph 6 of the Doha Declaration, negotiations between WTO Members, meeting within the TRIPS Council, took place throughout 2002 and early 2003. As during the earlier negotiations on the TRIPS Agreement, the US and European Communities (EC) took the lead. However, unlike the original TRIPS negotiations, the Paragraph 6 process was also marked by a far greater degree of involvement on the part of Non-Governmental Organisations (NGOs), acting in support of the developing country cause.[11]

Such organisations included Consumer Project on Technology (CPTech), a US-based NGO focusing on information technologies, intellectual property and research and development, and Health Action International (HAI), a global network of health, development, consumer and other public interest groups, based in the Netherlands. CPTech and HAI have been active in the debate surrounding patents, access to medicines and public health since the mid-1990s. The Quaker UN Office has also played a key role through the work of its consultant Geoff Tansey and the influential report it commissioned from Frederick Abbott in the run-up to the Doha Ministerial Meeting,[12] which itself reflected the comments of James Love and Ellen t'Hoen of NGOs CPTech and MSF respectively, together with academics Carlos Correa and Jerome Reichman. Oxfam was also active through briefing papers such as the 2002 publication *TRIPS and Public Health: The Next Battle*.[13] This involvement of

---

[10]   Sykes, A.O. (2002) 'TRIPS, Pharmaceuticals, Developing Countries, and the Doha "Solution"', *John M. Olin Law and Economics Working Paper No. 140* at 9.

[11]   See Sell, S.K. (2002) 'TRIPS and the Access to Medicines Campaign', paper prepared for 'Access to Medicines for the Developing World: International Facilitation or Hindrance?' Conference sponsored by the University of Wisconsin Law School, Madison, Wisconsin, 9–10 March 2002 at 15.

[12]   Abbott, above n 5.

[13]   Available at: http://www.oxfam.org.uk/policy/papers/15trips/15trips.html.

NGOs and academic experts was crucial in two respects. First, it highlighted the relationship between TRIPS and public health in the public's mind and, second, it acted as a support mechanism for developing country delegates seeking to influence the negotiating process during the Paragraph 6 negotiations. Nevertheless, despite the increased engagement of NGOs, the EC and the US continued to play an influential role as negotiations progressed.

Scope of exemptions from Article 31(f)

On 5–6 November 2002 the EC, having reportedly lobbied for support from China, Brazil and India, presented compromise proposals in the run-up to the Sydney WTO Mini-Ministerial Meeting that took place on 14–15 November 2002. The EC proposed that any solution which allowed an exemption to existing TRIPS rules under Article 31(f) that require generic drugs produced under a compulsory licence to be 'predominantly' for domestic use should be limited to the production of medicines 'where the gravity of public health problems afflict developing and least-developed countries, especially those resulting from HIV/AIDS, tuberculosis, malaria and other epidemics'. Product coverage would include patented pharmaceuticals and diagnostic test kits needed to address public health problems.

The US adopted a more restrictive approach. In late 2002, Assistant United States Trade Representative (USTR) for Africa, Rosa Whitaker, wrote to all African countries, urging them to support the US position.[14] The Whitaker letter insisted that an exemption be limited to HIV/AIDS, tuberculosis and malaria with no scope for 'other epidemics' to be included. The US view was that broadening the exemption to cover any 'other epidemics', in keeping with the wording of the Doha Declaration, would risk the inclusion of 'lifestyle' illnesses such as obesity or the common cold that should not be excluded from the compulsory licensing provisions of the TRIPS Agreement. NGOs criticised the US approach on the grounds that half of the victims of non-communicable diseases (cardiovascular diseases, cancer, diabetes, chronic respiratory diseases etc.) are from the developing world, where access to expensive patented pharmaceutical products remains limited. The Whitaker letter also argued against allowing the full range of health care products (including diagnostic kits) to fall within a Paragraph 6 solution, as the EC suggested, on grounds that this would divert attention from access to medicines.

Beneficiary countries

The EC and US both took the view that countries benefiting from the exception should be limited to least-developed countries and nations classified by

---

[14]   See *The Washington Post*, 'Drugs for the Poor', 14 November 2002, p. A32.

the World Bank as low-income developing countries. High-income developing countries[15] would be able to benefit from the exemption only if the low-cost medicines were needed to address situations of 'national emergency or extreme urgency'. Eligible countries would also have to show that they have no or insufficient manufacturing capacity in the drugs sector (i.e. no plants manufacturing active ingredients) and that they would not be able to create such capacities in the short term. NGOs criticised the proposal to restrict the exemption to low-income economies on grounds that this condition denied equal rights of access to generic medicines for at least 72 developing countries that could not, with the probable exception of China, produce these generic versions of the new drugs for themselves, nor do so at a reasonable price.

Exporting countries
Another major sticking point arose over which countries should be allowed to qualify as exporters of low-cost essential medicines. While the EC proposed that all WTO Members should qualify, in the Whitaker letter the US suggested limiting exporters under the exemption to least-developed and developing countries. Permitting developed countries to be exporters would, in the opinion of the US, hinder technology transfer and pharmaceutical company investment in the developing world. This US proposal was criticised by NGOs as having the effect of reducing the number of potential suppliers of generic medicines that would be able to produce low-cost medicines. The main problem with this solution was that the company supplying cheap generic drugs would have to ask the government of its own country to override the relevant patent before any export could take place.[16] This would make the importing country dependent on the political will of another government and increase the administrative burden.

---

[15]   According to the World Bank classification of high-income countries among non-OECD economies are: Brunei, French Polynesia, Guam, Hong Kong China, Macao China, New Caledonia, N. Mariana Islands, Singapore and Taiwan, Slovenia, Andorra, Channel Islands, Cyprus, Faroe Islands, Greenland, Liechtenstein, Monaco, Israel, Kuwait, Qatar, United Arab Emirates, Aruba, Bahamas, Bermuda, Cayman Islands, Netherlands Antilles, and Virgin Islands.

[16]   Abbott, above n 5 at 28, suggested overcoming the problems created by Article 31(f) by creating 'streamlined parallel compulsory licensing arrangements' under which a country of export might choose to recognise the grant of a compulsory licence issued by an importing country by issuing a parallel grant of a compulsory licence in the country of export, but this has the drawback that the exporting country faces the limitation imposed by Article 31(f) requiring compulsory licences to be predominantly for the supply of the domestic market authorising such use.

Labelling, marking and packaging

The US was particularly concerned that generic medicines produced under an exemption could be diverted to developed country markets and sold illicitly for huge profits. In order to minimise the re-direction of low-cost medicines into developed country markets, the EC proposed that safeguards need to be put in place, with producers and importers taking necessary measures to prevent trade diversion, including making medicines produced under the exemption clearly distinguishable through labelling, marking and packaging.

Interim measures

Although WTO Members originally agreed at Doha that an agreement on access to medicines should be achieved by the end of 2002 at the latest, as it became clear that this deadline would not be met, the EC and US both proposed interim measures. In the absence of a permanent solution, the EC proposed that WTO Members immediately agree to waive the compulsory licensing rules under TRIPS, or alternatively accept a moratorium on challenges to the exemption scheme. Members would then agree on an amendment to the TRIPS Agreement, formally recognising the scheme, by the time the Doha Round of trade negotiations were due to end in January 2005. The US also advocated a temporary solution in the form of a short-term moratorium or waiver until the end of the Doha Round, at which time a permanent solution would be sought.

Developing country position

Developing countries opposed the suggestion that discussions on access to essential medicines could drag on for the duration of the Doha Round, negotiations becoming enmeshed within wider trade discussions on issues such as agriculture and textiles, with trade-offs and compromise deals the likely outcome.

The EC and US proposals that would have prevented high-income developing countries from benefiting from the new rules were also criticised by developing countries, including Brazil, India, South Africa, Kenya, Thailand, China and Egypt. These countries argued that proposals by the developed nations amounted to an attempt to differentiate among the potential beneficiary countries to an extent not agreed upon by Paragraph 6 of the Doha Declaration, which simply refers to countries with 'insufficient or no manufacturing capacities'. The developing countries argued that all WTO Members should be allowed to judge for themselves whether they meet these criteria.

The African Group of developing countries elaborated on this position, stating that differentiating between developing countries may not have a good basis in the Doha Declaration because in that text reference was made to all developing country Members as a category. But the African Group signalled flexibility on possible safeguards imposed on the country making the generic drug. They proposed that safeguards could include a requirement to export all of the production to the country issuing the licence and to require special labelling of the drug. But they argued that proposals to require special colouring and shaping of pills might increase production costs and should be avoided.

Chairman's draft

In the closing months of 2002, the debate became stymied by disagreement over the issue of which illnesses and medicines should be covered by an exception, which countries should be allowed to benefit from the exception, which countries should be allowed to produce generic equivalents of patented medicines for export, and whether the TRIPS Agreement should be formally amended.

Ambassador Eduardo Perez Motta, Chairman of the TRIPS Council, attempted to achieve progress with a compromise text on 16 December 2002,[17] under which the TRIPS Agreement would be amended so that any country with manufacturing capacities could export, while developing countries without manufacturing capacities in the pharmaceutical sector would be allowed to benefit from this system in the face of public health problems. Countries with sufficient capacity and/or financial means would not be able to use the exemption system, since this would only divert resources away from those countries that needed it most. Developed and high-income developing countries would opt out from the system entirely, while the disease scope would reflect the wording of the Doha Declaration.

Under the Chairman's draft, countries importing generic pharmaceutical products and using the Paragraph 6 mechanism would be expected to take measures to prevent re-exportation, provided such measures were 'reasonable', 'within their means' and 'proportionate' to their administrative capacities and the risk of trade diversion. Exporting countries would be obliged to require the beneficiary company of the compulsory licence (1) to export their entire production to the countries needed and (2) to clearly identify the products through labelling or marking and through special colouring or shaping of the products themselves.

At the informal TRIPS Council meeting on 17 December 2002, Ambassador Motta made it clear that the US had little option but to accept or

---

17 'Main Elements of the Chair's 16 December 2002 Draft Compromise Decision (Perez Motta Text)', European Commission (Trade and Development) Press Release, 9 January 2003, available at: http://europa.eu.int/comm/trade/csc/memo090103_en.htm.

reject the compromise text contained in the Chairman's draft.[18] Developing countries, including India, Brazil and Kenya, signalled a willingness to accept the Chairman's draft, much to the dismay of some NGOs, provided there was no move to further limit the scope of diseases.[19] But when the TRIPS Council met formally on 20 December 2002, the effective deadline for the conclusion of Paragraph 6 negotiations, there was deadlock. The US blocked an agreement on grounds that the scope of coverage in the Chairman's draft was too broad and went beyond the focus of HIV/AIDS, tuberculosis and malaria. The US felt that the compromise text could be interpreted as meaning that drug patents could be ignored on treatments for a wide range of diseases.[20] Negotiations were suspended and Ambassador Motta asked WTO Members to resume negotiations and report to the next meeting of the TRIPS Council, which took place on 10 February 2003.

EC compromise text

In the interim, on 9 January 2003, the EC launched a new initiative to break the deadlock.[21] The EC proposal was to remove WTO constraints requiring compulsory licences to be 'predominantly' for domestic supply in the case of medicines to combat a limited list of 22 infectious diseases (including tuberculosis, malaria and HIV/AIDS) that are generally recognised by health experts to have the most damaging impact on developing countries. For any health concern not explicitly covered by the initial list, WTO Members wishing to import medicines under compulsory licence terms would be encouraged to seek World Health Organisation (WHO) advice before doing so. Involving the WHO, with its public health expertise, was seen as a way of ensuring that the Doha Declaration could be used in good faith.

The TRIPS Council on 10 February 2003 failed to take the issue much further, the meeting lasting only two hours and ending in deadlock with no party willing to relinquish its key demands. At the next TRIPS Council meet-

---

[18] 'US Faces Touch Choice', *BNA WTO Reporter*, 18 December 2002: http://pubs.bna.com/ip/BNA/wto.nsf/is/A0A6G2B6C2.

[19] 'US Sticks to Hard Line on TRIPS, as Supachai Tries to Broker Deal', *Inside US Trade*, 20 December 2002.

[20] 'Consensus on TRIPS Unravels as US Blocks Deal on Scope of Diseases' *Inside US Trade*, 3 January 2002; see also 'US Wrecks Cheap Drugs Deal: Cheney's Intervention Blocks Pact to Help Poor Countries After Pharmaceutical Firms Lobby White House', The *Guardian*, 21 December 2002: http://www.guardian.co.uk/international/story/0,3604,864071,00.html.

[21] 'EU Seeks to Break the Current Deadlock on WTO Access to Medicines: A Multilateral Solution is Needed', European Commission (Trade and Development) Press Release, 9 January 2003, available at: http://europa.eu.int/comm/trade/csc/pr090103_en.htm.

ing on 4–5 June 2003, attempts were made to break the deadlock in the form of Communications submitted by the European Communities and their Member States and by the African, Caribbean and Pacific (ACP) states. The EC Communication stressed that full advantage should be taken of the available expertise on health matters, particularly from the WHO, in relation to implementing the Doha Declaration, and made clear that the principles of the Doha Declaration should be carried through to issues other than compulsory licensing or parallel imports, such as 'exceptions to exclusive rights or other policy options'.[22] This latter statement left open the possibility of future EC support for an Article 30 based solution to the Paragraph 6 problem in the future. The ACP Communication expressed disappointment at the failure to reach agreement on the 16 December 2002 Motta text and highlighted the need for technical assistance, in particular from the World Intellectual Property Organisation (WIPO), the WTO and the WHO.[23] The June TRIPS Council meeting ended without any substantial progress on a solution. However, following the June meeting, reports began to appear that the United States was prepared to abandon its earlier insistence that a Paragraph 6 solution cover only specific diseases (namely HIV/AIDS, tuberculosis and malaria), shifting its focus from disease coverage to limitations on eligibility aimed at low-income developing countries and least-developed nations, together with safeguards against the risk of commercial export of low-cost medicines into other markets.[24] This shift in the position of the US was crucial in securing agreement on a Decision of the WTO General Council, designed to resolve the issue, at the end of August 2003.

The 30 August 2003 Decision

The final breakthrough was achieved when Ambassador Motta's successor as Chairman of the TRIPS Council, Vanu Gopala Menon of Singapore, met with a small group of WTO Members to negotiate a solution to Paragraph 6. This group, comprising the United States, Kenya, Brazil, South Africa and India, succeeded in producing a draft Decision on 21 August 2003, followed by a

---

[22]   *The Implementation of the Doha Declaration on the TRIPS Agreement and Public Health*, Communication from the European Communities and their Member States, IP/C/W/402, 24 June 2003.

[23]   *Paragraph 6 of the Doha Declaration on the TRIPS Agreement and Public Health*, Communication from the African, Caribbean and Pacific Group of States (ACP), IP/C/W/401, 28 May 2003.

[24]   'Industry to Unveil Cheap Drugs Plan', Guy de Jonguières, *Financial Times*, 23 June 2003; 'US Rumoured to Consider Change in Tactic on TRIPS and Health', *Bridges Weekly Trade Digest*, 3 July 2003, http://www.ictsd.org/weekly/03-07-03/story4.htm.

revised draft, almost identical to the original version, on 26 August. Following approval by the TRIPS Council on 28 August, the General Council of the WTO was then presented with a final draft of the Decision on implementation of paragraph 6 of the Doha Declaration, which it adopted on 30 August 2003.[25]

The Decision provides for a temporary waiver of Members' obligations under Article 31(f) of the TRIPS Agreement, until such time as Article 31(f) is amended, which we now know will occur as soon as the 6 December 2005 agreement takes effect,[26] which is due to be by the deadline of 1 December 2007. Pharmaceutical products covered by the Decision include any patented product, or product manufactured through a patented process, of the pharmaceutical sector needed to address public health problems as recognised by Paragraph 1 of the Doha Declaration. This explicitly includes active ingredients necessary for their manufacture and diagnostic kits needed for their use.

Countries eligible to import under the agreement include any least-developed WTO Member and any other Member that has notified the TRIPS Council of its intention to use the system as an importer, it being understood that a Member may notify at any time that it will use the system in whole or in a limited way, for example only in the case of a national emergency or other circumstances of extreme urgency or in cases of public non-commercial use. A number of Members (Hong Kong China, Israel, Kuwait, Macao China, Mexico, Qatar, Singapore, Chinese Taipei, Turkey and the United Arab Emirates) have stated that, if they use the system, it will only be in situations of national emergency or other circumstances of extreme urgency (this statement carrying with it the significant implication that other Members may use the system more liberally in circumstances other than in situations of national emergency or other circumstances of extreme urgency). Furthermore, as regards applicant states for European Union membership, until their accession the Czech Republic, Cyprus, Estonia, Hungary, Latvia, Lithuania, Malta, Poland, the Slovak Republic and Slovenia had all agreed that they would only use the system as importers in situations of national emergency or other circumstances of extreme urgency and, upon their accession to the EC, would opt out of using the system as importers altogether. In addition, footnote 3 to Paragraph 1(b) of the Decision carries a list of developed country Members that will from the outset opt out of using the system as importers entirely.[27] As

---

[25]   'Cheap Drugs Deal Agreed as US Lifts Veto', Frances Williams, *Financial Times*, 1 September 2003, 8.

[26]   *Implementation of Paragraph 6 of the Doha Declaration on the TRIPS Agreement and Public Health*, above n 2.

[27]   Australia, Austria, Belgium, Canada, Denmark, Finland, France, Germany, Greece, Iceland, Ireland, Italy, Japan, Luxembourg, the Netherlands, New Zealand,

regards countries allowed to sanction the manufacture and export of low-cost essential medicines under the system, the Decision makes it clear that any Member may use the system set out in the Decision to produce pharmaceutical products for, and export them to, an eligible importing country.

The Decision then goes on to set out a number of safeguards designed to ensure that cheap drugs manufactured under compulsory licensing arrangements and intended for developing countries are not diverted to developed country markets. These anti-diversion measures require that medicines made available under the scheme be a different shape and colour from those sold for profit in developed country markets, while the TRIPS Council will review periodically whether the licensing arrangements are being abused.

A separate statement by WTO General Council Chairman, Carlos Pérez del Castillo, described Members' 'shared understanding' that the Decision will be interpreted and implemented on a 'good faith' basis in order to deal with public health problems and not for industrial or commercial policy objectives, and that issues such as preventing the medicines getting into the wrong hands are important.[28] It also stresses that Members recognise that the purpose of the Decision would be defeated if products supplied under its arrangements were diverted from markets for which they are intended and that all reasonable measures should be taken to prevent such diversion, such as special packaging and/or colouring or shaping of medicines and that such measures should not have a significant impact on price. Examples of 'best practice', based on existing anti-trade diversion detection measures already taken by donor pharmaceutical companies, are appended to the statement. The statement then goes on to stress the role of the TRIPS Council in settling disputes arising from these arrangements expeditiously and amicably, with the TRIPS Council explicitly given a new role in reviewing notifications made under the system and all information gathered on implementation of the Decision included in the TRIPS Council annual review of the Decision.

However, concerns remained that the added costs associated with altering packaging, pill size and colour will have a detrimental effect on the availability of essential medicines in developing countries, reducing the incentives for generic drug companies, which will find it less cost-efficient to produce identifiable pills, while there are also concerns that the administrative burden associated with the procedural arrangements for notifying the WTO of a decision

---

Norway, Portugal, Spain, Sweden, Switzerland, the United Kingdom and the United States of America.

[28]   The General Council Chairperson's statement on implementation of paragraph 6 of the Doha Declaration on the TRIPS Agreement and public health, 30 August 2003, http://www.wto.org/english/news_e/news03_e/trips_stat_28aug03_e.htm.

to use the mechanism and undergo TRIPS Council scrutiny will result in lengthy delays and prove costly for developing country governments.

There were also concerns that the Decision, which was warmly welcomed by the Office of the United States Trade Representative,[29] the European Communities,[30] the European Federation of Pharmaceutical Industries and Associations (EFPIA)[31] and the Pharmaceutical Research and Manufacturers of America (PhRMA),[32] set out burdensome procedural arrangements. The arrangements required that the importing country first attempt to obtain a voluntary licence from the patent holder on reasonable commercial terms for a reasonable period. If this is not possible, the importing country must then assess its generic industry's capacity to produce the medicine locally and, if capacity is deemed insufficient, then notify the WTO with a detailed justification of its decision. The importing country must then notify a potential importer, which must in turn seek a voluntary licence and, failing that, must seek a compulsory licence from its own government on a single-country basis, with compensation payable on standards of reasonableness in the importing country. Conversely, there are still some lingering concerns for individual companies operating in the proprietary pharmaceutical industry that some high- and middle-income developing countries will not opt out from the arrangements.

In practice, no notifications have been made that WTO Members have used the system either as an importer or as an exporter under the 30 August procedure.[33] Perhaps one reason that the system envisaged by the 30 August Decision has never been used is that it has been criticised, particularly by NGOs, as being overly complex and bureaucratic. However, the Decision did mark a step back from the more restrictive interpretation of a Paragraph 6 solution advocated by the EC and US in earlier negotiations. The arrangements

---

[29]   'Statement of US Trade Representative Robert B. Zoellick Following Agreement in WTO on Access to Medicines', 30 August 2003, http://www.ustr.gov/releases/2003/08/2003-08-30-rbz-statement.htm.

[30]   'Access to Essential Medicines: EU Strongly Welcomes WTO Deal on Generic Medicines', 30 August 2003, http://europa.eu.int/comm/trade/issues/global/medicine/medic010903_en.htm.

[31]   'EFPIA Statement on Compulsory License for Export ("Paragraph 6" of Doha Declaration on TRIPS and Public Health)', 30 August 2003, http://www.efpia.org/3_press/20030830.htm.

[32]   'Statement from Shannon Herzfeld, PhRMA's Senior Vice President, International Affairs in relation to successful conclusion of the negotiations on TRIPS and Public Health', 30 August 2003, http://www.phrma.org/mediaroom/press/releases/30.08.2003.841.cfm.

[33]   TRIPS and public health: WTO dedicated website for notifications, available at: http://www.wto.org/english/tratop_e/trips_e/public_health_e.htm.

outlined in the final text of the Decision do not limit the scope of diseases, nor as a general rule require a national emergency such as an epidemic to be identified before compulsory licences can be issued since public health problems can now routinely be dealt with under the agreed arrangements.

The final paragraph of the WTO Decision set out an important step that must be taken before the WTO Decision becomes a permanent solution to the compulsory licensing and manufacturing capacity problem, namely the amendment of the TRIPS Agreement in accordance with Paragraph 11 of the Decision of 30 August 2003.[34]

THE PARAGRAPH 11 NEGOTIATIONS

The 'permanent solution' mandated by Paragraph 11 of the WTO Decision required that WTO Members agree to an amendment to the TRIPS Agreement, as a follow-up to the temporary waivers of Article 31(f) and Article 31(h) of the TRIPS Agreement. It directed the TRIPS Council to prepare an amendment which 'will be based, where appropriate, on this Decision' and it is this wording that has led to problems in securing a permanent deal.[35] In addition Paragraph 11 of the Decision makes it clear that the TRIPS amendment will not become part of the wider Doha Round negotiations referred to in Paragraph 45 of the Ministerial Declaration.[36]

Despite claims that the WTO Decision was achieved largely through the efforts of major developing countries, specifically Brazil, India, Kenya and South Africa, as well as the United States,[37] during Paragraph 11 negotiations the African Group continued to view the provisions of the WTO Decision as only an interim solution.[38]

---

[34]   'This Decision, including the waivers granted in it, shall terminate for each Member on the date on which an amendment to the TRIPS Agreement replacing its provisions takes effect for that Member. The TRIPS Council shall initiate by the end of 2003 work on the preparation of such an amendment with a view to its adoption within six months, on the understanding that the amendment will be based, where appropriate, on this Decision and on the further understanding that it will not be part of the negotiations referred to in paragraph 45 of the Doha Ministerial Declaration (WT/MIN(01)/DEC/1).'

[35]   See also Sisule, F. Musungu (2004) 'Intellectual Property and Public Health: Will it be Peace or War?', *Journal of World Intellectual Property*, 7(2): 249 at 251.

[36]   *Declaration on the TRIPS Agreement and Public Health*, above n 1.

[37]   Noehrenberg, Eric (2004) 'Intellectual Property and Public Health. Will it be Peace or War?', *Journal of World Intellectual Property*, 7(2): 253 at 253.

[38]   See also South North Development Monitor (SUNS), 'Heated Discussions as TRIPS and Health Deadline is Missed', 5772, 4 April 2005, posted on ip-health-admin@lists.essential.org.

Until 6 December 2005, Paragraph 11 negotiations on a permanent amendment to TRIPS remained deadlocked. On the face of it, there were strong incentives to reach agreement on a permanent solution. While the Paragraph 11 negotiations remained stalled, there was a risk that the limited resources of developing country and NGO negotiators would remain focused on this issue, to the detriment of other policy areas. In addition, quick implementation of the Decision was considered desirable because it would reveal problems with the system that could themselves provide developing countries with grounds for wholesale renegotiation of the system set out in the Decision.

Notwithstanding these imperatives, the reality was that attempts to agree on a permanent amendment at the TRIPS Council meeting on 31 March 2005 ended without agreement and highlighted sharp differences between developing and developed countries' viewpoints, with the former using the negotiations as an opportunity to reflect preferred developing country interpretations of the WTO Decision and the latter refusing to deviate from the precise wording agreed on 30 August 2003.[39]

The Status of the Chairman's Statement in a TRIPS Amendment

In many respects it is the Chairman's Statement that has proved the sticking point in finalising the amendment. It will be recalled that the Statement was intended to appease WTO Members that were concerned that the 30 August Decision might be abused (for instance, for commercial purposes instead of for public health emergencies) and undermine patent protection. The Chairman's Statement therefore highlights the limitations of the provision and restates the list of developed countries that agreed not to opt out of using the system as importers, and those who agreed to use it for 'extreme urgency'. It will also be recalled that the Statement includes best practices used by business to minimise diversion of cheaper products. In terms of the future role of the Chairman's Statement, the options appeared to be: (i) leave the Chairman's Statement out of the permanent amendment; (ii) incorporate the Chairman's Statement into the TRIPS Agreement as interpretive text, perhaps as a footnote or appendix to the TRIPS Agreement itself; or (iii) fully incorporate the Chairman's Statement as part of the permanent amendment to the TRIPS Agreement.[40]

At the TRIPS Council meeting on 31 March 2005, WTO Members consid-

---

[39] Minutes of TRIPS Council Meeting held on 8–9 and 31 March 2005, IP/C/M/47, 3 June 2005.
[40] According to South Centre/Centre for International Environmental Law (CIEL) IP Quarterly Update: Second Quarter 2005, at 10. Available at: http://www.southcentre.org/info/sccielipquarterly/index.htm .

ered three communications: the first was from the delegation of Rwanda on behalf of the African Group providing arguments to support the African Group proposal on the implementation of Paragraph 11 of the Decision;[41] the second was from the delegation of Barbados on behalf of the Group of Commonwealth Developing Countries containing a report on the workshop on the WTO Decision that was organised by the Commonwealth Secretariat;[42] and the third was from the United States, commenting on the implementation of the WTO Decision.[43]

Speaking on behalf of the African Group, Nigeria proposed an amendment to Article 31 TRIPS based on the waivers in the WTO Decision, with modifications, but did not include the Chairman's Statement either as part of the amendment to Article 31 or as a footnote to it. Nigeria considered that the African Group's proposal to add a new paragraph to Article 31 would stand on sound legal ground in WTO law and that it would be uncertain whether or not a footnote could have the same substantive value as an embodiment into the text of the TRIPS Agreement.[44]

The African Group argued that it was necessary to leave out certain parts of the Decision that were redundant on grounds that the African nations agreed to the 30 August Decision on the understanding that it was only an interim solution, with Paragraph 11 of the Decision making clear that discussions on a permanent solution would continue and that the amendment did not need to be a direct transposition of the Decision and the Chairman's Statement.[45]

Furthermore, the African Group argued that the Chairman's statement

---

[41]   Communication from Rwanda on behalf of the African Group, 'The TRIPS Agreement and Public Health', IP/C/W/445, 6 April 2005; see also Communication from Rwanda on behalf of the African Group, 'Legal Arguments to Support the African Group Proposal on the Implementation of Paragraph 11 of the 30 August 2003 Decision', IP/C/W/440, 1 March 2005; and Communication from Nigeria on behalf of the African Group, 'Implementation of Paragraph 11 of the 30 August 2003 Decision', IP/C/W/437, 10 December 2004.

[42]   Communication circulated at the request of the Delegation of Barbados on behalf of the Group of Commonwealth Developing Countries and the Commonwealth Secretariat, 'Report on the Workshop on the WTO Decision on Access to Medicines at Affordable Prices for Countries with No or Insufficient Manufacturing Capacities, organised by the Commonwealth Secretariat in Co-operation with the ACP Geneva Office and the Agency for International Trade Information and Cooperation (AITIC) (Geneva 12–14 October 2004)', 23 February 2005 (IP/C/W/439).

[43]   Communication from the United States, 'Comments on Implementation of the 30 August 2003 Agreement (Solution) on the TRIPS Agreement and Public Health', IP/C/W/444, 18 March 2005.

[44]   Minutes of TRIPS Council meeting held on 8–9 and 31 March 2005, above n 39 at 21.

[45]   Communication from Rwanda on behalf of the African Group, above n 41.

should not be adopted as part of the permanent solution since its purpose was to provide comfort language for pharmaceutical companies concerned that the system would be abused in favour of generic drug manufacturers.[46] It was also felt at the time that a Chairman's Statement would help facilitate a quick conclusion of the interim solution, but that it was always recognised that a permanent solution would require more careful consideration, taking into account all aspects, including how the mechanism chosen could be put into practice.[47] The view of the African Group was that the temporary waiver of Article 31(f) was cumbersome and administratively complex.

The African Group also sought clarification at the 31 March 2005 TRIPS Council meeting about the legal status of a possible footnote to Article 31 TRIPS, referring to the Chairman's Statement. In any case, the African Group complained that the Statement had been added to the Decision without the express consent of the Members and that, when the WTO Decision was agreed to, there was no reference to the Chairman's Statement. This was corroborated by a senior official of the WTO intellectual property division, who confirmed that Members had not agreed to include the footnote in the Decision, and that was why the footnote uses an asterisk (unlike the Decision, which uses numbers), and it is in the introduction, not the Decision itself. Therefore, including or excluding the footnote did not affect the Decision or the legal status of the Chairman's Statement, but it was included as a means of providing useful information.[48]

In fact, the African Group argued that the Chairman's Statement should not be part of the TRIPS amendment nor a footnote, but suggested instead that it could be read out at the time of the amendment. The African Group proposal was supported by other developing countries, including India, Brazil, the Philippines, Sri Lanka, Argentina and Peru, while Zambia, on behalf of least-developed countries, also supported the African Group position on grounds that the WTO Decision had only been an interim solution, with Paragraph 11 indicative of the intention of Member States.[49] Zambia also expressed the view that there was never an agreement or any kind of understanding amongst WTO Members that all the elements of the Chairman's Statement would form part of the amendment.

Calling for a more appropriate 'permanent' solution to the Article 31(f) problem than the 'interim' solution set out in the WTO Decision, Rwanda, on behalf of the African Group, highlighted findings of a recent African Union Workshop on Patents and Access to Medicines, which had expressed concern

---

[46] South North Development Monitor (SUNS), above n 38.
[47] Ibid.
[48] Ibid.
[49] Ibid.

that the Decision imposes several conditions on importers and exporters who wish to make use of the waiver and which thus may affect the operational effectiveness of an exporting country's ability to supply generic medicines to WTO Members with insufficient or no manufacturing capacity.[50]

African Group Proposals on Redundant Provisions of the WTO Decision

Nigeria explained to the 31 March TRIPS Council meeting that the African Group proposal to amend Article 31 TRIPS would modify and eliminate provisions of the WTO Decision whose purpose had already been served or that would be redundant in the context of an amendment. These provisions would include: the Preamble; the last part of Paragraph 1(b), dealing with WTO Members that voluntarily decided not to use the system or to use it only in limited circumstances; Paragraph 6(ii) on regional patent systems; Paragraph 8 on annual reviews; Paragraph 9 on prejudice to other rights; and Paragraph 11 on the amendment process. Provisions whose purpose was served by other provisions of the TRIPS Agreement, such as those on enforcement and the existing provisions of Article 31 TRIPS, would also be eliminated.[51] According to the African Group, redundant enforcement provisions in the WTO Decision included most of the provisions of Paragraph 2 of the WTO Decision, except for the requirement under Paragraph 2(b)(ii) that products produced under the licence shall be clearly identified as being produced under the system set out in this Decision through specific labelling or marking. The latter provision would, under the African Group proposal, be retained so that suppliers would distinguish products through special packaging and/or special colouring/shaping of the products themselves, provided that such distinction was feasible and did not have a significant impact on price.

The African Group also proposed the elimination of the requirement, under Paragraph 4 of the WTO Decision, according to which eligible importing Members shall take reasonable measures within their means, proportionate to their administrative capacities and to the risk of trade diversion to prevent re-exportation of the products that have actually been imported into their territories under the system. The African Group suggested that Paragraph 4 was no longer relevant since the patent holder would already have sufficient avenues to prevent re-exportation of the patents manufactured under the system. Furthermore, since the Chairman's Statement was not part of the Decision, the view of the African Group was that it should not be part of the amendment to Article 31 TRIPS.

---

[50]   Ibid.

[51]   Minutes of TRIPS Council meeting held on 8–9 and 31 March 2005, above n 39 at 22.

The Developed Country Position on a TRIPS Amendment

Also at the 31 March 2005 TRIPS Council meeting, developed countries insisted that a permanent solution must be based on practically the whole of the WTO Decision and on the Chairman's Statement that was read out when it was adopted.[52] In the view of the United States,[53] the amendment to Article 31 TRIPS would have to preserve the entire agreement reached by consensus in August 2003 and, therefore, would have to include an express reference to both the Decision and the Chairman's Statement, or the principles included therein.[54]

In support of the United States, the European Communities confirmed that the amendment process should remain a purely technical exercise, without any re-opening of discussion on the subject since this would jeopardise the amendment process and, in the view of the European Communities delegation, certain WTO Members were trying to obtain what they were unable to achieve in August 2003.[55] The European Communities agreed that the footnote approach was not the most appropriate way to implement Paragraph 11 of the Decision, a footnote being acceptable only if its wording clearly sets out a legal exception to Article 31(f) TRIPS.

The European Communities delegation also agreed that the legal status of the Chairman's Statement should not be upgraded, but said that the link between the Decision and the Statement should be preserved, perhaps by taking up the African Group's suggestion that some form of the Chairman's Statement be read out at the time of the adoption of the amendment.[56] The representative of Switzerland agreed that, since there would have been no agreement on the WTO Decision without the Chairman's Statement, it needed to be reflected adequately in the amendment.[57]

TRIPS Council Meeting, 14 and 15 June 2005

At the next TRIPS Council meeting on 14–15 June 2005, the African Group, supported by several developing countries including Argentina, Brazil, China, India, Malaysia, and the Philippines, maintained their position that the perma-

---

[52] South North Development Monitor (SUNS), above n 38.
[53] Minutes of TRIPS Council meeting held on 8–9 and 31 March 2005, WTO, above n 39 at 24.
[54] Communication from the United States, IP/C/W/444, at 3.
[55] Minutes of TRIPS Council meeting held on 8–9 and 31 March 2005, above n 39 at 24.
[56] Ibid. at 25.
[57] Ibid. at 30.

nent solution should be an amendment of Article 31 TRIPS, based on waivers adopted in the WTO Decision with modifications, but that the Chairman's Statement should not be included as part of the amendment, either in the text of the TRIPS Agreement or as a footnote.[58]

Developed countries, including the United States, Switzerland, Japan, Canada and the European Communities, continued to call for references to the Chairman's Statement to be included in the amendment and argued that, since the Chairman's Statement was part of the consensus achieved on 30 August 2003, it would be difficult to achieve a permanent solution if the substance of the waiver were renegotiated.

In an attempt to break the deadlock, in July 2005 a European Communities proposal on the amendment to the TRIPS Agreement was circulated to WTO Members. Although not formally tabled, the European Communities proposal was widely discussed amongst WTO Members in the run-up to the October TRIPS Council meeting, which took place against the background of rising concerns that an avian flu pandemic would be exacerbated by shortages of the best available antiviral drug, Tamiflu, due to the exclusive licensing of the key patent to Swiss pharmaceutical company Roche.[59] The European Communities proposal argued that the link between the 30 August 2003 Decision and the Chairman's Statement should be preserved on grounds that there is a 'legal relationship' between the two. The European Communities proposal also called for the Chairman of the TRIPS Council to reiterate the statement at the time of the amendment's adoption. The EC proposal called for confirmation, upon adoption of the amendment, that the Chairman's Statement is a 'shared agreement'.[60]

Although there had been hope that an amendment of TRIPS could be agreed by the end of July 2005, ultimately this was not possible.[61] At the WTO General Council meeting on 27 July 2005, Chairman of the TRIPS Council, Choi Hyuck of Korea, reported that he had held private consultations with Members during July but that he did not have any breakthroughs to report. Instead, he identified the TRIPS Council meeting on 25–6 October 2005 as the next hope for an agreement.[62]

---

[58]   See South Centre/Centre for International Environmental Law (CIEL), above n 40 at 10.

[59]   *Pandemic Fears Raise Questions About WTO Health Waiver Opt-Out*, Intellectual Property Watch (27 October 2005) available at: http://www.ip-watch.org/index.php?res=800.

[60]   Intellectual Property Watch, 'Push for IP Deals Continues in Lead-up to WTO Ministerial', 9 August 2005, available at: http://www.ip-watch.org/index.php?res=800.

[61]   Trade Law Centre for Southern Africa (TRALAC), 'TRIPS Negotiations Have Stalled', 22 June 2005, available at: http://www.tralac.org/scripts/content.php?id=3744.

[62]   Intellectual Property Watch, above n 59.

TRIPS Council Meeting, 25 and 26 October 2005

At the TRIPS Council meeting on 25 and 26 October 2005, WTO Members remained divided on how to formally amend TRIPS. No substantive discussions took place on the issue during the meeting and, with Members' positions largely unchanged since the 14–15 June meeting, Chairman Choi Hyuck suspended the TRIPS Council session, without having reached an agreement, on 26 October.[63] Some developing countries, particularly Brazil and India, were reported to have complained that they had been left out of consultations taking place and reiterated their support for the proposal of the African Group as a good basis for negotiations towards a solution and, while the United States continued to insist that a permanent solution must include the Chairman's Statement, Brazil, India and other developing countries argued that this would upgrade the Chairman's Statement to a higher legal status than it had on 30 August 2003.[64]

A Draft Text of the Permanent Amendment Emerges

By late November 2005, press reports began to emerge indicating that the African Group and the United States were close to agreement on a permanent amendment to TRIPS.[65] Developing countries including Argentina, Brazil, India and the Philippines voiced their concerns.[66] By 29 November 2005, a draft text of the permanent amendment, in the form of an Article 31*bis* and an Annex, began to circulate.[67]

Agreement on an amendment to TRIPS was finally reached on 6 December 2005 when Chairman Choi Hyuck reconvened the TRIPS Council, indicating

---

[63]   See Bridges Weekly Trade News Digest, 9(36) *TRIPS Council Still Divided on Public Health Amendment*, available at: http://www.ictsd.org/weekly/05-10-26/index.htm.

[64]   *Impasse on Talks on TRIPS and Health 'permanent solution'*, Third World Network Info Service on WTO and Trade Issues (28 October 2005), available at: http://www.twnside.org.sg/title2/twninfo286.htm.

[65]   *TRIPS and Public Health Agreement Appears to be in Sight*, Intellectual Property Watch (5 December 2005), available at: http://www.ip-watch.org/weblog/index_test.php?p=165.

[66]   *Chances Diminish for Solution on TRIPS and Public Health Before Hong Kong*, Intellectual Property Watch (22 November 2005), available at: http://www.ip-watch.org/weblog/index_test.php?p=147.

[67]   *Draft text of TRIPS and Public Health informal consultations*, posting on IP-Health list server (2 December 2005), available at: http://lists.essential.org/pipermail/ip-health/. See also *TRIPS and Public Health Agreement Appears to be in Sight*, Intellectual Property Watch (5 December 2005), available at: http://www/ip-watch.org/weblog/index.php?p=165&res=1280&print=0.

that he was seeking a successful outcome before the 13–18 December 2005 Hong Kong WTO Ministerial Meeting. After a short meeting of the TRIPS Council, Members agreed to submit to the WTO General Council, in accordance with paragraph 1 of Article X of the Marrakesh Agreement Establishing the World Trade Organisation, a proposal for a decision on an amendment to the TRIPS Agreement.[68]

Although the text of the agreement on a TRIPS amendment does not mention the Chairman's Statement, thus securing a key objective of many developing countries, particularly the African Group, in effect the Chairman's Statement remains by virtue of the process that will be followed to amend TRIPS, when the re-reading of the Statement by the Chairman of the General Council of the WTO will take place. Chairman Choi Hyuck's reportedly secured agreement on the 'choreography' for re-reading the Chairman's Statement at the time that the amendment is confirmed.[69]

In so doing there are potential grounds for arguing that the Chairman's Statement is the legal context for interpreting the amendment in the event of subsequent WTO dispute settlement proceedings.[70] The ambiguous status of the Chairman's Statement is further enhanced by the inclusion in the WTO press release announcing the agreement on a TRIPS amendment of a link, alongside that to the 6 December 2005 agreement itself, to the Chairman's Statement and its accompanying 'best practices' guidelines, the latter setting out examples of how pharmaceutical companies have often used special labelling, colouring, shaping or sizing to differentiate products supplied through donor or discounted pricing programmes from products supplied to other markets.[71]

Procedurally, the 6 December 2005 agreement will become an amendment to the TRIPS Agreement once two thirds of WTO Members have ratified the change, with a deadline of 1 December 2007 set for achieving this. The temporary waiver of Article 31(f) will remain in place until this is done.

---

[68]   *Implementation of Paragraph 11 of the General Council Decision of 30 August 2003 on the Implementation of Paragraph 6 of the Doha Declaration on the TRIPS Agreement and Public Health*, IP/C/41 (6 December 2005) available at: http://www.wto.org/english/news_e/pres05_e/pr426_e.htm.

[69]   *African Countries Ready to Accept TRIPS and Public Health Deal*, IP-Watch (6 December 2005) available at: http://www.ip-watch.org/weblog/index_test.php?p=166.

[70]   *Members Strike Deal on TRIPS and Public Health; Civil Society Unimpressed*, Bridges Weekly Trade News Digest, 7(42) (7 December 2005), available at: http://www.ictsd.org/weekly/05-12-07/story1.htm.

[71]   *Members OK Amendment to Make Health Flexibility Permanent*, WTO Press Release 426 (6 December 2005), available at: http://www.wto.org/english/news_e/pres05_e/pr426_e.htm.

The 6 December agreement, which essentially formalises the 29 November draft, consists of a proposal from the TRIPS Council for a Decision on an amendment to the TRIPS Agreement, which in turn is attached to a General Council Decision which adopts the Protocol and opens it for WTO Members to accept by 1 December 2007.

The Protocol, setting out the procedural aspects of amending the TRIPS Agreement, is followed by the actual amendment to the TRIPS Agreement in three parts: the Annex to the Protocol, which sets out the five paragraphs of the new Article 31*bis*, the new Annex to the TRIPS Agreement and the Appendix to the Annex to the TRIPS Agreement.

The five paragraphs that form the new Article 31*bis* and that will form an additional article to Article 31 TRIPS are as follows. The first paragraph allows pharmaceutical products to be exported to WTO Members lacking production capacity, by way of a derogation to Article 31(f) TRIPS. The second paragraph sets out provisions to avoid double remuneration to the patent owner in the importing and exporting countries. The third paragraph deals with regional trade agreements, at least half of the current membership of which is made up of least-developed countries, and provides that Article 31(f) TRIPS shall not apply to the extent necessary to enable a pharmaceutical product produced or imported under a compulsory licence in that WTO Member to be exported to the markets of those other developing or least-developed country parties to the regional trade agreement that share the health problem in question, provided this does not prejudice the territorial nature of the patent rights in question. The fourth paragraph sets out a moratorium on non-violation complaints against measures taken in accordance with the amendment, so ensuring that WTO Members will not launch complaints based on the loss of an expected benefit caused by another Member's actions if they do not actually violate WTO law. The fifth deals with retaining all existing flexibilities under Articles 31(f) and (h) TRIPS.

The new Annex to the TRIPS Agreement sets out the terms for using the system and contains: definitions of 'pharmaceutical product', 'eligible importing Member' and 'exporting Member'; terms for notification of use of the Article 31*bis* system in relation to the content of the notification to the TRIPS Council by the eligible importing Member, the conditions to be fulfilled by the compulsory licence issued by the exporting Member, and the content of the notification to the TRIPS Council by the exporting Member; details of anti-diversion measures required of eligible importing Members; an undertaking that developed country Members will provide technical assistance under Article 67 TRIPS to assist with the establishment of systems for the granting of regional patents; and a requirement that the TRIPS Council shall undertake an annual review of the system and report on its operation to the General Council.

An Appendix to the Annex sets out the criteria for assessing lack of manufacturing capacity in the pharmaceutical sector and reproduces the text of the Annex to the 30 August 2003 Decision.

Although the WTO press release on 6 December 2005 stresses that the agreement on an amendment to the TRIPS Agreement is designed to match the 30 August waiver as closely as possible,[72] one significant change from the Annex to the 30 August 2003 Decision is apparent. This is in respect of the list of WTO Members that will not use the system as importing countries. The change is that reference to the European Communities in footnote 3 no longer contains the names of all EC Member States. These have been deleted and replaced with 'European Communities', with the effect that the opt-out from using the mechanism will apply automatically to all applicant states on accession to the EC.[73]

Reactions to the Agreement of 6 December 2005

Initial reactions to the agreement of 6 December 2005 were mixed. The proposed amendment to TRIPS was welcomed by the Office of the United States Trade Representative,[74] the European Commission,[75] the UK Department of Trade and Industry,[76] the Pharmaceutical Research and Manufacturers of America (PhRMA)[77] and the International Federation of

---

[72]   *Members OK Amendment to Make Health Flexibility Permanent*, WTO Press Release 426 (6 December 2005), available at: http://www.wto.org/english/news_e/pres05_e/pr426_e.htm.

[73]   'Australia, Canada, the European Communities with, for the purposes of Article 31*bis* and this Annex, its Member States, Iceland, Japan, New Zealand, Norway, Switzerland, and the United States', Proposal for a Decision on an Amendment to the TRIPS Agreement, IP/C/41 (6 December 2005): Paragraph 3, footnote 3 of the proposed Annex to the TRIPS Agreement.

[74]   *United States Welcomes Negotiations Leading to Positive Outcome on Enhancing Access to Medicines*, Office of the United States Trade Representative Press Release (6 December 2005), available at: http://www.ustr.gov/Document_Library/Press_Releases/2005/December/United_States_Welcomes_Negotiations_Leading_to_Positive_Outcome_on_Enhancing_Access_to_Medicines.html.

[75]   *EU Welcomes Permanent WTO Solution on Generic Medicines*, European Commission Press Release IP/05/1537 (6 December 2005), available at: http://europa.eu.int/rapid/pressReleasesAction.do?reference=IP/05/1537&format=HTML&aged=0&language=EN&guiLanguage=en .

[76]   *Johnson Welcomes Boost for Global Health*, DTI Press Release (8 December 2005), available at: http://www.dti.gov.uk/news/newsarticle091205a.html.

[77]   *PhRMA Welcomes TRIPS and Public Health Agreement*, PhRMA Press Release (6 December 2005), available at: http://www.phrma.org/mediaroom/press/releases/06.12.2005.1335.cfm.

Pharmaceutical Manufacturers and Associations (IFPMA).[78] WTO Director-General, Pascal Lamy, heralded the agreement as confirming 'once again that Members are determined to ensure that the WTO's trading system contributes to humanitarian and development goals . . .'.[79] Supporters of the agreement on a permanent amendment have suggested that conditions for the waiver will improve once transposed into the TRIPS Agreement, arguing that while the waiver remained temporary under the 30 August Decision mechanism, legal certainty was absent.[80]

However, the agreement of 6 December 2005 was criticised by NGOs.[81] In particular, MSF expressed alarm at the decision to amend TRIPS based on a mechanism that has failed to prove it could increase access to medicines with, to date, not one patient benefiting from use of the mechanism.[82]

It is certainly true that the effectiveness or otherwise of the mechanism will not be known until WTO Members have adopted legislation to bring the system into operation and there is concrete evidence, based on use of these new arrangements, to indicate how efficiently the system works in practice.[83]

GLOBALISING INTELLECTUAL PROPERTY RIGHTS REVISITED

In 2002 I suggested that the TRIPS Agreement was made possible by a negotiating space that granted global corporate interests and key developed country governments (notably the US and the EC) a relatively 'free run' during the Uruguay Round of multilateral trade negotiations.[84] With few, if any, non-state actors opposing the TRIPS Agreement in a concerted way and developing

---

[78]   *TRIPS Amendment Permanently Resolves Export Compulsory License Issue*, IFPMA News Release (6 December 2005), available at: http://www.ifpma.org/News/NewsReleaseDetail.aspx?nID=3951.

[79]   WTO Press Release 426, above n 72.

[80]   *African Countries Ready to Accept TRIPS and Public Health Deal*, IP-Health (6 December 2005), available at: http://www.ip-watch.org/weblog/index_test.php?p=166.

[81]   *TRIPS Health Amendment Evokes Harsh NGO Reaction, Industry Caution*, IP-Health (7 December 2005), available at: http://www.ip-watch.org/weblog/index_test.php?p=169.

[82]   *Amendment to WTO TRIPS Agreement Makes Access to Affordable Medicines Even More Bleak: MSF Expresses Concern that Patients the World-Over Will Have to Pay the Price*, MSF Campaign for Access to Essential Medicines Statement (6 December 2005).

[83]   See also Musungu, above n 35 at 251.

[84]   Matthews, D. (2002) *Globalising Intellectual Property Rights: The TRIPs Agreement*, London: Routledge, at 139.

country governments experiencing not only information deficiencies but also negotiating fatigue, pressure to avoid bilateral trade sanctions and an imperative to achieve compromise deals in a multilateral context, sustained opposition to TRIPS was not readily apparent. Yet I concluded with the view that, post-TRIPS, the negotiating space would become populated by a wider range of actors bringing new issues, priorities and concerns to the negotiating table. The window of opportunity that emerged when global corporate actors seized the initiative and galvanised a broad range of interests in support of intellectual property protection would, I suggested, be unlikely to be re-opened. Instead, NGOs, industries previously excluded from negotiations (in particular the generic drug companies), international institutions (including the WHO and the United Nations agencies) and developing countries themselves would become fully engaged with the issue of international intellectual property rights once the more adverse effects of the TRIPS Agreement, and particularly its impact on drug pricing and availability, became widely understood. So, in the light of the 6 December 2005 agreement on an amendment to TRIPS, how far have those predictions been borne out in the post-TRIPS negotiating environment?

In part, the predictions have been realised. Developed country governments and the global corporate interests of multinational proprietary pharmaceutical companies have indeed found that public awareness of the more adverse effects of the TRIPS Agreement has grown, with resultant opposition to TRIPS in relation to its perceived impact on access to medicines and public health. Yet in many other respects what is perhaps more surprising is that so little has changed since the TRIPS negotiations in the mid-1990s. On the one hand, NGOs, generic drug companies[85] and international institutions have certainly played a more significant role in seeking to re-define and re-align the rules of international intellectual property law but, conversely, particularly during the debate over the Paragraph 6 mechanism of the Doha Declaration on the TRIPS Agreement and Public Health, the US (and, to a lesser extent, the EC) have remained key actors.

While there are certainly similarities between negotiations leading to the TRIPS Agreement and those involved with attempts to resolve the access to medicines issue, there are also significant differences between the negotiation

---

[85]   For example, on 2 December 2002, Jerome Smith, Chief Executive Officer of Mepro Pharmaceutica, South Africa, wrote to Members of the TRIPS Council on behalf of African generic drug manufacturers, commenting on negotiation of paragraph 6 of the Doha Declaration and urging negotiators to adopt a solution that encourages the further development of domestic value added companies in Africa, and which enables competition for the supply of pharmaceuticals, vaccines and other health care inventions.

of the original TRIPS Agreement and attempts to resolve the access to medicines issue. The higher profile and increased coordination of NGOs is one aspect of this, but the greater engagement of international institutions – particularly the WHO, UNICEF and UNAIDS[86] with concerns relating to public health and WIPO with its attempts to encourage greater dialogue with industry and the private sector[87] – is also important. Finally, industry itself appears to be responding to the public health imperatives relating to the TRIPS Agreement in new ways – generic drug companies on the one hand and proprietary pharmaceutical companies on the other – through public–private partnership initiatives in response to public and, most recently, investor pressure.

As during the original TRIPS negotiations, the role of the EC and the US has been central to the progression of negotiations on compulsory licensing, access to essential medicines and public health. But, unlike the original TRIPS negotiations during the Uruguay Round of GATT, the deliberations on a TRIPS amendment have been marked by a higher profile for NGOs and developing countries. Developing countries themselves, although initially 'emboldened'[88] to seek greater recourse to compulsory licences and importation, as during the TRIPS negotiations, ultimately lessened their opposition to the formula put before them by developed countries.[89] It is somewhat ironic that, in the final instance, NGOs that had been active in support of developing country delegates during both Paragraph 6 and Paragraph 11 negotiations, ultimately criticised those same developing countries for agreeing to a TRIPS amendment on 6 December 2005 on grounds that the agreement will make permanent the 30 August 2003 temporary waiver of Article 31(f) of TRIPS at a time when the mechanism still remains untried and untested. The lesson from the negotiation of an amendment to the TRIPS Agreement on compulsory licensing and access to medicines must ultimately be that there are limits to the extent that developing countries will act in harmony with the NGO community on access to medicines negotiations at the TRIPS Council.

---

[86]   For example partnership initiatives between the WHO, the United Nations International Children's Emergency Fund (UNICEF), the Joint United Nations Programme on HIV/AIDS (UNAIDS) and generic drug manufacturers, such as Apotex, to produce cheap and readily available medicines for developing countries.

[87]   For instance the World Intellectual Property Organisation (WIPO) Industry and Private Sector Forum on IP and the Knowledge Economy, which was due to meet in Beijing on 24–6 April 2003 (although due to the SARS outbreak, this meeting was subsequently postponed): http://www.wipo.int/summit-china/en/index.html.

[88]   Sykes, above n 10 at 2.

[89]   Matthews, above n 84 at 44.

13. The international protection of geographical indications yesterday, today and tomorrow*

Gail Evans and Michael Blakeney

The future protection of geographical indications (GIs) in the World Trade Organization (WTO) seems as intractable a problem as the agricultural negotiations to which it is inevitably linked.[1] During the last 20 years the international protection of GIs has experienced a notable worldwide resurgence. Given the ancient provenance of the modern geographical indication, it is a matter of historical irony that the reasons for this increase may be found in a local reaction to the industrialization and globalization of agricultural production. The current development of the law of geographical indications has been spurred by both the greater need and the additional opportunities offered by the global marketplace for the diversification of agricultural products and foodstuffs.

The industrialized model of agriculture based on the Green Revolution of the twentieth century[2] proved capable of producing prodigious food surpluses that might feed the world, but the resulting economies of scale simply made it uneconomical for small producers to continue to cultivate the land. As plentiful supplies of commodities such as sugar and cotton in Europe and the US threatened the incomes of their farmers and the stability of rural regions, their

---

* An abbreviated version of this chapter was first published in the *Oxford Journal of International Economic Law*, 9(3), 2006, pp. 575–614.

[1] The term 'geographical indication' will be used in its widest sense, covering indication of source, geographical indication (within the meaning of Article 22.1 of the TRIPS Agreement) and appellation of origin.

[2] A term coined by the director of the US Agency for International Development William Gaud ('The Green Revolution: Accomplishments and Apprehensions', Agency for International Development Department of State, Shorehan Hotel, Washington, D.C., 8 March 1968, available: <http://www.agbioworld.org/biotech-info/topics/borlaug/borlaug-green.html>) with respect to the movement to increase yields by using new crop cultivars, irrigation, fertilizers, pesticides and mechanization.

governments responded with subsidies and artificially inflated returns.[3] Yet, even with a sizeable commodity-producing acreage farmers still had difficulty making a predictable profit given the large-scale distribution, monopolistic state marketing agencies and the power of large-scale buyers such as supermarket chains.

Accentuating the trend to mass production of agricultural and food products, the revolution in agricultural biotechnology of the twenty-first century means that innovation, knowledge and technology are increasingly affecting the competitive base.[4] This latest transformation is further affecting the structure and location of agricultural production.[5] In the past, competitive position in agri-food production was based on high-quality land and capital-intensive production processes. That is changing, with knowledge becoming the defining factor in much of the food industry.[6] Institutional economic theory[7] suggests that over time the research, commercialization and even production activities of an innovative industry will converge on relatively few locations.[8]

In the developing world such concentration and protectionism has become untenable. Forty-three developing countries depend on exports of a single

---

[3]   WTO trade ministers agreed at the Hong Kong Ministerial Conference 'to ensure the parallel elimination of all forms of export subsidies and disciplines on all export measures with equivalent effect to be completed by the end of 2013': Sixth Session, Hong Kong, 13–18 December 2005, Ministerial Declaration, adopted on 18 December 2005, WT/MIN(05)/DEC.

[4]   Although biotechnology applications have existed for many centuries, modern, Mendelian plant breeding has, since 1973, been increasingly influenced by new molecular biology techniques (Organisation for Economic Co-operation and Development – OECD, 1999). In the knowledge-based agri-food sector commodities are differentiated by their transgenically-based nature, for example the canola sector: Stuart Smyth, George G. Khachatourians and Peter W.B. Phillips, 'Liabilities and Economics of Transgenic Crops', 20 *Nature Biotechnology*, 2002, 537 at 538–9.

[5]   For example western Canada's competitive position in agri-food production was formerly based on high-quality land and capital-intensive production processes. That is now changing, with knowledge becoming the defining factor in much of the food industry, ibid.

[6]   Ibid.

[7]   Given that knowledge-based innovations are usually transferable at low or no marginal cost, this creates significant economies of scale, which yields declining average costs and a major barrier to imitators: See generally, Shapiro, Carl and Hal Varian, *Information Rules*, Harvard Business School Press, Cambridge, M.A., 1999.

[8]   The evolving theory of 'institutional' economics helps to define the potential for industrial structure to adapt to the market opportunities. R.H. Coase ('The Nature of the Firm', *Economica*, 4, 1937, 386–405) posits that firms exist to manage risk – namely those risks and uncertainties related to price discovery, negotiation and monitoring of transactions. This theoretical approach has been further pursued by Oliver Williamson (*The Economic Institutions of Capitalism: Firms, Markets, Relational Contracting*, Free Press, 1985) who argues that contracting is not costless.

agricultural commodity for more than 20 percent of their total revenues from merchandise exports. Three-quarters are classified as least-developed countries. Most common among the commodities they depend on are coffee, cocoa, cotton, sugar and bananas. For non oil-exporting countries, agricultural exports represent the mainstay of foreign exchange earnings. Nearly all of Malawi's agricultural exports, for example, come from tobacco and tea. Benin depends on cotton for over 80 percent of its merchandise export earnings. Ethiopia relies on coffee for over 70 percent of agricultural exports.[9]

When farmers in the developing world attempt to export their produce, they are likely to be met with protectionism in the form of higher tariffs, and non-tariff barriers such as quotas and sanitary regulations from industrialized countries, and what is more, increasingly from developing countries as well.[10] They cannot export their agricultural products to the OECD markets because the tariff barriers faced by them are ten times or more those on typical inter-OECD trade.[11] In 2001, the agricultural subsidies and other support in the OECD economies amounted to $US311 billion, which was 1.3 percent of the gross national product of this country group. The level of support to the agricultural sector has not reduced much since 1986.[12] The magnitude of support, which led to large agricultural output in the OECD economies, tends to depress the international prices of those commodities that low-income developing economies are attempting to export.[13] As a result, the pattern of food imports has changed as developing countries have shifted from being net exporters to net importers of food and the long-term downward trend in agricultural

---

[9] For an overview of price trends and other developments affecting global markets for food and feed commodities see Food and Agriculture Organization of the United Nations, 'Roundup', *Food Outlook*, 4, December 2005 for both cereals and coffee at: http://www.fao.org/giews/english/fo/.

[10] See *Chile – Price Band System and Safeguard Measures Relating to Certain Agricultural Products*, WTO Dispute Settlement: Dispute DS207, Appellate Body Report, September 2002 at http://www.wto.org/english/tratop_e/dispu_e/cases_e/s207_e.htm. Argentina disapproved the measures adopted by Chile in order to comply with the DSB rulings. As a result, Argentina asked for the establishment of a compliance panel in January 2006 (WT/DS207/16).

[11] The Organisation for Economic Co-operation and Development (OECD) is a forum of 30 developed 'market democracies' who meet to address world socio-economic problems; oecd.org.

[12] Maria Soledad Bos, 'The Impact of OECD Members' Agricultural Subsidies on Welfare and Food Security in Sub-Saharan Africa', January–May 2003, at p. 8, http://www.ictsd.org.

[13] Alan V. Deardorff and Robert M. Stern, 'Enhancing the Benefits for Developing Countries in the Doha Development Agenda Negotiations', Davidson Institute Policy Brief No. 1, August 2003, at http://www.wto.org/english/forums_e/ngo_e/william_davidson_e.pdf (visited 2 August 2007).

commodity prices for commodity dependent countries threatens the food security of their populations as many farmers and exporting countries still find themselves trapped by their dependency in producing and exporting more, but earning less than they did formerly.

Coffee prices provide a dramatic example of low commodity returns to farmers. Significant oversupply and sluggish demand growth in the world market resulted in coffee prices falling by 58 percent between 1998 and 2001 to an all-time low of 45.67 US cents per pound.[14] Prices have remained weak since and although some rises occurred in the interim period, it was only in February 2005 that prices actually reached the same level that they averaged in 1999 of more than 85 US cents per pound.[15] In addition, structural changes have occurred in the coffee market as a result of depressed conditions including the exit from the industry of higher-cost producers and several major developments in the retail sector, including auctions of gourmet beans and increasing quantities of fair trade coffee beans being sold.

In the wake of the gene revolution, the increasingly influential role of intellectual property rights in agricultural and food production also plays a significant part in sustaining the asymmetry of markets between developed and developing countries. In the 1980s and 1990s, as private seed and agrochemical companies, headquartered chiefly in North America and Europe, began to invest in crop science, the international protection of intellectual property became central to the development and commercialization of production in the agri-biotech sector. Confirming the trend to economies of scale and tightly integrated production systems and two-way trade in differentiated products, institutional economic theory suggests that innovation-driven industries are inherently imperfectly competitive because large up-front research and development costs and low marginal costs yield rapidly increasing returns to scale in production.[16]

Given the significance of intellectual property to the knowledge-based agricultural sector, dramatic changes to international intellectual property laws might have been anticipated. The year 1994 saw the promulgation of universal minimum standards within the Agreement on Trade-Related Aspects of Intellectual Property Rights (TRIPS).[17] Such an unprecedented development

---

[14]   FAO, Food Outlook, April 2005, http://www.fao.org/documents/show_cdr.asp?url_file=/docrep/007/j5051e/j5051e04.htm (visited 13 June 2006).

[15]   Preliminary returns point to a similar crop size in 2004–2005 as that harvested in 2003–04 and a continued upward trend in prices: http://www.ico.org/coffee_prices.asp.

[16]   P.W.B. Phillips and G.G. Khachatourians, note 4, at pp. 6 ff.

[17]   Final Act Embodying the Results of the Uruguay Round of Multilateral Trade Negotiations, Marrakesh Agreement Establishing the World Trade Organisation, signed

in international intellectual property law marked the new found primacy of intellectual property rights (IPRs) within the global information economy. Throughout the following decade the capacity of IPRs to restructure and control markets for agricultural commodities became manifest as millions of patients in developing countries struggled to obtain life-saving drugs, and as subsistence farmers in the poorest parts of the developing world opposed to transgenetic seed licensing practices of the transnational corporations (TNCs) fought for the right to save and exchange seed, and breed their own crops from their seeds.[18]

The response to such a highly industrialized, privatized and technocratic means of agricultural production dominated by science and technical expertise might be anticipated. Local farming communities and their respective governments have responded by seeking a complementary means of legal control – the geographical indication (GI). The definition accorded geographical indications in TRIPS favours associations of small producers being a category of intellectual property chiefly applicable to agricultural products and foodstuffs that originate in a specific place and possess qualities, a reputation, or other characteristics that are essentially attributable to that place of origin.[19]

In view of certain adverse developments regarding access to medicines and the distribution of transgenic plant resources, the protection of GIs has gained a certain moral authority that weighs in favour of developing countries having the freedom to exploit their available knowledge. Where necessary the international enforcement of GIs might permit developing countries to reclaim intellectual property rights from previous usurpation. India, for example, possesses well-known geographical names for such staple commodities as 'Darjeeling' tea and 'Basmati' rice.[20] Yet tea from Kenya or Sri Lanka has

---

at Marrakesh (Morocco), 15 April 1994 (hereinafter WTO Agreement), Annex IC, Agreement on Trade-Related Aspects of Intellectual Property Rights (hereinafter TRIPS Agreement or TRIPS), reprinted in *The Results of the Uruguay Round of Multilateral Trade Negotiations-The Legal Texts*, 1–19, 365–403 (GATT Secretariat, Geneva 1994).

[18]   See M. Blakeney 'Intellectual Property and Agriculture', in L. O'Brien and R.J. Henry (eds), *Transgenic Cereals*, AACC, St Paul, Minnesota, MN, 2001, at pp. 285–6. See generally, Rafael V. Mariano, 'Benefits and Shortcomings of Intellectual Property Rights For Small Scale Farmers In Developing Countries', http://www.infoagrar.ch/ipr-symposium/documents/paper_mariano.pdf.

[19]   TRIPS Article 22.

[20]   'Basmati' is the customary name for certain varieties of rice that are grown exclusively in specific areas of the Indo Gangetic Plains, which currently includes the Punjab (a province which has borders with both India and Pakistan); Kasturi Das, 'Protection of India's "Geographical Indications"', 2006, at http://www.gdnet.org/fulltext/Das_Protection%20_india.pdf. Since both countries have traditionally inherited rights over the basmati the EC is of the view that it should be registered in the European

often been passed off abroad as 'Darjeeling tea'.[21] Corporations in France and the US have been producing rice based on 'Basmati' varieties in those countries, and registering trade marks that refer to 'Basmati', thereby seeking to gain from this renowned geographical name. The US patent on 'Basmati Rice Lines and Grains' granted to Texas-based Rice Tec Inc., which triggered a lot of controversy in the recent past, is a glaring example of wrongful exploitation of a renowned GI.

Not surprisingly, there is an increasing trend in such countries which are producers of such well-known and identifiable commodities to rely on geographical indications (GIs) to protect their markets both at home and abroad. Many developing-country governments and NGOs, cognizant of the potential commercial advantage inhering in local geographical names and the marketing of agricultural products are now desirous of ensuring the 'repatriation' of rights that historically may have gone inadvertently to distributors in the earlier industrialized countries of Europe or North America. Given the potential of GIs to attract price premiums, in 1999 India enacted separate legislation to protect geographical indications.[22] Following the WTO ruling of 2005 that served to clear the way for registration of foreign GIs within the European Union, that same year the coffee producers' agency Café de Colombia applied to register the geographical indication of 'Café de Colombia' (Colombian coffee) as a protected designation of origin (PDO) under EC Regulation 2081/92.[23]

It is symptomatic of the changes in the political economy of intellectual property that India and Brazil, which were formerly so opposed to the TRIPS Agreement, should subsequently at the launch of the Doha Round espouse GIs as the best available means of exploiting their traditional knowledge.

While GIs constitute a separate category of intellectual property within the TRIPS Agreement, their further harmonization is problematic since the means and extent of protecting GIs is not consistent within the domestic legal systems of WTO members. The origins of this regulatory problem are to be found in the historical development of the international protection of

---

market under a joint GI. Further, see 'Islamabad Plans to Move WTO over IPR of Basmati rice', 13 January 2007, at http://www.hinduonnet.com/businessline/blnus/14131701.htm.

21   Darjeeling is a tea-growing region in West Bengal.

22   The Geographical Indications of Goods (Registration and Protection) Act, 1999: the 'Geographical Indications Registry' in Chennai has national jurisdiction.

23   Pursuant to Article 7 of Council Regulation (EC) No 510/2006 notice of the right to object to the application, has been published in the *Official Journal*, 28 December 2006. Assuming there are no objections from third countries, only producers complying with the PGI will be permitted to trade in the EU under the designation 'Café de Colombia'; http://ec.europa.eu/agriculture/foodqual/protec/firstpub/index_en.htm.

geographical indications. The inclusion of geographical indications within the TRIPS Agreement marked a turning point in their long and often controversial journey towards recognition and protection in the treaties of the nineteenth and twentieth centuries. However, questions associated with different means of protecting GIs between civil and common law jurisdictions were not resolved during the Uruguay Round, so that, in witness to the strength of the divide, the TRIPS Agreement itself contains a provision requiring continuing negotiation.

The Hong Kong Ministerial Declaration affirmed the 'central importance of the development dimension in every aspect of the Doha Work Programme'. Following Doha, the results of the multilateral trade negotiations must be seen to make economic development 'a meaningful reality, in terms both of the results of the negotiations on market access and rule-making and of the specific development related issues' identified in the Work Programme.[24] In the case of geographical indications the regulatory difficulties of harmonization are further compounded by the fact that continuing negotiations must take account of the 'Doha mandate' in favour of providing ways and means to promote economic development among the world's poorest peoples.

The Doha Declaration signalled that the necessary rebalancing of trade concessions could only be achieved with substantial concessions regarding special and differential treatment for the agricultural commodities and manufactures of the developing world, supplemented by technology transfer and technical assistance. In accordance with Clause 18 of the Declaration, members are to pursue negotiations concerning the establishment of a multilateral register for wines and spirits, and consider the extension of GI protection beyond wines and spirits. The principal protagonists in negotiations are the European Community, which favours an expanded international regime, and the United States, which argues that current trade mark protection is sufficient. The EC and its supporters would see major reform in the introduction of a multilateral system for the registration and enforcement of GIs. June 2005 saw the European Community (EC) submit a radical proposal to amend the TRIPS Agreement to provide global protection for GIs in a multilateral system of registration.[25] This proposal seeks to bring international protection for GIs

---

24   Clause 2, Doha Ministerial Declaration, 14 November 2001, WT/MIN(01)/DEC/1.

25   In June 2005 the EC submitted a proposal for amending Section 3 of the TRIPS Agreement with a view to extending the regime of protection available for geographical indications on wines and spirits to geographical indications on all products ('extension'), and in addition a proposal for the inclusion of an annex to the TRIPS Agreement establishing a multilateral system of notification and registration of geographical indications (GIs). World Trade Organization, General Council, Trade Negotiations Committee, Council for Trade-Related Aspects of Intellectual Property

into conformity with the European Union where a Community-wide system for their registration is considered an indispensable part of agricultural policy, serving both to preserve the incomes of small to medium-sized producers and to guarantee the sustainability of the rural economy. Given the fact that it possesses over 700 registered geographical indications,[26] sophisticated institutional infrastructure and technical prowess, the European Union is exceptionally well placed to leverage the benefits of an expanded international system of GI protection. On the other hand, the US and its supporters favour voluntary multilateral registration and the choice of the means of protection – whether by special system or by utilization of the established trade mark system.

However, it would be wrong to think that the general question of whether protection should be afforded and indeed expanded is a simple North–South debate between the old industrialized and the developing worlds. Newly industrializing and leading developing countries such as India, China and Kenya are well placed to take advantage of intellectual property protection afforded to agricultural GIs. On the other hand, given the cost in establishing and maintaining the institutions necessary to intellectual property protection, doubts remain over the ability of less advanced or less advantageously placed developing countries to take advantage of GI protection.

Although these differing capacities and needs have been recognized since WTO negotiations on the establishment of a multilateral register started in 1997, no ready solution to the further global harmonization of GIs has been found. WTO members are divided as to their capacity to take advantage of GI protection no less than they are radically divided as to the means of regulation. Whereas the current TRIPS provisions allow member states to choose the means by which they protect GIs, the deep transatlantic division between the major powers of the EU and the US over the method of protection risks retarding further progress on harmonization for the foreseeable future.

Rights, Special Session on Geographical Indications, Communication from the European Community 14 June 2005, WT/GC/W/547, TN/C/W/26, TN/IP/W/11. See earlier submissions of the EC, 22 June 2000, IP/C/W/107/Rev.1 with respect to the register, and submission of 2002 in respect of the extension, IP/C/W/353 24 June 2002.

26 'Since 1993, more than 700 names, designating *inter alia* over 150 cheeses, 160 meat and meat-based products, 150 fresh or processed fruits or vegetables and 80 types of olive oil, have been registered in this context. The Commission has also received over 300 further applications for the registration of names and/or amendments to specifications from Member States and third countries', Proposal for a Council Regulation on the Protection of Geographical Indications and Designations of Origin for Agricultural Products and Foodstuffs, Commission of the European Communities, Brussels, 5.1.2006, para. 3.

While agricultural policy remains a highly controversial issue among WTO members, we are unlikely to see any lessening of pressure by the EC and supporting WTO Members for the extension of specific GI protection for an unlimited range of agricultural commodities and foodstuffs. For many developing countries faced with competition from industrialized food production, GIs provide a potential vehicle for the commercialization of their traditional knowledge in crop cultivation, fishing, and animal husbandry. Consistently with this objective, the text of the Doha Declaration recognizes 'the need for all our peoples to benefit from the increased opportunities and welfare gains that the multilateral trading system generates'.[27] GIs, pertaining to both agriculture and handicrafts, may contain traditional knowledge which is capable of exploitation in sophisticated consumer markets as natural medicinal, culinary, cosmetic or lifestyle products.

Nevertheless, the United States, Australia, Canada and Argentina are among those countries which are adamantly opposed to the proposal, being of the view that international protection of GIs is adequate as it stands and that such a drastic development would only serve to undermine future gains in market access for non-European food and agricultural products.[28] Developing countries are similarly divided. On the one hand, those who support the US and Australia have serious misgivings concerning the additional costs of implementing a distinct system of GI protection in addition to the TRIPS obligations that are outstanding. On the other hand, India and Kenya, possessing GIs that are already known, as well as the financial means and know-how to institute their protection, are among those developing countries which support the EC proposal.

Regrettably, the Hong Kong Ministerial Declaration of December 2005 did not record any notable progress concerning the extension of the protection of geographical indications to products other than wines and spirits, or the multi-

---

[27]   Clause 2, Doha Ministerial Declaration, 14 November 2001, WT/MIN(01)/DEC/1.

[28]   See US Submissions on GIs at the WTO TRIPS Council: 'Joint Proposal for a Multilateral System of Notification and Registration of Geographical Indications for Wines and Spirits', Communication from Argentina, Australia, Canada, Chile, Ecuador, El Salvador, New Zealand and the United States, TN/IP/W/9, 13 April 2004; and 'Multilateral System of Notification and Registration of Geographical Indications for Wines (and Spirits)', Communication from Argentina, Australia, Canada, Chile, New Zealand and the United States, TN/IP/W/6, 29 October 2002; and 'Proposal for a Multilateral System for Notification and Registration of Geographical Indications for Wines and Spirits based on Article 23.4 of the TRIPS Agreement', Communication from Argentina, Australia, Canada, Chile, Colombia, Costa Rica, Dominican Republic, Ecuador, El Salvador, Guatemala, Honduras, Japan, Namibia, New Zealand, Philippines, Chinese Taipei, and the United States, TN/IP/W/5, 23 October 2002.

lateral register for geographical indications for wines and spirits.[29] Admittedly, the momentum of negotiations was derailed by US and Australian requests for consultations with the European Community concerning the discriminatory nature of the European registration system. In the aftermath, the ruling of the WTO Panel of March 2005 in the case of *EC – Geographical Indications* has done little to quell the strength of this regulatory dispute. The decision in that case proved a victory for the United States. It successfully challenged Council Regulation (EEC) No 2081/92 on the protection of geographical indications for agricultural products (EC Regulation) as discriminatory of foreign rightholders. In fact, the decision, which nonetheless sanctioned the substantive provisions of the EC Regulation, only appears to have emboldened the EC's bid to see its system of GI protection promulgated within the TRIPS Agreement.[30]

To this end, the EC proposal of June 2005 would extend GI protection to all agricultural products as well as indigenous handicrafts, and see their notification in a mandatory multilateral register.[31] The emergence of the first truly global intellectual property rights would constitute an unprecedented departure from the classical system of international intellectual property law, based as it is on the territorial principle of national systems of registration for GIs and trade marks. In addition, it would entail an erosion of the property rights of trade mark owners and the corresponding capacity of member states to determine economic policy.

The future global regulation of GIs is now at a crossroads. The Agreement on Trade-Related Aspects of Intellectual Property Rights (TRIPS) is widely recognized as having set new standards for the international protection of GIs, having succeeded at one stroke in recognizing GIs as a major category of intellectual

---

[29] Clauses 29 and 39, Sixth Session, Hong Kong, 13–18 December 2005, Ministerial Declaration, adopted on 18 December 2005, WT/MIN(05)/DEC. Further, see Special Session of the Council for TRIPS Report by the Chairman, Ambassador Manzoor Ahmad, to the Trade Negotiations Committee, 23 November 2005, TN/IP/14, in which he laments the lack of progress at para. 5.

[30] Following the decision, EU Trade Commissioner Mandelson summed up the EC's position: 'By confirming that geographical indications are both legal and compatible with existing trade mark systems, this WTO decision will help the EU to ensure wider recognition of geographical indications and protection of regional and local product identities, which is one of our goals in the Doha Round of multilateral trade negotiations', http://www.delcan.cec.eu.int/en/press_and_information/press_releases/2005/05PR009.shtml

[31] World Trade Organization, General Council, Trade Negotiations Committee, Council for Trade-Related Aspects of Intellectual Property Rights, Special Session on Geographical Indications, Communication from the European Communities 14 June 2005, WT/GC/W/547, TN/C/W/26, TN/IP/W/11.

property alongside patents, copyright and trade marks.[32] While we may have agreement as to the fundamental principles of protection, the European proposal for a multilateral register for GIs raises complex legal issues concerning the relationship between any such international system and the national systems of registration that are currently in place throughout the world.

We have a subject matter that is complex and uncertain due to its lack of systematic development and to considerable variations in the law within different jurisdictions. A priori, given its legal and moral authority, negotiations must also take account of the Doha Declaration that is intended to make it easier for developing countries to adopt measures that are conducive to their economic development.[33] Ambitious claims associating the protection of GIs with economic development are now made by those developing countries that support the international protection of geographical indications. This is put forward as a means of sustaining rural communities by helping to guarantee food security for those without cash incomes, to avert natural environmental disasters and to promote biodiversity.[34]

To what extent then, we may ask, has the rationale for, and implications of protecting GIs been lost in the heated debate that has ensued in the decade since the conclusion of the TRIPS Agreement? While geographical indications have been promoted as a 'development-friendly' form of intellectual property, there are also costs to consider, not only to the public in higher prices and reduced competition, but also to those developing countries who are not well placed to implement further protection.[35] All intellectual property rights by

---

[32]   M. Blakeney, 'Stimulating Agricultural Innovation', in K.E. Maskus and J.H. Reichman (eds), *International Public Goods and Transfer of Technology under a Globalized Intellectual Property Regime*, Cambridge: Cambridge University Press, 2005, pp. 367–90. G. Evans, 'Intellectual Property As A Trade Issue: The Making of the Agreement On Trade Related Aspects of Intellectual Property', *World Competition, Law and Economics Review*, 18 (2), 1994, pp. 137–80.

[33]   At the fourth ministerial meeting of the World Trade Organization in Doha, Qatar during 9–13 November 2001 ministers agreed to 'undertake [a] broad and balanced work programme . . . that incorporates both an expanded negotiating agenda and other important decisions and activities necessary to address the challenges facing the multilateral trading system', paragraph (11), Doha Ministerial Declaration, 14 November 2001, WT/MIN(01)/DEC/1.

[34]   See UNDP, Environmental Mainstreaming Strategy, A strategy for enhanced environmental soundness and sustainability in UNDP policies, programmes, and operational processes, June 2004, at 8, http://www.undp.org/fssd/docs/envmainstrat.doc.

[35]   TRIPS Article 22, and Doha Declaration paragraph 18 as follows: members 'agree as part of the Doha mandate, to negotiate to establish a multilateral system of notification and registration of geographical indications for wines and spirits'. In accordance with paragraph 12 of the Doha Declaration an extension of the protection of geographical indications provided for in Article 23 to products other than wines and

their nature are restrictive of competition. The rationale is based on the notion that a temporary restriction is justified in providing an incentive and a return to the inventor or entrepreneur.[36] The question is whether these demands for extended protection and a mandatory multilateral register can be justified. Preferring therefore to err on the side of caution, this chapter argues in favour of an incremental approach in order to allow developing countries the flexibility to adjust the protection of GIs according to their level of economic development.[37]

And where will tomorrow lead? Before moving forward it behoves us to reflect on the past. Accordingly, Sections 1, 2 and 3 review the provenance and development of geographical indications from their appearance in medieval commerce as geographical marks, to their inclusion in the TRIPS Agreement of 1994. The review concludes with a description of the dual model of regulation promulgated worldwide under the TRIPS Agreement. Sections 4 and 5 examine the European model of *sui generis* regulation of GIs for agricultural products and foodstuffs, including the nature and extent of litigation concerning its application. Section 6 considers the opposing model of transnational regulation advanced by the United States that would protect GIs as a subset of the established trade mark system. It does so by analyzing the way in which the WTO Panel dealt with the conflicting regulatory models in *EC – Protection of Trademarks and Geographical Indications*. Finally, in the light of the Doha Declaration, Sections 7 and 8 discuss possible future developments in the protection of GIs, including the extension of eligible subject matter and the introduction of a mandatory multilateral register. In so doing, it keeps the light of the Doha mandate firmly to the foreground, so that at the end, we may better discern the outline of the road ahead.

---

spirits, is to be addressed in the TRIPS Council forum: further, see text at http://www.wto.org/english/thewto_e/minist_e/min01_e/mindecl_e.htm.

[36]   See K. Maskus, 'Encouraging International Technology Transfer, Intellectual Property Rights and Sustainable Development May', 2004, UNCTAD, Issue Paper No. 7, at p. 31; P. Drahos, 'An Alternative Framework for the Global Regulation of Intellectual Property Rights', *Austrian Journal of Development Studies*, Centre For Governance Of Knowledge And Development Working Paper, October 2005, at p. 14, http://cgkd.anu.edu.au/menus/workingpapers.php. See generally, John Braithwaite and Peter Drahos, *Global Business Regulation*, Cambridge, Cambridge University Press, 2000.

[37]   Bernard M. Hoekman, Keith E. Maskus and Kamal Saggi, 'Transfer of Technology To Developing Countries: Unilateral and Multilateral Policy Options', World Bank Policy Research Working Paper 3332, June 2004, develops a typology of country types and appropriate policy rules as a guide to both national policymakers and rule-making in the World Trade Organization (WTO). See summary table at p. 32.

1   PROVENANCE OF GEOGRAPHICAL INDICATIONS

The Collective Goodwill of Medieval Geographic Indications

Historically, GIs have been described has having led a 'shadowy or subter-
ranean existence, rarely emerging in solid form'.[38] This reputation is, no
doubt, largely due to the varying concepts under which they are protected as
well as the considerable diversity of definition. Geographical indications are
protected on the national and regional levels under a wide range of different
principles, such as protected appellations of origin, registered geographical
indications, protection under trade mark law, and unfair competition or passing off. Such conceptual variety is reflected in the diversity of applicable
terminology that distinguishes between 'geographical indications', 'indications of source' and 'appellations of origin'.[39] Geographical indications are
more broadly defined than appellations of origin. In other words, all appellations of origin are geographical indications, but some geographical indications
are not appellations of origin. 'Indication of source' is the broadest term. It
comprises geographical indications and appellations of origin. Indications of
source only require that the production in question originates in a certain
geographical area.[40]

As with the trade mark, the main function of the geographical indication is
to distinguish goods originating from a certain source. As distinct from trade
marks, geographical indications distinguish the goods for which they are used
through a reference to the place where they were made, and not through a
reference to their manufacturing source. The reference to the place of manufacturing or production is inherent to geographical indications. Unlike trade

---

[38]   N. Dawson, 'Locating Geographical Indications – Perspectives from English
Law' (2000) 90 Trademark Reporter 590. Further on the relationship between registered trademark systems and the protection of geographical indications, see at 590–601.

[39]   Article 1(1) of the Madrid Agreement on Indications of Source defines what
is meant by the term 'indication of source': it can be defined as an indication referring
to a country or to a place situated therein as being the country or place of origin of a
product. Note that this definition does not require that the product in question has a
certain quality or characteristics, which are derived from its geographical origin. The
term 'appellation of origin' is defined in Article 2 of the Lisbon Agreement for the
Protection of Appellations of Origin and their International Registration, of 1958
(Lisbon Agreement). An appellation of origin can be regarded as a special kind of indication of source because the product for which an appellation of origin is used must
have a quality and characteristics which are due exclusively or essentially to its
geographical environment; for example 'Bordeaux' for wine or 'Jaffa' for oranges.

[40]   Indications of source whose use on products does not imply a particular quality, reputation or characteristic of those products appear not to be covered by the definition of geographical indication under the TRIPS Agreement.

marks, geographical indications are not chosen arbitrarily and the reference to the geographical origin cannot be substituted.

Part II, Section 3 of the TRIPS Agreement is dedicated solely to the protection of geographical indications. It is a matter of historical irony that under the TRIPS Agreement, geographical indications should constitute a separate category distinct from trade marks, the very category of intellectual property from which they trace their provenance. Trade mark historians have attributed those very elements that characterize the modern trade mark, goodwill and an individual interest in the quality of the goods, to the geographical or collective mark of the Middle Ages.[41] The notion of a collective goodwill enjoyed by a given locality or organization and of the protection of a mark or seal as the symbol of that collective goodwill was common in the history of medieval as well as of modern commerce. In the competition to earn revenues from the international trade, which was developing at that time, it became apparent that the products of particular regions were more saleable than comparable products from other regions, because of their superior quality. This superior quality was said to be the result of either natural geographic advantages, as in the case of wine from Burgundy, or food processing techniques local to a region such as ham from Parma, or indigenous manufacturing skills as in the case of lace from Bruges. To take advantage of the commercial attractiveness of these local reputations, goods were branded with marks which designated the place of origin of these products. These brands were tantamount to a warranty of the quality of the goods, and goods to which they were affixed were sold merely upon the strength of the marks without the formality of opening or carefully scrutinizing the bales or bolts to which they were affixed. The mark of the town of Osnabrück, the center of the Westphalian linen industry, was held in such great respect and esteem abroad that, in England, in the middle of the fifteenth century, linen bearing this mark commanded a price 20 per cent higher than other Westphalian linens.[42] The law followed commercial practice, seeking to protect the commercial reputation of traders in such geographical localities. In Yugoslavia, for example, a charter of Steven I governed the sale of wine as early as 1222, permitting only products emanating from the region to carry the geographic indication.

The conceptual variety that characterizes the protection of geographical

---

[41]   Sidney A. Diamond, 'The Historical Development of Trademarks', *TMR*, 73, 1983, p. 222; J.T. McCarthy and V.C. Devitt, 'Protection of geographical denominations: domestic and international', *TMR*, 69, 1979, p. 199; M.G. Coerper, 'The Protection of Geographical Indications in the United States of America, with Particular Reference to Certification Marks', *Industrial Property*, July/August, 1990, p. 232.

[42]   Frank I. Schechter, *The Historical Foundation of the Law Relating to Trade Marks*, New York, Columbia University Press, 1925, at pp. 40–42, 78 ff, 122.

indications and the commensurate difficulties currently encountered in their international harmonization give tacit support to the continuing role played by legal history and cultural tradition. In the rise of individual enterprise and trade mark protection in the New World, in its immigrants' use of European geographical descriptions and, equally, in the persistence of the notion of collective goodwill among producers of towns and cities of Europe, we can see the roots of the most intractable issues that have characterized the development of international protection.

During the Industrial Revolution, the mass production of standardized goods on a large scale led to the desire of traders to identify their particular enterprise, rather than the geographical place, as the place of origin of goods. New individualized forms of commercial and political organization saw the emergence of the modern trade mark as any distinct word, phrase or symbol capable of distinguishing the goods of one undertaking from those of another. In contrast to the early marks which collectively conferred public rights on producers in defined localities, registered trade mark systems were enacted to permit individual traders to enforce their marks in the form of personal property rights. Because traders in particular localities might legitimately wish to associate their products with that region, trade mark laws tended to remove the possibility of an individual trader establishing through registration a private monopoly in a geographical indication. Geographical indications could be incorporated into a composite trade mark, only where exclusivity in relation to that mark was disclaimed, or where the geographical element was not the primary signification. Geographical names per se became primarily geographically descriptive and hence unregistrable as a trade mark in the absence of secondary meaning.[43]

Nonetheless, while legislation creating registered trade mark systems became the norm for the majority of countries, such a development did not result in the disappearance of the geographic mark. In continental Europe, substantial processed foods markets and markets for alcoholic beverages remained dependent upon the continued recognition of geographical marks. In these countries national systems for the registration of geographical indications were established.[44]

---

[43]   Graeme Dinwoodie and Mark D. Janis, *Trademarks and Unfair Competition: Law and Policy*, New York, Aspen Publishers, 2004.

[44]   See for example French Legislation on Appellations of Origin, Article L.721–1; JO n° 200 of 30 August 2000: Decree n° 2000–826 of 28 August 2000 concerning examination proceedings for registration of protected appellations of origins and protected geographical indications.

2 THE RISE OF INTERNATIONAL PROTECTION FOR TRADE MARKS AND GEOGRAPHICAL INDICATIONS

Industrialization and internationalization of the economy brought increased intermediation to the supply and distribution chain, giving rise to problems of informational asymmetries between sellers and buyers abroad. Mass production, a rising market of consumers and improved transportation led to the need for the international protection of trade marks and laws against unfair competition. As goods moved across national borders so came the need to promote legitimate trade between nation states by preventing deceptive and misleading trade conduct.[45] In France, between 1870 and 1914, the commercial world was concerned about the increase in 'fraud' and 'counterfeiting' within the beverage and food industries, including artificially coloured wines, margarine passed off as butter, and watered down milk.[46]

Like trade marks, geographical indications are subject to the principle of territoriality insofar as they are protected for a given territory only and are subject to the laws and regulations applicable in that territory.[47] As a result, a particular geographical indication such as 'feta' for cheese may be protected in one country, whereas in another country the same geographical indication may be considered as a generic expression for the kind of products for which it is used. The territorial scope of a geographical indication can be extended through international agreements. In the later nineteenth century, therefore, the nations of Europe and America and their exporters moved to protect the quality and reputation of agricultural products by obtaining the extraterritorial

---

[45] The continuing need to regulate trade marks and trade practices on an international scale is reflected in the revisions of the Paris Convention (1883) at Brussels (1900), Washington (1911), The Hague (1925), London (1934), Lisbon (1958) and Stockholm (1967).

[46] Legislation protecting wine, butter and milk was enacted between 1887 and 1902; finally a general law on food adulteration was adopted in 1905: Alessandro Stanziani, 'Quality Rules: What For? Consumers' vs Lobbies Protection, the case of France', 19th Early 20 Century, paper delivered at XIV International Economic History Congress, Helsinki 2006, Session 9, available at: http://www.helsinki.fi/iehc2006/papers1/stanziani.pdf (visited 31 May 2007).

[47] World Intellectual Property Organization, Standing Committee on the Law of Trademarks, Industrial Designs and Geographical Indications, Possible Solutions for Conflicts Between Trademarks and Geographical Indications and for Conflicts Between Homonymous Geographical Indications: nonetheless, arguing that the unauthorized use of a famous geographical indication takes unfair advantage of, or is detrimental to the reputation of that geographical indication and, therefore, constitutes an act of unfair competition (see, for example, Article 3(1) of the WIPO Model Provisions on Protection Against Unfair Competition): SCT/5/3, at page 8.

application of laws against unfair competition and the infringement of trade marks and geographical indications.[48]

The Paris Convention for the Protection of Industrial Property

The Paris Convention for the Protection of Industrial Property of 20 March 1883[49] provides for the protection of trade marks, geographical indications and other indications of source against misleading use.[50] In this respect, Article 10 of the Paris Convention states that in cases of 'direct or indirect use of a false indication of the source of the goods or the identity of the producer, manufacturer or merchant',[51] Article 9 of the Paris Convention is to be applied. Article 9 provides that goods bearing a false indication of source are subject to seizure upon importation into countries party to the Paris Convention, or within the country where the unlawful affixation of the indication of source occurred, or within the country of importation.[52] Thereafter,

---

[48] The proscription of false indications of the source of goods was included within the Paris Convention of 1883. The significance of the subject can be seen from the fact that the first special agreement under the Paris Convention, the Madrid Agreement for the Repression of False or Deceptive Indications of Source of Goods 1891 (the Madrid Agreement) dealt with this subject; its continuing importance is reflected in the revisions of the Madrid Agreement at Washington (1911), The Hague (1924), London (1934), Lisbon (1958) and Stockholm (1967).

[49] As revised at Brussels on 14 December 1900, at Washington on 2 June 1911, at The Hague on 6 November 1925, at London on 2 June 1934, at Lisbon on 31 October 1958, and at Stockholm on 14 July 1967, and as amended on 28 September 1979.

[50] Note the breadth of the definition of industrial property in Article 1(3) of the Paris Convention for the Protection of Industrial Property, 1883 that stated: 'Industrial property shall be included within the broadest sense and shall apply not only to industry and commerce proper, but likewise to agricultural and extractive industries and to all manufactured or natural products, for example, wines, grain, tobacco leaf, fruit, cattle, minerals, mineral waters, beer, flowers and flour.'

[51] Article 10(2) states: 'Any producer, manufacturer, or merchant whether a natural person or legal entity, engaged in the production or manufacture of or trade in such goods and established either in the locality falsely indicated as the source, or in the region where such locality is situated, or in the country falsely indicated, or in the country where the false indication of source is used, shall in any case be deemed an interested party.'

[52] This seizure shall take place at the request of the public prosecutor, or any other competent authority, or any interested party. However, Article 9(5) and (6) of the Paris Convention allows that countries party to the Paris Convention whose national laws do not permit seizure on importation or inside the country to replace those remedies by either a prohibition of importation or by any other nationally available remedy. Note also the cases in which the use of an indication of source which is literally true may still be misleading or deceptive; as in the case where a given geographical name

Article 10*bis* of the Paris Convention provides the basic international standard for protection against acts of unfair competition. Although the use of false indications of source is not mentioned in the non-exhaustive list of acts which are prohibited under Article 10*bis*(3), such use may be considered an act of competition contrary to honest practices in industrial or commercial matters and liable to mislead the public.[53]

The Madrid Agreement on Indications of Source

Desirous of procuring market exclusivity for its wines and foodstuffs, France has long fought to obtain enhanced international protection of GIs. The Paris Convention afforded the prestigious champagne houses of France only 'limited protection' to indications of source, failing to define the conditions of protection, and prohibiting only 'cases of serious fraud'.[54] There are cases in which the use of an indication of source which is literally true may still be misleading or deceptive. This may be the case where a given geographical name exists in two different countries, but was used as an indication of source only for products originating from that place in one country. Use of that indication of source by producers from the other country cannot be regarded as use of a 'false' geographical indication, although consumers may be deceived by such use. The Madrid Agreement on Indications of Source provides for a remedy in such situations. Article 1 of the Madrid Agreement contains a prohibition on the use of misleading geographical indications, requiring that all goods 'bearing a false or misleading indication' to signatory country, or to a place in that country 'shall be seized on importation'. The Agreement prohibits even the non-misleading use of an indicator, such as 'Champagne-style cheese'.

Nevertheless, the established vintners of Europe did not garner widespread international support for the enhanced protection of indications of source. While 117 countries agreed to the original Paris Convention, subsequent attempts to establish a higher level of protection of GIs in the 1891 Madrid

---

exists in two different countries, but was used as an indication of source only for products originating from that place in one country. Use of that indication of source by producers from the other country cannot be regarded as use of a 'false' geographical indication, although consumers may be deceived by such use.

53   See Article 4(2) of the WIPO Model Provisions on Protection Against Unfair Competition.

54   In its original form, the Paris Convention only barred the use of geographic indicators or appellations of origin in cases of 'serious fraud': Murphy, Bodenhausen. However, it may be argued that Article 10*bis* of the Paris Convention also covers non-misleading use of geographical indications to the extent that such use is considered to constitute an act of unfair competition.

Agreement for the Repression of False or Deceptive Indications of Source on Goods ('Madrid Agreement')[55] failed to achieve the support of significant trading nations such as the USA, Germany and Italy.

The Lisbon Agreement

A further attempt to provide geographic indicators with an even higher standard of harmonized protection is contained in the Lisbon Agreement for the Protection of Appellations of Origin and Their International Registration of 1958. The Lisbon Agreement provides indications of source with stronger protection, although it is only applicable to a special kind of indication of source, namely to appellations of origin which are already protected on the national level of a state party to that Agreement.[56] Like the EC proposal of 2005 for the amendment of the TRIPS Agreement, it envisages a system whereby member states register geographic indications, which receive protection under the national laws of their country of origin, with a central office at the World Intellectual Property Organization in Geneva. After its registration, the appellation of origin is published and notified to all other states party to the Lisbon Agreement. Following receipt of that notification, those states may declare during a period of one year that they cannot protect the appellation of origin which was the subject of the notification.

The scope of protection for internationally registered appellations of origin is broader than the protection for indications of source under the Paris Convention and the Madrid Agreement on Indications of Source. Once an appellation of origin is internationally registered and the one-year objection period under Article 5(3) has expired, the appellation cannot, or can no longer, be used by third parties. In addition, Article 5(6) provides that, where in a state which is a party to the Lisbon Agreement, the internationally registered appellation of origin is already used by third parties, and a declaration according to

---

[55]   See Madrid Agreement for the Repression of False or Deceptive Indications of Source on Goods, Apr. 14, 1891, as amended July 14, 1967, 21 U.S.T. 1583, 828 U.N.T.S. 389 (hereinafter Madrid Agreement) (proscribing the false or deceptive use of indicators which suggest that a good originated in the territory of a member state, and granting national courts the discretion to determine whether an indicator has degenerated into genericism, except in the case of wines), available at: http://www.wipo.org Madrid Agreement.pdf.

[56]   The 'Lisbon Agreement' provides the most exclusive definition of geographic indications, which includes 'appellations of origin': Article 2(1) defines appellations of origin as 'the geographical name of a country, region or locality, which serves to designate a product originating therein, the quality and characteristics of which are due exclusively or essentially to the geographical environment, including natural and human factors'.

Article 5(3) has not been made, that state may grant such third parties a period not exceeding two years to terminate such use. This means that members must prohibit the use of registered geographic indicators, even if the labelling discloses the product's true place of origin or clearly denotes that the indicator is false (for example, by the use of language such as 'imitation' or 'style').

Thus not only misleading use of a protected appellation of origin is prohibited, but 'any usurpation or imitation [of the protected appellation of origin], even if the true origin of the product is indicated or if the appellation is used in translated form or accompanied by terms such as "kind," "type," "make," "imitation" or the like'. Needless to say, given its highly protectionist nature, the Lisbon Agreement failed to win broad international support. As of 1996, only 17 countries were party to the Lisbon Agreement, and again, the United States was not among them.

3 UNIVERSAL MINIMUM STANDARDS OF PROTECTION UNDER TRIPS

At the time of the Paris and Madrid conferences, the primary concern of those seeking to protect geographical indications was the protection of the European wine and spirit industries. This concern has remained constant right up to the promulgation of the first comprehensive international agreement for the protection of intellectual property: the TRIPS Agreement of 1994. Desirous of procuring market exclusivity for its wines and foodstuffs, the EU has long fought to obtain the international protection of GIs. As early as 1988, the EC submitted its views regarding the inadequacy of existing international protection and the deleterious effect on the marketing of Community products, the wine and spirits sector being one which is particularly vulnerable to usurpation, imitation or evocation. The EC draft text submitted to the Uruguay Round would have protected all foodstuffs, including wine, to the same high level, prohibiting use of such geographical indications in question even when accompanied by words such as 'type' or 'style' and in the absence of 'misleading use'.[57] The competing positions were those of the EU and Switzerland

---

[57]   Guidelines and Objectives Proposed by the European Community for the Negotiations on Trade Related Aspects of Substantive Standards of Intellectual Property Rights, MTN.GNG/NG11/W/26. The Swiss draft text defined a geographical indication as: 'any direct or indirect reference to the geographical origin of a product, including characteristics or qualities which are related to that origin', and an appellation of origin as, 'a qualified geographical indication denominating a country, region or locality indicating that a product is originating there from'. Standards and Principles Concerning the Availability, Scope and Use of Trade-Related Intellectual Property

which proposed a broad 'Lisbon-style' protection that would protect geographic indications for all foodstuffs, and the United States which favoured the protection of geographic indications through a certification mark system.[58] In the result the Draft Final Act of December 1991 shows a compromise. While the EC succeeded in having GIs recognized as a distinct category of intellectual property right within Section 3 of the TRIPS Agreement and in securing additional protection for wines and spirits, member states have the freedom to determine the legal means of protection for all other foodstuffs.[59] As the law stands, TRIPS mandates a two-tiered model of regulation, giving enhanced protection to wines and spirits, but for other agricultural products and foods leaving the legal means of protection to national governments.

Enhanced Protection for Geographical Indications for Wines and Spirits

Enhanced, additional protection is provided for geographical indications for wines and spirits by virtue of Article 23. This enhanced protection has two components:

1. protection for geographical indication for wines in the case of homonymous indications; and
2. the establishment of a multilateral system of notification and registration of geographical indications for wines eligible for protection in those members participating in the system.

Typically an application for registration of a geographical indication will specify the applicant, the appellation, the relevant geographical area, the products for which the appellation is used and the 'essential characteristic qualities of the product for which the appellation is used'.[60]

In order to accommodate the differing means of protection among member states, the TRIPS Agreement stops short of setting out the requirements for the registration of geographical indications. Article 23.2 addresses the issue negatively by permitting members to legislate to allow 'an interested person' to

---

Rights, Communication from Switzerland, MTN.GNG/NG11/W/38, 11 July 1989. See further T.P. Stewart (ed.), *The GATT Uruguay Round, A Negotiating History (1986–1992)*, Vols I–III, Deventer, Kluwer, 1993.

[58]   Draft Agreement on the Trade-Related Aspects of Intellectual Property Rights, Communication from the United States, MTN.GNG/NG11/W/70, 11 May 1990.

[59]   TRIPS, Article 22(2).

[60]   The provisions of Article 23.2 apply equally in respect of spirits. See further WIPO, Model Law for Developing Countries on Appellations of Origin and Indications of Source (1975), s.7.

request the refusal or invalidation of the registration of a trade mark which contains or consists of a geographical indication identifying wines or spirits which does not have the indicated origin. Such 'interested persons' will usually include relevant producers from the geographical location, representative associations from those areas, or even associations of consumers.

Prohibited Use

With respect to unauthorized use, Article 23.1 allows each member the flexibility to 'provide the legal means to interested parties to prevent the use of a geographical indication' identifying wines or spirits which do not originate in the place indicated by the geographical indication in question. Registration of trade marks falling under that provision has to be refused or cancelled, either *ex officio* if the applicable law so allows, or at the request of an interested party. In addition, this prohibition, borrowing from Article 3 of the Lisbon Agreement, includes indications which refer to the true origin of such goods, or where the geographical indication is used in translation, or where the geographical indication is 'accompanied by terms such as "kind," "type," "make," "imitation," or the like'. The scope of exclusivity granted GIs for wines and spirits approximates dilution-style protection for trade marks. For example, it is prima facie an infringement of a GI to use it for any similar product, or other product or service, if the use is likely to result in an appropriation of the reputation of the geographical indication, or in the weakening of its reputation.[61]

Homonymous Geographical Indications for Wine

Conflict may arise where products on which homonymous geographical indications[62] are used are sold into the same market. The problem is accentuated where the homonymous geographical indications in question are used on identical products. In the case of homonymous geographical indications for wine, Article 23.3 permits each member to 'determine the practical conditions under

---

[61] For example applying Belgian law on geographical indications and fair trade practices, in 2003, the Nivelles Commercial Court ordered SA de Landtsheer Emmanuel to cease using the word 'champagne' in relation to its new product, as well as the slogan 'the beer world's answer to Veuve Cliquot' (RG A/02/01496).

[62] Homonymous indications are those which are spelled and pronounced alike but which are different in meaning and which are used to designate the geographical origin of products stemming from different countries. For example, Rioja is the name of a region in Spain and in Argentina and the expression applies for wines produced in both countries.

which the homonymous indications in question will be differentiated from each other, taking into account the need to ensure equitable treatment of the producers concerned and that consumers are not misled'. Honest use of such geographical indications should be possible, because the indications designate the true geographical origin of the products on which they are used. However, concurrent use of homonymous geographical indications in the same territory may be problematic where the products on which a geographical indication is used have specific qualities and characteristics which are absent from the products on which the homonym of that geographical indication is used. In this case, the use of the homonymous geographical indication would be misleading, since expectations concerning the quality of the products on which the homonymous geographical indication is used are not met.[63]

General Protection for Other Foodstuffs and Traditional Handicrafts

Insofar as GIs generally are concerned the flexibility of Article 22 permits members to provide 'interested parties' with comprehensive protection by the 'legal means' of their choice. Article 22 facilitates a high standard of protection by the unprecedented breadth of the definition it accords GIs, allowing members to accord protection 'where a given quality, reputation or other characteristic of the good is essentially attributable to its geographical origin'. This definition expands the Lisbon Agreement concept of appellation of origin to protect goods which merely derive a reputation from their place of origin without possessing a given quality or other characteristics which is due to that place. In addition, while a geographical indication to be eligible for protection has to identify goods as originating in a particular territory, it does not necessarily have to be a geographical name. Thus, 'Basmati' for example, is taken to be an indication for rice coming from the Indian subcontinent, although it is not a place name as such.

Codifying existing international protection against unfair trade practices, Article 22.2 prohibits any use which 'constitutes an act of unfair competition under Article 10*bis* of the Paris Convention'. TRIPS extends the ambit of Article 10*bis* to a geographical indication 'which, although literally true as to a territory, region or locality in which the goods originate, falsely represents to

---

[63]   The WIPO Standing Committee on the Law Of Trademarks, Industrial Designs And Geographical Indications recommended that, it may be considered to extend this principle to geographical indications regardless of the kind of products for which they are used. WIPO Standing Committee On The Law Of Trademarks, Industrial Designs and Geographical Indications, 'Possible Solutions For Conflicts Between Trademarks and Geographical Indications and For Conflicts Between Homonymous Geographical Indications', WIPO Doc. SCT/5/3, 8 June 2000.

the public that the goods originate in another territory'. Article 22.2 is supplemented by Articles 22.3 and 22.4. The former deals specifically with the registration of trade marks, containing or consisting of a geographical indication, for goods not originating in the territory indicated, if the use of those trade marks for such goods would be misleading as to the true place of origin of the goods.[64] The remedy available in that situation is refusal or invalidation of the trade mark registration, either *ex officio*, if the applicable law so allows, or at the request of an interested party. Thus, if an application for a trade mark containing the name 'Parma ham' were submitted to the Canadian trade mark office, or indeed any other national trade mark office, with the exception of Italy, it must be refused. The latter, Article 22.4, stipulates that the protection under Articles 22.1–3 must also be made available in respect of the use of deceptive geographical indications, that is, geographical indications that are literally true, although they falsely represent to the public that the goods on which they are used originate in a different territory.

General Exceptions

Article 24 contains a number of exceptions to the obligations under Articles 22 and 23. Generally speaking, there are three categories of exceptions, namely continued and similar use of geographical indications for wines and spirits, prior good faith trade mark rights, and generic designations.[65]

The first exception under Article 24.4 gives the right to WTO members to allow continued and similar use of a particular geographical indication of another member identifying wines or spirits, in connection with goods or services by any of its nationals or domiciliaries who have used that geographical indication in a continuous manner with regard to the same or related goods or services in the territory of that member either for at least ten years preceding 15 April 1994, or in good faith preceding that date.

The second exception under Article 24.5 relates to rights in trade marks that contain a GI, where such marks have been in use in a Member State prior to the date of application of the TRIPS Agreement. It stipulates that the obligation to protect GIs under Articles 22 and 23 is without prejudice to the 'eligibility for or the validity of the registration of a trade mark, or the right to use a trade mark, on the basis that such a trade mark is identical with, or similar to, a geographical indication. Such trade mark owners were not provided with

---

[64]   Ibid. at p. 11.

[65]   Note also: 'Fair use' of personal names in Article 24.8 preserves 'the right of a person to use, in the course of trade, that person's name or the name of that person's predecessor in business, except where such name is used in such a manner as to mislead the public.'

an indefinite dispensation however, since, Article 24.7 allows no more than a five-year window of opportunity to register or enforce their rights. The following conditions must be fulfilled:

1. An application for the registration of such a trade mark must have been filed, or the trade mark must have been registered; or,
2. where the right to the trade mark was acquired by use, that trade mark must have been used, in good faith, by the WTO member concerned, before the TRIPS Agreement became applicable to that member, or
3. before the geographical indication in question is protected in its country of origin.

The third exception in Article 24.6 is related to geographical indications of a WTO member which are considered by another WTO member to be a term customary in common language as the common name for goods or services or, where the geographical indication is used for products of the vine, it is identical with the customary name of a grape variety existing in the territory of that member as of the date of entry into force of the TRIPS Agreement.

In sum, while European negotiators failed to attain the high level of protection they desired, the very inclusion of geographical indications as a distinct category of intellectual property within the TRIPS Agreement marked a milestone in their international protection.

4   REGIONAL PROTECTION OF GEOGRAPHICAL INDICATIONS IN EUROPE

While Europe has had only mixed success in obtaining the higher standard of international protection desired, the autonomous protection of geographical indications across the European Economic Area became an early feature of the Commission's agricultural policy. The formation of the European Community enabled the European Commission to make the international protection for geographical indications an integral part of the Common Market's rural policy.[66] Council Regulation 2081/92 on the Protection of Geographical

---

[66]   In addition to amended Regulation 510/2006 (formerly Regulation 2081/92), there are a series of regulations dealing with designations for wines and spirits including: Regulation 1493/1999 of 17 May 1999 on the common organization of the market in wine (OJL 179, 14 July 1999, p. 16); Regulation 1576/89 of 29 May 1989 laying down general rules on the definition, description and presentation of spirit drinks, OJL 275, 25 April 1989, p. 1; OJL 208, 24 July 1992, p. 1, as amended by 535/97 of 17 March 1997, OJL 83, 25 March 1997, p. 3, and Council Regulation 2082/92 on certifi-

Indications and Designations for Agricultural Products and Foodstuffs[67] notes in its seventh recital that in view of the

> diversity in the national practices for implementing registered designations of origin and geographical indications . . . a Community approach should be envisaged . . . a framework of Community rules on protection will permit the development of geographical indications and designations of origin since, by providing a more uniform approach, such a framework will ensure fair competition between the producers of products bearing such indications and enhance the credibility of the products in the consumers' eyes.[68]

Like trade marks, geographical indications are subject to the principles of 'specialty', insofar as they are only protected in regard to the kind of products on which they are actually used. The subject matter of this Regulation is described as being applicable to certain agricultural products and foodstuffs for which a link between product or foodstuff characteristics and geographical origin exists.[69]

European Definition of Geographical Descriptions

The Regulation defines two different types of geographical description, namely protected geographical indications and protected designations of origin.

---

cates of specific character for agricultural products and foodstuffs. OJL 208, 24 July 1992, p. 9.

[67]   Entered into force on 25 July 1993: its fifth recital states in the relevant part: 'the labelling of agricultural products and foodstuffs is subject to the general rules laid down in Council Directive 79/112 of 18 December 1978 . . . in view of their specific nature, additional special provisions should be adopted for agricultural products and foodstuffs from a specified geographical area'.

[68]   The purpose of protection is to promote agriculture's role in protecting the rural environment, in producing safe and high-quality food and in contributing to maintaining the attractiveness of rural areas for the young and new residents. To encourage applications for GIs, a special fast-track system was initially provided in Article 17. In 2003 however this was abandoned in favour of financial incentives. In addition, financial incentives are offered to EC producers to apply for geographical indications protection: Rural Development in the EU, 2003: http://www.eu.int/comm/agriculture/publi/fact/rurdev2003/en.pdf. See also EC investment programme 17/01/2006. Approval of a €25.5 million programme to support the promotion of agricultural products reflects growing concern over global competition; http://www.foodanddrinkeurope.com/news/printNewsBis.asp?id=65149.

[69]   Council Regulation On The Protection Of Geographical Indications And Designations Of Origin For Agricultural Products And Foodstuffs (EC) No 510/2006 of 20 March 2006.

Protected geographical indication (PGI)

Article 2(1) defines a protected geographic indication to mean:[70]

> the name of a region, a specific place or, in exceptional cases, a country, used to describe an agricultural product or a foodstuff:
> * originating in that region, specific place or country, and
> * which possesses a specific quality, reputation or other characteristics attributable to that geographical origin and the production and/or processing and/or preparation of which take place in the defined geographical area.

Definitional questions concerning a particular specification for a geographical indication are critical since any initial grant of exclusive rights of use to certain producers of agricultural or foodstuffs in accordance to geographic region, is unlikely to go unchallenged by producers of those products outside the designated zone.

Protected designation of origin (PDO)

For the purposes of the Regulation, Article 2(1) provides that protected designation of origin means:[71]

> the name of a region, a specific place or, in exceptional cases, a country, used to describe an agricultural product or a foodstuff:
> * originating in that region, specific place or country, and
> * the quality or characteristics of which are essentially or exclusively due to a particular geographical environment with its inherent natural and human factors, and
> * the production, processing and preparation of which take place in the defined geographical area

It will be noted that qualifying for a PGI is less stringent than qualifying for a PDO, since the product need not originate entirely from within the designated region and need only have one particular quality (rather than the majority of the food's characteristics) that is attributable (rather than exclusively due to) the geographical area.

Registration Procedure

The EU registration system for PGIs and PDOs requires applicants file a specification with the EC.[72] Citizens from member states must initially apply to the

---

[70]   Ibid.

[71]   Under the amended Regulation registration is open to 'the geographical indications of third countries where these are protected in their country of origin': Recital 13.

[72]   Articles 5 to 7 of the Regulation.

relevant national government agency in which the geographical area is located. For applicants in the United Kingdom the relevant agency is the Department for Environment, Food and Rural Affairs.[73] As part of the scrutiny process, the member state is to initiate a national objection procedure ensuring adequate publication of the application and providing for a reasonable period within which any third party having a legitimate interest may lodge an objection to the application. In the absence of any objection and appeal, the member state shall forward the specification to the Commission.[74]

Rights Conferred

Assuming the specification satisfies the requirements of Article 4 concerning the specification, the Commission shall register the designation in accordance with the committee procedure laid down in Article 15. Once registered, a registered geographical indication enjoys the broad description of exclusive rights that are provided in Article 13.1. It provides that registered names shall be protected against:

(a) any direct or indirect commercial use of a name registered in respect of products not covered by the registration in so far as those products are comparable to the products registered under that name or insofar as using the name exploits the reputation of the protected name;

(b) any misuse, imitation or evocation, even if the true origin of the product is indicated or if the protected name is translated or accompanied by an expression such as style, type, method, as produced in, imitation or similar;

(c) any other false or misleading indication as to the provenance, origin, nature or essential qualities of the product, on the inner or outer packaging, advertising material or documents relating to the product concerned, and the packing of the product in a container liable to convey a false impression as to its origin;

(d) any other practice liable to mislead the public as to the true origin of the product.

This prohibits not only food products from outside the region from using the geographical name, but also denies use of the name to products within the region that do not meet the standards set forth in the application. The latter

---

[73] Department for Environment, Food and Rural Affairs responsible for the administration of the policy on regional, local and speciality food and the EU Regulations on the Protected Food Names Schemes http://www.defra.gov.uk/foodrin/foodname/intro.htm

[74] Article 5 paragraphs (4) and (5). Since examination of an application for registration by the Commission takes a certain amount of time, pending a decision on the registration of a name, a member state may, on a transitional basis only, grant protection at national level to the name: Article 5(6).

prohibition on exploitation may extend to include even dissimilar products which attempt to trade on the cachet of the registered products, as where a French court found that a comparable regulation governing wine appellations prohibited the use of 'Champagne' for a perfume as a misappropriation of the registered designation.[75] In this respect, the protection goes beyond that accorded to trade marks, which is limited, except in the case of the most famous, to the goods in which the mark is registered or those sufficiently similar to cause confusion.

Furthermore, the prohibition as to 'any misuse, imitation or evocation, even if the true origin of the product', prevents the use of PDOs and PGIs in conjunction with qualifiers such as 'style' or 'method'. EU member states may allow continued use of these qualifiers for a transitional period of five years, if the products had previously been marketed in such a manner for at least five years and the true origin of the product is clearly labelled.[76] Perhaps most significantly, the Regulation prevents any protected name from becoming generic. Although a designation may be altered, or even lost, as a result of changes in technology or processing techniques, it cannot be lost as a result of changes in understanding or usage of the protected name.[77]

5   PERSISTENT PROBLEMS IN THE INTERNATIONAL HARMONIZATION OF GEOGRAPHICAL INDICATIONS

Since the introduction of the EC's specialized system for the protection of geographical indications in 1992 over 700 foods and beverages have been approved by the Commission for GI registration, with another 320 applications under consideration.[78] In the decade since the Regulation was implemented, recurrent litigation has borne witness to a number of problems that are likely to be replicated should similar protection be adopted on an international scale.

---

[75]   Cour d'appel Paris 1st ch. A., 15 December 1993.

[76]   As far as potential actions for infringement are concerned, Article 13(3) provides for a transitional period of up to five years for adjustment where the products in question have been legally on the market for at least five years preceding the date of the publication provided for in Article 6(2).

[77]   Article 13(2).

[78]   As of 25.10.2005, 36 UK products have been registered with the EU including Stilton Cheese, Cornish Clotted Cream and West Country Farmhouse Cheddar. A further 18 applications are being considered: http://www.publications.parliament.uk/pa/cm200506/cmhansrd/vo051025/text/51025w03.htm.

Conflicts Concerning Trade Marks and Geographical Indications

Potential conflicts concerning trade marks and geographical indications in respect of agricultural products and foodstuffs have proven problematic in cases where there exists a high level of supply-side substitutability and a high likelihood of conflict between trade marks and geographical indications: the market for mineral waters being a notable example. Formerly protectable as a PGI under EC Regulation 2081/92, complications surrounding the interaction of trade marks and GIs for such products caused the Commission to remove 'mineral and spring waters' from the list of registrable items in 2003.[79]

The market for mineral waters appears not best suited to protection by separate systems for geographical indications and trade marks. It is characterized by a high level of supply-side substitutability that tends to militate in favour of a single product market. Thus it appears that practically the whole body of Italian bottlers can bottle both still and sparkling water, and a large number of them seem to use the same brand for both. There are relatively low production switching costs involved in a change from sparkling to flat water or vice versa. With respect to time and financial expenditure, these costs do not amount to a significant barrier. The European market for mineral water is an intensely competitive market.[80] Because of high consumption rates, prices and competition on prices are the driving factors of the market.[81]

Annex I of Regulation (EEC) No 2081/92, listing the types of foodstuff that may be registered, until recently included natural mineral waters and spring waters. The Commission's examination of applications for registration of these products revealed several difficulties. In particular, the use of identical names for different mineral waters and of invented names that were not covered by the provisions of the Regulation, proved problematic. There was considerable potential for litigation concerning the conflict between the respective rights of use of the trade mark owners and those of the owners of geographical indications. The decision to withdraw mineral waters was undoubtedly made in view of the likelihood of consumer confusion as a result of the application of the principle of coexistence between

---

[79] Mineral waters are no longer registrable and old registrations are only valid until 2013: Regulation (EC) No 692/2003. However, there is a provision for a 10-year transitional period to avoid any injury to waters already registered.

[80] In terms of pro capita consumption, Italy is by far the largest consumer of mineral water, with 127 litres in 1996, against 34 litres for Portugal, 82 litres for France, 62 litres for Spain, 90 litres for Germany and 8 litres for the United Kingdom.

[81] See Case No IV\M.1065 – Nestle/San Pellegrino Merger Procedure, Article 6(1)(b) Decision, Commission Of The European Communities, Brussels, 16 February 1998, Case No IV\M.1065.

the two sets of rights, as provided in Articles 13(5) and 14(2) of the above Regulation.[82]

These difficulties led to conflicts of interests in the course of the implementation of former Regulation 2081. The case of *Gerolsteiner Brunnen GmbH & Co. v Putsch GmbH*,[83] for example, concerned the use of the words 'Kerry Spring' on mineral water bottles, which might be in conflict with the mark 'Gerri' for products of the same description. The defendant argued that the prominent display of 'Kerry Spring' on the product was justified under Article 6(1)(b) since the water came from a source in County Kerry, Ireland. The German Federal Supreme Court referred to the ECJ, the question as to whether Article 6(1)(b) is only applicable if the sign is not used 'as a mark', that is, in a manner which could be mistaken as indicating a commercial source; and, whether the fact that the sign had been used 'as a mark' should be taken into account for the purpose of assessing use in accordance with honest commercial practice.

The ECJ concluded that Article 6(1)(b) does not distinguish between the possible uses of the indications to which it refers. The only test in the Article is whether the indication of geographical origin is used in accordance with honest practices in industrial or commercial matters, equating to a duty to act fairly in relation to the legitimate interests of the trade mark owner. Thus, 'the mere fact that there exists a likelihood of confusion between a word mark registered in one Member State and an indication of geographical origin from another Member State is . . . insufficient to conclude that the use of that indication in the course of trade is not in accordance with honest practices'. As a result, trade marks and geographical indications had to coexist to the effect that where an alleged infringing mark is used to indicate the geographical origin of the goods in question, the ability to escape liability for infringement depends on whether the use is in accordance with honest practices in industrial or commercial matters and not whether the indication is being used as a trade mark.[84]

---

[82]   Mineral and spring waters are already the subject of Council Directive 80/777/EEC of 15 July 1980 on approximation of the laws of the member states relating to the exploitation and marketing of natural mineral waters. Council Regulation (EC) No 692/2003 of 8 April 2003 amending Regulation (EEC) No 2081/92 on the protection of geographical indications and designations of origin for agricultural products and foodstuffs.

[83]   The European Court of Justice in its decision of 7 January 2004, in the case of *Gerolsteiner Brunnen GmbH & Co. v Putsch GmbH* (Case C-100/02).

[84]   It is for the national court to carry out an overall assessment of all the relevant circumstances to determine whether the producer of the product bearing an indication of geographical origin is unfairly competing with the proprietor of the trade mark.

Questions Concerning the Definition of Geographical Indications

The course of the Regulation shows that definitional questions are likely to be the subject of recurrent challenge. Both geographical indications and designations of origin mean 'the name of a region, a specific place or, in exceptional cases, a country, used to describe an agricultural product or foodstuff'.[85] In both cases the production, processing or preparation take place within the 'defined geographical area'. The case of *Northern Foods Plc* v *The Department For Environment, Food And Rural Affairs* has emerged as a ground-breaking case over the EU's geographical indications (GI) system and the problems it can pose for competitor manufacturers outside the defined geographical area. Northern Foods Plc, sought to challenge the decision of the defendant, the Department of the Environment, Food and Rural Affairs (DEFRA) to forward to the European Commission an application by the Melton Mowbray Pork Pie Association ('MMPPA') for the registration of 'Melton Mowbray Pork Pie' as a protected geographical indication ('PGI') under EC Council Regulation 2081/92/EEC. On 21 December 2005, the High Court dismissed Northern Foods' application, allowing the application to the Commission to proceed. Mr Justice Crane[86] ruled that Northern Foods' main contention concerning the proposed 'region' of 1800 square miles going far beyond Melton Mowbray, was misconceived. The proposed area includes Leicester, where Samworth Brothers make 62 percent of Britain's Melton Mowbray pies, compared with the 28 percent share held by Northern Foods.

European case law indicates that, when considering the grant of a defined geographical area, the size of the area is immaterial.[87] *Commission of the European Communities* v *The Federal Republic of Germany*[88] concerned an application by the Federal Republic of Germany reserving the appellations 'Sekt' and 'Weinbrand' to sparkling wine and brandy produced in Germany. The ECJ ruled that 'an area of origin which is defined on the basis either of the extent of national territory or a linguistic criterion cannot constitute a geographical area capable of justifying an indication of origin', particularly as the products in question could be produced from grapes of indeterminate origin. In November 2006 Northern Foods withdrew an application to appeal

---

[85] Article 2(2).
[86] *Northern Foods Plc* v *The Department For Environment, Food And Rural Affairs* [2005] EWHC 2971.
[87] See concerning the definitional breadth of the specified geographic area Case T-109/97, concerning the PDO 'Altenburger Ziegenkäse' (goats' cheese made in the Altenburg region, which must contain a minimum percentage of goats' milk), which was registered by Germany under Regulation No 2081/92.
[88] Case 12-74, Judgment, 20 February 1975.

after an assurance from the Department for Environment, Food and Rural Affairs (DEFRA) that, in the event that the European Commission decides to approve 'Melton Mowbray' as a PGI, business will be allowed a five-year period to transfer production into the designated zone.[89]

Generic Indications

Throughout the development of international protection, geographic names which have become generic have proven a repeated stumbling block. EC Regulation, Article 3(1) defines a 'name that has become generic' as the name of an agricultural product or a foodstuff which, although it relates to the place or the region where this product or foodstuff was originally produced or marketed, has become the common name of an agricultural product or a food-stuff.[90] European migration in the eighteenth and nineteenth centuries to the colonies of the New World invariably resulted in new entrepreneurs hoping to capitalize on the success of their traditional European food products and processes. Two popular American foods – hamburgers and frankfurters – reveal much about the culinary and cultural history of America.

Consequently, the 'deal-breaker' has invariably been the inability of nations to exempt geographical indications which had arguably become generic within their borders. During the twentieth century, increasingly international trade, a global marketplace and sophisticated marketing techniques have rendered the historical adoption of Old World names by New World immigrants an urgent problem of legal harmonization. In an attempt to preserve GIs further from usurpation, the Madrid Agreement of 1891[91] prohibited members from allowing geographical indicators to become generic without a decision by a national court. Thus, valid wine appellations might never lose protection. As an indication of the difficulty of the issue, over 100 years later only 31 states had

---

[89]   On 20 February 2007, the Court of Appeal informed the ECJ that it was withdrawing its request for a preliminary ruling. Legally, it is regrettable that the case was removed from the court's register, since a ruling might have clarified the situation regarding the method of defining geographic area: Case C-169/06 at http://curia.europa.eu.

[90]   For instance, the names 'Mozzarella' and 'Camembert' for cheese are not currently protected as geographical indications in the EC or elsewhere and are therefore not entitled to protection in third countries under TRIPS provisions.

[91]   See the Madrid Agreement for the Repression of False or Deceptive Indications of Source on Goods, 14 April 1891, as amended 14 July 1967, 21 U.S.T. 1583, 828 U.N.T.S. 389 proscribing the false or deceptive use of indicators which suggest that a good originated in the territory of a member state, and granting national courts the discretion to determine whether an indicator has degenerated into genericism, except in the case of wines, available at http://www.wipo.org Madrid Agreement.pdf.

signed the agreement. Subsequently the Lisbon Agreement attempted to prevent the degeneration of registered appellations of origin into genericism, provided they continued to receive protection in their country of origin. This ambitious attempt to extend the scope of protection was also a failure. As of 1996, only 17 countries were party to the Lisbon Agreement, and again, the United States was not among them.

And so it is that today the issue of generic names has the potential to cause the greatest unease in negotiations for increased international protection. The European Commission has submitted to the TRIPS Council a proposal to extend enhanced protection of geographical indications beyond that currently accorded to wines and spirits, to agricultural products and foods. This would mean for example that Wisconsin producers, could no longer use 'feta' cheese as a generic or customary term in the trade.

Among some 700 geographical indications registered under the European Regulation, a considerable number comprise formerly generic terms. In fact, a high proportion of the litigation concerning the grant and use of geographical indications concerns the contested genericism of the applicant PGI or PDO. The GI Regulation is intended 'to protect agricultural products or foodstuffs which have an identifiable geographical origin . . . to achieve a better balance between supply and demand on the markets'.[92] However, the registration of GIs may exclude producers who were using what they thought was a generic name for their products, or who hoped to capitalize on the success of traditional foods.

As recently as October 2005, the ECJ ruled that the term 'feta', which is used to refer to the soft white cheese made from sheep or goat's milk, is not a generic name, thereby restricting the use of the 'feta' name to producers in the designated region of Greece. The ruling means that all non-Greek EU feta producers had to change the name of their cheese by 2007 or be forced to stop production if unable or unwilling to do so.[93] The ruling dramatically illustrates the breadth of the EU Regulation and its capacity to offer protection to terms previously considered generic. The Regulation prevents any protected name from becoming generic. Although a designation may be altered, or even lost, as a result of changes in technology or processing techniques, it cannot be lost as a result of changes in understanding or usage of the protected name.[94]

---

[92]　Recitals 6 and 2 respectively.

[93]　Greece produces about 85 per cent of the feta consumed in the EU, or about 115 000 tonnes a year. Danish dairies produce about 27 000 tonnes of feta a year; Germany from 20 000 to 40 000 tonnes. France produces 8000 to 20 000 tonnes a year. Further, see 'UK Dismay as Greeks Win Feta Cheese Rights', *Financial Times*, 25 October 2005, http://www.ft.com/cms/s/a01bdebe-4571-11da-981b-00000e2511c8.html.

[94]　Art. 13(3).

'Feta' had originally been registered as a PDO under Regulation (EEC) No 2081/92 (2) in 1996. Following objections from several member states, the decision was subsequently annulled by the Court of Justice in 1999 on the basis that the Commission had paid insufficient attention to the situation existing in other member states when assessing the possible generic character of the 'feta' designation.[95] Following the court's decision, the Commission subsequently invited member states to provide exhaustive information on production, consumption and other available knowledge on the denomination of 'feta'. Article 15 of the former Regulation provides that the Commission shall submit a proposed course of action to a committee of the member nations. If the committee agrees, the Commission may proceed. If not, the proposal is submitted to the Council for action. Should the Council fail to act within three months, the Commission may proceed with its proposal. In the case of feta cheese it was unable to achieve a consensus regarding registration. In June 2002, due to the absence of opinion by the relevant committee, the proposal was transmitted for adoption to the Council. According to comitology procedure, the Council had three months to take a decision and, as there was no decision, the Commission formally adopted the regulation in October.

The ruling upholds the EC's decision to grant Greek feta cheese producers protected designation of origin (PDO) status in 2002. The European Court of Justice ruling of 26 October 2005 in favour of the grant of PDO status to 'feta' that prohibits cheese makers outside of designated areas in Greece from calling their products 'feta' emphasizes the danger to food processors of making branded products based on local traditions. The granting of PDO status to feta was contested by Germany and Denmark, who were supported by France and the UK. Germany, Denmark, France and the UK applied for annulment of the registration of 'feta' as a PDO for Greece, arguing that the name had become a generic term, like 'cheddar'. France and Denmark have been producing feta-type cheeses since the 1930s. German companies began in 1972. The failure of their challenge and the character of the court's reasoning as to the entitlement of formerly generic terms to PDO status indicate the breadth of protection offered by the EC Regulation. The European Court of Justice ruled that white cheese soaked in brine and called 'feta' must originate from specified areas in Greece.

The court found that 'the interplay between the natural factors and the specific human factors, in particular the traditional production method, which requires straining without pressure, has thus given feta cheese its remarkable

---

[95]   In the event of an objection, and if an agreement cannot be worked out between the parties involved, the Commission may determine whether to proceed with the registration in consultation with a committee of the member nations or the Council.

international reputation'. It concluded that the name 'feta' had not become the common name of the product, and that it continued to evoke a Greek origin. The court found that while white cheeses soaked in brine have been produced for a long time, not only in Greece but in various countries in the Balkans and the southeast of the Mediterranean basin, those cheeses are known in those countries under names other than 'feta'. The court noted that in other member states, feta is commonly marketed with labels referring to Greek cultural traditions and civilization. Thus, the court concluded that consumers in those member states perceive feta as a cheese associated with Greece, even if in reality it has been produced in another member state. As regards Denmark, the court noted that the relevant 'Danish legislation does not refer to "feta" but to "Danish feta", which would tend to suggest that in Denmark the name "feta", by itself, had retained a Greek connotation.'

The feta decision therefore gives exclusive rights to feta producers in mainland Greece and the department of Lesbos to market the cheese in the EU using the 'feta' designation. GI status having been granted, other food makers must either stop calling the products by the protected name, or move production to the designated area using the same sourced ingredients and processes.

Generic Names under TRIPS

The dual protection of the TRIPS Agreement reflects the transatlantic divide over the scope of protection granted geographic indications. Under TRIPS a term that is considered to be generic and not an indication of a specific origin need not be protected; that is, a WTO member need not extend protection to a GI if it is 'customary in common language as the common name for such goods' in that WTO member, without regard to the situation in the territory of export. In the case of GIs which have become generic in their country of origin, TRIPS Article 24.9 provides that there is no obligation under the TRIPS Agreement to protect geographical indications 'which are not or cease to be protected in their country of origin, or which have fallen into disuse in that country'.

Exceptions with Respect to Wines and Spirits

That is not to say of course that, given the global nature of markets, US and other New World cheese producers may be in a more certain position in the event that Article 23-style protection were to be adopted and they were able to invoke the kinds of international rules that presently pertain to wines and spirits. In an endeavor to accommodate the registration and use by members of geographical indications in relation to wines or spirits, TRIPS Article 24.4 exempts members from having to 'prevent continued and similar use of a particular geographical indication of another Member identifying wines or spirits in connection with goods or services' where that geographical indication has been used 'in a continuous manner with regard to the same or related goods or services' in the territory of that member either for at least ten years preceding 15 April 1994 (the date of entry into force of the TRIPS Agreement) or where the continuous use has been in good faith.

As an illustration of the sorts of matters falling within the exceptions contained in Article 24, reference may be made to the protection of geographical indications for wines and spirits undertaken by the US Bureau of Alcohol, Tobacco and Firearms (BATF).[96] Its regulations permit the use of 'semi-generic names' such as 'Champagne', 'Burgundy' and 'Chablis' if 'the correct place of origin is directly conjoined to the name'.[97] This practice may fall within the Article 24.4 exception or within the exception in Article 24.6 which exempts the geographical indications of a member 'with respect to the products of the vine for which the relevant indication is identical with the customary name of a grape variety existing in the territory of that Member as at the date of entry into force of the WTO Agreement'.

However, the possible closing-off of future market access opportunities for emerging industries, and uncertainty concerning the continued use in existing markets, would be equally real under such rules, since the exceptions under Article 24.6 apply on a per-member basis. Thus, if a term is generic (Article 24.6 exception) in one WTO member, it may be a protected geographical indication in other WTO members. For example, if the EC concludes sufficient bilateral agreements for absolute protection of the term 'feta', producers in a WTO member where 'feta' is a generic term will nonetheless be precluded from exporting to any WTO member with whom the EC has concluded such a bilateral agreement. Therefore, the producers in the WTO member where the term is generic would not be able to export that product using the generic term to other markets.[98]

---

[96]   See generally, Peter Brody, 'Protection of Geographical Indications in the Wake of TRIPS: Existing United States Laws and the Administration's Proposed Legislation', *TMR*, 84, 1994, 520.

[97]   Ibid., at p. 530.

[98]   See EU–Chile Association Agreement, 2002, Wines and Spirits, Section 6: http://europa.eu.int/comm/external_relations/chile/assoc_agr/ip02_1696.htm.

6 THE REGULATORY STRUCTURE OF GEOGRAPHICAL INDICATIONS AS A MATTER FOR WTO DISPUTE SETTLEMENT

US v EC – Protection of Trade Marks and Geographical Indications

In view of the global markets at stake in the agricultural and food processing sectors, the US and Australia became so concerned at the systematic discrimination its trade mark owners faced in enforcing their rights against European registered GIs that they invoked the WTO dispute settlement procedure.[99] On 18 August 2003, the US and Australia requested the establishment of a WTO dispute settlement panel to review the consistency of EU Regulation 2081/92 with the rules of the TRIPS Agreement and the General Agreement on Tariffs and Trade (GATT).[100]

The US and Australia argued that the EU scheme for the protection of geographical indications failed to comply with TRIPS in three chief respects. Firstly, they claimed the EC Regulation was discriminatory and in violation of the national treatment obligations and the most-favored-nation obligations in Articles 3 and 4 of the TRIPS Agreement and Articles I and III of the General Agreement on Tariffs and Trade 1994. The TRIPS Agreement requires that members accord most-favoured-nation treatment to the GIs of fellow member states and national treatment to the geographical indications of their citizens. The US and Australia argued that:

1. Regulation 2081/92 does not provide the same treatment to other nationals and products originating outside the EC that it provides to the EC's own nationals and products.
2. The Regulation does not accord immediately and unconditionally to the nationals and products of each WTO Member any advantage, favour, privilege or immunity granted to the nationals and products of other WTO Members.
3. It diminishes the legal protection for trade marks.

---

[99]   The statement of the United States (US) to the WTO in a WTO trade policy review of the European Union expressed the concern that 'foreign persons wishing to obtain protection for their GIs in the EU itself face a non-transparent process that appears to come into some conflict with the EU's TRIPS obligations' and that 'EU rule-making processes are often perceived by third countries as exclusionary, allowing no meaningful opportunity for non-EU parties to influence the outcome of regulatory decisions', WTO Trade Policy Review of the European Union, Statement by the United States to the WTO, 24 July 2002, http://www.state.gov/e/eb/rls/rm/2002/12242.htm.

[100]   See documents WT/DS174/20 and WT/DS290/18.

4.   It does not provide any legal means for interested parties to prevent the misleading use of a geographical indication.
5.   It does not define a geographical indication in a manner that is consistent with the definition provided in the TRIPS Agreement.
6.   It is not sufficiently transparent.
7.   It does not provide adequate enforcement procedures.

As a result of the alleged violation, in the event that US holders of geographic indications such as 'Florida oranges' and 'Idaho potatoes' sought registration under the EC Regulation, they were subject to a requirement of reciprocity and equivalence. Although expressed to be 'without prejudice to international agreements', Article 12 states that the Regulation

> may apply to an agricultural product or foodstuff from a third country provided that:
> *   the third country is able to give guarantees identical or equivalent to those referred to in Article 4,
> *   the third country concerned has inspection arrangements and a right to objection equivalent to those laid down in this Regulation,
> *   the third country concerned is prepared to provide protection equivalent to that available in the Community to corresponding agricultural products for foodstuffs coming from the Community.

Secondly, they claimed that the grant of exclusive rights in the use of the mark provided by virtue of TRIPS Article 16.1 required member states to make available to earlier trade mark owners rights against GIs. The United States argued that the Regulation was inconsistent with the exclusivity of the trade mark owners' rights under Article 16.1 of the TRIPS Agreement because it did not ensure that a trade mark owner may prevent uses of GIs which would result in a likelihood of confusion with a valid prior trade mark.[101]

Thirdly, they argued that Regulation 2081/92 was inconsistent with the EC's obligations under Article 24.5 of the TRIPS Agreement, since the Regulation failed to provide sufficient protection to pre-existing trade marks that were similar or identical to a geographical indication.

In short, food exporters in the United States were concerned that geographical indications should not be given precedence over trade mark rights. The issue was one of priority between a coexisting GI and a trade mark and whether the principle of 'first-in-time, first-in-right' should be enforced as it is in the trade mark law of the United States. In contrast, in the European Union, trade marks are required to coexist with geographical indications. As we noted in the Gerolsteiner case, under European law a trade mark owner's rights

---

[101]   See variously, United States' first written submission, paras 137–140, 170; United States' first oral statement, paras 42–43.

cannot prevail over a third party using a duly registered GI in accordance with honest business practices.[102] As a result, private trade mark suits brought by US litigants against European-owned GIs might well result in the US trade mark owner having to forfeit valuable rights to priority and exclusivity. Thus, trade mark wars over the competitive European market for beer, had seen US trade marks 'Budweiser' and 'Bud', subject to termination in various member states of the European Communities because the European law holds 'Budweiser' and 'Bud' to be geographical indications for beer from the Czech Republic.[103] The cancellation of the Budweiser and Bud trade marks for beer in Europe caused unease among US trade mark owners. The obstacles to registering US certification marks as GIs in Europe gave rise to further uncertainty about the security of protection and conditions of competition.

The Panel Report in the dispute concerning *European Communities – Protection of Trademarks and Geographical Indications for Agricultural Products and Foodstuffs*, was adopted at a meeting of the Dispute Settlement Body on 20 April 2005.[104] Concerning the discriminatory conditions regarding the registration of foreign GIs and the requirement for reciprocity of protection, the panel gave a resounding decision in favour of the US and Australia. Pursuant to Article 19.1 of the DSU, the Panel recommended that:[105]

1. The European Communities bring the Regulation into conformity with the TRIPS Agreement and GATT 1994.
2. The European Communities could implement the above recommendation with respect to the equivalence and reciprocity conditions, by amending 'the Regulation so as for those conditions not to apply to the procedures for registration of GIs located in other WTO Members'.

---

[102] *Gerolsteiner Brunnen GmbH & Co.* v *Putsch GmbH* (Case C-100/02).

[103] The battle over the right to the name 'Budweiser' has pitted the world's largest brewer, Anheuser-Busch of the United States, against the 'boutique' Czech brewer Budejovicky Budvar. The latter, based in the Czech town of Ceske Budejovice (also known as Budweis), claims it has been brewing a beer under the name since the thirteenth century, although the American beer has gained broader international reputation in recent years. See WTO, 1999: Preparations for the 1999 ministerial conference – Agreement on TRIPS: Extension of the additional protection for geographical indications to other products. Communication from the Czech Republic. WT/GC/W/206.

[104] WT/DS290/R.

[105] *European Communities – Protection of Trademarks and Geographical Indications for Agricultural Products and Foodstuffs*, Complaint by the United States, (*EC – Trademarks and Geographical Indications*) Panel Report, WT/DS174/R, adopted 20 April 2005, at p. 167.

However, as far as the future protection of GIs as a discrete form of intellectual property is concerned, a substantive victory went to the EC. In an affirmation of the geographical indication as intellectual property, the Panel endorsed the European principle of their coexistence with all but the most famous of prior trade marks. The panel concluded that while the Regulation is inconsistent with Article 16.1 of the TRIPS Agreement, this derogation is justified by Article 17 of the TRIPS Agreement.

The Interrelationship of Geographical Indications and Trade Marks

The WTO ruling on the interrelationship of GIs and trade marks has important implications for current debate in the TRIPS Council concerning the possible extension of protection to all agricultural products and foodstuffs. One of the key concerns of those who oppose an extension of GI protection is the potential conflict between geographical indications and identical or similar trade marks.

In the event that there is a conflict between a trade mark and a GI, TRIPS Article 24 appears to offer certain protections for trade mark owners who use or register marks in good faith. A trade mark that has been used or registered in good faith in one jurisdiction cannot be pre-empted by a later-established GI that conflicts with the trade mark. As to whether this meant that the later geographical indication could not even be used in the event that it conflicted with an earlier-established, good-faith trade mark, this was by no means certain. The question called for the Panel to examine the scope of the general principle *prius in tempore, potior in jure* (first in time, stronger in right) in relation to the scope of protection accorded GIs on the one hand and prior marks, containing an identical or deceptive geographical name, on the other.

Coexistence under Article 14(2) of the EC Regulation

In response, the European Community successfully argued before the WTO that the boundary between GIs and trade marks as independent but equal forms of intellectual property is defined by TRIPS Article 24.5, which provides for coexistence with earlier trade marks.

Under Community law the system for the registration of GIs is required to coexist alongside the Community Trade Mark system.[106] The term 'coexis-

---

[106] In point, Art. 159 of the CTM as amended provides as follows: 'This Regulation shall not affect Council Regulation (EEC) No. 2081/92 on the protection of geographical indications and designations of origin for agricultural products and foodstuffs of 14 July 1992, and in particular thereof.' The Community Trade Mark Regulation (CTM) and the Harmonization Directive contain stipulations ensuring that

tence' refers to a legal regime under which a GI and a trade mark can both be used concurrently to some extent even though the use of one or both of them would otherwise infringe the rights conferred by the other. Article 14.2 of the EC Regulation is intended to implement Article 24.5 of the TRIPS Agreement.[107] It provides as follows:

> With due regard for Community law, use of a trade mark corresponding to one of the situations referred to in Article 13 which was registered in good faith before the date on which application for registration of a designation of origin or geographical indication was lodged may continue notwithstanding the registration of a designation of origin or geographical indication, where there are no grounds for invalidity or revocation of the trade mark . . .

Article 14(2) begins with the introductory phrase '[w]ith due regard to Community law'. This is a reference to the Community Trademark Regulation and the First Trademark Directive,[108] both of which provide that trade mark registration confers the right to prevent 'all third parties' from certain uses of 'any sign', including uses where there exists a likelihood of confusion.[109] Prima facie, the trade mark owner's exclusive rights under TRIPS Article 16.1 cannot be exercised against a person who uses a registered GI in accordance with its registration where the trade mark is subject to Article 14(2) of the Regulation.

With the exception of well-known marks, Article 14 privileges the GI to the extent that the rights conferred by a trade mark registration against 'all third parties' and uses of 'any sign' do not prevail over a third party using a GI in accordance with its European registration.[110] It will be recalled, for example,

---

the GI prevails over a registered trade mark. Article 142 of the original Council Regulation (EC) No. 40/94 was renumbered Article 159 by Article 156(5) of Council Regulation (EC) No. 1992/2003.

[107]   Paragraph 11 of the recitals to the April 2003 amending Regulation explained that the dates referred to in Article 14(2) should be amended in line with Article 24.5 of the TRIPS Agreement. Article 14(2) has been interpreted once by the European Court of Justice, in Case C-87/97, *Consorzio per la tutela del Formaggio Gorgonzola* v *Käserai Champignon Hofmeister GmbH & Co Kg* [1999] ECR I-1301, concerning the trade mark, 'Cambozola' for cheese and the GI 'Gorgonzola'.

[108]   European Communities' response to panel question No. 138. The 'Community Trademark Regulation' refers to Council Regulation (EC) No. 40/94 on the Community trade mark, as amended by Council Regulation (EC) No. 1992/2003 and Council Regulation (EC) No. 422/2004.

[109]   Article 9 of the Community Trademark Regulation, and Article 5 of the First Trademark Directive.

[110]   The scope of Article 14(2) is confined in time to those trade marks applied for, registered or established by use either before the GI is protected in its country of origin or before the date of submission to the Commission of an application for GI registration. Art. 14(3) stipulates that a designation of origin or geographical indication shall

that in *Gerolsteiner Brunnen GmbH & Co* v P*utsch GmbH*,[111] the European Court of Justice (ECJ) in accordance with the principle of coexistence of the trade mark and GI systems, ruled that trade mark owners cannot stop others from using similar-sounding geographical indications where they are used honestly in industrial or commercial matters.[112]

Earlier Trade Mark Owners' Rights of Priority

In respect of the earlier trade mark owners' rights of priority, the European Communities argued that Article 14.3 of the Regulation, together with the criteria for registrability of trade marks applied under EC law, prevent the registration of a GI, use of which would result in a likelihood of confusion with a prior trade mark. Article 14.3 provides as follows:

> A designation of origin or geographical indication shall not be registered where, in the light of a trade mark's reputation and renown and the length of time it has been used, registration is liable to mislead the consumer as to the true identity of the product.

It can be invoked before the courts after registration of a GI, including trade mark infringement proceedings brought against a user of the GI.[113] It amounts to a condition for the registration of a GI, as it provides for the refusal of registration of a GI that is liable to mislead the consumer as to the true identity of the product in light of certain factors relevant to a prior trade mark. This, in effect, provides that a prior trade mark may prevail over a later application for GI registration under certain conditions. For example, 'Bayerisches Bier' was registered as a protected geographical indication in 2001 subject to the proviso that the use of certain prior trade marks, for example, 'Bavaria' and 'Høker Bajer', was permitted to continue under Article 14(2). The GI refers to a beer and the trade marks are registered in respect of beer. The GI and the trade

---

not be registered where, in the light of a trade mark's reputation and renown and the length of time it has been used, registration is liable to mislead the consumer as to the true identity of the product.

[111]   Case C-100/02.

[112]   Trade Mark Directive, 1989, Article 6(1) defence.

[113]   A trade mark owner may raise the invalidity of the measure before the courts under the preliminary ruling procedure in Article 234 of the EC Treaty. Depending on the factual circumstances of each case, a trade mark owner may also have standing to bring an action in annulment under Article 230 of the EC Treaty, if a GI registration were considered to affect adversely specific substantive trade mark rights. Under both procedures, judicial review is available on points of fact and law. The cancellation procedure is set out in Article 11a of the Regulation and the grounds mentioned in Articles 11 and 11a are exhaustive. Further, see European Community responses to Australia's question Nos 2 and 3 after the second substantive meeting, and European Community responses to panel question Nos 67 and 142; rebuttal submission, paras 294–7; second oral statement, paras 174–9.

marks are, respectively, the words 'Bavaria' or 'Bavarian beer' rendered in the German, English and Danish languages. Upon its registration, the EC Council concluded that the GI would not mislead the public as to the identity of the product, which is the standard embodied in Article 14(3) of the Regulation.

In respect of the operation of Article 14.3, the Panel found that the United States had a prima facie case that Article 14.3 limits the exclusive rights of trade mark owner insofar as it cannot prevent all situations from occurring in which Article 14(2) would operate to limit the rights provided in TRIPS Article 16. The EC Regulation therefore was found to limit the availability of that right for the owners of trade marks which are subject to Article 14(2). The Panel therefore concluded that, under Article 16.1 of the TRIPS Agreement, members are required to make available to trade mark owners a right against certain uses, including uses as a GI. Although Article 16 does not specifically exclude use of signs protected as GIs, the Panel found no implied limitation *vis-à-vis* GIs in the text of Article 16.1 on the exclusive right which members must make available to the owner of a registered trade mark. That right may be exercised against a third party not having the owner's consent on the same terms, whether or not the third party uses the sign in accordance with GI protection, subject to any applicable exception.

GIs as an Exception to Trade Mark Rights

The EC successfully argued that the general exception as to trade mark rights in TRIPS Article 17 constitutes a valid and affirmative defence against derogation of the trade mark owner's exclusive rights in the EC Regulation.[114] Article 17 permits members to provide limited exceptions to the rights conferred by a trade mark, which include the right provided for in Article 16.1 of the TRIPS Agreement. The panel found that Art. 14.2 of the EC Regulation constituted a limited exception within the purview of TRIPS Article 17. The Panel held Article 14(2) of the Regulation to be a 'limited exception' because it only allows use by those producers who are established in the geographical area on products that comply with the specification. The trade mark owner retains the exclusive right to prevent use by any other persons. Coexistence falls within the example of 'fair use of descriptive terms' because GIs are descriptive terms, even where they consist of a non-geographical name, and

---

[114]   Generally, on the interpretation of TRIPS exceptions see Panel reports on *US – Section 110(5) Copyright Act*, para. 6.239, and *Canada – Pharmaceutical Patents*, para. 7.16. The Panel in the latter case observed that a respondent cannot demonstrate that no legitimate interest of a patent owner has been prejudiced until it knows what claims of legitimate interests can be made by the complainant. Similarly, the weight of legitimate third-party interests cannot be fully appraised until the legitimacy of the patent owner's legitimate interests, if any, are defined: see para. 7.60 of the Report.

their use to indicate the true origin of goods and the characteristic associated with that origin is 'fair'.[115]

With respect to the construction of the term 'limited exceptions' the Panel had regard to previous TRIPS jurisprudence concerning the exceptions provided for copyright and patents, but was of the view that as the text differs in certain respects, it was important to interpret Article 17 according to its own terms. The Panel proceeded in its decision-making on the literal basis of the text of Article 17 insofar as it requires: (1) a 'limited exception' permitting only a small diminution of rights; and[116] (2) one that is subject to the proviso that 'such exceptions take account of the legitimate interests of the owner of the trade mark and of third parties'.

Foreign trade mark holders derive some relief from the finding that registration as a European GI does not confer a positive right to use any such other signs or combination of signs or to use the name in any linguistic versions not entered in the register.[117] As a result of the Panel's interpretation of Article 24, not only may the trade mark continue to be used, but the trade mark owner's right to prevent confusing uses remains unaffected, except with respect to the use of a GI as entered in the GI register in accordance with its registration.[118]

---

[115]　European Community first written submission, paras 315–18; rebuttal submission, paras 333–8, 348–50: available at http://trade.ec.europa.eu/doclib/docs/2004/august/tradoc_118312.pdf. Under traditional trade mark law, geographical marks such as 'Parma ham' are routinely denied registration on the grounds of non-distinctiveness: for example dry-cured ham produced in Parma has to be marketed as 'super ham' or 'No 1 ham' in Canada because a Canadian company holds the local trade mark rights to the Parma name; see dismissal of application to expunge in *Consorzio del Prosciutto di Parma* v *Maple Leaf Meats Inc.* November, [2001] 2 F.C. 536: http://reports.fja.gc.ca/fc/src/shtml/2001/pub/v2/ 2001fc28097.shtml.

[116]　With respect to the construction of the term 'limited exceptions' the panel had regard to previous TRIPS jurisprudence concerning the exceptions provided for copyright and patents. The Panel cited the opinion of the Panel in *Canada – Pharmaceutical Patents*, which interpreted the identical term in Article 30, that '[t]he word "exception" by itself connotes a limited derogation, one that does not undercut the body of rules from which it is made': see *Geographical Indications*, Panel Report, WT/DS174/R at paras. 7.650 and 7.662–3.

[117]　The European Communities explained that '[t]he positive right extends only to the linguistic versions that have been entered into the register' in its response to Panel question No. 140 at para. 301; see also its rebuttal submission, paras 288 and 293; response to panel question No. 137 and comment on US response to that question: European Communities – Protection of Trademarks and Geographical Indications, Second Written Submission: at http://ec.europa.eu/trade/index_en.htm. A different 'linguistic version' means a translation which renders the name differently. Some GIs are registered in more than one linguistic version.

[118]　The United States appears to acknowledge that the GI registration does not extinguish the trade mark owner's rights against other third parties, although it alleges

EC Compliance with the WTO Ruling: Amended Regulation 510/2006

'Council Regulation (EEC) No 2081/92 of 14 July 1992 on the protection of geographical indications and designations of origin for agricultural products and foodstuffs' was repealed and replaced by 'Council Regulation (EC) No 510/2006 on the protection of geographical indications and designations of origin for agricultural products and foodstuffs' of 20 March 2006. It came into force on 31 March 2006. It is designed to ensure that the Community regulation on registering GIs and designations of origin implements the recommendations of the WTO Dispute Settlement Body. Accordingly, the EC was required to amend the Regulation with respect to the equivalence and reciprocity conditions so as for those conditions apply to the procedures for registration of GIs located in other WTO members.[119] The key amendments introduced by the new Regulation are as follows:

Amended registration procedure for PDOs and PGIs from producers in third countries

The provisions concerning equivalence and reciprocity for products from third countries have been deleted in order to allow names corresponding to geographical areas in those countries to have access to the European system for the protection of GIs. In accordance with Article 5, registration is open to associations of producers from third countries on proof that the name is protected in its country of origin. Under the amended procedure, foreign applicants will no longer have to seek examination and transmission of applications from their national governments. From 3 April 2006, applications for registration of PDOs and PGIs from producers in third countries may be made directly with the European Commission on a single form, reducing the time needed for the application and approval process.[120]

---

that use of the GI will affect the distinctiveness of the trade mark: see Protection of Trademarks and Geographical Indications, Oral Statement of the United States at the First Substantive Meeting of the Panel, June 23, 2004, para. 75 and Answers of the United States to Questions posed by the Panel to the Parties in Connection with the Second Substantive Meeting of the Panel, August 26, 2004, paras 63, 69: http://www.ustr.gov.

[119]   The Commission's Proposal required approval by the Council of Ministers and the European Parliament by the WTO deadline of April 2006. See Commission of The European Communities, Proposal for a Council Regulation on the Protection of Geographical Indications and Designations of Origin for Agricultural Products and Foodstuffs, Brussels, COM (2005) 2005/0275 (CNS) 5 January 2006, Corrigendum and 'New rules ease foreign access to protected name status', 5 January 2006.

[120]   The application form and product classifications (Annex V, Classification of Products for the Purposes of Council Regulation (EC) No 510/2006) are available at

Amended objection procedures applicable for groups and individuals in third countries

With respect to the objection procedures, insofar as they formerly required verification and transmission of objections by third-party governments,[121] the amended Regulation provides the opportunity for any natural or legal person having a legitimate interest, established or resident in a third country, to object to the proposed registration by lodging a duly substantiated statement.[122] From 3 April 2006, therefore, objections to applications by groups, organizations or individuals in third countries, can be made directly to the European Commission on a single form statement of objection.[123]

Amended inspection requirements in respect of third-country registrations

The requirements of government participation in the inspection structures and the provision of the declaration by governments under the former Regulation[124] have been amended by Article 11.2, according to which verification of compliance with the specifications, before placing the product on the market, shall be ensured by one or more public authorities designated by the third country and/or one or more product certification bodies.

Notwithstanding the above amendments, the impact of the WTO decision in *EC – Geographical Indications* and consequent amendments remains to be seen. To what extent can developing countries benefit from the European model of GI protection? Will the outcome make it easier for third countries, in particular developing countries, to protect their GIs in Europe? More broadly, in view of the Commission's aim to obtain, by means of the TRIPS Agreement, the international promulgation of the European regulatory model, can it offer developing countries the advantages indicated?

---

http://ec.europa.eu/comm/agriculture/foodqual/protec/thirdcountries/index_en.htm. Further see generally Regulation (EC) No 1898/2006 of 14 December 2006 containing rules of implementation for Regulation (EC) No 510/2006: available at http://ec. europa.eu/agriculture/foodqual/quali1_en.htm.

[121]   Producer groups within the EU, by contrast, are obliged first to submit their applications to their national governments for approval, Article 5(4).

[122]   Article 7(2).

[123]   See Article 7 concerning objections and decisions on registration and Article 12 concerning cancellations. Statement of objection form at: http://ec.europa.eu/comm/agriculture/foodqual/protec/thirdcountries/index_en.htm.

[124]   Article 12a(2)(b).

7 FUTURE DIRECTIONS IN THE PROTECTION OF GEOGRAPHICAL INDICATIONS

Extension of Eligible Subject Matter

No doubt emboldened by the affirmation of GI rights in the WTO decision, the EC proposal of June 2005 would amend Section 3 of the TRIPS Agreement with a view to extending the regime of protection currently available for geographical indications on wines and spirits to geographical indications on all products. As far as the 'extension' is concerned, the amendments to Article 23 of the TRIPS Agreement seek to extend their scope to geographical indications for all products. In short, the obligation to provide the legal means to interested parties to prevent certain types of imitations,[125] as well as the obligation to refuse or invalidate trade marks including geographical indications, are extended to any situation in which the trade mark or the imitation concerns a product of the same kind as the one protected by the geographical indication.[126] In addition, the provision on homonymous GIs would apply to geographical indications on all products.[127]

In support of the extension, a number of developing countries have identified GIs as a category of intellectual property from which they might profit. Prior to the Seattle Ministerial, a submission by Turkey of 9 July 1999 proposed the extension of GIs in TRIPS beyond wines and spirits.[128] Endorsing this proposal, an African group of countries, including Kenya, Nigeria and South Africa, requested that the protection of GIs be extended 'to other products recognizable by their geographical origins', notably agricultural, food and handicraft products.[129] This proposal was also adopted by Cuba, the Czech Republic, the Dominican Republic, Honduras, India, Indonesia, Nicaragua, Pakistan, Sri Lanka and Venezuela. These developing countries support an extended GI regime for food in order to facilitate market differentiation for a variety of common commodities such as tea, coffee and rice. Significantly, the protection of GIs has been identified as a useful legal instrument for the protection of traditional knowledge[130] insofar

---

[125] Article 23.1.
[126] Article 23.2.
[127] Article 23.3.
[128] WTO Doc No WT/GC/W/249, 13 July 1999.
[129] Preparations for the 1999 Ministerial Conference the TRIPS Agreement Communication from Kenya on Behalf of the African Group, WTO Doc WT/GC/W/302, 6 August 1999.
[130] D. Downes and S. Laird, *Innovative Mechanisms for Sharing Benefits of*

as such products have a strong association with the land and reflect historical links between a particular region and the products of that region.

Opponents of the proposal, led by the United States, warn that the extension of Article 23(1) would oblige members of the WTO to protect the GIs of all other members at an enhanced level of protection and that 'this could involve a considerable burden, particularly in view of the fact that some Members, such as the European Communities, have many hundreds of domestic geographical indications'.[131] The opponents, including Australia, Chile and Guatemala, further point out that the extension of Article 23(1) to cover other products 'will undoubtedly be accompanied by claims from certain producer groups that they have the exclusive rights to particular terms. Any grant of exclusive rights to one group of producers necessarily involves depriving others of the right to use those terms'. The example of 'feta' cheese, which is produced by a range of companies including Australia, Canada, Denmark, Greece, New Zealand and the United States, is given in the Communication as an example of the way in which the extension of Article 23(1) might cause conflicts between WTO members.

In view of the disquiet that the concept of coexistence causes among WTO members who rely exclusively on the trade mark system, the EC proposal of June 2005 advances a number of proposals regarding the exceptions of Article 24 of the TRIPS Agreement. The EC proposes the following:

1. The proposal would remove the reference to 'Article 23' in Article 24.1 TRIPS as redundant, since all products would enjoy the additional protection of Article 23 of the TRIPS Agreement.
2. The date to which Article 24.3 refers should be supplemented in order to take account of new developments in GI protection at the national level between the entry into force of the TRIPS Agreement and the date on which the TRIPS Agreement will be amended.
3. The EC proposal of June 2005 advances a number of proposals regarding the exceptions of Article 24 of the TRIPS Agreement. The grandfathering clause of Article 24.4 TRIPS would have a second paragraph to cover other products. This provision would prevent the protection of a geographical indication to prejudice the use of such indication in the territory of a third country, in certain prescribed circumstances.

Biodiversity and Related Knowledge: Case Studies on Geographical Indications and Trademarks, Geneva: UNCTAD, 1999; M. Blakeney, 'Proposals for the International Regulation of Geographical Indications', *Journal of World Intellectual Property*, 4, 2001, pp. 629–52.

   [131]   'Communication from Argentina, Australia, Canada, Chile, Guatemala, New Zealand, Paraguay and the United States', 29 June 2001, WTO DOC. IP/C/W/289 at para. 18.

4. To add a sentence to Article 24.5 TRIPS to ensure that the effects of 'extension' do not prejudice the registration, validity and use of trade marks that were to remain unprejudiced under Article 22.3, because they would not mislead the consumer as to the origin of the product.

In view of the political climate of North–South relations 'post-TRIPS', if no consensus is possible on the extension of subject matter eligible for higher protection, there is unlikely to be any progress on negotiations for a multilateral register for wines and spirits.[132] On the other hand, if negotiations prove successful, the effect of this provision would be to incorporate within TRIPS the registration scheme established under the Lisbon Agreement.

The debate in the TRIPS Council regarding the question of extension is further beset by procedural difficulty. It is said to lack the requisite negotiating mandate, since it is part of the 'built-in agenda' concerning implementation issues. Controversy therefore surrounds the interpretation of Article 24, which somewhat ambiguously obliges members to enter into negotiations 'aimed at increasing the protection of individual geographical indications under Article 23', while simultaneously ensuring that there is no reduction in 'the protection of geographical indications that existed in that Member immediately prior to the date of entry into force of the WTO Agreement'.[133]

Nevertheless, the two issues are incontrovertibly linked in the current political economy. As evidence of this effect, Clause 39 of the Hong Kong Ministerial Declaration exhorts WTO members to redouble their efforts to find appropriate solutions to 'outstanding implementation-related issues' including 'the extension of the protection of geographical indications provided for in Article 23 of the TRIPS Agreement to products other than wines and spirits'.

The Multilateral Register for Geographical Indications

Associated with the extension of eligible subject matter, debate has focused on a proposal by the EC for a multilateral register that would be open to

---

[132] Note the further obstacle arising from a difference of opinion among WTO members concerning the scope of the negotiating mandate. Whereas the multilateral register for wines has the express negotiating mandate of Article 23.4 of the TRIPS Agreement, in comparison, the question of extension of the higher level of protection (Article 23) to other products is addressed in para. 18 of the Doha Declaration where it is noted that the matter is to be discussed in the Council for TRIPS.

[133] Article 24.3.

geographical indications on all products.[134] The EC submission of June 2005 sets out provisions for a centralized register that would be compulsory and have legal effect.[135] It envisages multilateral registration as a three-step process as follows:

- First, WTO members would notify their GIs and the WTO Secretariat would publish all notifications.
- In the second phase, members would have 18 months to examine the notifications and would have the right to object to the registration of a notified GI. In such a case, the members concerned would start bilateral negotiations aimed at resolving the disagreement.
- In the third phase, the notified GI would be registered in the multilateral register with reference to any challenge.[136]

A registration, under the EC proposal, would have legal effects insofar as a registered GI could no longer be claimed:

1. not to be in conformity with the definition of GIs in the TRIPS Agreement; or
2. to be false homonymous (literally true but misleading); or
3. to be a generic name.

In addition, registration would create a rebuttable presumption of eligibility for protection. Members would be free to decide whether they wished to participate in the notification system. The non-rebuttable legal effects flowing from registration, however, would apply to all members.

Opponents of the EC proposal, including the USA, Chile and Argentina, disagree with the creation of a mandatory multinational system of notification and registration of geographic indications for wines and spirits, or any other products. They advocate a system of voluntary notification and registration with no obligation to protect registered GIs. The reasons for their

---

134   General Council, Trade Negotiations Committee, Council for Trade-Related Aspects of Intellectual Property Rights, Special Session geographical indications WT/GC/W/547 TN/C/W/26, TN/IP/W/11, 14 June 2005.

135   Communication from the European Communities (TN/IP/W/11) 14 June 2005. This proposal maintains the level of ambition of the EC as regards both 'extension' and the multilateral register of GIs, as contained in its earlier proposals in documents IP/C/W/107/Rev.1 (on the GI register) and IP/C/W/353 (on 'extension').

136   EC June 2005. Finally, it should be noted that paragraph 3.4 is slightly modified to clarify that the negotiation is a possibility given to the notifying member, but not an automatic consequence, in line with Article 24.1 of the TRIPS Agreement.

opposition are not only legal, but also related to the cost of implementing a mandatory system of registration and extended protection.

Legally, those countries where geographical indications are protected as certification or collective marks would find it more difficult to comply with the EC proposal for a mandatory multilateral register. Consistent with the principle of territoriality that characterizes trade mark law, there is no agreement on whether the determination of whether a geographical indication conforms to the definition should be left to individual members solely. The US and its supporters argue that the protection of GIs is granted according to the criteria established in the national laws of members.

The EC proposal of June 2005 aims at meeting the demands of those WTO members who have expressed concerns over geographical indications. In respect of the preservation of the territorial principle, the proposal preserves each WTO member's prerogative to determine whether a certain sign, indication or geographical name does indeed meet the TRIPS definition of a geographical indication.[137]

The cost of implementing the TRIPS Agreement and any subsequent amendments remains a vital concern to the majority of developing countries, for whom the balance of concessions was not adequately met during the Uruguay Round. Consequently, the EC submission of June 2005 contains some additional provisions that are intended to meet this concern. It includes a recommendation for a system of financing the multilateral register. The draft treaty text provides for a system of fees which allows a WTO member to recoup the costs incurred in complying with the obligations regarding trade marks, through a system of fees to be paid by the notifying WTO members. This mechanism is self-explanatory, and largely inspired by the existing system embodied in the Madrid Protocol for the international registration of trade marks, divides fees among:

1. A basic fee: to cover the administrative functioning of the system, including setting-up costs.
2. An individual fee: to cover the upon-request obligations to monitor past or future trade marks.[138]

Even assuming costs of implementation are accommodated, the foregoing overview of international protection during the last 200 years indicates that there are not only historical and cultural constraints to increased harmonization, but also persistent legal problems. The negotiating history of the

---

[137] Paragraph 3.2(a).
[138] Included in paragraph 9.4 et seq.

Madrid and Lisbon Agreements indicates that questions surrounding the definition and the eligibility of geographical indications for international protection are likely to continue to be problematic.

Should the extension and multilateral register be approved, despite the consensus concerning the definition of 'geographical indications' in TRIPS Article 22.1, problems are likely to reappear in questions involving the ability of developing countries to register their GIs, whether by way of objection to the multilateral registration, or alternatively in the registers of third countries.

As the European experience indicates, when those seeking protection for a specific name in the territory of a third party discover that protection is denied, because the term does not meet the definition of 'geographical indication' or because it is considered generic, litigation is likely to ensue.[139] It is very doubtful whether the current WTO dispute settlement mechanism would have the capacity to deal with conflicts of that character and probable extent.

8   TAKING ACCOUNT OF THE DOHA AGENDA FOR ECONOMIC DEVELOPMENT

Are Geographical Indications 'Development-Friendly'?

In light of the Doha Declaration, WTO Director-General Pascal Lamy affirmed that 'current negotiations must integrate the issues and concerns of developing countries "in every stage"'.[140] Yet finding the means by which each member is able to leverage some benefit from the protection of GIs, as the lack of progress in negotiations since 2001 evinces, will be no easy task. On the one hand, proponents of the GI extension and multilateral register observe that it is to ensure that GIs will only be used for products actually originating from the place indicated by the GI, that is, to prevent their usurpation in third countries.[141] Certainly, an enhanced system of registra-

---

[139]   The Secretariat has provided a summary in JOB(00)/5619 of 19 September 2000 of the responses to the Article 24.2 questionnaire on the differences in national law standards for determining what is entitled to protection as a geographical indication.

[140]   See 'Lamy Highlights Doha Round's Development Benefits', in a speech in Lima, Peru on 31 January 2006, <http://www.wto.org/english/news_e/sppl_e/sppl17_e.htm.

[141]   See WTO Doc. TN/C.W/14, 'Geographical Indications – The Significance of Extension in the TRIPS Agreement and Its Benefits for WTO Members'. See also IP/C/W/204/Rve.1, IPC/C/W/247/Rev.1 and IP/C/W/353.

tion for geographical indications would have been useful for dealing with the kinds of controversies involving Basmati rice, Neem, Enola beans and Ayahuasca. Classic intellectual property law gives value to knowledge that is innovative and capable of industrial or commercial application. Geographical indications however are capable of transforming traditional knowledge into intellectual capital. In this respect, the Doha discussions relating to geographical indications recognize that knowledge related to food has existed for a long period in Africa and can be found in foods linked to a particular location. For some African nations, this food origin link offers a means to promote small businesses, exports, and rural development.

Discerning the Road Ahead

There are no commercial, economic or legal reasons to limit effective GI protection exclusively to wines and spirits or to avoid extending such protection to all other products. The developing-country proponents of extension are justified in their criticism that industry-specific TRIPS protection is untenable. They argue that Article 23 is discriminatory insofar as it gives additional protection and unfair advantage to wines and spirits. When France accorded protection to appellations of origin for wines it was justified on the basis that the industry had long been subject to deceptive and dishonest practice. Given the significance of the industry to France, additional protection could be justified. However, when similar protection is advocated on a global basis for an industry that is limited in reach and application, the policy appears to be self-serving.

Extension would create a level playing field in the TRIPS Agreement for all products in the sense that legally all members have an equal opportunity to provide enhanced protection. Developing countries that have products of unique characteristics, quality and reputation could potentially benefit from GI protection.[142] On the other hand, not all developing countries have the means to take advantage of such an opportunity. In order for Korhogo fabrics from Côte d'Ivoire or Gabon sweet potato or Mananara vanilla from Madagascar to become well known in the global market, there must be investment in modern manufacture, packaging, distribution and promotion of their having unique geographical attributes.

Both regulatory and developmental differentials among WTO members dictate caution and suggest the wisdom of an incremental approach. Legally

---

[142] For example in Kenya, the products that could benefit from GI extension include agricultural products such as Kericho tea, Kikuyu grass, Mombasa mango, and Muranga bananas. Livestock products that could benefit from GI extension include Molo lamb and Omena fish.

speaking, even if the status quo were maintained, developing countries might take further advantage of the flexibilities offered by TRIPS Article 22 protection. Few WTO members' nationals have made full use of the protections provided under Article 22.2. Article 22.2 also prohibits any use which 'constitutes an act of unfair competition within the meaning of Article 10*bis* of the Paris Convention'. The ambit of Article 10*bis* is extended to geographical indications 'which, although literally true as to a territory, region or locality in which the goods originate, falsely represent to the public that the goods originate in another territory'.

In any event, in the decade since the conclusion of TRIPS, further harmonization has been occurring from the bottom up. In a bid to comply with both TRIPS and TRIPS Plus[143] obligations, WTO members are moving towards the statutory protection of geographical indications by three distinct but related means: countries such as the US protect geographical indications as an integral part of the trade marks regime; countries such as the EU and India have chosen to enact specialized geographical indications systems of protection; and countries such as Japan have moved to implement a system of collective regional marks as a subset of their trade marks regime. Regional and bilateral trade agreements (RTAs) such as the United States FTAs and EU Economic Partnership Agreements (EPAs) further serve to reinforce this effect by exporting their preferred means of protection in so-called TRIPS Plus provisions. By this means the EU and the US are building a critical mass of support for their preferred means of GI protection, utilizing RTAs with member states throughout Africa, South America, Asia and the Middle East.[144]

It is not only a question of deciding which group – the EC or the US and supporters – has the most convincing case for harmonization, but equally one of determining what constitutes a principled case for increased protection of geographical indications. In the case of GIs these questions are all the more pertinent due to the intersection of this form of intellectual property with a number of policy areas critical to the needs of economic development, including agricultural policy, rural regeneration, cultural heritage and environmental conservation.[145]

---

[143]   The term given to the higher standard of protection often required by the EC and the US in bilateral and regional trade agreements.

[144]   For example Central America–Dominican Republic–United States Free Trade Agreement, Final Text, ch. 15, Intellectual Property, http://www.ustr.gov/Trade_Agreements/Bilateral/CAFTA/Section_Index.html and EU Chile Association Agreement above note 98.

[145]   Keith Maskus and Carsten Fink (eds), *Intellectual Property and Development*, World Bank and OUP, Washington DC, 2005, Chapter 2 at pp. 19 ff.

Critical also because most IPRs are concerned with legal rights to prevent other people doing certain things and are therefore to some extent restrictive of trade. IPRs are, as the Preamble to the TRIPS Agreement reminds us, 'private rights' residing not in the public but in a natural or legal person. A geographical indication may be exploited to the potential benefit of a collective of landholders, who may or may not comprise a group of nationals indefinitely, without the capacity to assign or license the intellectual property for use on the domestic market or internationally.

Further, it must be recognized that the rights granted by the intellectual property laws, when combined with market power, can be used for anti-competitive ends. This occurs when the rights are used to claim for the owner not merely a share of the efficiency gains society obtains from the creation, but also extra profits that ultimately reduce social output. We have previously noted, in the case of mineral waters, that in markets where there is a high level of substitutability on the supply side, geographical indications may not be the optimal form of protection.

The potential for anti-competitive conduct is the reason why opponents of extended protection warn of the possible closing-off of future market access opportunities for emerging industries, and uncertainty concerning the continued use of geographically descriptive terms in existing markets. Many such countries and their industry associations are concerned that, depending on the outcome of discussions and the scope of any agreement, they might have to relabel products and forego names or words that are well known to their consumers. In this regard the European case of feta cheese previously examined is instructive. These label changes could be required by a new rule regarding the geographical indications–trade mark interface or because the use of certain traditional or generic expressions would be prohibited. An example given by the Grocery Manufacturers of America is the consumer consternation and confusion that would be caused if manufacturers have to replace 'Parmesan' on cheese labels with a generic description.

CONCLUSION: TOMORROW?

The demand for increased protection of geographical indications is unlikely to abate. As we observed, its roots are to be found in the untenable nature of agricultural production and distribution for small farmers and developing countries. The foregoing analysis has shown that due to historical reasons there exist considerable differences in the legal concepts which are applied for the protection of geographical indications. These differences have a direct bearing on important questions such as conditions of protection, entitlement to use and scope of protection.

Fierce competition among nations for the most lucrative markets, a deep division between Europe and the United States as to the manner in which GIs should be regulated, and a concomitant difference among WTO members that transcends the customary developed–developing divide, are likely to ensure that the protection of GIs remains a contentious issue for some time to come. If the opportunities and risks, the benefits and burdens of the continued harmonization of GIs are to be legitimately assessed and, in the event that protection is extended, its implementation appropriately planned, lawmakers must begin by having a better understanding of the project upon which they are about to embark.

PART III

Traditional knowledge, technology and resources

14. Knowledge and other values – Intellectual property and the limitations for traditional knowledge

Johanna Gibson

> Knowledge is and will be produced in order to be sold, it is and will be consumed in order to be valorized in a new production: in both cases, the goal is exchange Knowledge ceases to be an end in itself, it loses its 'use-value.'[1]

INTRODUCTION

The international enthusiasm for achieving a framework not only for the protection but also, implicitly, for the commodification and understanding of traditional knowledge, has been channelled largely through intellectual property perspectives. As distinct from what are arguably diverse community perspectives upon the generation and exchange of such knowledge, intellectual property frameworks confine traditional knowledge systems to a possessory and individualistic rendering of culture as property, as commodities. Importantly, however, this potential conflict with intellectual property models does not justify dismissing the types of 'ownership' at work within communal models. Indeed, it is necessary to acknowledge the way in which that 'ownership', or that personal relationship to knowledge, is achieved through traditional systems of development, access, and incremental change. This chapter will consider this relationship between value generation and knowledge commodities. What is the value at stake in the protection of traditional knowledge? And what is the value generated by the application of intellectual property frameworks?

---

[1]   Lyotard, J-F (1984) *The Postmodern Condition: A Report on Knowledge*, G. Bennington and B. Massumi (trans), Minneapolis, U of Minnesota P: 4–5.

INTELLECTUAL PROPERTY, 'VALUE ADDING'

Possessory models of knowledge commodities, in an industrialised system, are articulated upon the exchange of 'value' – that is, the possession of knowledge is relevant in terms of the value realised in the commercial exchange of that knowledge. Knowledge is without value until it is recognised and transferable within intellectual property frameworks. As Jean-François Lyotard explains: 'Knowledge ceases to be an end in itself, it loses its "use-value"'.[2] In contrast, traditional knowledge systems, where the relationship of a community and its members to the knowledge in question is built upon a kind of exchange of knowledge as an end in itself, this construction of 'value' is not necessarily relevant. In particular, given the way in which transferable and competitive value is created and maintained by economic structures of exchange, 'value' is then not readily registered in traditional knowledge until it is transformed in this way. This is seen in particular in the way in which discussions have marginalised forms of ownership in traditional communities, as the conventional recognition of possessory authority of knowledge, mobilised by these kinds of exchanges, is not applicable. Thus, the concepts of ownership and the ambitious self of Western economic models obscure the kinds of 'ownership' argued for by traditional communities. Therefore, it is important to acknowledge that traditional development of knowledge is nevertheless through a kind of exchange, through access, but access which is appropriate according to the differentiation of a particular group. This kind of incremental change through the communication of knowledge as an end, rather than the exchange of knowledge in order to manifest value and creatorship, is what has been argued to be unregistered within intellectual property regimes.

INTELLECTUAL PROPERTY – AN ACCREDITATION SYSTEM FOR KNOWLEDGE

An understanding of the legitimation and institutionalisation of the intellectual property narrative provides a critical insight into the fundamental conflicts generated by the assimilation of traditional knowledge within intellectual property laws in preference to the recognition of parallel customary systems of knowledge generation and exchange. The intellectual property system makes known the creative and innovative output of society and registers it within its system of recording and regulating the dissemination of that information – a system in which traditional knowledge occupies at best the periph-

---

2   Lyotard (1984): 5.

ery, the 'history' of knowledge.[3] The stability of tradition, the value which motivates knowledge as an end in itself, and the source of legitimacy for community and traditional innovation, are figured as contrary to creativity within governing models of advancement: 'When innovation is valued as a defining characteristic of the creative process, tradition often becomes set up against it as inevitably static and unchanging. In this view, tradition inhibits, and is seen as an impediment to be overcome.'[4]

In particular, a critical conflict between intellectual property models of creativity/innovation and traditional and indigenous practices is the necessary simplification and commodification of innovation in the former. Precepts of authorship, self-expression, individuality, and control presume all individuals (and communities) desire the same experience of their creativity and will be rewarded in the same way. The 'difference' of the community is suspect, unreliable, and unenforceable, whereas intellectual property law is seen to be certain, replicable, and predictable. Indeed, this 'suspicion' is arguably underpinning the persistent repetition of arguments against community authority which maintain that the community is not readily identifiable, consultable, and, thus, knowledgeable. At the same time, intellectual property frameworks render the creative process a singular and simplified event (through principles of authorship, originality, inventiveness, novelty, and so on), producing 'the illusion of singularity and therefore of universality'.[5]

INTELLECTUAL PROPERTY AND THE NARRATION OF CULTURE

In its instrumental role as the mechanism by which knowledge is translated into 'value', intellectual property literally narrates the story of innovation. In this way, intellectual property operates as a kind of 'grand narrative',[6] justifying itself as progress, harmonised, and total in its rendition of

---

[3]   Althusser L. (1970) 'The Errors of Classical Economics: An Outline for a Concept of Historical Time', in Althusser L. and Balibar E., *Reading Capital*, London, New Left Books: 91–118.

[4]   Negus K. and Pickering M. (2004) *Creativity, Communication and Cultural Value*, London, Sage: 91.

[5]   Wright (2001): 130. Similarly, see the discussions of freedom of expression and the problematic application of this 'right' to arguments against the customary control over traditional knowledge and restrictions upon its dissemination, in Gibson J. (2005) *Community Resources: Intellectual Property, International Trade and Protection of Traditional Knowledge*, Aldershot, Ashgate (Chapter 5).

[6]   Lyotard (1984).

knowledge.[7] In other words, intellectual property frameworks may be understood as comprising the grand narrative of innovation, and indeed of knowledge. In this way, intellectual property laws are rendered the *de facto* authors of legitimate 'Culture' in Western society. Furthermore, the internationalisation of intellectual property is the mechanism by which that particular cultural watermark is held up to cultures throughout the world. Thus, cultures are recognised and authorised, and rendered legitimate information for trade according to the model presented by a Western intellectual property imperative. In this way, the creation of intellectual property becomes synonymous with not only innovation, but also culture, 'as though there were some overarching legal recognition of originality'.[8]

In stark contrast, attempts to decipher traditional knowledge through the lens of intellectual property present it as un-authorised, un-original, and illegitimate according to this world view.[9] In its application, intellectual property law inevitably decides the distinction between art and artifact, invention and imitation, trade mark and decoration. Intellectual property is therefore not only documenting, as it were, the cultural progress and civilisation of society, but also simplifying culture as a uniform and universalised model. In this way, the very selectiveness of this process is disguised.

Thus, intellectual property judgements also influence the recognition of a particular cultural output as authentic. But in rendering the 'authenticity' of traditional knowledge within this narrative of innovation, the quality and value of that knowledge is arguably overlooked. The 'branding' of value through the intellectual property system indeed necessarily transforms a community's role and responsibility with respect to its knowledge. In rendering 'value' through this kind of model, the 'loss' of knowledge suddenly has a commercial and tangible effect. And the 'blame' for that loss of knowledge, now re-made as property, is constructed as resting with the 'identity' of the indigenous and traditional group:[10] 'the failures of public sympathy, state institutions, and lawful forms of property become the failures of local people to maintain their "culture"'.[11] According to the narratives within which it is authenticated, if traditional knowledge (particularly ancient knowledge) is used by community it is almost a waste.[12] In other words, traditional 'use' is compromising the

---

[7]   Ibid.

[8]   Strathern M. (1999) *Property Substance and Effect: Anthropological Essays on Persons and Things*, London, Athlone P: 168–9.

[9]   See the critique of the classical opposition between tradition and society in Negus and Pickering (2004): 91–114.

[10]   See the discussion of identity and ownership in Gibson (2005) (Chapter 1).

[11]   Povinelli E.A. (2002) *The Cunning of Recognition: Indigenous Alterities and the Making of Australian Multiculturalism*, Duke UP, Durham: 189.

[12]   See Simpson M.D. (2001) *Making Representations: Museums in the Post-*

'value' that is otherwise consolidated by reading that knowledge and consumption through intellectual property frameworks. According to this modelling, traditional knowledge has no 'use-value' other than that precipitated by these laws. The value of that knowledge, within Western legal and cultural frameworks, is ascertained through constructions of its authenticity, its collectabilility, its objectification and commodification. And this construction arguably is effected by intellectual property perspectives.

While such traditional use is therefore 'waste', by way of contrast, preservation comes through the commodification of knowledge as a fixed and legitimate object of 'Culture', not as a performative and generative value with particular cultural effects for communities: '"culture" appears to denote a form of property'.[13]

This has interesting connections to the criticism of 'authenticity' in art exhibitions and museum curation. The process of self-legitimation that occurs through the categorisation of 'intellectual property' might be understood through the process of categorisation that occurs with cultural artifacts for the purpose of identifying authenticity in 'art'. That which cannot be reconciled within that framework is 'inauthentic', and museums will 'choose that which *authenticates* over that which is authentic':[14]

> Authenticity . . . remains the rationale for a great deal of art-historical and museum practice. How has it got away with it? . . . It is done through the apparently down-to-earth business of identification and classification, which must always impose theoretical assumptions on whatever is classified, but without the assumptions necessarily being obvious. As natural historians found out before art historians, any identification system more ambitious than just numbering items as they turn up involves putting things into categories of some kind, and it is impossible to devise an extended system of categorisation without some theory about the subject under investigation. So early taxonomic schemes in natural history assumed that species were stable entities and could be described in terms of constant characteristics, but the constancy has turned out to be an untenable theoretical assumption.[15]

Similarly, intellectual property systems assume the constancy of the criteria for determining 'intellectual property', and their applicability to all developments in forms of knowledge. The over-arching principles of the market and of what will be described as origination and in-imitativeness, present

---

Colonial Era, London, Routledge: 198–9. Simpson discusses the way in which repatriation is almost presented as a threat to preservation of that knowledge.

[13]   Tamen M. (2001. *Friends of Interpretable Objects*, Cambridge, Mass, Harvard UP: 73.

[14]   Schwartz H. (1996) *The Culture of the Copy: Striking Likenesses, Unreasonable Facsimiles*, New York, Zone: 279.

[15]   Phillips D. (1997). *Exhibiting Authenticity*, Manchester, Manchester UP: 96.

significant obstacles for the realisation of community resources within intellectual property frameworks.

TRADE RELATIONS

It remains a fact, however, that intellectual property presents the key framework to which efforts to achieve protection for traditional knowledge currently refer, in so far as intellectual property laws are an intrinsic part of the international legal structure of trade. Intellectual property laws are justified and interpreted in terms of facilitating trade – that is, in terms of facilitating that fundamental exchange in which value subsists. Indeed, for intellectual property to apply, the starting-point is, *de facto*, that knowledge must be capable of trade in order to warrant protection:

> The relationship of the suppliers and users of knowledge to the knowledge they supply and use is now tending, and will increasingly tend, to assume the form already taken by the relationship of commodity producers and consumers to the commodities they produce and consume – that is, the form of value.[16]

It is the economic value of knowledge that justifies its protection, and the need to sustain the market that motivates the broadening of that protection.[17] Thus, while credited as motivating and encouraging creativity and innovation, intellectual property law must also ensure the marketplace exists for those ideas. To maintain the market, intellectual property law creates an artificial scarcity for information, for a 'public good'.[18] The system creates the scarcity that ensures the need for exchange, the circumstances in which value materialises. In a sense, intellectual property frameworks create the desire for the information in the marketplace. In this way, such frameworks are in and of themselves intrinsically commercial, effective 'brands' for the significance of knowledge. This is particularly clear in the way in which knowledge is significant where it has this economic impression, where it is adequately branded: 'Cultural production can be seen as just that, production of commodities for the marketplace'.[19]

---

[16]   Lyotard (1984), *The Postmodern Condition: A Report on Knowledge*, G. Bennington and B. Massumi (trans), Minneapolis, University of Minnesota Press: 4.

[17]   Dutfield G. (2003) *Intellectual Property Rights and the Life Science Industries: A Twentieth Century History*, Ashgate, Aldershot: 66, 208–10.

[18]   The construction of information as a global public good persists throughout the open access debates. For a discussion of information as a public good, and the relationship to intellectual property laws, see Vaver D. (1997) *Intellectual Property Law: Copyright, Patents, Trademarks*, Toronto: Irwin Law: 3–6. See further the discussion of open access models in Gibson (2005) (Chapter 5).

[19]   Wright S. (2001) *International Human Rights, Decolonisation and Globalisation: Becoming Human*, London, Routledge: 116.

The production of value is therefore not only the effective product of the application of intellectual property laws, but also provides the self-legitimation of the application of those laws to expanding subject matter and, in the present case, to traditional knowledge. In other words, intellectual property rights arise, or at least become meaningful, only through their transfer, only through the fundamental value of the system, the value of exchange. Intellectual property laws facilitate that exchange, and intellectual property requires this exchange with the 'other' in order to come into being.

RISKY EXCHANGES

Among the many justifications that are presented for intellectual property laws, the 'risk' associated with creativity and innovation has become increasingly predominant in discussions. This kind of reasoning, together with the expansion of the scope of protection, comes from the increasing significance of investment in innovation, the supporting industries for that innovation, and the perceived justice in mitigating the risk involved in developing transactional knowledge commodities. The calculation of regulatory mechanisms by which to manage risk, such as the creation of specific terms of monopoly in intellectual property law, corresponds not only to decisions on the risks inherent in innovation, but also to the 'value' of those risks (the 'opportunity costs', as it were) and indeed the 'Culture' produced: 'To one extent or another, all risk assessments involve the calculation not just of odds, but of the value of those odds ... Cost, however, is a subjective matter.'[20] In other words, the public discourse of risk has been appropriated as a universalising rhetoric of regulation.[21]

In this context, the exclusion, according to customary law, of certain aspects of traditional knowledge from the public domain, provokes reactions reliant upon risk, and predictions of chaos where access to that information is denied. Indeed, the public domain is invoked as legitimating ongoing appropriation of traditional knowledge as 'archaic', public goods. Constructing traditional knowledge as public goods in this way, it is sometimes argued to be legally (and morally) impossible to exclude access. In this way, arguments for access to traditional knowledge are seemingly ethically privileged over arguments for recognition of the importance of traditional knowledge as cultural resources, by virtue of the construction of the public domain around the 'good'

---

[20]   Steele J. (2004) *Risks and Legal Theory*, Oxford, Hart Publishing: 24.

[21]   For instance, intellectual property paradigms appear to confer certainty and predictability upon the creative process and indeed upon new and emerging technologies: for example, gene technology.

of traditional knowledge rather than the diversity and internal governance of community.[22] But arguably this somewhat obscures the 'economic' privilege attached to such arguments, which are indeed anchored upon the intrinsic value of exchange in this system.

Indeed, the very construction of traditional knowledge as 'public' common knowledge within the public domain is built upon essentially commercial concerns for that public. The public domain is, in and of itself, a question of commercial construction, comprised as it is of those goods for which the monopoly (as an assessment of the value in time required to recover the 'costs' in the risks of creativity and innovation) has expired. It is this 'vacuum' of the public domain that drives the exchange underpinning the value of the intellectual property system. It is therefore implied that the commercial utility of anything within the public domain has passed, while the value and priority continues to attach to knowledge that is protected by intellectual property rights.[23] Traditional knowledge recognised and governed as resources of and by the community, and acknowledgement and application of the specific 'public domains' that operate within specific communities, are thus rejected, as it were, by both the commercial interests seeking access to the creation of intellectual property rights and by certain aspects of campaigns for greater public access. In other words, by reading knowledge through this dominant narrative, traditional and customary systems of management are rejected from not only an ethically justified but also economically advantaged standpoint.

RISKING TRADITION?

These underlying principles of the present system appear to mark the irrelevance or inapplicability of intellectual property frameworks and economic models to the particular problems posed by traditional knowledge. This form of 'social contract' or quid pro quo suggested by economic analyses of intellectual property, and the balance between users and producers, is 'inefficient' in a community context. While all members of a community may not necessarily contribute to a 'product', as realised by intellectual property models, this does not justify differences in the distribution of custodianship with respect to that knowledge. Custodianship is not individualised, and is not personal, but

---

22   For further discussion on the notion of resources as a means of individual communities, as distinct from discrete products or goods to be identified through trading relationships, see Gibson (2005).

23   Nwokeabia H. (2001) 'Why Industrial Revolution Missed Africa: A "Traditional Knowledge" Perspective', Economic Commission for Africa, ECA/ESPD/WPS/01/02: 15.

is according to shared values within the community. Custodianship is not defined according to the actors in a commercial exchange, but according to a responsibility to the knowledge as an end in itself.

Distinct from this globalisation of risk, for traditional and indigenous communities the value of resources is constituted by the intrinsic relationship between community and resources; not, as it were, in the community-to-community exchange, the trade that is facilitated by the commodification of that knowledge. In other words, the value is, by contrast, materialised in the expression of culture and the responsibility to tradition. Through the imposition of intellectual property frameworks upon traditional knowledge development, the protection of traditional knowledge as the responsibility of the community, to be managed according to customary law, is displaced as the global risk of natural and cultural resources, and the means by which the value of trade may come to be realised. The ultimate consensus on that risk is summarised in the development of intellectual property laws. The international harmonisation of laws marks the attempt to achieve consensus on that risk in a global trading context. Thus, the responsibilities of indigenous and traditional communities to tradition are deferred by the priority attached to a 'global' system.

ETHICAL 'VALUE'

As identified from the outset, the ongoing conceptualisation of traditional knowledge and its protection within a system that facilitates its appropriation and removal is the central paradox of this debate. Indeed, it is this very articulation of the subject matter that at the same time eschews any ethical accountability for the knowledge systems and communities involved. There is, quite rightly perhaps, no ethical accountability built into systems of intellectual property. But quite troubling is the way in which intellectual property has come to be relied upon as the ethical arbiter of knowledge and the circumstances for its creation.

In the articulation of traditional knowledge, intellectual property laws, as a very characteristic of their appropriate functioning, necessarily disguise the subject matter of protection as uniform, pure, and discrete. As discussed earlier in this chapter, in representing the truth or authenticity of objects of information with such 'authority', the institution of intellectual property is also incriminated in the process of authenticating traditional knowledge, such as indigenous art works, for the purposes of realising its 'value' as a commodity of exchange. The means by which to do so come from conventional intellectual property models, where the 'otherness' (and creatorship) of these exotic objects is authenticated, authorised, and legitimised for exhibition to the knowledge economy. The 'difference' in these objects is refined, scripted, and authored by the means by which it is recognised and registered.[24]

Efforts to achieve equitable frameworks for dealing with traditional knowledge,[25] such as mandatory disclosure of origins in traditional knowledge, nevertheless risk the simplification of the critical relationship between the community and its knowledge resources, and the offence and harm caused by the assumption that such taking is fundamentally just. The context of scientific progress and innovation make the taking appear inherently just, that is, part of the advancement of society and of the dissemination of 'Culture'. Therefore, in that the fundamental value is that of exchange, discussions invariably cooperate with that objective. Protections offered by geographical indications, trade marks, and so on are not readily available other than through efforts to 'exclude' certain material from trade mark registration[26] or to anonymise communities within national publics (as in the use of geographical indications). Any efforts within these models depend upon a presumption of the importance of safeguarding the knowledge as cultural artifact, rather than recognising community and respecting and giving effect to customary law. It is critical that attention remains on the value that is at stake, not the value that is to be created. Indeed, without this awareness discussions between governments and traditional and indigenous groups are in effect negotiating upon different subject matter. Therefore, in addition to the asymmetry of the relationship itself, there may also be a fundamental misunderstanding as to the stakes of those negotiations in many instances.

It is essential that the authority to manage knowledge, as distinct from knowledge commodities, vests in the communities themselves. Without adequate and meaningful recognition of customary law in the context of the diversity of cultures and 'publics' of traditional knowledge, these complex questions are reduced to 'properties' and communities are rendered 'propertyless'.

---

[24]   See also Appiah K.A. (1992) 'Identity, Authenticity, Survival: Multicultural Societies and Social Reproduction', in A. Gutmann (ed.), *Multiculturalism and 'The Politics of Recognition'*, Princeton, Princeton UP.

[25]   In particular, see the development of protection on an international level in the documents of the World Intellectual Property Organization (WIPO) Intergovernmental Committee on Intellectual Property and Genetic Resources, Traditional Knowledge and Folklore (IGC).

[26]   Problems persist in relying on exclusions of emblems and symbols, in that these must be fixed and repeatable for protection. Such defensive mechanisms cannot capture methods in cultural expressions (such as dot painting).

15. Checking the lie of the land: Current trends in bioprospecting related laws

Florian Leverve

Bioprospecting is the systematic search, classification and investigation for commercial and scientific purposes of new sources of biochemical compounds, genes and other products with present or potential value. It seeks compounds of interest that originate in the complexity of biodiversity.[1] The latter seems to be more pronounced in 'southern' countries, whereas exploitation of it occurs mainly in the 'north'. Its commercial applications are seen in various sectors such as the enhancement of crops, the improvement of technologies, the design of natural personal care products and cosmetics, and the development of new drugs.[2]

The Rio Earth Summit was held in June 1992 during which the Convention on Biological Diversity (CBD) was promulgated. Although it mainly addressed the protection of biodiversity, general guidance was also specified concerning the means to regulate access to biological resources. No real harmonization exists worldwide. In particular, the specificities of each country associated with a recent legal development lead to a certain variability.[3]

---

[1]   CBD Art 2 biodiversity: 'the variability among living organisms from all sources including, inter alia, terrestrial, marine and other aquatic ecosystems and the ecological complexes of which they are part; this includes diversity within species, between species and of ecosystems'.

[2]   See S.A. Laird and K. ten Kate, 'Biodiversity prospecting: the commercial use of genetic resources and best practice in benefit sharing' in *Biodiversity and Traditional Knowledge. Equitable Partnerships in Practice*, London, Earthscan, 2002, 241–86.

[3]   The type of bioprospecting regulations can be divided into five areas (Glowka L., Environmental Policy & Law paper series, No 34, *A Guide to Designing Legal Frameworks to Determine Access to Genetic Resources*, IUCN, 1998): A general environmental law concerned with the protection of the biodiversity more than the development of bioprospecting activity (*National Environmental Management Act from Gambia, 1995; Environmental Management Bill of Malawi, 1996; National Environmental Preservation Act from the Republic of Korea, 1994; National environmental statute from Uganda, 1995*), A legal framework for sustainable development,

Nevertheless, the nature of the resources associated with the worldwide dialogue shaped a sort of common ground.

This chapter is concerned with the way bioprospecting is being regulated in so called southern countries. It is constructed around three key steps: request for access to a site and contractual arrangements, authorized actions and obligations over sought resources, and further utilization and associated rights over acquired material and knowledge. The approach taken is based on a patchwork of provisions gathered in national or regional laws, whether in force or not. Therefore, it is in itself not practical as this would require a focus on a single country, but instead provides a review of the potential legal implications associated with this activity at a national and regional level. The intention is to create a snapshot of current trends in bioprospecting related laws. Finally, the examples of law provided in the footnotes are merely illustrative of the legislative responses to the specific bioprospecting problems tackled here, rather than being an exhaustive list of laws on such issues.

ACCESS TO RESOURCES

Protected Subject Matter

A first issue to determine is if the subject matter is under any protection. Two main types of law may be distinguished. Some will solely enforce the protection of biodiversity against activities that might potentially affect it[4] rather than considering the subject-matter of the bioprospecting activity as such. In that case, any wild species might be assumed to be owned by an official body or person and transfer of ownership to a bioprospector will occur unless acquired in contravention of any rules.[5] If protected species are involved, a

---

nature conservation, biodiversity access and contractual arrangements related thereto (*Wildlife Conservation Law of Costa Rica, 1992; Draft Sustainable Development Bill from Fiji, 1997; Law for the Conservation and Sustainable Use of Biodiversity of Peru 1997*), Stand alone national laws or decrees on access to genetic resources (*Supreme Decree No 24676 of Bolivia, Department Administrative Order No 96-20 of the Philippines, Legislative Assembly Law No 2*), Modification of existing laws to be consistent with the characteristic of access to resources and related use (*Draft national park decree 1996 to modify the existing National Park Acts 1991; Proposal to revise the Code of Federal Regulations Title 36(2.5)*), Regional level action (*Decision 391 of the Andean Pact, 1996, Law applicable in Bolivia, Colombia, Ecuador, Peru and Venezuela*).

    4   Malawi, National Park and Wildlife Act; section 27: 'The purposes of national parks and wildlife reserves shall be; (a) to preserve selected examples of biotic communities of Malawi and their physical environment; . . . (c) to preserve populations of rare, endemic and endangered species of wild plants and animals'.

    5   Malawi, National Park and Wildlife Act; section 4(2).

licence agreement or authorization, warranting that non-adverse consequences occur within the area, should secure the lawfulness of the activity and the ownership of the acquisition.[6]

When laws are more specific to bioprospecting, it is the activity as such that will be thoroughly addressed. In that case, it is more likely that any access will be regulated with specific emphasis on the actual sampled resources. Not only protection of the area will be at stake, but also biodiversity will be viewed as a valuable resource to trade.

Since biological resources have become more specific valuable assets, legislation concerning the protection of biodiversity has become more concerned with clarifying the concept of regulated access to samples rather than merely the site of access.

Seeker

The requirements enforced upon a person, institution or any entity regarding their ability to access resources might or might not be dependent on their status. Local legislation might only require foreigners to apply for access.[7] Contrarily, citizenship combined with place of residency, thus favouring sourcing countries, might allow privileges such as an exemption to request for access.[8] In the case of body corporate, associations, etc., registration within the sourcing country might be a prerequisite to enjoying such a privilege, but foreign participation or capital might preclude it.[9]

Privileges granted to local participants or institutions can be justified on three grounds. First, a local actor is more likely to be involved in developments beneficial for the country. Second, its actions might be more respectful towards and affected by the customs of its locality. Finally, in the case of misbehaving, the local authority can enjoy direct jurisdiction.

The activity of the entity is also important. When the purposes behind bioprospecting activity are for research[10] or other non-profit purposes, preferential treatment could be granted under different contractual agreements[11] or free access.[12] Such preferential treatment will mostly be provided to

---

[6]   Malawi, National Park and Wildlife Act; section 4(3).
[7]   Brazil, Provisional Measure No 2.186-16, Art 12.
[8]   India, Biological Diversity Act 2002, section 3(2) (a) and (b).
[9]   India, Biological Diversity Act 2002, section 3(2)(c).
[10]   Malawi, National Park and Wildlife Act, section 53(a).
[11]   Organization of African Unity Model Legislation for the Protection of the rights of local communities, farmers and breeders, and for the regulation of access to biological resources, Art 13(1).
[12]   Brazil, Provisional Measure No 2.186-16, Art 16 §4.

local universities, governmental and inter-governmental entities duly recognized.[13]

Even though it is harder nowadays to differentiate research from commercial purposes, these provisions support the vision of the Food and Agriculture Organization concerning multilateral access, emphasizing the need to maintain biological resources as freely accessible, while excluding the creation of exclusive rights on the exchanged material.[14]

National Competent Authority

The right to permit, control and enforce appropriate development of bioprospecting activity should be vested in a national competent authority. Such authority should receive applications, examine requests ensuring that they comply with the regulation, negotiate or provide advices when other parties have control over negotiations, ensure the legality of the right granted to the seeker, follow the development of the activity and so on. Their authority could be transferred to a local institution in order to ease the process of access permits.

Prior Informed Consent (PIC)

A central requirement to request access is the prior informed consent of the legitimate holders of the resources.[15] This is some sort of agreement between the holders of resources and the seeker in which most provisions concerned with the requested activity should be disclosed. It is not an agreement to enter into any activity as such, but acts as a basis for the access agreement. The way it is developed might be precisely regulated in order to ensure the fairness of the action. Also, it is most likely that a specified language will be required such as the national language of the country, but also dialect, in order to ensure that all potential actors might have a role.[16]

Prior means that consent should be acquired before any potential user may gain access to any resources. Again it it emphasized that such consent will not act as a right to access but as a foundation for further negotiation.

---

[13]   Philippines, Executive Order No 247, section 3.
[14]   Leverve F., *Bioprospecting and Intellectual Property Rights*, IPR Helpdesk Action Line [2004], www.iprhelpdesk.org.
[15]   Philippines, Executive Order No 247, section 6(1)(3); Brazil, Provisional Measure No 2.186-16, Art 11(IV)(a).
[16]   Bangladesh, Biodiversity and Community Knowledge Protection Act, Draft, Art 13(8).

Informed implies that the prior consent is premised on a full and frank disclosure[17] by users about all their relevant details, purpose, means of proceeding, targeted resources, and interests. The means of informing could be specified such as community assembly held in a language or dialect understandable by all participants.[18]

Consent emphasizes the requirement that an official and/or community authority approves. It should involve community holders of resources, especially when their knowledge is at stake.[19] Some laws might impose upon the bioprospector the burden to demonstrate the intention to share resources with the community,[20] but also to what extent they understand that to share their resources might result in a loss of control over its subsequent use.[21]

The parties

The parties to the prior informed consent procedure can be divided into three groups: the state, the seeker, and possibly any other parties that are linked with the resource.

The state, under a competent national authority, will first have a role by virtue of being the owner of some or all resources under its national sovereignty. When indigenous communities are the main party, a competent national authority or other entitled institution might provide assistance to them in order to ensure that they are properly represented.

The seeker of resources will obviously be part of the PIC and should provide consequently various information such as its identification, name, address, activity . . . Any links with other companies or organizations could be required. The applicant might have to prove that he is in a legal capacity to contract,[22] that he is financially sound and that he is not himself nor is any member or partner thereof a person convicted of an offence involving fraud or dishonesty or an undischarged bankrupt.[23] Where the seeker is living or based

---

17 Andean Pact, Art 15.

18 Philippines, Executive Order No 247, section 7(2)(2).

19 Model Law for the Protection of Traditional Ecological Knowledge, Innovations and Practice, Draft 201, Pacific Forum, section 10(1)(a).

20 Model Law for the Protection of Traditional Ecological Knowledge, Innovations and Practice, Draft 201, Pacific Forum, section 3(2)(a); Bangladesh, Biodiversity and Community Knowledge Protection Act, Draft 1998, Art 7(4).

21 Model Law for the Protection of Traditional Ecological Knowledge, Innovations and Practice, Draft 201, Pacific Forum, section 3(2)(d).

22 Decision 391 of the Andean Pact, Art 26(a); Organization of African Unity Model Law, Art 4(2)(a)(i).

23 Gurdial Singh Nijar, Draft Model Law: Collectors of Biological Resources Act, In Defence of Local Community Knowledge and Biodiversity: A Conceptual Framework and the Essential Elements of a Rights Regime, 1996.

outside of the sourcing country, he might have to be represented by a legal representative resident in the country.[24]

The other parties might be the owner of some private land, communities' holders of specific resources, or the director or any official entity in charge of a national park or any protected areas. They can be party to the PIC when access is sought to resources they are associated with.[25] They can request that access be denied to resources within the area they inhabit.[26] When indigenous communities are involved, a relevant representative of the community should be recognized. The head of the community or medicine holder might hold the right or knowledge over resources to decide matters affecting their community. Or, it could be required that the whole community be invited to participate in the consultation.[27]

Whereas it appears reasonable to admit local communities or actors at the stage of the PIC, maybe it is not the most appropriate forum for them to deploy their views. The PIC might be more efficient as a first stage for information transfer from the potential seeker to the national authority. The information could then be used as a foundation for the access contract negotiation concerning whether local communities or actors should have a substantial role.

Subject matter

The subject matter has to be defined precisely, such as the species at stake and all the taxonomic information and scientific data associated with its characterization. Where this is not possible, other type of contracts might be entered into. Also endemic, rare, threatened or endangered species will likely be the subject of higher requirements for access, or excluded for any access.

The subject matter, when specified, can add more precision to the purpose of access. Apart from differentiating between commercial and non-commercial purposes, it can also highlight the industry within which it is intended to be used and consequently the specificities of the industry. For example, the constraint of innovation and the likely outcome directly derived from the accessed resources are different between the pharmaceutical and agriculture industry and therefore might lead to different terms of access.

Event of collection

The way the collection is to be acquired, the time of the proposed collection,

---

24   Costa Rica, Biodiversity Law 7788 of Costa Rica, Art 63(5).
25   Brazil Bill No 306/95, Chapter II, Art 5(III); Costa Rica, Biodiversity Law, No 7788, Art 63(1).
26   Brazil, Bill, Art 46.
27   Philippines, Executive Order No 247, section 7(2)(2).

the geographical area of collection, the name of the individual or team involved in the collection and the quantity sought should be specified.

The event of collection, whereas not given too much focus within national legislation, is in fact landmark information. If properly addressed, it can be used as a complex tool to substantiate the extent of collection and veracity of the seeker.

Potential use
The PIC is also an important means of requesting the purpose of the activity. The potential use acting as the foundation for the possible benefit sharing will also restrain the use made of the resource once accessed. It might encompass the extent and probability of results and benefits, the planned use of information and samples, the likely end product, if any intellectual property rights might be sought in relation to the acquired sample, the primary destination of the resource and possible further destinations, where the research and development will take place, how the research and development are to be carried out, the possible third party implications and the budget involved in this activity.

Again, this information should be compared to that provided on the subject matter, extent of collection, and so on, in order to ascertain the reliability of the information provided.

Technology transfer and benefit sharing
The transfer and benefit sharing represent the compensation that the sourcing country in general will negotiate against the potential grant of access and further use or development made of its resources. Those terms will be mostly developed with regard to the characteristics included within the request, and therefore a certain freedom should be enjoyed within the terms of the contract. Meanwhile some terms or general benefits might be imposed at this stage, such as benefits that will enhance protection of biodiversity.[28]

Time of issuance of the PIC
A time of issuance of the PIC might be imposed on communities or other stakeholders, meanwhile ensuring an appropriate cooling period allowing relevant stakeholders to reflect on their decision.[29]

---

[28] Bangladesh, Biodiversity and Community Knowledge Protection Act, draft, section 13(2); Costa Rica, Biodiversity Law 7788, Art 63(4).
[29] Philippines, Executive Order No 247, section 7(2)(3).

Involvement of third parties

One of the features of the procedural aspect of the PIC is to make the request publicly available. With the primary aim of involving public concern over such potential agreement, it will also be an act of transparency. This could be achieved through publication in the mass media or within a registration system. All the information exchanged could appear in a public file accessible to everybody for an unlimited time,[30] or only for a set period.[31] There could be discrimination on access by third parties with respect to their citizenship.[32] The information provided to the public might itself be restricted: for example, publication of an abstract of the request or a summary of the profile of the project.[33] Transparency over such an agreement might only be enforced through a public notice of approval;[34] or even, with less frequency, by periodical disclosures of authorizations of access.[35]

Confidentiality terms

Even when public disclosure is enforced under the legislation, a request for certain information to be kept confidential might be granted. In order to enjoy such treatment the information shall present the potential of being used in an unfair commercial way if made public.[36] The applicant should provide the relevant authority with a non-confidential summary to be made public.[37] Trade secrets are likely to be protected from disclosure unless there are considerations of biosafety.[38]

In some cases confidentiality will be restricted, and should not encompass certain terms, such as: the application, identification of the applicant, supplier of the resource and national support institution or individual; the locality or area in which access will be made, the methodology of access, project proposal;[39] hence reflecting the requirement to rendering the application public as previously described.

Meanwhile, some regulations might assume all information to be confiden-

---

[30]   Decision 391 of the Andean Communities, Art 18; Philippines, Executive Order No 247, section 7(1)(1).
[31]   Pakistan, Legislation on Access to Biological Resources and Community Rights, Draft, Article 4(2)(b); Organization of African Unity Model Law, Art 4(2)(b).
[32]   Bangladesh, Biodiversity and Community Knowledge Protection Act, Draft, Art 13(10).
[33]   Brazil, Provisional Measure No 2.186-16, Art 22.
[34]   India, Biological Diversity Act 2002, section 19(4).
[35]   Brazil, Provisional Measure No 2.186-16, Art 14(IV).
[36]   Andean Pact, Art 19.
[37]   Andean Pact, Art 19.
[38]   Costa Rica Biodiversity Law 7788, Art 67.
[39]   Andean Pact, Art 19.

tial and therefore will exclude any access from third parties except with the express permission of both parties.[40]

Whereas confidential treatment obviously hinders transparency and the participation of third parties, it has commercial value in that it keeps the field of development of the seeker unknown to direct competitors. If biological resources are to be considered as valuable commercial resources, confidentiality might enforce provisions friendly to the downstream business.

PIC as Foundation

Again, the PIC will act as a pre-agreement and most of the provisions agreed within the PIC must be reiterated under the formal agreement. It is only after being granted a PIC associated with the required documents for application that the seeker will be allowed to enter into negotiation for access to the resources, the related knowledge, and the possible further transfer and all associated terms.

Review of Request

The regulation might enforce the evaluation of the whole application by the competent national authority within a limited time, such as a maximum of 30[41] days or 60[42] days. In addition, provisions within the regulation might provide means to extend the time of reviewing for another limited time either under a justified request,[43] or at the discretion of the national competent authority.[44]

The application form can be considered as incomplete, the applicant being still allowed to improve it. If the request for access is denied, means of opposition might be anticipated within the law.[45] When considered complete, an official statement should follow and the applicant will be allowed to start negotiating for access to the resources.[46]

The access agreement will be more thorough than the PIC as its purposes are to specify access and the potential use of the acquired resources. While negotiating the access agreement, all the interested parties should enter into negotiation. The indigenous community might then gain more weight in the

---

[40]   Peru, Law No 27811, Art 28.

[41]   Decision 391 of the Andean Communities, Art 29; Peru, Law No 27811, Art 30.

[42]   Brazil, Bill 306/95, Art 17.

[43]   Supreme Decree No. 24676 of Bolivia, Art 24.

[44]   Brazil, Bill 306/95, Art 17.

[45]   Bolivia, Supreme Decree No. 24676, Art 26.

[46]   Brazil, Bill 306/95, Art 18.

negotiating process, especially regarding access to their knowledge, which is of value in terms of the results deriving from a bioprospecting activity. In this respect the ability to negotiate might need to be enhanced in order for the indigenous communities to have their interests fully protected.[47] A mediator could be appointed for the development of the negotiations.[48]

An access agreement may be cancelled after it has been granted when it can be shown that the grant was in violation of any legal provision, or that essential data might be inaccurate or false.[49] Meanwhile the bioprospector might be entitled to rectify. It might be enforced that the bioprospector be made aware of the coming cancellation within a minimum time, like 30 days, before a final decision is held, providing him with the chance to rectify or settle the issue.[50]

Definitions

Definitions have to be precisely stated in the contract, especially those relating to the subject matter and the derivatives. Most laws will specify terms, and therefore, assuming that those contracts will be developed under their jurisdiction and that the freedom to negotiate will be framed under national laws over this specific subject matter, it is strongly advised to employ the same ones.

Grant of Access

The right of access will be effective when granted by the national competent authority.[51] Such grant might enter into force once an agreement is signed between the applicant and the authority,[52] whether on behalf of the community[53] or not. In addition, it might be required before being in force that a resolution should have been published with an extract of the contract in an official newspaper or a newspaper with a wide circulation.[54]

---

[47]   COP VI Decision VI/24 Art 20(b).
[48]   WIPO/GRTKF/IC/1/9 Art 15(1).
[49]   Peru, Law No 27811, Art 34.
[50]   Peru, Law No 27811, Art 36.
[51]   Brazil, Provisional Measure No 2.186-16, Art 29.
[52]   Pakistan, Legislation on Access to Biological Resources and Community Rights, Draft, Art 4(3)(b); Organization of African Unity Model Legislation for the protection of the rights of local communities, farmers and breeders, and for the regulation of access to biological resources. Art 7(2): Philippines, Executive Order No 247, section 3.
[53]   Bangladesh, Biodiversity and Community Knowledge Protection Act, Draft, Art 13.
[54]   Decision 391 of the Andean Communities, Art 38; Brazil, Provisional Measure No 2.186-16, Art 28.

Fees

While various monetary terms could be defined through the agreement under the benefit-sharing provisions, some fees are likely to arise when entering such agreement. They could be fixed,[55] or elaborated as a function of the expenses in relation to the necessary evaluations required to grant access.[56] The expenses of publication might also be taken into consideration. Finally, the amount of the fees perceived might be based on a percentage of the research budget.[57]

BIOPROSPECTION AND TRANSFER OF RESOURCES

Once access is granted under a specific agreement, the activity as such will start. What will now be emphasized are the precise controls and duties effective during the course of the activity that might be enforced within the law.

Different Types of Contract and Authorized Sampling Activity

The access agreement or material transfer agreement is the main contract. It might integrate all provisions or be associated with accessory contracts, which will then specify issues connected with access to resources such as transfer, benefit sharing and associated rights.[58] It is central; thus, if declared void, any supplementary contracts will also be void. On the other hand, a void accessory agreement will not affect the access agreement unless it is held to be indispensable.[59]

The purpose of access should differentiate between types of permit. An academic research permit might enjoy less stringent conditions for access compared to a commercial permit, in the meantime limiting any commercial development. The amount of samples over the specified resources will in general be limited. This provision might be of little importance when one is seeking genetic resources, where a low amount might ensure their effective use. On the other hand, prospectors interested in biochemical or biological compounds might require a higher amount of samples; hence a commercial exploitation permit should better reflect requirements for higher supplies.[60]

---

55 Philippine, Executive Order No 247, section 5(j).
56 Bolivia, Supreme Decree No 24676, Art 29.
57 Costa Rica, Biodiversity Law 7788, Art 76.
58 Andean Pact, decision 391, Art 41.
59 Andean Pact, decision 391, Art 44.
60 Organization of African Unity Model Legislation for the Protection of the

Some permits, or concessions, will also allow for constant use of and access to the resources.[61]

In a case where a bioprospector is interested in having a right to randomly screen resources of interest, a provisional bioprospecting contract[62] might be granted. The terms under those contracts are more rigorous, such as a shorter period of time for access and non-renewability. In addition, commercial use of the product might be prohibited and would require the seeker to enter into another agreement. A duty will be imposed to send a detailed report of the bioprospecting activity within a limited time after completion of the agreement. Meanwhile, the seeker might enjoy some preferential terms such as a priority right to request access under a more conventional agreement, or that the research report remain confidential for a limited time after the end of the contract.

The length of authorized access will in general be for a period of three years, to be renewable.[63]

Transfer or Technology

Transfer of technology and information is one of the key features of benefit sharing because it will increase the sourcing country's ability to use fully its own resources. This can be facilitated through equipment purchases, donations and other infrastructure developments from the seeker. Particular emphasis will be placed on knowledge and technology that are relevant to the recognition, handling, sustainable utilization and conservation of biodiversity.[64]

The contractual terms of technology transfer should reflect contractual freedom rather than being too rigidly framed. Indeed, the variability of purpose, type of industry, characteristics of the seeker exclude a one-size-fits-all treatment.

Associated National Institution

The participation of a national institution might be mandatory to ensure that access and acquisition of resources are done properly.[65] Moreover it could also

---

Rights of Local Communities, Farmers and Breeders, and for the Regulation of Access to Biological Resources, Art 13(1).

[61]   Costa Rica, Biodiversity Law No 7788, Art 75.

[62]   Brazil, Bill 306/95.

[63]   Brazil, Bill 306/95, Art 23; Costa Rica, Biodiversity Law 7788, Art 70.

[64]   Bangladesh, Biodiversity and Community Knowledge Protection Act, draft, section 13(2); Costa Rica, Biodiversity Law 7788, Art 63(4).

[65]   Brazil, Provisional Measure No 2.186-16, Art 16 §5; Bangladesh, Biodiversity and Community Knowledge Protection Act, draft, section 13(23); Philippines, Executive Order No 247, section 5(h).

be enforced that national actors be involved actively and substantially in the access to and research into the resources, as well as locating the research within the sourcing country, when appropriate. This will increase the transfer of knowledge, while keeping some of the basic research development within the sourcing country. This should act as a buffer to the loss of information associated with the resources; limiting it to what the bioprospector specifically seeks. The associated cost could then be assumed by the applicant.[66]

Depository of Duplicate

The bioprospector might be required to collect additional samples of each specimen and to provide them to a designated institution.[67] The samples should encompass any associated material that has been gathered. The deposit of a duplicate could be made legally compulsory,[68] or enforced within the contractual arrangement under a guarantee.[69] A breach of such a provision will render the access contract void. Also, a control might be added by prohibiting any export of single samples.[70]

The main objectives are to provide means of monitoring which specimen as accessed by the bioprospector and to develop an *ex situ* collection within the sourcing country.

Environmental Impact Assessment

One of the main concerns in regulating bioprospecting is to preserve the existing biodiversity. The activity of collecting might affect to some extent the specimen sought and its surrounding ecosystem. The potential risks incurred in such activity should then be specified by an environmental impact assessment (EIA).[71]

---

[66] Bangladesh, Biodiversity and Community Knowledge Protection Act, draft, section 13(23); Philippines, Executive Order No 247, section 5(h).

[67] Philippines, Department Administrative Order No 96-20, section 8(1)(2) and (3).

[68] Andean Communities, Decision 391, Art 17(g).

[69] Bangladesh, Biodiversity and Community Knowledge Protection Act, draft, section 13(15)(d).

[70] Brazil, Bill 306/95, Art 22(IX).

[71] Costa Rica, Biodiversity Law, No 7788, Art 7(18) 'Evaluation of environment impact: Scientific and technical procedure which permits the identification of the effects which an action or specific project will have on the environment, as well as quantifying and considering them in order to take decisions. Includes the specific effects, their overall evaluation, the alternatives for greater environmental benefit, a program for control and minimisation of the negative effects, a monitoring program, a recovery program, as well as the guarantee of proper environmental execution'.

An EIA might be requested prior to any access contract;[72] or only when some doubts are held.[73] Endemic, rare, threatened or endangered species[74] that enjoy specific protection are likely to increase the requirement for a prior EIA. Such a procedure could be undertaken alongside development of the activity,[75] ensuring that no adverse consequences happen at any stage;[76] or at the request of a third party when it has sufficient reason to believe negative effects are occurring.[77]

If an adverse effect results from bioprospecting activity, issues of liability might arise.[78] What is at stake are the potential consequences that might be assumed under the responsibility of the bioprospector, whether unpredicted (erroneous EIA) or unpredictable. Associated with recognition of liability are the issues of damages or compensation. The bioprospector could be forced to indemnify the owner of the area in the event of a disaster occurring.[79] Issues of ecological or environmental costs could also be addressed in a wider manner in order to ensure the rehabilitation of the affected area.[80] The purposes for which a bioprospector sought access, such as direct or indirect commercial use, may also increase its liability.[81]

Monitoring

Again the activity of the bioprospector has to be monitored to ensure that no adverse effect on biodiversity is occurring as specified above under the requirement for continuous EIA or allowing third parties to present complaints. A status report on the progress of the activity might also be

---

[72]   Philippines, Executive Order No 247, section 6(1)(4).

[73]   Peru, Bill for the Regulation of Access to Genetic Resources, 1999, Art 16.

[74]   Convention on International Trade and Endangered Species of Wild Flora and Fauna (CITES) aims at providing protection of endangered species. But it mainly affects the trading, and transport of such species. CBD Art 8(k): 'Develop or maintain necessary legislation and/or other regulatory provisions for the protection of threatened species and populations'.

[75]   Bangladesh, Biodiversity and Community Knowledge Protection Act, draft, Art 13(15)(g).

[76]   Philippines, Executive Order No 247, section 5(g).

[77]   Malawi, National Park and Wildlife, Act No 11, section 23(1).

[78]   CBD Art 14 (2): 'The Conference of the Parties shall examine, on the basis of studies to be carried out, the issue of liability and redress, including restoration and compensation, for damage to biological diversity, except where such liability is purely internal matter'.

[79]   Brazil, Provisional Measure No 2.186-16, Art 16 §10.

[80]   Bangladesh, Biodiversity and Community Knowledge Protection Act, draft, Article 7(5).

[81]   Ibid.

requested at the end of it[82] ensuring its conformity with the access contract. In a more rigorous manner, the bioprospector might, at the end of his work in each area, have to sign a declaration with the owner or representative of the area, which will list the material accessed.[83]

Access, being the only right truly vested in the state to control its biological resources, ensures that monitoring the activity becomes a necessary means of enforcement of the regulation of access.

Transfer of Resources

The resources sought might be of a different nature and different 'rights' are potentially embodied within them. A first distinction should be made between tangible and intangible resources. Tangible resources are those presenting the characteristics of being concrete, touchable, physical, corporeal. One has to take possession of them in order to enjoy any use. The primary purpose for any bioprospecting activity is to access such resources in their tangible form. On the other hand, intangible resources are the opposite: they comprise information, knowledge, ideas, entities that are of a non-scarce nature. The resource might embody intangible information such as genetic information or biochemical structure. In addition, the knowledge of the people in relation to those resources should be added .

Whereas the primary purpose of a bioprospecting activity is to access resources of interest, the right vested in the resources and especially the transfer of any rights is a key point of those agreements. With highly developed intellectual property rights that address the issue of ownership of intangible resources, there should be concern over what a bioprospector will actually access.

Transfer of ownership
Sovereignty of the state or people over their resources will be enforced, with the consequence that assignment of ownership will be barred in general.[84] This will ensure perpetual ownership by the sourcing country, excluding therefore any restriction on further use of the resource, which will keep customary use safe. Nevertheless what might be granted is the right of the bioprospector to use his acquisition in the manner he stated, and most probably when a commercial entity is involved, the bioprospector's entitlement to seek intellectual property

---

[82] Philippines, Executive Order No 247, section 5(g).
[83] Brazil, Provisional Measure No 2.186-16, Art 16 §1.
[84] Philippines, Department Administrative Order No 96-20, section 8(1)(16); Bangladesh, Biodiversity and Community Knowledge Protection Act, draft, Art 6(1).

rights regarding further developments might be acknowledged. The latter will obviously restrain some of the further uses that could be made by the sourcing country. There could also be an issue when patent law is not in synergy with legislation affecting bioprospecting, especially when customary use was confined within an indigenous community. Under such circumstances, the customary may not form part of the state of the art and thus still manifest novelty, which is one of the requirements for the patentability of an invention. The indigenous community will not be restrained because of their privilege in prior use, but the rest of the sourcing country might have to take into consideration the right of the patent.

Export of tangible material
Transport of material once acquired lawfully might be regulated, either under laws regulating access to resources[85] or under other bodies of laws like those concerned with transport, import and export.[86] A transport or postal clearance might be required while transferring any biological or genetic resources,[87] which will enforce control not only at the border but also within the country. Transfer might be solely controlled at the border through an export permit, which should comprise disclosure of the species, associated scientific information and geographical origin. Some further laws could be involved when there are certain peculiarities of the specimen. If endangered species are at stake, then one has to carefully consider the provisions of the CITES,[88] which could lead to an export ban.[89]

Measures of strict quarantine might occur, ensuring that any specimen collected from the wild is free from any potential disease.[90] Generally such measures relate to imports and therefore will be specified under the legislation of the destination country, but they could also be considered at the export stage.

---

[85]   Bangladesh, Biodiversity and Community Knowledge Protection Act, draft, Art 13(28).

[86]   Malawi, National Park and Wildlife Act No 11, section 99.

[87]   Department Administrative Order No 96-20 of the Philippines, section 8(1)(7).

[88]   'The Convention on International Trade in Endangered Species (CITES) is an international agreement concerned with the survival of wild animals and plants threatened by over exploitation as a result of international trade in specimens. Today, more than 30,000 species of animals and plants are accorded various type of protection against abusive trade. It provides protection by imposing a compulsory authorizing licence requirement for all import, export, re-export and introduction from the sea of the selected species', available at www.cites.org (accessed 01/2007).

[89]   Philippines, Department Administrative Order No 96-20, section 8(1)(5).

[90]   Philippines, Department Administrative Order No 96-20, section 8(1)(1).

Transfer of intangible resources

Practical transfer of intangible resources will occur immediately when information, like traditional knowledge, is transmitted, and from the physical transfer of samples embodying information. The latter is the easiest to control as one has to transfer the material sample in order to enjoy the information contained within it. Once transferred, any further uses or limitations should have been anticipated within the access contract. The transfer of associated traditional knowledge should be more complex to control because of its nature.

Traditional knowledge might highlight specimens of interest and provide guidance for potential use. It is generally valuable to bioprospector in order to increase their chances of successful screening and corresponding applications, and therefore should influence negotiations over benefit sharing. The only means of securing the transfer of such knowledge is in close supervision of the exchanges between communities and bioprospectors. In particular, thorough provisions within the access contract should specify the information exchanged, delimit its potential use and indicate whether it could be disseminated or should remain confidential. In addition, the legal status of such information needs also to be assessed such as its non-assignability[91] and its repatriation.[92] Communities' ownership of their knowledge might be held to be inalienable and non-transferable with the effect of rendering the contract void.[93] Again, such provisions should act as safeguards ensuring the continuous enjoyment by the community of their customs and should not restrain developments based on it.

UTILIZATION OF RESOURCES

Potential Utility of Accessed Resources

Different factors could motivate a bioprospecting activity. A distinction is usually made between commercial and non-commercial intent. However, even when research is carried out without any thought of profit, downstream developments that were not intended could lead to a more lucrative path. With respect to commercial activity, two main uses of the acquired sample could be specified. The sample might be used in order to conduct research, or its commercial application might already be known and what is of interest is exploitation of the resource in a quantitative manner.

---

[91] Brazil, Bill 306/95, Art 5(V).
[92] CBD, Art 17(3).
[93] Model Law for the Protection of Traditional Ecological Knowledge, Innovations and Practices, Draft, Pacific Forum, section 8(1)(a).

Associated with use of the resource is what the sourcing country is prepared to surrender. The potential developments will lead to different consequences in order to ensure enjoyment of what one was interested in. Use made of acquired resources could be of a different nature: publication of the acquisition, development of knowledge, product, and applications for intellectual property rights; events that are likely to limit the sourcing country in some future developments and therefore should be carefully weighed up against what is offered in exchange.

Technology Transfer and Information

Technology transfer could occur first under provisions that will trade material, facilities, knowledge etc. against the right to access resources as stated previously. With respect to resources as such, commitment to provide all research reports and related results might be enforced;[94] possibly in a language understandable by the sourcing country and communities involved.[95] Those measures might run counter to commercial interests favouring secrecy; a minimum time before disclosure should then be ensured. Enhancement of participation in product development with potential co-inventorship, co-authorship and even joint ventures might be specified, especially when the development is located within the sourcing country. Unrestricted licences for any further development made by the seeker could be imposed. The seeker might also be required to incorporate within its research program fields of interest to the sourcing country, such as screening for therapies against endemic diseases.

Monetary Benefits

Compensation should be required for grant of access. Fees, acting as up-front payment in return for the right to access and to collect, are a first step. Concerning the resources as such, when the seeker is interested in a quantity, the price is easier to set and tune. When research is to be conducted, the outcome is more uncertain and monetary provisions will be harder to set. The central idea is to share the benefits that might arise later and to ensure that the access contract anticipated it. The law might request that the access contract include provisions specifying how it is intended to share benefits,[96] thus precluding highly unfavourable deals.

---

94   Brazil, Bill 306/95, Art 22(VII).
95   Bangladesh, Biodiversity and Community Knowledge Protection Act, Draft, Art 13(7).
96   Bangladesh, Biodiversity and Community Knowledge Protection Act, Draft, Art 13(15)(f); Philippines, Department Administrative Order No 96-20, section 8(1)(14); Andean Community, Decision 391, Article 35.

Such benefit sharing could be made by means of division of profits, lump sums and payments of royalties when intellectual property rights are sought. A system of licence fees could also be developed differentiating the various possible uses. All of this could be included within a milestone payment scheme that will identify achievements and be more relevant than stipulating the possible benefits. When a potential commercial development is reached where the contract excluded any commercial use, a means of entering into further negotiations should be foreseen.

The amount to be shared might be framed; a minimum of 5 to 10 per cent of the benefits resulting from goods, gross sales before tax, which were developed directly or indirectly, could be enforced, especially when community knowledge is involved.[97] In that case, one should carefully assess, in an endeavour to respect the community hierarchy and customs, to whom payment should be made. In contrast, the law might require the benefits to be shared on a communitarian basis.[98]

Other monetary terms could be included such as special fees to be paid to trust funds supporting conservation and sustainable use of the biodiversity, salaries in case of joint development, research funding etc.

Intellectual Property Rights (IPR)

The development of commercial by-products based on the accessed resource might involve the creation of IPR. In fact this will most generally be a prerequisite for a private investor. Meanwhile, the right of the primary holder of the resource must be enforced against a certain misappropriation of the information embodied. Once the material has been accessed, all physical controls from the source will be lost. This should be anticipated within the access contract reflecting both interests: the stakeholder's and the bioprospector's. Otherwise legislation might still stipulate that any further development requires that the holder of a resource was aware of such use,[99] thus ensuring restriction even when non-specified.

The resource might, before accession, already be associated with specific knowledge and the degree of human improvement and innovation upon the whole transmitted information is hard to delimit. The disclosure of traditional knowledge might be valuable in the future development of the resource. On

---

[97] Peru, Law No 27811, Art 27(c); Pakistan, Access to Biological Resources and Community Rights, Draft, Art 5(4); Bangladesh, Biodiversity and Community Knowledge Protection Act, Draft, Art 6(5).

[98] Peru, Law No 27811, Art 8.

[99] Model Law for the Protection of Traditional Ecological Knowledge, Innovations and Practices of the Pacific Forum, section 3(2)(c).

the contrary, when bioprospecting is done in a random manner, it is hard to adduce any role, under a standard IPR regime, coming from outside the recipient. But the notion of contribution in terms of conservation might enforce certain rights; such as benefit sharing of any related future IPR.[100] If a certain partnership is agreed, issues of joint inventorship or joint authorship will appear. The latter should not be a problem whereas joint inventorship is unlikely when private investment is involved.

What has to be stressed, in addition, is to what extent the scope of protection granted by IPR might restrain the customary use of the community. Legislation will be likely to enforce continuous enjoyment by those communities, with the consequence that intellectual property laws might be rendered void where inconsistency occurs.[101] The issue could be of more interest when an improvement is made. In that case patent rights should prevail. Nevertheless, if patent law is properly set, one should not be able to claim property over what was enjoyed before.

Monitoring

Monitoring is not only important during access and transfer but should also address further developments. This could mainly be achieved by regular reports on any subsequent research flowing from the bioprospecting activities,[102] development of any products,[103] notification of any IPR sought, and admittance to *ex situ* facilities of genetic resources and database. Terms may also be included on the possible transfer of such resources.[104]

Previous to the grant of IPR, an assessment could be made as to whether the applicant had acquired the said resource in compliance with laws on access and that the agreement allowed the applicant to apply for IPR on by-products.[105] This is not applied under European, Japan and US patent law, and therefore is unlikely to be of substantial weight.

---

[100]   India, Protection of Plant Varieties and Farmers' Rights Act 2001, Art 26 enforces compensation when a new variety is registered and has been developed from an existing one over which the role of a community in providing such variety is proved.

[101]   Model Law for the Protection of Traditional Ecological Knowledge, Innovations and Practices of the Pacific Forum, section 8(1)(a).

[102]   Brazil, Bill 306/95, Art 22(VII).

[103]   Brazil, Bill 306/95, Art 22(VI).

[104]   Brazil, Bill 306/95, Art 22(VIII).

[105]   Pacific Forum, Model Law for the Protection of Traditional Ecological Knowledge, Innovations and Practices, section 14(a).

Transfer to Third Parties

It is particularly important to restrain third party involvement, first to increase the potential commercial bargaining power of a sourcing country, but also because the provisions that bind the bioprospector will not affect a third party. The transfer of specimens, information or any associated knowledge could be excluded under any circumstances.[106] Or the contract of access granted to the applicant might always be specific to the collector, therefore excluding any form of subcontracting.[107] Meanwhile some flexibility might be required and in some places provisions for the act of sublicensing could be allowed.[108]

Transfer of knowledge should be carefully considered. Under a contractual term, information may be deemed confidential and held as a trade secret. Its disclosure might be regulated by imposing a consent requirement or by requiring a minimum time before a recipient could start publishing. On the seeker side, keeping information confidential held a few important commercial advantages such as keeping the research secret and preventing the devastating effect on patent of a prior disclosure.

Whereas enforcement will generally be on the contractor side, the third party in its accession to this kind of knowledge might also be held liable. When the acquisition was made without the requirement held in the laws regulating access to resources and associated knowledge, the act of access to the specimen or information might be alleged to be an offence.[109] Under trade secret protection, a third party might not be allowed to enjoy access to any information when said information was protected under confidentiality provisions, and also where the third party knew the nature of the information and the limitation that was made over access from third parties or had reason to believe it.

In cases where the means of access by a third party to the information cannot be held to be unlawful on his side and where the laws of access do not have jurisdiction over the third party, which is mostly the case when a third party is not within the sourcing country, then the chances of repatriating the knowledge or limiting its potential use are small.

Finally, the authorities entitled to grant IPR, or the regulation specifying the grant of such a right, might require or be required, when assessing whether an

---

[106] Bangladesh, Biodiversity and Community Knowledge Protection Act, Draft, Art 13(16).

[107] Bangladesh, Biodiversity and Community Knowledge Protection Act, Draft, Art 13(14).

[108] Peru, Law No 27811, Art 33.

[109] Pacific Forum, Model Law for the Protection of Traditional Ecological Knowledge, Innovations and Practices, section 8(2).

application is deemed valid or not, to request or ensure that access was done properly with regard to the laws in force.

Unlawful Acquisition

When a bioprospector unlawfully accesses resources without authorization or by breach of the contract for access;[110] he will commit an offence.[111] Punishment most generally would require the offender to pay a fine.[112] The fine imposed could target a person's income, between one to twelve months of salary,[113] or the economic exploitation of the product or process that is related – an indemnity of at least 20 per cent of the benefits or royalties.[114] When the offender persists in failing to comply, criminal proceedings could even be initiated.[115]

To ensure the effectiveness of the punishment, especially when the offender is not under state jurisdiction and is simultaneously involved in another contract in force or at the request stage, he might be under the constraint of a possible revocation of the existing contract and incapacitation to enter into any further contract. This might hold until the offender has fulfilled his duty, but also if he is a recidivist.[116] A register of any offence might be kept publicly available to monitor potential recidivists[117] and to provide parties wishing to enter into negotiation with a potential seeker with information about the honesty and reliability of the contractor. Such information being held public, the publicity that might arise over companies and their misbehaviour might be detrimental to their image with consequences that might potentially affect their business worldwide.

The way an applicant behaved in other countries might be addressed when access is sought in one country. When a bioprospector is accused of irregular or unauthorized action or transaction in one country, he might be refused access in another.[118]

In practice, these provisions might be useless. Indeed the market for biological resources is international and developed countries are the main recipient

---

[110]   Costa Rica, Biodiversity Law 7788, Art 112.
[111]   Model Law for the Protection of Traditional Ecological Knowledge, Innovations and Practices of the Pacific Forum, section 8(2).
[112]   Peru, Law No 27811, Art 62.
[113]   Costa Rica, Biodiversity Law 7788, Art 112.
[114]   Brazil, Provisional Measure No 2.186-16, Art 26.
[115]   Peru, Law No 27811, Art 62.
[116]   Bolivia, Supreme Decree No 24676, Art 60(d).
[117]   Peru, Law No 27811, Art 61.
[118]   Bangladesh, Biodiversity and Community Knowledge Protection Act, Draft, Art 13(3).

of the transfer of products within that market. Therefore, without corresponding enforcement of access within developed countries, the sourcing country
will lose any possible jurisdiction over the alleged trespasser, who then might
not be substantially affected by his misbehaviour.

Illegitimate IPR

Illegitimate IPR will occur when, irrespective of the contract or the law under
which it was agreed, the seeker still applies for and obtains exclusive rights
over a product or process derived from accessed resources. When the seeker is
outside the sourcing country, then he might be required to meet his obligations
in accordance with his contractual liability. Again issues of jurisdiction could
be problematic.

Pre-emptive solutions can be anticipated: that is, specific requirements for
the grant of IPR. When an application is related to a biological entity, intellectual property laws could require disclosure of the geographical origin of the
resources, thereby providing a means to track back the access.[119] More inva-
sively, the relevant institution concerned with the grant of IPR might be
responsible for securing during the assessment of the application that it has
been made in compliance with the access contract or regulation ruling the
access contract.[120] An applicant might also need, when his invention is related
to biological resources endemic to the country, to be granted an approval from
another national institution prior to any filing.[121] The extent of information to
be provided might also encompass identification of communities either when
they are directly involved, or also if the biological sample originates from the
area they inhabit.[122]

Failure to do so or a false statement might result in an invalidation of the
right as part of the grounds for revocation. Or, the validity of the right might
not be revoked and compensation imposed to be paid to the community in relation to which the claimed product has been developed.[123]

Again, to effectively regulate illegitimate IPR, corresponding provisions
should be enforced within recipient countries.

Dispute and Relevant Law

The contract should again specify means of settling disputes. Of particular

---

[119] India, Patents Act, section 10(4)(d).
[120] Costa Rica, Biodiversity Law 7788, Art 80.
[121] India, Biological Diversity Act, section 6(1).
[122] India, Plant Breeders and Farmers' Rights Act, Art 26.
[123] Ibid.

interest is the law that should be in force. It is likely that national regulations ruling access will prevail over the freedom to contract by requiring that any contract to be granted should identify the national law as the relevant one.[124] Also alternative means could be anticipated such as arbitration. When privileged links exist between the sourcing country and the seeker, some preferential ways of settling the dispute could also be emphasized.[125]

CLOSING REMARKS

The review of the various laws, being either implemented or proposed in southern countries, is somehow drawing the landscape of a coming harmonized appreciation and regulation of access and use of biological resources held within a country.

The activity of bioprospecting is not in itself new but it is only recently that higher concerns were raised over the regulation of access. More than the protection of biological diversity, what was of interest was the qualification of such resources as property, especially forecasting commercial interests. The corresponding legal response, even though disparate, mainly tackled the regulation of access rather than defining property in the resource as such. Framing natural biological resources within a property regime appears extremely problematic and would require a worldwide recognition which is far from being achieved. Regulating access is more appropriate currently as it can be fully controlled by a state.

Bioprospecting is representative of a market that expands outside of state boundaries. It appears that most of the sourcing countries are developing countries whereas the market and technology to appropriate the wealth of those resources are held within developed countries. For the activity to be properly regulated in the future, greater harmonization worldwide will be required. Such harmonization should occur on two levels. First, southern countries must ensure implementation of related legislations; it is only when access is properly regulated on the spot that further actions can be taken. Second, at the level of developed countries, more effort should be made to harmonize the existing rights affecting the end product of bioprospecting activity with the recognition of said regulations over biological resources. This could occur by creating safeguards for the granting of certain intellectual property rights, like patents. The current lack of recognition of disclosure of origin, for various reasons, is

---

[124]   The ASEAN Framework Agreement on Access to Biological and Genetic Resources, Art 9.
[125]   Ibid.

somehow blocking the effectiveness of regulating access by foreclosing any further action within the country of use.

Finally, national legislation within sourcing countries should reflect a certain flexibility in order to accommodate commercial reality. If legislation becomes too burdensome for commercial practice, then the potential for exchange will be hindered. This can be seen in the Philippines, for example, where, in spite of natural biodiversity, highly complex legislation has allowed only two access agreements over the last ten years.

16. Avenues to ensure full participation of rural communities in access authorisation processes in Cameroon and South Africa

Marcelin Tonye Mahop*

This chapter considers Cameroon and South Africa, two countries rich in biological and cultural diversity, as sources of materials used in scientific research with potential commercial applications. Field activities and an intensive literature search aimed at assessing biodiversity research activities and the existing regulations were carried out in Cameroon and South Africa. The main issues investigated include the usefulness of biological resources and traditional knowledge to rural communities and the extent to which their local management practices achieve sustainability; the extent to which the existing regulations in Cameroon and South Africa exclude rural communities from the decision-making processes pertaining to access; cases of scientific and commercial use that have stimulated the depletion of resources, raising concerns about sustainability. Following this assessment, this chapter discusses some workable avenues aimed at ensuring the full participation of rural communities in the decision-making processes pertaining to access to biological resources for corporate use. The proposed full participation is meant to provide incentives to rural communities to strengthen their commitment to biodiversity conservation at the local level.

*   I am thankful to Queen Mary Intellectual Property Research Institute, Queen Mary, University of London for providing the Herchel Smith fellowship, without which this contribution would not have been produced. Special thanks to Graham Dutfield, Michael Blakeney and Duncan Mathews for their attention to this research.

1. ASSESSMENT OF THE USEFULNESS OF BIODIVERSITY TO RURAL COMMUNITIES AND THEIR SUSTAINABLE RESOURCES MANAGEMENT PRACTICES

Across the world, rural communities depend on Non-Timber Forest Products (NTFPs) for their food, agricultural and medicinal needs (de Jong and Campbell 2001). Traditional societies' reliance on genetic resources and traditional knowledge to meet their food and agricultural needs go back millennia. Farming in sub-Saharan Africa began in Ethiopia between 4,000 and 6,000 BC, and rapidly extended to what are now Tanzania and Kenya through the migration of pastoral peoples. In West Africa, millet cultivation started in Mauritania around 1,000 BC, and the cultivation of rice in the valley of the Niger River started 100 years later. Simultaneously, the communities started cultivating yam and oil palm (Austen 1987).

Over time, rural communities have developed complex agricultural systems allowing them to address their food needs on the basis of their traditional knowledge of crop selection and their farming practices. For example in Swaziland, the Suazi communities nurture and use 200 plant species while the Tembe Thonga communities of Southern Africa use an estimated 106 plant species on a daily basis (Mooney 1996, p. 85). Southern African women have an impressive knowledge of seed selection and storage, allowing them to store seeds from ten ecotypes of sorghum and pearl millet at any given period in their homestead granaries (Musa 1998).

It therefore follows that like other parts of the developing world, the great majority of people in Africa are still largely dependent on plant genetic resources for their agricultural and food needs. Indeed recent estimates suggest that overall 70 percent of peoples in sub-Saharan Africa are largely dependent on agriculture and depend on seeds cultivated within their own communities for as much as 90 percent of their seed needs (Food and Agriculture Organisation of the United Nations (FAO) 1995).

The usefulness of genetic resources to rural populations can also be assessed on the basis of their reliance on traditional medicine. According to the World Health Organisation (WHO), traditional medicine is 'the sum total of knowledge, skills, practices based on the theories, beliefs and experiences indigenous to different cultures, whether explicable or not, used in the maintenance of health as well as the prevention, diagnosis, improvement or treatment of physical and mental illnesses' (WHO 2000). This definition indicates that traditional medicine is indeed deeply rooted in the tradition of certain communities. This knowledge is held by traditional peoples, is passed from one generation to another and is understood to have been tested during centuries of accumulated learning. Many populations in developing countries largely depend on traditional medicine for their primary health needs. In India, for example, it is reported that 65 percent of the population depend on traditional medicine while 80 percent of the African population is highly dependent on traditional medicine (WHO 2002). But it should also be indicated that, increasingly, other forms of medicine, including traditional medicine, are gaining ground in industrialised countries where they are known as alternative or complementary medicine (Eisenberg *et al.* 1993, p. 246).

As mentioned above, traditional societies also depend on genetic resources and associated traditional knowledge (TK) for securing an income. Indeed, rural communities are generally involved in a wide range of activities constituting their 'livelihood portfolio'. It is very common for people to be involved in more than one activity, such as livestock-raising, growing a large variety of subsistence and cash crops and gathering non-timber forest products (NTFPs) for their use and sales in local markets (Nnadozie *et al.* 2003). Their activities may also involve exchanging goods with neighbouring communities. Usually some household members are involved in off-management employment to earn income for the family and some are involved in small industrial activities such as brick burning, carpentry, craft production and local beer brewing (de Jong and Campbell 2001).

The role that local communities can play in the conservation and sustainability of biodiversity has led some commentators to argue that biodiversity conservation and the exploitation of its components will only be successful if these activities address primarily the concerns of the poorest and ensure their full participation in decision-making processes (Bell 1987, p. 79; Wells 1995). Indeed, the future and sustainability of some traditional societies is highly dependent upon the conservation of specific biomes (Bell 1987, p. 79).

This issue may be considered in the context of the lifestyle of the Pygmies, ancient hunter-gather societies inhabiting the rainforest of the Congo Basin. To be successful, conservation initiatives and extraction of biogenetic resources in Central Africa or more widely in the Congo Basin must take into account the concerns of the Pygmies because these communities have a wealth of knowledge that they apply to the management and use of their resources. Indeed, despite permanent access to and heavy reliance by the Pygmies on these resources, they can hardly be considered as depleted. This suggests that perhaps their traditional methods are sustainable, and if adopted by conservationists, may be most effective for biodiversity conservation. In a wider dimension, it is reported that throughout Africa, conservation and traditional management practices of rural communities are regulated by local rules, otherwise known as customary laws, that usually provide for sanctions against wrongdoers within a given community. For example, in the Miombo region of Southern Africa the cutting of fruit trees growing around a specific water spring is prohibited. Sacred groves and other forest stands are maintained for important ceremonial reasons as the residence of the souls of ancestors, as a source of medicinal plants and as the source of natural water springs (Clarke *et al.* 1996, p. 102). Not only are such areas a source of NTFPs useful to society at large and to specific rural societies in particular, but they also perform important ecological functions (Hughes 1998, p. 101).

Having broadly examined the extent to which bio-resources are useful to rural populations and the fact that the sustainability of these resources is not under threat despite the heavy reliance of rural populations, this chapter turns to the specific case studies, Cameroon and South Africa.

2. BIOLOGICAL AND CULTURAL DIVERSITY IN CAMEROON AND SOUTH AFRICA

Cameroon is a country rich in biological diversity,[1] as demonstrated in its diversity of plants and animals. The flora of Cameroon comprises about 8,000 plant species, of which 156 are endemic to Cameroon, i.e. they are only found in Cameroon, and about 45 are specifically endemic to the Mount Cameroon area (Thomas and Cheek 1992; Fomete and Tchamou 1998). With regard to cultural diversity, the outcomes of the 1998 national census suggested that the population of Cameroon was estimated at 14 million, with a 2.3 percent annual growth rate.[2] The population is divided into 200 ethnic groups practising an estimated 286 local languages.[3]

According to Fomete and Tchamou (1998), the biological diversity richness is reportedly under the threat of depletion due to the overexploitation of timber resources. On the other hand, the gradual loss of traditional knowledge held by rural communities is also reported, due to the gradual extinction of local languages. There is no specific evidence to demonstrate a link between the

---

[1] Article 2 of the Convention on Biological Diversity (CBD) defines biodiversity as 'the variability among living organisms from all sources including, *inter alia*, terrestrial, marine and other aquatic ecosystems and the ecological complexes of which they are part; this includes diversity within species, between species and of ecosystems'. See Convention on Biological Diversity (Rio de Janeiro, 5 June 1992).

[2] More details on the socio-cultural and economic data on Cameroon can be found at: http://www.afdb.org/en/content/download/%20383/1851/file/cameroon_basicindicators.pdf.

[3] Recent studies of local languages in Cameroon suggest that, out of the 286 national languages, 279 are living languages, three are second languages without mother tongue speakers and four are completely extinct. These statistics were confirmed by one senior researcher in the Cameroon branch of the International Linguistic Society in October 2003 in Yaoundé.

depletion of biological resources and the associated traditional knowledge held by rural communities. However, the link between the preservation of local languages and the preservation of traditional knowledge emerged during discussions with some traditional healers in Cameroon. Some of them complained that it is becoming more and more difficult to pass their traditional medicinal knowledge and practices to youngsters who live in cities, because most of them do not understand or speak native languages (Maffi 2001; Twarog and Kapoor 2004).

South Africa is an attractive land for bioprospecting activities because of the country's rich biodiversity.[4] The country hosts between 250 000 and 1 000 000 species, with a large number being endemic to South Africa. In terms of plant diversity, South Africa hosts 18,000 vascular plant species, among which 80 percent are endemic to South Africa. South Africa is reportedly the only country on earth to have within its borders, an entire plant kingdom, known as the Cape Floral Kingdom. In terms of animal diversity, South Africa hosts 5.8 percent of the world's total mammal species, 8 percent of the bird species, 4.6 percent of the global diversity of reptile species, 16 percent of the total world marine fish species and 5.5 percent of the world's insect species (Kidd and Mayet 2003, p. 231).

Like other biodiversity-rich countries, South Africa is also characterised by its impressive cultural diversity in terms of its diversity in ethnic groups and languages. It is estimated that 45 million people populate South Africa, among whom nearly 31 million are black people, 5 million are white, 1 million coloured and 1 million Indians. A further breakdown suggests that the black population is divided into four major ethnic groups including the Nguni, Sotho, Shangaan-Tsonga and Venda. There are also a number of sub-ethnic groups, among which the Zulu and Xhosa are two subgroups of the Nguni. In respect of language diversity, the total number of languages in South Africa is estimated at 31, among which 25 are still living languages, three are second languages without mother tongue speakers and three are reportedly extinct.[5] These ethnic groups have a significant wealth of knowledge and practices in the use of medicinal plants for example, such knowledge and practices that can be of interests to bioprospectors (Grace *et al.* 2003, p. 301).

With such impressive wealth, not surprisingly, scientific and commercial activities have posed a threat to the sustainability of some specific biological

---

[4]   See Section 1.2.1 of the White Paper on the Conservation and Sustainable Use of South Africa's Biological Diversity, Government Gazette, Republic of South Africa, Vol. 385, No. 18163, General Notice 1095 of 1997, found at: www.polity.org.za/govdocs/white_papers/diversity.html.

[5]   For more details, see Languages of South Africa, available at: www. ethnologue.com/show_country.asp?name=South+Africa.

materials useful to rural communities in Cameroon and South Africa. Therefore, it is necessary to ensure the conservation of such biological materials by promoting traditional management practices of rural communities and empowering them to monitor access at the local level. A legal incentive that will encourage rural communities to engage in biodiversity conservation is needed and this chapter investigates the avenue of full participation by rural communities in the decision-making processes pertaining to access as an appropriate legal inventive for their commitment to conservation. Full participation may be achieved through the establishment of proper consultation processes within the framework of the permit mechanisms. The remainder of this chapter discusses: the existing legal procedures for access authorisation as they exclude rural communities from decision-making in Cameroon and South Africa; concrete cases of commercial use that have caused the depletion of resources in Cameroon and South Africa; and the suggested avenues through which the full participation of rural communities may be achieved and incentivised to engage in sustainability at a local level.

3.   CURRENT ACCESS AUTHORISATION PROCESSES IN CAMEROON AND SOUTH AFRICA

A number of regulatory instruments in Cameroon have provisions about access to plant genetic materials for research purposes. The Decree No. 95-531-PM of 23 August 1995 to Determine the Conditions of Implementation of Forestry Regulations (hereinafter 'the 1995 Forestry Decree') sets out the legal basis for access to and collection of forest products for scientific research and other purposes. Articles 13 to 14 of the 1995 Forestry Decree state that the issuance of an authorisation to carry out scientific or commercial activities based on forest resources is a joint responsibility of that country's Ministry of Scientific and Technical Research (MINREST) and the Ministry of Environment and Forestry (MINEF). But, in practice, MINEF makes decisions about plant collection permits for scientific and cultural purposes upon the recommendation of MINREST, while MINREST makes decisions about research authorisation. The application process for research authorisation is as follows. A researcher or research body willing to carry out research activities must submit its application to MINREST. For biodiversity-related research, applications for research authorisations (or research permits) are assessed against any potential environmental impact – stressing the quantity of materials required and the harvesting methods – and the potential benefits to Cameroon.

Foreign operators wishing to apply for a research authorisation must establish partnerships with national operators because through such collaboration, training can be provided to the local counterpart. After the field research (e.g. plant collection and interviews with local communities) is completed, a preliminary written report must be submitted to the national counterpart who will transfer it with comments to MINREST where a copy will be kept at the documentation centre. A fuller report with details of the research results and relevant recommendations will later on be submitted to MINREST through the national counterpart. In addition, voucher specimens of plants collected during field activities will be kept at the national herbarium, or at the herbarium at the Limbe Botanical and Zoological Gardens.[6] But with its lack of research infrastructure and skilled human resources, Cameroon is not fully benefiting from the potential of its biodiversity because the research partnerships are likely to favour the foreign counterpart that will end up with the materials overseas.

The basis for the exploitation of bio-resources is provided under Law No. 94/01 of 20 January 1994 on Forestry, Wildlife and Fisheries (hereinafter '1994 Forestry Law'). Section 41(2) of the law stipulates that: 'forest exploitation rights may be granted only to natural persons resident in Cameroon or to companies whose registered offices are in Cameroon and whose shareholders are known to the forestry services'. Apparently, the law does not stress the nationality of the natural person, but allows in principle anybody who can be qualified as forest exploiter and who resides in Cameroon to carry out forest exploitation. A special department in the office of the Prime Minister assesses applications for the status of forest exploiter and in Cameroon, applications for the status of forester exploiter are received from companies or associations. The names, nationality, occupation and place of residence of the owners of the company or the head of the association must be provided. Also the name, articles of an association or a company and the location of its head office, registered capital and its distribution, and the capital invested must be provided.[7] These requirements make it difficult for rural communities to qualify as forest exploiters, because, although they are natural persons residing in Cameroon, they may not be able to provide proof of professional experience or qualifications in forest exploitation, neither will they be able to provide proof of a statistical and trade registration number as a company.

If approved as a forest exploiter, the second step is to seek a *permis d'exploitation* from the Ministry of Environment and Forestry (MINEF). Section

---

[6]   These specific requirements are not provided by the 1995 Forestry Decree (ibid.), but they were brought to the attention of the author of this chapter during an interview with one senior officer of the department in charge of processing applications for research authorisations at MINREST (Yaoundé, October 2003).

[7]   For details of the requirements that an applicant for the status of forest exploiter must fulfil, see Art 36(1) and Art 36(2)(A)(B)(C) of the 1995 Forest Decree.

56(1) of the 1994 Forestry Law stipulates that: 'an exploitation permit . . . shall mean an authorization to exploit or harvest specific quantities of the forest products in a given zone. The products concerned may be special products according to section 9 (2) of the law, timber whose volume does not exceed 500 gross cubic meters, fire wood or poles for commercial ends'. The permit is granted following the recommendations of a competent commission for a maximum period of one year and it is renewable. However, the Minister of Environment and Forestry can also issue a permit for the exploitation of certain forest products by mutual agreement, as stipulated under Section 56(3) of the 1994 Forestry Law.

The existing legal framework regulating biodiversity activities in South Africa does not have any statutory procedure at the national level to streamline the permit scheme across the country. Access to bio-materials for scientific or commercial purposes is, however, subject to the acquisition of a permit or licence issued by provincial conservation departments. Each provincial conservation department has its own set of procedures, although there may be similarities in some respects. There are three instances under which research or plant collection permits are applied for at the provincial level (Burgener 2003, p. 82):

- where the applicant states that he/she wants to collect biological materials for research purposes;
- where the applicant states that the collection is for purely personal, non-commercial and non-research purposes; and
- where the applicant states that the intention is to collect for commercial purposes.

With regard to plant collection for research purposes, whether or not the applicant is a South African citizen, he/she should be affiliated to a South African institution. The application must include the research proposal, detailing the type of species that will be collected, the quantity and the area where collection would take place. During the field collection, the researcher must be accompanied by a senior staff member from the provincial nature conservation office. After the collection, the applicant must provide the department with duplicates of voucher specimens and copies of their research results (Burgener 2003, p. 82). Depending on each provincial nature conservation department, the permit is issued either by the head of the departmental nature conservation office or by the head of the regional and district nature conservation offices. For example, in the four provinces of Gauteng, Kwa-Zulu Natal, Free State and North West, the departmental head office issues the permit, but in three of the other five provinces (Western Cape, Northern Cape and Mpumalanga) permits are issued by regional and district head offices, copies of which are sent to the departmental head office, while in the remaining two provinces (Eastern Cape and the Northern Province) copies are not sent to the departmental head office (Burgener 2003, p. 82).

In its present format, the South African permit system is patchy, characterised by a lack of harmony among all the provincial nature conservation departments. This lack of harmonisation may not be efficient in promoting biodiversity conservation because different access procedures cannot ensure effective monitoring of access and collection of plant genetic resources throughout the territory. Also, in their existing format the mechanisms employed in the examination of applications for research or plant collection permits and ultimately the grant of such legal authorisations in the various provinces do not provide for the full involvement of local communities. Consequently, so long as the applicants fulfil the conditions of the departmental nature conservation offices, they may be granted research or plant collection permits, without any consultative process through which the consent of rural communities is properly sought and acquired.[8]

In their existing format, the biodiversity regulations in Cameroon and South Africa exclude rural communities from the decision-making processes, while they may be allowing access to the resources for scientific or commercial activities that are causing threat to the sustainability of the resources.

4.   SCIENTIFIC AND COMMERCIAL USE OF VALUABLE RESOURCES AND THREAT TO SUSTAINABILITY

Table 16.1 presents the key events in the acquisition of traditional knowledge on Hoodia by the South African San communities to its use for scientific and commercial purposes. It must be noted that the San communities are the most ancient indigenous communities in Southern Africa. With the possible exception of the aborigine communities in Australia, the San peoples may be the longest continuously living populations in one location in the history of mankind (Crawhall 2001; Stephenson 2003). The currently identified species of Hoodia include *Hoodia currorii, Hoodia gordonii* and *Hoodia flava*. They

---

[8]   Section 82 of the Biodiversity Act No. 10 of 2004 deals evasively with the prior informed consent of private landowners and rural communities. The Act seems to have secured the *de facto* PIC of rural communities and private land owners to permit seekers, because the Act does not give them the opportunity to accept or refuse the activities before the final approval authorising access. See Section 82 of the South African Act No 10. of 2004, National Environmental Management: Biodiversity Act, Government Gazette, Republic of South Africa, Vol. 467, No. 2636, Cape Town, 7 June 2004.

Table 16.1   Acquisition and exploitation of the San traditional knowledge on Hoodia

Date(s)	Event
1796	Francis Masson, botanist who visited the Cape in South Africa (1772–74 then 1786–95) was first to record the use of Hoodia species by the 'Hottentots'.
1937	White and Sloane publication of account of Dutch ethnobiologist, R. Marloth, of the traditional thirst and appetite suppressant uses of the Hoodia plant.
1945	CSIR established as South Africa's central scientific research and development resource.
1963–71	Hoodia investigated by scientists of the then National Food Research Institute under CSIR's direction, initially as part of a project on edible, indigenous plants of South Africa. Laboratory studies at CSIR at that time provided evidence of the appetite-suppressant properties contained in extracts of the Hoodia plant. Literature combined with laboratory tests on mice fed Hoodia led scientists to identify Hoodia as a non-toxic appetite suppressant. But these data were hardly enough to enable scientists to file patent.
1971–82	Apparent hiatus in Hoodia research at CSIR due to technical challenges facing the project at that time. But it is also reported that the research was halted by the death in 1968 of the leading scientist on the project.
1982	National Chemical Research Laboratories of CSIR acquire state-of-the-art equipment for isolation and characterisation of natural products, which assists in the discovery of the appetite-suppressant agent in Hoodia.
1990	Phytopharm plc founded in UK by its current CEO.
1996	CSIR begins the process of filing patent applications around the world to protect its discoveries related to the appetite-suppressant agent P57 derived from Hoodia.
January 1996	The Working Group of Indigenous Minorities in Southern Africa (WIMSA) holds its first official meeting.
July 1996	South African San Institute (SASI) formed at the request of WIMSA and interested individuals working with the San.
4 April 1997	SA Patent No. 983170 filed by CSIR; pharmaceutical with appetite-suppressant activity.
June 1997	CSIR signs an agreement with the UK drug research company Phytopharm that would allow Phytopharm to take the P57 product through development and the initial stages of clinical trials.
1998	CSIR obtains UK patent GB2338235 and world patent WO 98/46243 covering the 'raw materials, active substances and mode of action' of P57.

Table 16.1 Continued

Date(s)	Event
August 1998	Phytopharm signs a sub-licensing agreement with US drug manufacturer Pfizer that would allow Pfizer to take P57 through development and commercialisation.
2 October 1998	CSIR publishes its Bioprospecting Policy that declares its commitment to the equitable sharing of benefits that might be derived from its research based on biodiversity and any associated traditional knowledge.
27 October 1999	GB Patent 9925457 filed; patent pertains to gastric acid secretion.
May 2001	WIMSA informed by Survival International regarding the patenting of P57.
18 June 2001	The San confirm information regarding the P57 project through an article appearing in *The Observer*.
22 June 2001	Lawyer meets on behalf of WIMSA with CSIR representatives.
September 2001	Interim South African San Council established (!Xun, Khwe, and +Khomani San communities represented on the Council).
27 November 2001	Adoption of constitution by South African San Council; the Council becomes official.
29 November 2001	WIMSA confirms agreement in principle (Memorandum of Understanding 'MOU') between CSIR and the San Council regarding the San's rights with respect to the P57 project.
December 2001	Phytopharm announces completion of the proof of principle clinical study for P57 using raw materials manufactured in South Africa; also notes that the US market for treating obesity is estimated at well in excess of US$3 billion.
1 February 2002	P57 Memorandum of Understanding formally executed by CSIR and the San Council.
22 February 2002	CSIR meets the San Council in Upington to share information on its P57 project.
18–19 March 2002	CSIR and the San Council meet in Pretoria for further P57 negotiations; MOU modified and announced to the public; San visit CSIR laboratories.
11 April 2002	Phytopharm announces that it has completed the installation of a new botanical supplies unit in South Africa to expand the manufacturing capacity for P57.

23 April 2002	United States Patent and Trademark Office officially approves CSIR's P57 patent application and assigns it US Patent No. 6,376,657.
23 May 2002	CSIR and the San meet for second time to negotiate benefit-sharing arrangements under terms of MOU (third meeting overall to date).
23 May 2002	+Khomani San Land Claim Treaty signed.
22 July 2002	Pfizer announces intention to acquire Pharmacia; according to industry press, the acquisition, when finalised, will make Pfizer the largest (presumably in gross revenue) pharmaceutical company in the world. But Phytopharm would develop semi-synthetic versions of the active molecules and be free to seek other partners to commercialise these products.[1]
13–14 June 2002	The San (WIMSA and South African San Council, as well as traditional San leaders), CSIR scientists and policy developers, South African Government officials and representatives of Biowatch and First Peoples Worldwide meet at a Kalahari workshop. The purpose of the workshop was to provide the San with information on P57 development and related matters to facilitate their future benefit-sharing negotiations with CSIR.
22–3 August 2002	Members of the San communities and CSIR participate in a panel discussion of the P57 case at a Biopiracy workshop in Johannesburg, one of the pre-Summit meetings leading to the 2002 World Summit on Sustainable Development.
6 November 2002	CSIR and South African San Council meet in Kimberley to discuss benefit-sharing models.
March 2003	Negotiations concluded on the benefit-sharing terms between the major stakeholders, including CSIR, the San representatives, Phytopharm, Pfizer.
30 July 2003	Phytopharm announces that Pfizer has indicated the return of rights of P57.[2]

Notes:
1 Phytopharm (30 July 2002), 'Future development of P57', press release. http://www.phytopharm.com/news/PressReleases2002/press067-200200730.shtlm.
2 Phytopharm (30 July 2003), 'Pfizer returns Rights of P57'. http://www.phytopharm.co.uk/press/Rel%2080finalfinal.htm

Source: Adapted from Stephenson (2003).

355

belong to the family of Asclepiadeae. Local names of Hoodia plants include Ghaap and !Khobab (in Khoi language). Hoodia plants are cactus-like leafless succulents with thick fleshy finger-like stems that branch near the ground. Hoodia has traditionally been used as appetite and thirst suppressants by the San communities of Southern Africa from time immemorial (van Wyk and Gericke 2000).

This chronology indicates that as far back as the 1930s, the San's knowledge was beyond their control as it was collected and documented through ethnobotanical research. Scientific and commercial users could therefore access such valuable information and use it in applied research, which, in the legal context of the 1960s, did not necessarily require the prior informed consent of the San communities. Arguably, the ethnobotanical studies that led to a publication by White and Sloane (1937) on the properties of Hoodia and the San's knowledge were not carried out with commercial intent in the first place. It is reported that the first recorded use of Hoodia was carried out by the botanist Francis Masson who visited the Cape in South Africa twice (1772–4 then 1786–95). He recorded findings about *Stapelia gordoni* and indicated that the San ate the stems of *Trichocaulon piliferum*. As stated by Wynberg (2004, p. 851), it is apparently this knowledge recorded in the literature and other field work that motivated the South African Council for Scientific and Industrial Research (CSIR) to include Trichocaulon species in its research programme for the determination of the nutritional and possible toxic properties of 'foods from the veld'. Furthermore, it is hard to figure out how the scientists who retrieved this knowledge from a publication would have thought to seek permission from the San people before starting their research.[9] In this respect, it is difficult to sustain arguments suggesting that the CSIR refused to seek the prior informed consent of the San before using their knowledge associated with Hoodia.[10]

However, significant changes occurred in South Africa in the 1990s, and should have been taken into consideration by the CSIR in the subsequent processes involving Hoodia and the associated knowledge of the San communities. In 1994, the African National Congress (ANC) acquired political power by winning the first democratic elections in South Africa. The subsequent

---

[9]   Just to remind ourselves that the political context in South Africa during that period did force the San people to hide their identity especially with the passage of the Coloured Registration Act No. 68 of 1955, which officially excluded the San communities as an identifiable ethnic group.

[10]   It is also worth noting that, during this period, there was no international environmental treaty such as the Convention on Biological Diversity requiring the prior informed consent of the communities before accessing and using their knowledge, innovations and practices relevant to the conservation of biodiversity. See Article 8(j) of the 1992 Rio Convention on Biological Diversity, ibid., *supra,* footnote 1.

reforms included the abolition of the segregation system called apartheid and the development of a new constitution allowing ethnic minorities to reassert their identity.[11] Despite these internal changes and the growing international debates about commercial use of biological resources and associated traditional knowledge of indigenous communities, the CSIR continued to sideline the San in all activities related to Hoodia, including the characterisation and patenting of P57,[12] and in all negotiations with industrial counterparts for possible development of pharmaceuticals based on P57. It is reported that the CSIR repeatedly said to its international partners that the San people had all died. When challenged on this issue, the CSIR submitted that the reluctance to engage the San peoples in the discussions was because they might have raised demands that would have been difficult to satisfy (Barnett 2001).

Reasonably, being aware that the San communities were still alive and that this valuable knowledge, taken from a publication, was still used by the remaining San peoples, the CSIR, for ethical reasons, should have sought the informed consent of the San before using it in commercial activities. In this respect, the San communities were arguably denied participation in the processes that led to the utilisation of their assets and therefore, their rights to control and to determine the grounds for such use were seriously undermined.[13]

The involvement of the San communities in the decision-making processes was also very limited in the subsequent developments related to the exploitation of Hoodia, especially the exploitation of P57. In order to secure access to and acquisition of the Hoodia plants for the production of P57, CSIR applied for and was granted plant collection permits by the Northern Cape Directorate of Nature Conservation. These permits allowed CSIR to collect 80 specimens of *Hoodia gordonii* in 1998; 200 plant specimens in 2000; 1350 kg of specimens between 2001 and 2002; and 19,000 kg of specimens in 2002 (Wynberg 2003, p. 56). Even if the issuing body was satisfied with the application submitted by the CSIR, for instance in respect of the potential environment impact of the collection on the wild population of *Hoodia gordonii*, there is no

---

[11]   See Table 16.1 above. Such reforms allowed the creation of the Working Group of Indigenous Minorities in Southern Africa (WIMSA) and the South African San Council in 1996.

[12]   The P57 is an appetite suppressant, an active ingredient isolated and characterised from Hoodia through research carried out by the CSIR. This element was deemed novel, non-obvious and industrially applicable, which is why the CSIR was granted a South African patent No. 983170 in 1997 (see Table 16.1).

[13]   It should be mentioned that only in 2001 were the San informed about all these processes when a civil society organisation, Survival International, informed the Working Group of Indigenous Minorities on the Patenting of P57 (see Table 16.1 above).

indication that the San peoples were consulted prior to the grant of such a permit.[14] Not only did the context in which the knowledge of the San peoples associated with Hoodia was acquired not provide any legal requirement for these peoples to be consulted, subsequent events related to scientific and commercial use of the plant have also excluded the San peoples. Presently, wild sources of Hoodia are undergoing such serious depletion due to commercial exploitation, as to stimulate the inclusion of Hoodia in Annex II of the Convention on International Trade in Endangered Species of the Wild Fauna and Flora (CITES).[15]

Prunus africana is an evergreen mountain forest species that occurs in 22 countries across Africa where it contributes to the social and economic well-being of rural populations. Traditionally it is used in many ways, including traditional medicine for the treatment of stomach ache, malaria and other diseases; it is also used in modern medicine in the treatment of Benign Prostatic Hyperplasia, prostate disorders affecting men in some cases as early as in their late thirties (Graham 1960).

Commercial exploitation of *Prunus africana* in the Mount Cameroon area can be traced back to the early 1970s when Plantecam Medicam had an exclusive permit to exploit this species in the area. The company brought labourers from other areas, especially from the Western Province of Cameroon. A number of issues were unacceptable to the communities living in the Mount Cameroon area. These communities were not legally allowed to commercially exploit *Prunus africana* themselves, which according them is their property because it grows on their traditional lands and they were not even employed by the company (Ndam and Tonye 2004; Tonye 2005). Also, the process that led to the approval and issuance of an exploitation licence to the

---

[14]   It should be mentioned that the CBD places all biological resources within the national territory legally under the sovereignty of the state (Art 3 of the Convention on Biological Diversity). In this respect, access to and acquisition of these resources should be subject to the state's authorisation. Indeed, Art 15(5) of the Convention on Biological Diversity establishes that access to the country's genetic resource is subject to that country's prior informed consent, unless the country establishes otherwise. This indicates that the CBD has not defined the prior informed consent procedure and leaves it to the states to do it themselves. National legislations can therefore ensure that the custodians of the resources are empowered to control access at local level and are consulted prior to granting any legal authorisation for access to the resources that are valuable to them. However, whether or not such collections were to take place in the traditional land of the San peoples, this research suggests that for sustainability purposes, the decision-making processes pertaining to access to valuable species for scientific and commercial purposes should involve the communities to whom the resources are traditionally useful.

[15]   Amendments of Appendix II of CITES, proposal to the Thirteenth Meeting of the Conference of the Parties, Bangkok, Thailand, 2–14 October 2004.

company did not involve the communities nor was their consent sought in that process.

Consequently, local communities embarked on illegal exploitation, making deals with middlemen to whom they were supplying the products, most of the time harvesting overnight. In addition to the legal exploitation activities carried out by the company, the illegal practices of rural communities increased the threat to the sustainability of *Prunus* in this area. Across its geographical area of distribution in Africa, the exploitation of *Prunus africana* for international trade caused a depletion of wild resources which, similar to the Hoodia case in Southern Africa, stimulated the inclusion of *Prunus* in Annex II of CITES in 1994 during a meeting held in Harare, Zimbabwe (Cunningham *et al.* 1997).

5. RECOMMENDATIONS OF NEW ACCESS PROCEDURES IN OUR CASE STUDIES

In Cameroon, biodiversity research and collection of biological materials are illegal, if they are done without proper legal authorisation in the form of a research permit or a *permis d'exploitation*. Some local realities contribute to illegal activities, including the lack of awareness on the part of local communities about the existing regulations and their poor living conditions. If the communities knew that biodiversity researchers and the collectors of biological materials need biological resources and the associated traditional knowledge as much as the communities need compensation, the latter would oppose unauthorised activities and resist illegal deals.

One of the suggestions for shaping an improved access procedure in this contribution is that the opinions of community members must be considered in the process through which access authorisations are approved. The communities must be able to refuse participation in a project as well as its execution on their traditional lands. The role of the authorities in making the final approval of the research permit or the exploitation licence remains. However, such a final approval must henceforth be heavily grounded on the consent of the communities.

Some practical options may be explored in an attempt to secure the full participation of rural communities in the permit processes. One may consider the decentralisation of the existing authorities that assess applications for research permits or exploitation licences. If these authorities are very close to the communities, applications for access authorisations submitted to them will be assessed in consultation with the communities concerned. The local authorities will then help the communities to understand the activities in question, but avoid forcing the communities to accept the proposed activities. The report of such a local assessment will be channelled to the central authority for the final approval or refusal of the authorisation.

The creation of an institution that will bring about coordination in this sector, having among other responsibilities the approval and grant of exploitation licences and research permits, is highly recommended. As the National Biodiversity Authority (NBA), such an independent biodiversity authority will play the role of the National Competent Authority defined under Articles 57 and 58 of the OAU (now African Union) Model Law[16] and shall be composed of officials selected from the government departments currently responsible for permitting issues. Two major advantages would result from the establishment of an independent biodiversity body. It would ensure the coordination of the access-related responsibilities currently shared between the Ministry of Scientific and Technical Research and the Ministry in charge of Forestry and it would minimise the corrupt practices observed in existing administrations (Nguiffo 2003).

If a national biodiversity authority such as this is created, the mechanism allowing community involvement in the decision-making process may operate in a two-way system. Applications would be submitted to the authority, which would then assess them in respect of the potential environmental and social impacts of the related activities to the areas and the communities concerned. The authority would issue a letter requiring the applicant to carry out consultations with the communities concerned. Applicants may express difficulties in identifying all the communities, but practical mechanisms could be designed in this respect. For example, communities can be used to identify other communities that may be impacted. Also, the involvement of anthropologists in the processes can prove to be useful. The cost of all these activities must be paid for by the applicants for the research permit. The outcome of the consultations would determine the actual decision on the granting or refusal of authorisation. The authority would operate using a database to ensure that all applicants for research or authorisation for access are registered and are consistently monitored. Knowing that anybody without a letter from the authority is attempting illegal activities, the communities would refrain from negotiations with such operators and might even report such operators to the authority. In turn, the authority would ensure that each applicant is not trying to shop around, using many communities and trying to collaborate with those who may not implement the law properly. The creation of an independent

---

[16]   See African Model Legislation for the Protection of the Rights of Local Communities, Farmers and Breeders, and for the Regulation of Access to Biological Resources. Organisation of African Unity (now African Union)/Scientific Technical and Research Commission (Ouagadougou, July 1998), found online at: http://www.twnside.org.sg/title/oau-cn.htm.

body that would coordinate the permit procedures in itself would contribute to minimising corrupt practices that are currently observed. Empowering civil society organisations to challenge malpractices of the authority could also prove useful in the fight against corruption.

In South Africa, the current permit scheme lacks harmonised procedures throughout all the provincial nature conservation departments. This situation is inadequate for proper control over access to biological resources across the national territory and is therefore ineffective at achieving conservation and sustainability. Furthermore, the system does not adequately ensure the involvement of rural communities in the decision-making processes through which permits are approved and issued at the provincial level. So long as the traditional societies living where plant collection and ethnobotanical interviews take place are excluded from such processes, there will be persistent doubts about the issuing authority's ability to ensure that researchers or bioprospectors to whom the authorisation is issued will respect the local systems of resource management of traditional societies and address their expectations during their activities. The Biodiversity Act No. 10 of 2004 fails to address these issues properly.

In order to achieve changes in the permit scheme in South Africa, it is necessary for a harmonised set of permitting rules and procedures to be established, administered by a single institution at the national level which oversees implementation. Section 10 of the Biodiversity Act No. 10 of 2004 suggests the establishment of a National Competent Authority, defined as the National Biodiversity Institute. One avenue through which harmonisation may be achieved is by assigning the National Biodiversity Institute with, among other responsibilities, the establishment of the rules and procedures for the permit scheme, as well as the final approval of access authorisations in consultation with other stakeholders and rural communities. The National Biodiversity Institute would then establish provincial representations, entrusting them with the responsibility to receive and examine applications for access authorisation, approving and issuing permits for scientific and academic research, with the consent of the communities if the proposed activities impact on identifiable communities in one way or another. However, for applications related to typical commercial or scientific research with potential commercial applications, the provincial representation of the National Biodiversity Institute must forward the application to the national authority, which will make the final decision. Nonetheless, whether or not a permit is granted at the provincial level, copies of applications and appropriate notifications should be forwarded to the national authority. In order to handle such responsibilities at both the national and provincial levels, the National Biodiversity Institute must have access to a pool of skilled human resources. The required skills include strong botanical assessment capacities, strong negotiation skills, good understanding of the commercial environment of products resulting from biodiversity research, and good understanding of the implications of intellectual property rights as applied to the products or processes derived from the exploitation of biological resources and associated traditional knowledge.

There are potential difficulties in relation to assigning the above-mentioned responsibilities to the National Biodiversity Institute.[17] For instance, the Biodiversity Act No. 10 of 2004 has not given such responsibilities to the National Biodiversity Institute. The Act establishes the National Biodiversity Institute as an advisory body, to provide recommendations to the Minister in charge of Environmental Issues regarding applications for access. The Act gives a great deal of decision-making power to the Minister, as reflected in the long list of regulations he or she is entitled to decide upon, for example, '. . . the designation of State's organs as permit issuing authorities . . .'.[18] Consequently, not only did the Biodiversity Act No. 10 of 2004 narrow the decision-making power of the National Biodiversity Institute, it has failed to identify the central administration that will be responsible for the permit system. The fact that the Minister is empowered with the discretion to make certain decisions leaves the permit system at square one, meaning that the system remains fragmented and patchy.

Furthermore, the National Botanical Institute should not be the institution to handle the responsibilities associated with the permit system because this institution cannot at the same time act as judge and party. Indeed, the National Botanical Institute is largely known for its involvement in bioprospecting activities in South Africa. Also, the National Botanical Institute does not have the required skills mentioned above. Moreover, as highlighted by one policy expert who has been observing the evolvement of biodiversity policy in South Africa, 'the National Botanical Institute may not even accept such responsibilities'.[19]

In light of these difficulties, a second and key suggestion is to identify a coordinating authority at the Department of Environmental Affairs and Tourism (DEAT) and assign responsibilities associated with the permit scheme. The existence of strong civil society organisations in South Africa

[17]   See Chapter 2, Part 1, Sections 10 to 12. Biodiversity Act, ibid., *supra*, footnote 8, dealing with the establishment, powers and duties of the South African National Biodiversity Institute. The Minister of Environmental Affairs and Tourism announced the transformation of the National Botanical Institute into the National Biodiversity Institute provided by the law.

[18]   See Chapter 8, Part 1, Section 97(b)(i), The Biodiversity Act, ibid.

[19]   This statement was made by Sarah A. Laird, during discussion with her in London in October 2004. Sarah A. Laird is an international consultant on biodiversity policy making.

will ensure that the activities of the identified authority at the DEAT are consistently monitored and properly criticised.[20] Practically speaking, the implementation of the rules and procedures of the permit scheme can rest with the provincial conservation departments. However, there should be a division of responsibilities between the central and provincial services. The central authority at the DEAT will only be responsible for issuing bioprospecting-related permits while the provincial nature conservation departments will be issuing academic research-related permits. Considering the need to involve rural communities in the decision-making processes, how is the model going to work in practice?

Applicants will submit their permit applications for bioprospecting and academic research activities to the provincial nature conservation department. All applications will be assessed at the provincial level in order to establish whether the related activities are for pure scientific or academic research, or bioprospecting or scientific research with potential commercial implications. The permit applications must clearly indicate the type and quantity of resources needed, the areas where the materials will be collected and whether the knowledge of the communities will be sought through interviews during field activities. If it is established that the permit application is for academic research only, it will be wholly processed and possibly approved and the provincial nature conservation department may therefore issue the permit.

The permit applicants will be urged to conduct consultations with specific communities in the areas where they intend to undertake field work. In the course of such consultations, they will assure the communities that their knowledge and resources that are going to be collected are for research only and that they will be acknowledged in the final reports or in the resulting articles published in scientific journal, as the providers the raw materials. This is an important approach because it will give the applicants for research permits the opportunity to provide the communities with clarifications about their real intent, and will give the communities the opportunity to understand the issues

---

[20]   Such non-governmental organisations (NGOs) established in South Africa include Biowatch South Africa, which carries out research activities on biodiversity policy making and contributes to the improvement in the livelihoods of rural populations in South Africa. This NGO was very instrumental in bringing the Hoodia case to the attention of the public at large and has been strongly involved, alongside other stakeholders, in the negotiation processes aimed at addressing the expectations of the San communities in relation to the commercial exploitation of their traditional knowledge. More information on Biowatch South Africa can be found at: http://www. biowatch.org.za/; and the African Institute of Corporate Citizenship, which is an NGO committed to promoting responsible growth and competitiveness in Africa by changing the ways companies do business in Africa: See the website at: http://www. aiccafrica.com/.

at stake and decide whether to accept or refuse the research activity if they find it disrespectful to their traditional systems of resource use and management. The report of such a consultative process, clearly establishing the consent of the communities, will be sent to the provincial nature conservation department and will form the basis for the final approval or refusal of the permit.

If the project or activities for which the permit is required are academic research only, there should not be any requirement to identify all the communities that might be sharing the same knowledge because this will be burdensome to academic research. There should not be a requirement for a comprehensive benefit-sharing agreement because the activities have no commercial intent. There should not be any requirement for an Environmental Impact Assessment (EIA) because the materials needed will be in very small quantities and, equally, there should not be a requirement for the permit applicant to invest in *ex-situ* or *in-situ* plant conservation. However, the permit will only be issued when the applicant has paid the required fees, which will be established by the central authority at the DEAT and harmonised throughout the territory. Whether or not the permit is granted, the provincial nature conservation department will send copies of applications to the central authority at the DEAT where a database will be developed and consistently managed, allowing proper monitoring of biodiversity research activities throughout the national territory.

If it is established that the permit application is for bioprospecting activities or that the research is likely to lead to some form of commercial applications, for instance, research conduced in the academic context leading to the production of cosmetics or other unpatented phytomedical products, a preliminary assessment of the application will be carried out at the provincial level but the central authority at the DEAT must be involved in order to ensure that certain issues are addressed before the permit is eventually granted. The central service will ensure that applicants for bioprospecting activities have developed a comprehensive benefit-sharing agreement with the communities whose knowledge and resources are targeted. The communities living in the specific area where field activities are carried out will primarily be consulted. However, in order to ensure that potential conflicts among communities do not arise in the future, all the communities likely to share the knowledge must be identified. The first communities consulted will be used to identify other communities while the involvement of social scientists such as anthropologists will also be useful. As plant collection for commercial use can be detrimental to the sustainability of the resources, the EIA should be carried out by the National Botanical Institute. The central authority at the DEAT will ensure that the bioprospector is committed to investing in *in-situ* and *ex-situ* conservation of the resources sought. Overall, all such processes will be carried out at the expense of the permit applicant.

During consultations with the communities, permit applicants will clearly present their project and disclose their intended commercial activities, including the application of patents to the products or processes derived from the transformation of their resources. The consultation processes will therefore give an opportunity to the communities to accept or refuse the proposed activities. Staff of the central authority at the DEAT or the provincial nature conservation department will be responsible for facilitating the consultation processes and will therefore assist the communities to understand the issues at stake and make informed decisions. Once the central authority is satisfied with the outcomes of all these consultations, it will either issue the permit or request the provincial department to do so. This approach will ensure that permits are granted only if the communities have agreed upon the activities that will be using their assets, and that such permits are only granted when all the conditions are satisfied and that the permits are not granted unconditionally[21] by the issuing authorities.

One may argue that this system is bringing an additional bureaucratic burden that will likely slow down research activities in South Africa. Such arguments were put forward in other instances such as in the case of Botswana, where it is argued that the current administrative procedures regulating plant collection for research purposes are lengthy and complicated and have slowed down academic research (Burgener 2003, p. 82). From the perspective of this chapter, the process of filing and eventually being granted a patent for an innovation based on biological resources is constraining and very expensive. With this in mind, why is it that a research institute, a business or a corporate body will agree to go through such constraints to obtain a patent, but would like to have readily available the raw materials used in the research process that will likely produce a patentable outcome? There is no intention whatsoever for the permit scheme discussed in this chapter to complicate access to plant genetic resources and traditional knowledge in South Africa. Instead the issue here is essentially about empowering rural communities, to some extent, to control access because they can better promote biodiversity conservation.

6. CONCLUSION: OPTIONS FOR WIDER APPLICABILITY BY OTHER COUNTRIES

In Cameroon, South Africa and very likely in most biodiversity-rich countries,

---

[21]   See the Biodiversity Act of 2004, ibid., *supra*, footnote 8. Chapter 7, Part 1, Section 88 (2)(c) dealing with application for permits.

access procedures exclude rural communities from decision-making. However, when access is authorised for commercial activities, such activities tend to cause depletion of the resources. The suggestions in this chapter are tailored to the specific contexts of our case studies, while also being directed to other countries whose contexts are similar to our case studies.

Some countries may consider, as is suggested for Cameroon, the establishment of an independent biodiversity authority that will ensure the harmonisation of the access-related responsibilities currently shared between two government departments. As an independent body, the National Biodiversity Authority would have local representations whose role would be to assist rural communities in the consultation processes. The creation of such an independent body would also contribute to fighting other issues such as corruption.

On the other hand, some countries may consider, as is suggested for South Africa, assigning the administration of access authorisation processes to a central authority under the government department in charge of biodiversity issues, perhaps because in this context, there is a strong civil society that can criticise government wrongdoings. In any case, there should be mechanisms allowing the full participation of rural communities in the processes leading to the grant of access authorisations as, under this approach, the communities have the appropriate incentive to control access and monitor illegal activities at the local level.

REFERENCES

Austen, R. (1987), *African Economic History. Internal Development and External Dependency*, James Currey Ltd, London.

Barnett, A. (2001), 'In Africa the Hoodia cactus keeps men alive. Now its secret is stolen to make us thin', The *Observer*, 17 June.

Bell, R.H.V. (1987), 'Conservation with a human face: conflict and reconciliation in African land use planning', in Anderson, D. and Grove, R. (eds), *Conservation in Africa: People and Practice*, Cambridge University Press, Cambridge, p. 79.

Burgener, M. (2003), 'A review of the existing South African administrative systems for permitting and overview on benefit sharing schemes', in IUCN (ed.), *Developing Access and Benefit Sharing Legislation in South Africa: A Review of International and National Experiences*, IUCN, Gland, Switzerland, p. 82.

Clarke, J., Cavendish, W. and Coote, C. (1996), 'Rural households and Miombo woodlands: use, value and management', in Campbell, B. (ed.), *The Miombo in Transition: Woodlands and Welfare in Africa*, Centre for International Forestry Research, Bogor, Indonesia, p. 102.

Crawhall, N. (2001), *Written in the Sand: Auditing and Managing Cultural Resources with Displaced Indigenous Peoples, A South African Case Study*, South African San Institute/UNESCO, Rondebosch, SA.

Cunningham, M., Cunningham, A.B. and Schippmann, U. (1997), 'Trade in *Prunus africana* and the implementation of CITES', German Federal Agency for Nature Conservation.

de Jong, W. and Campbell, B. (2001), *The Role of Non-timber Forest Products in Socio-economic Development*, CABI Publishing, Wallingford.

Eisenberg, D.M., Kessler, R.C., Foster, C., Norlock, F.E., Calkins, D.R. and Delbanco, T.L. (1993), 'Unconventional medicine in the United States – prevalence, costs and patterns of use', *New England Journal of Medicine*, 328(4), p. 246.

FAO (1995), *A Synthesis Report of the Africa Region – Women, Agriculture and Rural Development*, prepared under FAO's Programme of Assistance in Support of Rural Women in preparation for the fourth World Conference on Women.

Fomete, T. and Tchamou, Z. (1998), *La gestion des ecosystemes foretiers du Cameroun a l'aube de l'an 2000*, vol.1, IUCN, Yaoundé.

Grace, O.M., Prendergast, H.D.V., Jager, A.K. and Staden, van J. (2003), 'Bark medicines used in traditional healthcare in KwaZulu-Natal, South Africa: an inventory', *South African Journal of Botany*, 69(3), p. 301.

Graham, R.A. (1960), *Rosaceae. Flora of Tropical East Africa*, Crown Agents, London.

Hughes, J.D. (1998), 'Sacred groves of the ancient Mediterranean area: early conservation of biological diversity', in Ramakrishnan, P.S., Saxena, K.G. and Chandrashekhara, U.M. (eds), *Conserving the Sacred: For Biodiversity Management*, UNESCO and Oxford & India Book House, New Delhi, p. 101.

Kidd, M. and Mayet, M. (2003), 'Access to genetic resources in South Africa', in Nnadozie, K. *et al.* (eds), *African Perspectives on Access to Genetic Resources. A Handbook on Laws, Policies and Institutions*, Africn Union/Environmental Law Institute, Washington, DC, p. 231.

Maffi, L. (ed.) (2001), *One Biocultural Diversity: Linking Languages, Knowledge and the Environment*, Smithsonian Institution Press, Washington, DC.

Mooney, P.R. (1996), 'The parts of life: agricultural biodiversity, indigenous knowledge and the role of the third system', *Development Dialogue*, 1(2), p. 85.

Musa, T. (1998), 'Farmer seed systems', in *Proceedings of the International Workshop on Developing Institutional Agreements and Capacities to Assist Farmers in Disaster Situations to Restore Agricultural Systems and Seed Security Activities*, FAO, Rome, Italy, 3–5 November.

Ndam, N. and Tonye, M.M. (2004), 'Chop, but no broke pot: The case of *Prunus africana* on Mount Cameroon', in Sunderland, T. and Ndoye, O. (eds), *Forest Products, Livelihoods and Conservation: Case Studies of Non-Timber Forest Products Systems*, vol. 2, CIFOR NTFP, Bogor, Indonesia.

Nguiffo, S. (2003), 'Law, transparency, responsibility and rights of citizens in Cameroonian forests', in Center for Environment and Development/The Rainforest Foundation and Forests Monitor (eds) *Forest Management Transparency, Governance and the Law: Case Studies from the Congo Basin*, Report prepared for the Ministerial Conference on Africa Forest Law Enforcement and Governance (AFLEG), Yaoundé, 13–16 October, p. 55.

Nnadozie, K., Lettington, R., Bruch, C., Bass, S. and King, S. (eds) (2003), African Perspectives on Genetic Resources. A Handbook on Laws, Policies and Institutions', African Union/Environmental Law Institute, Washington, DC.

Stephenson, D.J. Jr. (2003), 'The patenting of P57 and the Intellectual Property Rights of the San peoples of Southern Africa', South African San Council/First People Worldwide. Paper distributed during the international conference on Biodiversity, and Biotechnology and the Protection of Traditional Knowledge, organised at Washington University, St Louis, Missouri in April 2003.

Thomas, D.W. and Cheek, M. (1992), 'Vegetation and plant species on south side of

Mount Cameroon in the proposal Etinde reserve', Project RBG Kew/Gov. Cameroon/ODA, cyclotyled.

Tonye, M.M. (2005), 'The *Prunus africana* (Hook, f) Kalkman', presented at the regional ABS Capacity-building Workshop for Eastern and Southern Africa, Addis Ababa 2–6 October 2005, found at: <http://www.abs-africa.info/index.php?id=14>.

Twarog, S. and Kapoor, P. (eds) (2004), 'Protecting and promoting traditional knowledge: systems, national experiences and international dimensions', UNCTAD/DITC/TED/10.

van Wyk, B. and Gericke, N. (2000), *People's Plants: A Guide to Useful Plants of Southern Africa*, Briza Publications, Pretoria, South Africa.

Wells, M.D. (1995), 'Biodiversity conservation and local people's development aspirations: new priorities for the 1990s', Rural Development Forestry Network Series No. 18d.

White, A. and Sloane, B.L. (1937), *The Stapelieace*, vol. III, second edition, Abbey San Encimo Press, Pasadena.

WHO (2000), *General Guidelines for Methodologies in Research and Evaluation of Traditional Medicine*, Geneva: World Health Organisation.

WHO (2002), *Traditional Medicine Strategy 2002–2005*, Geneva: World Health Organisation.

Wynberg, R. (2003), 'A review of benefit-sharing arrangements for biodiversity prospecting in South Africa', in IUCN (ed.), *Developing Access and Benefit Sharing Legislation in South Africa: A Review of International and National Experiences*, IUCN, Gland, Switzerland, p. 56.

Wynberg, R. (2004), 'Rhetoric, realism and benefit-sharing – use of traditional knowledge of Hoodia species in the development of an appetite suppressant', *Journal of World Intellectual Property*, 7(6), p. 851.

17. NERICA, food security and intellectual property: From the Green to the Gene Revolution

Muriel Lightbourne

The new varieties of rice for Africa (known under the acronym 'NERICA') developed at the West Africa Rice Development Agency are raising big hopes in terms of food security, to the extent of being qualified as tools in a Green Revolution in Africa. NERICAs refers to seven different varieties, with different characteristics to suit different tastes, and mostly designed for upland (i.e. dry) breeding systems. However, some on-going trials aim at developing NERICAs varieties for wet conditions. Located in war-torn Côte d'Ivoire, the West African Rice Development Agency (WARDA) could not fully complete the field trials or communicate the results of such trials. Thus, cultivation standards, such as required quantities of fertilizers, are not known. Moreover, field trials conducted with one of these varieties, namely NERICA 4, showed stability problems. Thus, according to prominent members of non-governmental organizations (NGOs) involved in the development of these varieties, two criticisms can be made of the latter: first, available data are not sufficient to guarantee the success of their wide use; secondly, rice represents only 20 per cent of the African diet, the main staple food in Africa being maize. However, NERICAs has allowed a country such as Guinea for instance to save $13 million on its rice imports bill.[1]

As the phrase 'new Green Revolution' is widely used in respect to NERICAs, it may be worth recalling the history of the advent of the Green Revolution, before appraising its long-term effects and the wider resort made to biotechnologies in agriculture.

---

[1]   Consultative Group of the International Agricultural Research (CGIAR), September 2004, available at http://www.cgiar.org/languages/lang-french.html.

FROM THE CREATION OF HYBRIDS TO THE GREEN REVOLUTION

Henry A. Wallace, an American geneticist, became convinced of the virtues in terms of vigour of hybrid seeds and set up in 1926 a company that came to be called Pioneer Hi-Bred International, to develop and sell hybrid maize seed. According to Dr William Brown,[2] a geneticist with Pioneer Hi-Bred who was to become the company's president,

> [The] introduction of U.S. hybrid maize into Europe following World War II saved countless lives and transformed agriculture in that part of the world in an incredibly short period of time. The methodology of hybrid development quickly spread from the United States throughout the developed world, and U.S. genetic materials, where adapted, greatly enhanced the rapid development of commercial hybrids. Many persons deserve credit for this revolution, among the foremost is H.A. Wallace.

Indeed, Henry Wallace was also credited as the initiator of the so-called Green Revolution. On returning from a trip to Mexico to attend the Mexican presidential inauguration, Henry Wallace, the then vice-president to F.D. Roosevelt, contacted the Rockefeller Foundation to draw its attention to the situation of Mexican agriculture production. The Rockefeller Foundation then funded a programme set up in 1943 in collaboration with the Mexican Ministry of Agriculture, whose goal was to assist farmers in Mexico to increase their wheat production. As one of the fathers of the Green Revolution, Dr Norman Borlaug explains,

> We spent nearly 20 years breeding high-yield dwarf wheat that resisted a variety of plant pests and diseases and yielded two to three times more grain than traditional varieties. Eventually, in the 1960s, we were able to expand the program and teach local farmers in Pakistan and India to cultivate the new wheat properly. The results were wonderful . . .[3]

Accordingly, the total volume of annual harvest of grain (wheat and rice compounded) per hectare of the same land in India had risen from 2.5 metric tons to 12 metric tons over a few years.

Another father of the Green Revolution, Monkombu Sambasiwvan

---

2   Quoted by John Hyde's Remarks (p. 3) at the Hoover Library, 26 October 2002, available at http://hoover.archives.gov/programs/4Iowans/Hyde-Culver.html, visited 4 August 2004.

3   'Biotechnology and the Green Revolution – Interview with Norman Borlaug', *ActionBioscience*, November 2002, available at http://www.actionbioscience.org/biotech/borlaug.html, visited on 22 July 2004.

Swaminathan, brought into India seeds developed by Norman Borlaug. After cross-breeding them with Japanese (in particular Norin 10, a very dwarf wheat) and Indian species, Dr M.S. Swaminathan obtained in 1966 a wheat plant with a much higher yield than local species, and a stronger stem. Later, the International Rice Research Institute (IRRI) created in the Philippines and jointly financed by the Ford and Rockefeller Foundations in collaboration with the government of the Philippines, and which M.S. Swaminathan headed for some time, accomplished the same for rice, with the high-yielding dwarf variety IR-8. As Norman Borlaug recalls,

> In 1968, when the administrator for the U.S. Agency for International Development (USAID) wrote in his annual report that there was a big improvement in Pakistan and India, he said, 'It looks like a Green Revolution.' That is how the label 'The Green Revolution' got started . . ., which is all about alleviating world hunger.[4]

APPRAISAL OF THE GREEN REVOLUTION

Notwithstanding its humanitarian goals, the Green Revolution provoked much criticism, owing to its heavy reliance on water resources, chemical fertilizers and pesticides. As Norman Borlaug aptly expresses it, '[i]f the high yielding dwarf wheat and rice varieties are the catalysts that have ignited the green revolution, then chemical fertilizers is the fuel that has powered its forward thrust'.[5] Effectively, pesticide consumption in India increased nearly 50-fold between 1958 and 1975, and was around 330 g/ha in 1973–74, to be compared to 1483 g/ha in the USA and 1870 g/ha in Europe.[6]

Thus, environmentalists have raised some concerns, warning of soil erosion, as well as genetic erosion (i.e. the loss of plant genetic resources, no longer cultivated, or wiped-out by specific pathogens). Borlaug objects to at least one of these criticisms, saying that

> Contrary to a widespread and erroneous opinion, the original dwarf wheat imported from Mexico definitely carried a wider spectrum of disease resistance than the local Indian types that they replaced. But the newer Indian varieties are even better in resistance and of a different genetic type than the original introductions. . . . From such a program a constant flow of new high-yielding disease-resistant varieties can be developed to checkmate any important changes in the pathogens[7]

---

[4]   Ibid.

[5]   *The Green Revolution, Peace and Humanity*, Nobel Lecture (1970), p. 7, available at http://nobelprize.org/peace/laureates/1970/borlaug-lecture.html, last visited 20 June 2005.

[6]   According to Avcievala (1991), quoted by Edwin D. Ongley (1996), 'Control of water pollution from agriculture', FAO irrigation and drainage paper no. 55.

[7]   Nobel Lecture, p. 9.

Nevertheless, several problems have been identified: in particular, the fertilizers used to grow the new seeds are very rich in nitrogen, the excess of which remains in the soil and decreases its fertility. Pesticides put a toll on the health of people handling them, and harm the natural balance of pollinators, predators – some of which are killed off by the pesticides – and pests, which tend to become more and more resistant. Less trivial than it may appear, the situation of pollinators is a matter for concern, as perhaps one-third of our diet is dependent on insect-pollinated plants, in particular fruits and vegetables.[8]

Fertilizers' and pesticides' runoff from farmlands into rivers and lakes constitute another source of pollution, and fresh and ground water supplies are being depleted. Pesticides are carried by dust over impressive distances: the United Nations Food and Agriculture Organization (FAO) gives the example of tropical/subtropical pesticides found in Artic mammals.[9] Moreover, modern crop varieties require important irrigation systems. These systems constitute a breeding ground for vectors of diseases, such as mosquitoes responsible for malaria or dengue fever. Both China and India are currently implementing programs in order to reduce the levels of water supplies to be used for crops. The Chinese government has encouraged farmers to move away from grain crops towards higher-value crops like fruit and vegetables. Albeit the latter use more water than grain, they require less land area, which should translate into water saving. According to Jurgen Vögele, an agricultural specialist at the World Bank in Beijing, quoted by the *Far Eastern Economic Review*,[10] '[i]f China imports 10 million tonnes of grain, that would [solve] about half of the North China water shortage'. Similarly, China's soybean imports have soared over the decade 1994–2004 and are expected to amount to roughly 30 million tonnes annually by 2010. In Punjab, the government is trying to entice farmers to replace wheat and rice crops with oil seed on one million hectares, with a view to saving 14.7 billion m^3 of water per year.[11]

Apart from the question of genetic erosion itself, which will be addressed in the next sub-section, some criticism raised underlines the level of indebtedness and unemployment amongst farmers entailed by the mechanization of agriculture. Moreover, systems of loans sometimes force farmers to adopt specific plant varieties. In India, a bill aimed at removing farmers' indebtedness has been drafted and introduced in the Rajya Sabha (Higher House of

---

   [8]   See S.E. McGregor (1976), *Insect Pollination of Cultivated Crop Plants*, USDA, chapter 1, p. 1, available at http://gears.tucson.ars.ag.gov/book/econ.html, visited 17 August 2004.
   [9]   Ongley (1996), op. cit., p. 11.
   [10]   Dated 22 July 2004, p. 55.
   [11]   *The Hindu*, quoted by *Courrier International*, dated 29 July 2004, p. 50.

Parliament) on 19 July 2002. It is argued in the statement of objects and reasons for this Bill that

> Most of the farmers have to take loans from the Banks and other financial institutions for purchasing seeds, fertilizers, bullocks, tractors, tubewells, livestock . . . but despite their best intentions they cannot repay the loans in time. . . . The Government should take lead in this matter by writing off the loan amounts particularly of those farmers who have paid back the principal amount. Similarly in cases of natural calamities the loan recovery should either be stopped or be recovered in a way that the farmer does not face hardships.[12]

Another criticism was that the Green Revolution was concerned mainly with three or four crops, leaving aside many others that were critical to some regions. Initially, no research or elite germplasm was available for many of the crops grown in less favourable agro-ecological zones, such as sorghum, millet, barley, cassava and pulses. However, since the 1980s, modern varieties have been developed for these crops, with improved yields. Overall, for all developing countries, wheat yields rose by 208 per cent from 1960 to 2000, rice yields, 109 per cent, maize yields, 157 per cent, potato yields, 78 per cent and cassava yields, 36 per cent.[13] This resulted, according to the FAO (2004), in a fall in real prices of staple food products.

Yield improvements made a dramatic difference to the lives of poor farmers. However, they are not a general panacea for development problems (such as educational needs etc.) and they are accompanied by health and environment issues. As will be addressed later, some of these issues are being reduced by the advent of biotechnologies.

GENETIC EROSION: MYTH OR REALITY?

There is no official definition of the notion of genetic erosion. According to the Crucible Group,[14] this definition varies owing to the operators concerned.

---

[12]   Available at http://rajyasabha.nic.in/bills-ls-rs/2002/XLIII_2002.pdf, visited 16 August 2004 (and still pending, according to India Parliamentary Bills Information System, accessible at http://164.100.24.167:8080/bills/listbills.asp, last visited 22 January 2007). It may be interesting to note that this law has a retroactive effect, as it is 'deemed to have come into force on the 15th day of August, 1947'. Practically, this does not make much sense for farmers who have meanwhile finished repaying their loan, or for those who, unable to do so, took their lives.

[13]   FAOSTAT (2003), quoted by FAO (2004), *The State of Food and Agriculture 2003-2004*, chapter 3, p. 4, available at http://www.fao.org/docrep/006/y516e/y5160e08.htm, visited 18 August 2004.

[14]   The Crucible Group (1994), *People, Plants and Patents – The Impact of Intellectual Property on Trade, Plant Biodiversity, and Rural Society*, IDRC, Canada.

From the viewpoint of agricultural research centres and gene banks, genetic erosion occurs when multiplication material is not easily available in germplasms. As to farmers, they are faced with genetic erosion when multiplication material is no longer present in fields or in local markets.

The first alarm was sounded during the International Agricultural and Forestry Congress in Vienna in 1890 by two German scientists, Franz Schindler and Emanuel Ritter von Proskowetz. Von Proskowetz, who had carried out extensive research on barley landraces in Moravia, was convinced that if no action was taken, they could disappear forever.

Later on came Nikolai Ivanovich Vavilov, a Russian scientist, who in 1926 developed the theory that crops had both a centre of origin in specific regions of the world where their cultivation started, and centres of diversity. The latter are areas where variation within a given crop is strongest. Vavilov and his colleagues travelled the world, documenting crop diversity and gathering one of the world's largest collections.

After him, Harry V. Harlan and M.L. Martini, of the National Research Council of the National Academy of Sciences, in 1936 issued a warning about the on-going loss of diversity in barley crops. Nevertheless, it was three decades before the concept emerged forcefully, as a result of the technical meeting held in Rome in 1967 and jointly organized by the FAO and the International Biological Programme (IBP). This conference on the Exploration, Utilization and Conservation of Plant Genetic Resources confirmed the existence of a consensus on the need for more efforts for *ex situ* and *in situ* conservation.[15] The establishment of a global network of *ex situ* collections was thus decided. As a follow-up, a Plan of Action presented during the 1973 FAO/IBP Technical Conference on Plant Genetic Resources was published by Frankel and Hawkes in 1975.[16] In this book, the authors recommended sampling techniques, methods of exploration in seed crops, vegetatively propagated crops and tree species, and long-term storage of seed and pollen.[17] In the meantime, a new alarm was raised in 1972 by a report

---

[15]   Pursuant to Art. 2 of the Convention on Biological diversity:

- '*Ex situ* conservation' means the conservation of components of biological diversity outside their natural habitats;
- '*In situ* conservation' means the conservation of ecosystems and natural habitats and the maintenance and recovery of viable populations of species in their natural surroundings and, in the case of domesticated or cultivated species, in the surroundings where they have developed their distinctive properties.

[16]   (1975), *Crop Genetic Resources for Today and Tomorrow*, Cambridge University Press, Cambridge, 1975.

[17]   See G.T. Scarascia-Mugnozza and P. Perrino (2002) *The History of* ex situ

published by the USA National Research Council, entitled *Genetic Vulnerability of Major Crops*, and by Jack Harlan, Harry Harlan's son. J. Harlan's article, 'Genetics of Disaster',[18] insisted on the vulnerability to epidemics that resulted from genetic uniformity. That same year, the United Nations Conference on Human Environment (UNCHE) was held in Stockholm. It was agreed on this occasion that both *in situ* and *ex situ* conservations were needed, and that whereas genetic resources of value for agriculture should be maintained in *ex situ* collections, wild relatives of crop species would be maintained in their natural environment. Drawing on Harlan's article, Cary Fowler and Pat Mooney have developed the concept of genetic erosion. As these authors explain,

> Varieties are unique combinations of genes. It is possible that some, most, or all of the genes of an extinct variety still exist in another variety, though not in that particular combination. . . . Given the fact that none of the 'functionally extinct' varieties was studied prior to disappearance, however, it is impossible to say there have been no losses of genes. And given the magnitude of variety loss, one might even argue that many distinct genes and characteristics have been lost.[19]

C. Fowler and P. Mooney illustrate the necessity to preserve genetic diversity with the example of Harlan's wheat variety. In 1948, Jack Harlan had collected in Turkey a variety of 'miserable-looking' wheat that later proved resistant to several diseases, and 'is now used in all breeding programs in the Northwestern states of the U.S. and saves farmers millions of dollars each year'.[20] Another instance is provided by rice:

> In Thailand, populations of wild rice (*Oryza rufipogon*) grew in ditches along roads. A rapid progress of modernization and industrialization all over the country resulted

---

Conservation and Use of Plant Genetic Resources, IPGRI, pp. 5–6, available at http://www.ipgri.cgiar.org/Publications/727/podf/0851995225Ch1.PDF, accessed 22 January 2007.

18   In *Journal of Environmental Quality* 1: 212–25; in another well-known article, 'Agricultural Origins: Centers and Noncenters', published in 1971 in *Science*, 174: 468–74, J. Harlan revisits the Vavilovian theory: 'I propose the theory that agriculture originated independently in three different areas and that, in each case, there was a system composed of a center of origin and non-center, in which activities of domestication were dispersed over a span of 5 000 to 10 000 kilometers. One system includes a definable Near East center and a non-center in Africa; another system includes a North China center and a non-center in Southeast Asia and the South Pacific; the third system includes a Mesoamerican center and a South American non-center. There are suggestions that, in each case, the center and non-center interact with each other. Crops did not necessarily originate in centers.'

19   C. Fowler and P. Mooney (1990), *Shattering: Food, Politics, and the Loss of Genetic Diversity*, University of Arizona Press, Tucson, p. 62.

20   Ibid., p. 13

in expansion of major roads and destruction of wild rice populations recently. To learn about the situation, wild rice populations at 17 sites along the road from Bangkok to Nonkai were observed in respect to their size and density in 1983 and 1991. At the same time, replacement of indigenous rice cultivars with improved ones during the eight years was observed at 19 sites, so as to estimate the level of genetic erosion in cultivated rice. During the eight years, six wild rice populations observed either were destroyed or reduced in size and/or density. In particular, four sites within 150 km of Bangkok were heavily disturbed by the expansion of the road, or by construction of factories, resulting in disappearance of the wild rice.[21]

The above-mentioned IR-26 rice variety developed by IRRI illustrates this point even more. IR-26 was a 'super-hybrid that turned out to be exceptionally resistant to almost all Philippines diseases and insect pests. But it proved fragile for the island's strong winds, whereupon plant breeders decided to try an original Taiwan strain that had shown unusual capacity to stand up to winds – only to find out that it had been all but eliminated by Taiwan farmers as they planted virtually all their ricelands with IR-8.'[22]

According to Norman Borlaug,[23] a similar situation prevails in Sri Lanka and Malaysia. J. Harlan sums up the situation prevailing in the early 1970s by asserting that the 'destruction of genetic resources is caused primarily by the very success of modern plant breeding programs'.[24]

Two decades later, based on CIMMYT (the International Maize and Wheat Improvement Centre, based in Mexico) and IRRI data, quoted by Melinda Smale,[25] roughly 80 per cent of the wheat area in developing countries was sown to semi-dwarf varieties in 1997, as was about 75 per cent of the rice area in Asia. In sub-Saharan Africa, rice landraces are still cultivated to a greater extent than modern varieties. Oddly, a much lower proportion of the maize area in developing countries is planted to modern varieties, whereas maize being an open-pollinating crop, incentives for privatization of research have been stronger than for rice and wheat.

Modern varieties are designed so as to produce high yields and be resistant to a wide range of pathogens. However, it seems that, very much like what can

---

[21]   Songkran Chitrakon, Y.I. Sato, H. Morishima and Y. Shimamoto (1992), 'Genetic Erosion of Rice in Thailand', in Gramene, *Rice Genetics Newsletters*, vol. 9, available at http://www.gramene.org/newsletters/rice_genetics/rgn9/v9p73.html, visited 26 February 2004.

[22]   Fowler and Mooney (1990), chapter 4.

[23]   Nobel Lecture, 11 December 1970, p. 13.

[24]   Harlan (1972), quoted in CIMMYT, *Dimensions of Diversity in CIMMYT Bread Wheat from 1965 to 2000*, p. 1 and in Melinda Smale (2000), 'Economic Incentives for Conserving Crop Genetic Diversity on Farms: Issues and Evidence', paper prepared for EXPO 2000, p. 2.

[25]   Smale (2000), p. 2.

be observed in the field of pharmaceuticals with antibiotics, a race is constantly run between plant breeders and pests. As Tom Hash of ICRISAT formulates it, 'by the time the poorer farmers in a given region decide to adopt a particular variety, its days are usually numbered'.[26] However, against pest adaptation or more generally, against genetic erosion, modern varieties and gene banks alike are only a partial answer. Accordingly, if seeds kept in gene banks are not regenerated for a long time, only a small percentage germinate and the genetic material is at risk; conversely, if they are regenerated frequently, mutations may occur, transforming this genetic material. It seems thus that preservation of genetic material in its original form is a romantic ideal, whose implementation is problematic.

REVISION OF THE CONCEPT

It was argued not so long ago that the genetic erosion hypothesis is 'plausible but nowhere documented'.[27]

The CIMMYT starts by conceding that many 'of the semi-dwarf wheat varieties grown in developing countries today have as ancestors the green revolution wheat varieties', before showing that 'the number of advanced wheat lines produced and distributed by CIMMYT over 1996–1997 is estimated to be more than 30,000'.[28]

Along the same lines, Daniel Charles[29] retraces the tangled pedigree of rice variety IR-36, developed from the crossing of numerous local rice varieties and cross-bred rice varieties from India, China, Taiwan, the Philippines and the USA. According to S. Brush,

> [The] concept of genetic erosion of crops can be traced to a period when crop population biology was still in an exploratory stage and before the availability of ecological analysis of crop populations in their centers of diversity. A review and a revision of this concept are long overdue, especially because the concept has important implications for conservation policy.[30]

---

[26] FAO (2004), p. 6. ICRISAT stands for *International Crops Research Institute for the Semi-Arid Tropics.*

[27] Stephen Brush (1992), 'Reconsidering the Green Revolution: Diversity and Stability in Cradle Areas of Crop Domestication' in *Human Ecology*, 20: 145–67, quoted in CIMMYT, *Dimensions of Diversity in CIMMYT Bread Wheat from 1965 to 2000*, p. 2.

[28] CIMMYT, *Dimensions of Diversity*, quoting a personal communication from S. Rajaram, p. 3.

[29] Daniel Charles (2001), 'Seeds of Discontent' in *Science*, 294(5543): 772–5, 26 October.

[30] S. Brush (1999), 'Genetic Erosion of Crop Populations in Centers of Biodiversity: A Revision', FAO Technical Meeting, Prague 1999, p. 1.

The CIMMYT challenges the genetic erosion hypothesis on the basis of 'two "dimensions" of diversity: latent (unobservable) and apparent (observable) diversity. . . . For latent diversity, the indicator is an index constructed from molecular or coefficient of parentage data;[31] for apparent diversity, the indicator is a measure of performance'[32] with respect to grain yield, heat and drought tolerance, disease resistance, etc.

An unpublished thesis by J.V. Dennis quoted by Brush establishes that frequent variety turnover is a feature of traditional rice breeding in Thailand, with indigenous rice varieties being regularly acquired from distant locations. This study compares rice accessions found in six districts during the period ranging from 1950 to 1961 to those found in 1982–83. Of the 89 varieties found in the first period, only 15 were present in 1982–83, and 82 varieties were found in 1982–83 that were not present in these districts in 1950–61.[33] One of the conclusions reached by S. Brush is that 'crops in centers of diversity are not assemblages of locally endemic or relatively static populations'.[34] Moreover,

> Selection is influenced by the heterogeneity of a farming system – natural, social and economic. Yield is an important criterion, but only one of several that are weighed in choosing crops and varieties. The genetic erosion hypothesis fails to anticipate this heterogeneity in farming systems, selection criteria, and market conditions. This failure limits the hypothesis' ability to foresee limits to the diffusion of modern varieties.[35]

Starting at the farm level, the analysis of genetic diversity has to be extended to metapopulations. Following Brush,

> While the extinction of landraces in a single farm or village may not threaten the entire landrace, the extinction of a metapopulation of the landrace is possible as the habitat of the landrace is degraded by modernization. . . . The mathematics of metapopulations are such that relatively high probabilities of extinction at the local level may be greatly reduced at the regional level.[36]

M. Smale insists that '[d]epending on popular notions of centers of origin and diversity to locate reserves may be misguided'. She further explains that farmers' choice is determined by risk-aversion, missing markets for the produce of

---

[31]   It must be borne in mind that uniform appearance may mask genotypic diversity.

[32]   CIMMYT, *Dimensions of Diversity*, p. 2.

[33]   Brush (1999), p. 6.

[34]   Ibid., p. 7.

[35]   Ibid. p. 10.

[36]   Ibid. pp. 17–18.

some landraces, and differential soil quality or nutrient response. 'Heuristically, three axes determine the probability that landraces will continue to be grown: population densities, the production potential of an area, and commercialisation. Predicted probabilities of landrace survival differ for rice, wheat, and maize, because of their biological properties.'[37]

THE CGIAR NETWORK AND THE FAO INTERNATIONAL TREATY

On the conservation front, according to Mary Footer,[38] the first initiative to streamline germplasm (gene banks) conservation and distribution was launched by the FAO in 1961. A third such meeting in 1973 defined sampling strategies for *ex situ* collections, in preference to *in situ* conservation. In parallel, as was mentioned earlier in reference to the Green Revolution, the Rockefeller Foundation financed the first *ex situ* collection of wheat and maize germplasm, and established the Consultative Group of the International Agricultural Research (CGIAR) in 1971. The FAO, the United Nations Programme for Development, the United Nations Programme for Environment and the World Bank now participate in the financing of the CGIAR, which federates 16 collections and research centres – some of which, like IRRI, created in 1960, CIMMYT in 1966, or the International Centre for Tropical Agriculture (CIAT) in 1967, predated the CGIAR. Countries freely contribute genetic resources to the CGIAR's centres and anyone can ask for free samples for research or breeding programmes. This results from a suggestion made to the CGIAR Technical Adviser Committee (TAC) during a meeting in Beltsville, Maryland, in 1972. This plan embraced several other proposals, such as the inclusion of new gene banks, the West African Rice Development Association (WARDA, 1971), the International Potato Centre (CIP, 1971) and the International Crops Research Institute for the Semi-Arid Tropics (ICRISAT, 1972), the creation of new regional gene banks in the Vavilovian centres of crop diversity, and of a coordinating centre, the International Board for Plant Genetic Resources, which was later succeeded by the International Plant Genetic Resources Institute, in 1991.

During the FAO 21st Conference, on 25 November 1981, the lack of an 'international agreement for ensuring the conservation, maintenance, and free exchange of genetic resources of agricultural interest contained in existing

---

[37]   Smale (2000), p. 8.
[38]   Mary Footer (1999), 'Intellectual Property and Agrobiodiversity: Towards Private Ownership of the Genetic Commons' in *Yearbook of International Environmental Law*, vol. 10, Oxford University Press, Oxford.

germplasm banks'[39] was underlined in the statement (e) of Resolution 6/81. Industrialized countries, in particular the USA, the United Kingdom and Australia, strongly opposed the resolution. However, the 22nd FAO Conference endorsed in 1983 the proposal for an International Undertaking and the establishment of the FAO Commission on Plant Genetic Resources (CPGR). The International Undertaking is one element of a subsequently elaborated global system on plant genetic resources, which also comprises, *inter alia*, a Code of Conduct for Plant Germplasm Collection and Transfer,[40] the World Information and Early Warning System on Plant Genetic Resources,[41] the Global Plan of Action for the Conservation and Sustainable Utilization of Plant Genetic Resources for Food and Agriculture, and the International Gene Fund. The latter, set up in 1989 and meant as an implementation of Farmers' Rights, had never become operational.

The International Undertaking on Plant Genetic Resources (IUPGR) was a non-legally binding instrument, based on the assumption that plant genetic resources were the common heritage of mankind and should be freely exchanged. Three resolutions (4/89, 5/89 and 3/91) have later been annexed to the Undertaking, respectively affirming the compatibility of plant breeders' rights with the multilateral system, recognizing Farmers' Rights and sovereign rights of nations on their genetic resources. According to the interpretation of the rationale underlying Resolution 5/89 given by Graham Dutfield (2002),

> Farmers' Rights under the Undertaking were designed to recognize that plant genetic resources were different from natural fossil resources, like coal and oil, since assuming that plant genetic resources were mere gifts of nature would have failed to give credit to the knowledge and resource management practices of traditional communities who nurtured them.[42]

---

[39]   Quoted by Scarascia-Mugnozza and Perrino (2002), p. 8.

[40]   Some of the goals of the 1993 Code of Conduct for Plant Germplasm Collecting and Transfer particularly worth mentioning consist in promoting the sharing of benefits derived from plant genetic resources between donors and users of germplasm, taking into account the costs of conserving and developing germplasm, in avoiding situations whereby benefits currently derived from plant genetic resources by local communities and farmers are undermined by the use made by others of these resources, or situations where significant material for genetic variation would be removed from the local gene pool.

[41]   The creation of this warning system was required by Article 7.1(e) and (f) of the International Undertaking, 'to draw rapid attention to hazards threatening the operation of ex situ collections, and to the danger of the extinction of plant species and the loss of genetic diversity throughout the world', in the opinion of Jerzy Serwinski, in 'World Information and Early Warning System on Plant Genetic Resources', FAO Technical Meeting on the method of WIEWS, held in Rabat, Morocco, 1–3 February 1999. The first report on the 'State of the World's PGR' was prepared for the Fourth International Conference on Plant Genetic Resources held in Leipzig in June 1996.

[42]   Graham Dutfield (2002), *Intellectual Property Rights, Trade and Biodiversity*,

According to Resolution 5/89, Farmers' Rights mean 'rights arising from the past, present and future contributions of farmers in conserving, improving, and making available plant genetic resources, particularly those in the centres of origin/diversity'. They aim to 'ensure that the need for conservation is globally recognized and that sufficient funds for these purposes will be available', and to allow farmers to benefit from the improved use of plant genetic resources.

In parallel, in 1989, the CGIAR Policy on Genetic Resources declared that the collections were being held in trust for the world community, with a view to increasing food security and alleviating poverty.

The FAO initiatives were being criticized, mostly by industrialized countries, although some developing countries were also starting to be weary of not being entitled to benefit from their plant genetic resources, gradually seen as a potential source of benefits. In particular, Article 2(1)(a) of the International Undertaking, encompassing landraces and wild relatives, as well as newly developed varieties, was the focus of this negative attention. As the polarization of antagonisms was threatening the exchange of genetic resources, William Brown of Pioneer Hi-Bred and others sought the mediation of the Keystone Center in Colorado. Several meetings were convened, first in Colorado in 1988, then in Madras, India and Oslo, Norway. As reported by C. Fowler,[43] the government of Norway asked for the three plenary documents resulting from the Keystone Dialogue to be formally considered by the UN Conference on Environment and Development in 1992.

In addition to the Keystone Dialogue input, the influence of the World Conservation Union (IUCN) was paramount. It was reported[44] that the UN Environment Programme (UNEP) insisted in 1987 to endorse the IUCN work (notably the 1982 World Congress on National Parks convened in Indonesia). The IUCN was the promotor of the Convention on Biodiversity (and more recently, of the so-called 'Bonn Guidelines').

In 1991, the FAO Conference considered that several issues, particularly those relating to access to plant genetic resources, had to be addressed during the Earth Summit organized by the Conference of the United Nations on Environment and Development in Rio in 1992. In reality, the Convention on Biological Diversity (CBD), which is one of the texts adopted during the Earth Summit, fell short of answering all the concerns previously expressed within

---

Earthscan, United Kingdom; endorsed by the WTO in document IP/C/W/175, indent 13.

  [43] C. Fowler (1993) 'International Conflicts in New Crops Policy', in J. Janick and J.E. Simon (eds), *New Crops*, Wiley, New York, pp. 22–7.

  [44] See the acts of the UNU-IAS/JBA Symposium on 'Commercial Prospects of Access to and Benefit-Sharing of Genetic Resources', Tokyo, Japan, 30 September 2003.

the FAO or within the framework of Agenda 21,[45] also adopted during the Earth Summit. For instance, issues regarding rights granted to farmers and conditions of access to *ex situ* collections created before the adoption of the CBD were still pending, although the CBD reaffirmed the principle of sovereign rights of nations on their genetic resources[46] (Art. 3) and the need to protect indigenous knowledge relating to the conservation of biological diversity (Art. 8 (j)). The FAO Conference then launched the Fourth International Technical Conference on Plant Genetic Resources, held in Leipzig in June 1996. The Leipzig Declaration insisted on the importance of the revision of the International Undertaking, which was completed on 3 November 2001.

Meanwhile, in October 1994, the FAO and 11 CGIAR centres which were depositaries of *ex situ* collections had signed agreements placing these collections under the auspices of the FAO and instituting an International Network of *Ex Situ* Collections, 'for the benefit of the international community, in particular the developing countries'.

The Joint Statement of FAO and the CGIAR Centres on the Agreement Placing CGIAR Germplasm Collections under the Auspices of FAO contains precisions as to the interpretation of some terms of the Agreement. Where the Agreement states (in Art. 3) that the 'Centre shall not claim legal ownership over the designated germplasm, nor shall it seek any intellectual property rights over that germplasm or related information', the words 'related information' cover in particular information on indigenous knowledge. Where the Agreement represents (in Art. 9) that the 'Centre undertakes to make available directly to users or through FAO, for the purpose of scientific research, plant breeding or genetic resources conservation, without restriction', these last two words shall not be interpreted in a way affecting the rights of countries of

---

[45]   Chapter 32 of Agenda 21 adopts a viewpoint slightly different from that of the FAO in that it insists on the need to encourage the adoption of environmentally sound technologies, the integration of negative externalities and the participation of farmers in the implementation of environmental and agricultural policies. However, Chapter 14G addresses more specifically issues relating to the conservation and sustainable utilization of plant genetic resources for food and agriculture.

[46]   According to Art. 2 of the Convention on biodiversity, 'genetic resources' means genetic material of actual or potential value. Under the FAO ITPGRFA, 'plant genetic resources for food and agriculture' means any genetic material of plant origin of actual or potential value for food and agriculture, and 'genetic material' means any material of plant origin, including reproductive and vegetative propagating material, containing functional units of heredity. The definition contained in the former International Undertaking in Plant Genetic Resources (Art. 2) was more sweeping, encompassing 'cultivars in current use and newly developed varieties, obsolete cultivars, primitive cultivars (land races), wild and weed species and special genetic stocks (including elite and current breeders' line and mutants)'. This gives the background for the adoption of Resolution 4/89.

origin under the CBD (for instance, when a country intends to protest the lack of prior informed consent). With respect to transfers of samples, the centres were to ensure by arrangements, such as material transfer agreements, that the recipients should not seek intellectual property protection on the material and that they pass on the same obligation to subsequent recipients. However, the source centre was under no obligation to monitor the compliance of the recipient with these undertakings.

The Second Joint Statement, adopted in 1998, acknowledges that violations by the recipients of germplasm of the prohibition against seeking intellectual property rights may occur, and it provides for proceedings to remedy such instances.[47]

Taking the CBD into consideration, the CGIAR adopted in 1999 Guidelines for Germplasm Acquisition Agreements, which hold that 'resources should be acquired in a way which would allow those resources and related information to be placed and managed under the terms of the agreement with FAO placing CGIAR germplasm collections in trust under the auspices of FAO'. As of 2004, the number of accessions (in other words, varieties contributed to or developed by these collections) covered by this agreement amounts to roughly 600 000.

Since then, the FAO Commission on Genetic Resources for Food and Agriculture (CGRFA), acting as interim committee for the International Treaty (entered into force end of June 2004) prepared terms of reference for a new version of the standard material transfer agreement. Regarding the 'sharing of monetary and other benefits of commercialisation', it identifies several questions:[48]

- What constitutes incorporation of material accessed from the Multilateral System?
- When will a product incorporating such material be considered available without restrictions on others over further research and breeding (and thus be exempted from compulsory payment to the fund which is to be instituted within the Multilateral System for benefit-sharing purposes)?

---

[47] See the System-wide Genetic Resources Programme (SGRP), CGIAR Centre Policy Instruments, Guidelines and Statements on Genetic Resources, Biotechnology and Intellectual Property Rights, Rome, September 2001.

[48] In CGRFA/MIC-1/02/REP, Appendix D, document prepared for the meeting of the CGRFA acting as Interim Committee for the International Treaty of October 2002. A Report on the outcome of the Expert Group on the terms of the standard Material Transfer Agreement – document CGRFA/IC/MTA-1/04/Rep, prepared for the second meeting of the CGRFA, Rome, 15–19 November 2004 – gathers the suggestions or recommendations made in relation to this initial document.

- Should small farmers in developing countries be exempted from such payments and if so, who qualifies as such?
- Should different levels of payment be established for various categories of recipients who commercialize such products?

Some of these questions clearly show that the MTA should be the interface between the FAO multilateral system and privately held intellectual property rights. Accordingly, when designated germplasm is integrated in a breeding programme and then transformed, intellectual property rights may be applied for, and payment (voluntary or compulsory, whether it is possible to access the result of such a breeding programme, or not) to the multilateral fund should be made.

During the first meeting of the Governing Body of the International Treaty, held in Madrid in June 2006, an African proposal on benefit-sharing was well-received and found its way, after discussion, into the final draft for the SMTA. Pursuant to this proposal, access to all products belonging to one of the crops listed under Annex I to the ITPGR may give rise to a payment to the MLS at a discounted rate, irrespective of whether the product has been developed from material received from the MLS or not. In return, the product developer shall be exonerated from any payment obligation under Article 6.7 of the draft SMTA (former Art. 7.10 of the April 2006 version) – i.e. payment upon commercialization of the product with restrictions attached to it. The Contact Group for the drafting of the SMTA agreed to a discounted rate of 0.5 per cent and a normal rate of 1.1 per cent of the gross product sales in case of commercialization with restrictions.[49]

With a wider use made of biotechnologies, and thus of intellectual property rights in order to recoup important investments, this provision of the FAO Treaty (Art. 13(2)(d)ii) should be quite significant.[50]

---

[49]   The STMA was adopted by Resolution 2/2006 of the Governing Body of the IT during its first meeting in Madrid in June 2006 – see FAO Document IT/GB-1/06/Report, June 2006, pp. 5–7.

[50]   Art. 5(3) of the 1978 Act and Art. 15 of the 1991 Act of the UPOV Convention make the requirement of payment to the multilateral system of the FAO Treaty non-applicable to varieties protected by breeders' rights in most situations (except for hybrids), insofar as protected varieties remain accessible for research purposes. Whereas it is possible, pursuant to the 1978 Act, to commercialize varieties derived from protected varieties without being authorized by the breeder of the initial variety, the notion of 'essentially derived variety' introduced by the 1991 Act of the UPOV Convention makes it mandatory for the subsequent breeder to obtain said authorization. Moreover, pursuant to Article 16.1 (ii) of UPOV 1991 Act, the breeder can oppose acts of re-export of his protected plant material into a country that does not offer protection for the genus or species of the plant concerned, unless the exported material is for final consumption purposes.

Shift from the Public to the Private Sector

Seeds had for long been considered as public goods, as they can reproduce, which makes their use non-excludable and non-rival (i.e. it is difficult to exclude anyone from using them and their use by one person does not preclude their use by another person). Thus, agricultural research was mainly conducted by public (international or national) research centres, or local experimental stations, not subject to the need to capture enough benefits to compensate research and production costs. Another reason for public funding of agricultural research is that public goods tend to be under-produced.[51]

While development assistance has been decreasing, private investment in agricultural research and development rose in the 1930s and 1940s with the advent of hybrid seed companies. A survey conducted at Iowa Tate University shows that while plant breeding research and development in the public sector has decreased by 2.5 scientist-years per year from 1990 to 1994, the annual growth for the private industry amounted to 32 scientist-years.[52] Still in the USA, in the mid-1990s, field crop breeding comprised around 80 per cent of the private sector effort.[53] In the UK, 'the overall effect of several related privatisation moves on research budgets for plant breeding and biotechnology was indeed negative, and the change shifted some of the burden of research from taxpayers to farmers'.[54]

Several shortcomings of such a shift have been pinpointed. First, the private sector may have a shorter time horizon than would be socially optimal, minor crops for which seed markets are limited may be neglected, there are less opportunities for breeders to be trained in near-market breeding, more and more conducted by the private sector.

However, it has been objected that '[p]ublic breeding programmes can be

[51] Timothy G. Reeves and Kelly A. Cassaday (2001), 'Global Public Goods for Poor Farmers: Myth or Reality?', CIMMYT, at 3, available at http://www.cimmyt.org/whatiscimmyt/globpublgoods/global_public.htm, last visited 10 January 2005.

[52] Survey by Ken Frey, quoted by Steven C. Price (University of Wisconsin-Madison) in 'Informal Survey on Impact of IPR on Plant Breeding', in *Nature Biotechnology*, 17, October 1999, p. 938, available at http://biotech.nature.com, last visited 28 October 2004.

[53] K.J. Frey (1996), *National Plant Breeding Study*, Special Report 98, Iowa State University, quoted by Paul W. Heisey, C.S. Srinivasan and Colin Thirtle, *Public Sector Plant Breeding in a Privatizing World*, Economic Research Service, US Department of Agriculture, Agriculture Information Bulletin no. 772, August 2001, p. 8.

[54] C.E. Pray 'The Impact of Privatising Agricultural Research in Great Britain: An Interim Report on PBI and ADAS', in *Food Policy*, 21(3) :305–18, quoted by Paul W. Heisey, C.S. Srinivasan and Colin Thirtle (2001), p. 9.

as protectionist as their private counterparts'.[55] Other authors signal as well that there is a 'rising pressure for public-sector institutions to behave like private institutions'.[56]

In this context, it seems necessary to understand and compare the reach of breeders' rights and of patents in the agricultural field, and to assess the 'freedom-to-operate' in future breeding programmes, knowing that there are 50 to 100 new plant biotechnology patent applications per month, according to ISAAA (2000).[57]

In particular, apart from the well-documented reinforcement of plant breeders' rights in the 1991 version of the UPOV Convention for the protection of plant varieties, and the growing number of plant-related patent applications filed to the US, Japanese and European patent offices,[58] it may be interesting to focus on the situation of hybrids, which were already protected by the 1978 version of the UPOV Convention. By covering the parental lines of a protected hybrid, it may be argued that plant breeders' rights potentially limit hybrid variability. Accordingly, for some plants, the progeny of the crossing of a given line A as the female line with line B as the male one differs from the result of the crossing of father A and mother B. It does not seem legitimate that the protection granted by plant breeders' rights on a hybrid obtained through one of the possible crossings should also cover the results, potentially different, from other crossings of the same parental lines. However, a recent position adopted in May 2006 by the International Seed Foundation seems to take into account the decision of the District Court of Wisconsin dated 27 October 2004 in *Advanta v. Pioneer Hi-Bred International*:

> Seed of proprietary parental lines may incidentally happen to be included in bags of commercial hybrid seed. Proprietary parental lines may also incidentally happen to be present in fields in which hybrids are grown. In both cases, this presence results from technicalities in producing and processing hybrid seed and does not reflect the owner's intent to make its parental lines available to the public.

---

[55]   Robert Tripp (2000), 'Can the Public Sector Meet the Challenge of Private Research? Commentary on "Falcon and Fowler" and "Pingali and Traxler"' in *Food Policy*, 27, at 241.

[56]   Reeves and Cassaday (2001), at 5.

[57]   R. David Kryder, Stanley P. Kowalski and Anatole F. Krattiger (2000), *The Intellectual and Technical Property Components of pro-Vitamin A Rice (GoldenRice™): A Preliminary Freedom-To-Operate Review*, The International Service for the Acquisition of Agri-biotech Applications (ISAAA), Briefs no. 20, Ithaca, NY, United States, at 6.

[58]   See for instance OECD Directorate for Science, Technology and Industry, Committee for Scientific and Technology Policy, *Overview of Recent Trends in Patent Regimes in United States, Japan and Europe*, 19–20 June 2003, Paris; OECD (2002) *Genetic Inventions, Intellectual Property Rights and Licensing Practices – Evidence*

Biotechnologies and Conservation Goals

The first use made of DNA-related knowledge consisted in forcing a cell to express a character of interest. The cell is induced to express characters differing from those it would normally produce.

However, systems able to integrate DNA are not universal. Thus, in the particular field of agriculture, the principal vector resorted to is *Agrobacterium tumefaciens*, a soil plant pathogenic bacterium. This bacterium has the exceptional ability to transfer a specific DNA fragment (Transfer-DNA or T-DNA) of a tumour-inducing plasmid into the nucleus of infected cells where it is then integrated into the host genome of dicotyledonous plants[59] and transcribed. The tumour-inducing gene can be removed or incapacitated before introducing any foreign DNA into the plasmid. What is used here is the capacity of the plasmid to be integrated in a plant host. Plant leaf cells then take up the modified plasmid, and can be grown into transgenic plantlets. A patent on such a 'plant vector' was filed with the USPTO in 1982, and granted under number 4,536,475 in August 1985.[60] This patent was addressed to both monocotyledonous and dicotyledonous plants. Subsequently, reproducible methodologies were established among others for rice (1994, 1998), corn, wheat and sugarcane (1997, 1998).[61] Since then, a patent (number 6,528,701) has been granted by the USPTO on 4 March 2003 for rice-derived promoters that 'can be used to drive expression of structural genes including but not limited to genes for herbicide resistance, resistance to pests, and tolerance to drought or other adverse environmental conditions'. There are three types of genetic modification methods:[62]

---

and Policies; Jayashree Watal (2001), *Intellectual Property Rights in the WTO and Developing Countries*, Netherlands, Kluwer Law International, chapter V, pp. 135–63; Dan Leskien and Michael Flitner (1997), 'Intellectual Property Rights and Plant Genetic Resources – Options for a Sui Generis System' in *Issues in Genetic Resources*, no. 6, IPGRI.

[59] Flowering plants having two embryonic seed leaves or cotyledons that usually appear at germination (cf. soybeans, potato, tobacco etc.); monocotyledonous plants have a single cotyledon in the seed (cf. rice, wheat, barley, maize etc.). A plasmid is a circular self-replicating non-chromosomal DNA molecule found in many bacteria, capable of transfer between bacterial cells of the same species, and occasionally of different species. Plasmids are particularly important as vectors for genetic engineering.

[60] See the US Patent and Trademark Office (1998), patent database at http://www.uspto.gov

[61] See G. de la Riva, J. Gonzalez-Cabrera, R. Vasquez-Padron and Camilo Ayra-Pardo 'Agrobacterium: a natural tool for plant transformation' in *Electronic Journal of Biotechnology*, 1(3), 15 December, at http://www.ejb.org/content/vol1/issue3/full, visited 31 March 2003.

[62] See FAO (2004), chapter 1, p. 9.

- 'tweaking', in which genes already present in a plant's genome are manipulated to change the level or pattern of expression,
- 'close transfer' in which genes are transferred from one species to another of the same kingdom,[63]
- 'distant transfer' in which genes belonging to a species of another kingdom are transferred into a plant (cf. bacteria genes into plants).

The third type of method is best illustrated by the uses made in agriculture of the *Bacillus thuringiensis* (Bt) bacterium. This bacterium, capable of producing specific proteins called delta-endotoxines, makes a natural insecticide and numerous patents have been filed for its introduction in plants such as maize, cotton or rice.

The first patent involving Bt genes and the production of delta-endotoxines was granted by the USPTO in May 1984 (no. 4,448,885) to the Board of the Regents of the University of Washington. Whereas this patent was concerned with the expression within plasmids of DNA sequences coding for delta-endotoxines, the numerous American patents subsequently granted on Bt genes dealt with the expression of lethal proteins for specific (and distinct) larvae first in micro-organisms colonizing (and protecting) plants, before covering methods of insertion of gene constructs directly into different plants.

Another frequent application of biotechnologies in agriculture, which also gives rise to numerous patents, consists in introducing resistance genes to glyphosate, a type of herbicide. Interestingly, the FAO 2004 report observes that

> Almost two-thirds of the field trials in industrialized countries and three-quarters of those in developing countries focus on two traits: herbicide tolerance and insect resistance or a combination of the two traits together. . . . Although insect resistance is an important trait for developing countries, herbicide resistance may be less rele-

---

[63] 'For crosses between distantly related species death of hybrid embryos often occurs at a very early stage.' These hybrid embryos can be removed from the endosperm and brought to germination in vitro ('[t]he endosperm is the tissue that nourishes the young embryo from fertilization to the time when the green leaves become functional.') Hai-Shan Chi (2002), 'The Efficiencies of Various Embryo Rescue Methods in Interspecific Crosses of Lilium' in *Botanical Bulletin of Academia Sinica*, 43: 139–46, p. 142. This technique has also allowed the crossing of high-yielding Asian rice *Oryza sativa* with an African variety resistant to weeds competition, moisture-stress, aluminium soil toxicity and diseases, giving birth to the NERICA, or the New Rices for Africa: M.P. Jones, (1999) 'Basic Breeding Strategies for High Yield Rice Varieties at WARDA', in *Japanese Journal of Crop Science*, 67: 133–6, quoted in Nuffield Council on Bioethics *The Use of Genetically Modified Crops in Developing Countries* (follow-up of the 1999 report), London, June 2003, p. 13. See also The Sasakawa Africa Association Newsletter, *Feeding the Future*, July 2003, p. 13.

vant in areas where farm labour is abundant. By contrast, agronomic traits of particular importance to developing countries and marginal production areas, such as
potential yields and abiotic stress tolerance (e.g. drought and salinity), are the
subject of very few field trials in industrialized countries and even fewer in developing countries.[64]

Moreover, biotechnologies provide tools for identification, and not only modification of genetic material. In the 1980s, the technique known as 'restriction fragment length polymorphism' (RFLP) allowed for the first molecular maps to be
drawn up and led to the discovery that related species have noticeably similar
gene maps. This property is called 'synteny'. Since the sequencing of the rice
genome has been fully completed,[65] it is possible, using synteny, to foresee that
key genes (for instance for disease resistance) will be present in other cereals,
including the so-called 'orphan crops', in the same order as in rice.

In more detail, RFLP is a technique that allows the differentiation of organisms by analysis of patterns of cleavage of their DNA. When two organisms
differ in the distance between sites of cleavage under the action of a specific
enzyme (i.e. a restriction endonuclease), the length of the DNA fragments
retrieved will also differ. These fragments are then separated by gel elec-
trophoresis. Less time consuming, albeit also less precise, the Random
Amplified Polymorphic DNA (RAPD) is broadly resorted to. It consists of
creating genomic fingerprints from species identifying some (randomly
chosen) stretch of unknown DNA to facilitate discrimination. These two techniques are the most used fingerprinting methods, and can be carried out in the
course of breeding programmes, to differentiate plants according to differences in their genotypes.[66] Nevertheless, these techniques remain costly and
far from being systematically used in order to determine the origin of plant
genetic resources, although this would facilitate the implementation of Article
13(2)(d) of the FAO Treaty.[67]

---

[64]   FAO (2004), chapter 3, p. 10.
[65]   In April 2000, Monsanto announced its intention to make available free of
charge to the scientific community the results of its research on the sequencing of the
rice genome. On 26 January 2001, the CGIAR declared it was deeply satisfied with a
similar public undertaking made by Myriad Genetics Inc. and TMRI, Syngenta
research centre, which have jointly drawn up the mapping of the rice genome.
[66]   For more precision, see J.A. Hardon, B. Vosman and T.J.L. van Hintum,
*Identifying Genetic Resources and their Origin: The Capabilities and Limitations of
Modern Biochemical and Legal Systems*, FAO Background Study Paper no. 4, Rome,
7–11 November 1994.
[67]   According to this provision, commercializing products that incorporate
genetic material accessed from the Multilateral System triggers the payment of a
contribution to the FAO Multilateral System of benefit-sharing, except where such
products are available without restriction to others for further research and breeding.

CONCLUSION

We are therefore witnessing a combination of traditional agricultural methods, relying on the labour force and on the knowledge of both local population needs and environmental conditions, with biotechnologies, which can be a complementary research tool to identify desirable traits from remotely related taxonomic groups. Such a trend should lead to the creation of a whole range of new varieties, better adapted to different ecosystems and consumer preferences, and more environment-friendly, which are conditions for sustainable development[68] called for as early as 1987 by the World Commission on Environment and Development, then chaired by the Prime Minister of Norway. *In situ* breeding programmes are not conducted exclusively by farmers, but also by breeders and multinational companies, likely to apply for intellectual property rights to protect the outcome of such programmes. Thus, there is a need for in-depth research on the effects of IPRs[69] on the implementation of the FAO Treaty.

---

[68] Concept defined as 'development which meets the needs of the present without compromising the ability of future generations to meet their own needs'.

[69] In particular, the notion of 'essential derivation' of the 1991 version of the UPOV Convention has to be assessed. A variety essentially derived from a protected variety is covered by breeders' rights. This can thus limit the 'freedom-to-operate' in future breeding programmes using the protected variety as starting material – legally, pursuant to UPOV Art. 15.1(iii). Thus, the notion of essential derivation has to be clarified, in relation to that of exploitation.

18. The appropriation of American Indian names and images in trade marks – The Washington Redskins Case

Daphne Zografos

INTRODUCTION

Over the years, the use of Native American names and images in sports teams' names, mascots and logos has been a widespread practice in both professional and amateur sports arenas in the United States. Whereas amateur teams do not usually own trade marks on those names and images, most professional teams have registered them as trade marks and it is estimated that the sale of professional team apparel generates over a billion dollars each year in licensed merchandise. High profile examples of uses of Native American names and images in sports teams' names, mascots and logos include the team name of the Atlanta 'Braves' professional baseball organisation and a fan ritual called the 'Tomahawk Chop', the Cleveland 'Indians' professional baseball team name and 'Chief Wahoo' mascot and perhaps the most controversial of all, the Washington 'Redskins' professional football team name. Over the past decades, Native Americans and other individuals have been campaigning to change this practice as they consider it to be disparaging, racially discriminatory and to perpetuate a racial stereotype.

This chapter will first set the context of the Redskins cases by examining Section 2(a) of the Lanham Trademark Act ('the Lanham Act') which enables the United States Patent and Trademark Office (USPTO) to refuse to register trade marks which contain immoral, deceptive, scandalous, or disparaging matter. In particular it will focus on trade marks which consist of or comprise scandalous matter and those which may disparage persons, living or dead, institutions, beliefs, or national symbols. It will then move on to examine the litigation involving the Washington Redskins trade marks and conclude by analysing the efficiency and usefulness of Section 2(a) of the Lanham Act in protecting traditional names and images and the potential implications of the Redskins cases.

SECTION 2(A) OF THE LANHAM TRADEMARK ACT

Unlike analogous sections in predecessor statutes, which only focused their attention on morality,[1] Section 2(a) of the Lanham Act is also designed to discourage the commercial use of offensive subject matter that may not directly implicate principles of morality or virtue.

Section 2(a) of the Lanham Act[2] provides that no trade mark by which the goods of the applicant may be distinguished from the goods of others shall be refused registration on the principal register on account of its nature unless it consists of or comprises (1) immoral, (2) deceptive, or (3) scandalous matter; or matter which may (4) disparage or (5) falsely suggest a connection with persons, living or dead, institutions, beliefs, or national symbols, or (6) bring them into contempt, or disrepute.

The language of the statute draws a distinction between scandalous, immoral, and deceptive marks on the one hand, and disparaging, contemptuous, and false connection trade marks on the other. While trade marks falling within the first grouping are refused registration when they consist of or comprise matter that actually *is* scandalous, immoral or deceptive, trade marks falling within the second grouping are refused registration when they consist of or comprise matter that *may* be disparaging, contemptuous, or suggestive of a false connection. In other words, registration will be refused even where the nature of the mark cannot be proven with certainty.

Scandalous Trade Marks

Because of the paucity of legislative history to aid in interpreting the term 'scandalous' in Section 2(a) of the Lanham Act, courts have found that they

---

[1]   The Trademark Acts of 1881 and 1882 did not expressly ban immoral subject matter from registration. The 1905 Trademark Act was the first federal statute to directly and explicitly forbid registration of scandalous and immoral trade marks. Section 5(a) of the 1905 Act provided 'That no mark by which the goods of the owner of the mark may be distinguished from other goods of the same class shall be refused registration as a trademark on account of the nature of such mark unless such mark – (a) Consists of or comprises immoral or scandalous matter . . .'. In 1947, the Lanham Act extended its definition of offensive matter in Section 2(a) to also forbid the registration of trade marks that consist of or comprise matter that may 'disparage' or bring into 'contempt' or 'disrepute' persons (living or dead), institutions, beliefs, or national symbols. See Baird S. R., 'Moral Intervention in the Trademark Arena: Banning the Registration of Scandalous and Immoral Trademarks', *Trade Mark Reporter*, 83, 666–7.

[2]   Section 2(a) of the Trademark (Lanham) Act of 1946, as amended, 15 USC § 1052(a) (1988).

must 'give the word "scandalous" its ordinary and common meaning'.[3] In particular, courts have looked to dictionary definitions existing at the time of the enactment of the Trademark Act in 1946. According to those definitions, the term 'scandalous' means 'giving offence to the conscience or moral feelings; exciting reprobation, calling out condemnation . . . Disgraceful to reputation . . .'; 'shocking to the sense of truth, decency, or propriety; disgraceful, offensive; disreputable, as scandalous conduct'. [4]

Academics have divided cases considering the scandalous issue into two separate approaches taken by reviewing bodies:[5] (i) the 'Rule of Association' approach, and (ii) the 'Anti-Contextual Approach' or the 'Per Se Rule'.[6] The 'Rule of Association' approach acknowledges that a mark is not scandalous on its face, but it may become scandalous when placed in a certain context. Consequently, where the association between the mark and the goods is offensive, registration will be refused. Where on the other hand the resulting association is innocent, registration will be allowed. Under this approach, an innocent term may therefore be considered scandalous because of its context, and an otherwise offensive mark may be registered because of its innocent context.[7] On the other hand, under the 'Anti-Contextual Approach' or 'Per Se Rule', a reviewing body need not examine the context of the mark. It will look at whether the mark is scandalous on its face.[8] However, decisions taken under the 'Per Se Rule', without the association between the marks and the goods,

---

3   See *In re Riverbank Canning Co.*, 95 F2d 328, 37 USPQ 269.
4   See *In re McGinley*, 660 F2d at 486 fn 11, 211 USPQ at 673.
5   Trade mark decisions in the United States can be made either by an administrative body or by a federal court.
6   See Zlotchew Ethan G. (1998), ' "Scandalous" or "Disparaging"? It Should Make a Difference in Opposition and Cancellations Actions: Views on the Lanham Act's Section 2(a) Prohibitions Using the Example of Native American Symbolism in Athletics', *Colum.-VLA J.L. & ARTS*, 22, 226 and Blankenship Justin G. (2001), 'The Cancellation of Redskins as a Disparaging Trademark: Is Federal Trademark Law an Appropriate Solution for Words that Offend?', *Columbia Law Review*, 72, 431.
7   For example, while the trade mark MADONNA is legitimate as a registration for a pop music star (US Trademark Reg. No. 1,473,554 (1988)), it may become scandalous when placed on a bottle of wine, because of the potential religious significance. See *In re Riverbank Canning Co.*, 95 F2d 327, 328, 37 USPQ 269. Similarly, in *Ex parte Martha Maid Mfg. Co.*, 37 USPQ 156 (Comm'r Patents 1938), it was held that the mark 'Queen Mary', while innocent enough on its face, took on a scandalous meaning when associated with women's undergarments. See Blankenship, *supra* note 6, 431–3.
8   This approach was taken in the case *In re Tinseltown*, 212 USPQ 863 (TTAB 1981) where the Board held that the trade mark BULLSHIT was scandalous per se and that its association with fashion accessories did not make it any more or less scandalous.

are more subjective and unpredictable than under the 'Rule of Association' approach.

It emerges from a thorough analysis of Section 2(a) case law interpreting the term scandalous, that there are seven distinct groupings of decisions: (i) decisions having in common marks with a religious nexus; (ii) decisions having in common marks that consist of or comprise racial slurs, insults or epithets; (iii) decisions having in common marks that consist of or comprise profane matter; (iv) decisions having in common marks consisting of or comprising vulgar matter; (v) decisions having in common marks that relate to sexuality; (vi) decisions having in common innuendo marks; and (vii) decisions having in common marks that suggest or promote illegal activity.[9]

The most relevant categories of decisions in the context of the protection of traditional names and images are those consisting of or comprising religious content and most importantly those concerning marks that consist of or comprise racial slurs, insults or epithets. Decisions with a religious content can be divided into three main categories:

- those identifying the name of the Supreme Being. In that situation, the scandal arises from the trivialisation and commercialisation of the name of the Supreme Being. This applies to the use of all names that designate the Supreme Being to any religious group, including minority groups, such as indigenous communities;
- those consisting of or comprising words or symbols of great religious significance. This is relevant for indigenous communities as words or symbols with religious or sacred significance have often been registered as trade marks by third parties, often causing great offence; and
- those that name or otherwise identify a known religious organisation or its members.

Cases involving trade marks that consist of or comprise racial slurs, insults, or epithets are relevant for the protection of traditional names and images as the use of such trade marks can be deeply offensive to indigenous communities. Indeed, it has been acknowledged that there is a public interest in protecting the sensibilities of those living in a minority status because the use of such matter perpetuates racial stereotypes against minority groups and degrades those individuals of the identified race.[10]

---

[9]   This analysis is based on decisions interpreting Section 2(a) of the Lanham Act as well as decisions interpreting the statutory sections that preceded Section 2(a) of the Lanham Act. See Baird, *supra* note 1, 704.

[10]   See Baird, *supra* note 1, 714–15. Additional concerns related to the use of racial slurs, insults and epithets include the facts that they might provoke responsive

Finally, there is no need for a majority of the general public to be shocked or offended to trigger the protection of Section 2(a). In *Maverty Media Group Ltd*, it was established that whether the trade mark comprises scandalous matter is to be ascertained from the standpoint of not necessarily a majority but a substantial composite of the general public, and in the context of contemporary attitudes.[11] Consequently, it is enough that a minority group, such as Native Americans, be shocked or offended for scandal to be raised.

Disparaging Trade Marks

There is relatively little published precedent or legislative history on the disparagement provision of Section 2(a) of the Lanham Act. Section 2(a) of the Lanham Act precludes registration of trade marks which consist of or comprise matter that may disparage (i) living or dead persons; (ii) institutions; (iii) beliefs and (iv) national symbols. As with scandalousness, it is presumed that Congress intended to adopt the ordinary and common meaning of the term 'disparage'. According to dictionary definitions of 'disparage' that were contemporary with the Trademark Act of 1946, 'disparage' means 'to speak slightingly of; to undervalue; to discredit', 'to dishonour by bringing discredit or reproach upon . . . depreciate, cheapen'.

For the purpose of determining Section 2(a) disparagement, the relevant public has been interpreted in most decisions[12] as consisting of those individuals who are described, identified, or implicated in some meaningful way by the subject matter of the registration at issue. Therefore, in order to demonstrate that a mark is disparaging to a particular group, such as Native Americans, in cancellation proceedings, claimants must show that (i) the trade mark is reasonably understood to refer to the claimants; and (ii) the 'substantial composite' associated with the mark find it disparaging or scandalous. In that case, the 'substantial composite' refers to the reasonable member of the relevant racial group, and not to any reasonable person.[13]

---

violence, they deeply wound those at whom they are directed and they have an insidious effect on social relations. Indeed, it is believed that they reinforce prejudice and contribute to unjust discrimination, generate resentment and undermine self-esteem among members of the group about whom the remarks are made. See Greenawalt Kent (1990), 'Insults and Epithets: Are They Protected Speech?', *Rutgers Law Review*, 42, 143.

[11]   See *In re Maverty Media Group Ltd.*, 31 USPQ 2d 1923, 1925 (1994).

[12]   Case law interpreting the disparagement provision of Section 2(a) makes clear that offensiveness is to be measured from the perspective of the potentially damaged group. See *In re Hines*, 31 USPQ 2d (BNA) at 1688, *In re In Over Our Heads, Inc.*, 16 USPQ 2d 1653 at 1654; *In re Condas S.A.*, 188 USPQ 544 at 544, *In re Anti-Communist World Freedom Congress, Inc.*, 161 USPQ 304 at 305 and *Doughboy Industries, Inc. v Reece Chemicals Co.*, 88 USPQ 227 at 228.

[13]   See *In re Hines* at 1688.

In contrast, in *Greyhound Corp. v Both Worlds, Inc.*,[14] the Board held that the claimants must establish that (i) the trade mark must be 'reasonably understood' to refer to the claimant and that (ii) a 'reasonable person of ordinary sensibilities' must consider the trade mark offensive or objectionable. Therefore, the second part of the Greyhound test is an objective standard. A reasonable person in society must find the trade mark offensive or objectionable. According to one commentator, the Board in Greyhound omitted a critical qualification, namely, that to be disparaging, the mark must be viewed as offensive by a reasonable person of ordinary sensibilities who faces circumstances identical to those faced by the person or group that the mark has identified.[15] To hold otherwise and to consider the perceptions of those who are not referred to, identified by, or implicated in some meaningful manner by the mark, inappropriately dilutes the significance of the perceptions of those who are the intended beneficiaries of the disparagement part of Section 2(a). Consequently offensiveness is to be measured from the perspective of the reasonable person of ordinary sensibilities who is identified by the questioned mark.

THE REDSKINS CASE: *HARJO v PRO-FOOTBALL INC.*

I am not a sports team mascot. With all due respect to the teams who want to honor me by having a Native American mascot. It is outdated. It's the wrong way.

Billy Mills, Oglala Lakota
US gold medal winner in the 10,000 metres at the 1964 Olympics (2005)

Introduction

Over the years, more than 2600 high school, college or professional teams in the United States have used Native American names and images as mascots, logos and team names.[16] Whereas most high school and amateur teams do not own trade marks on those names and images, most professional teams and many college teams have registered them as trade marks. Since 1969, over 600 high school, college, and minor league teams have eliminated these uses, most because of political pressures.[17] The University of Oklahoma was the first

---

[14]   *Greyhound Corp. v Both Worlds, Inc.*, 6 USPQ 2d 1635 (TTAB 1988).

[15]   See Baird, *supra* note 1.

[16]   See Behrendt Kristin E. (2000), 'Cancellation of the Washington Redskins' Federal Trademark Registrations: Should Sports Team Names, Mascots and Logos Contain Native American Symbolism?', *Seton Hall J. Sport L.*, 10, 396.

[17]   Other teams that have changed their names include the Dartmouth 'Indians' in 1974, the Saint John's University 'Redmen' in 1994, the Miami of Ohio 'Redskins'

major collegiate institution to eliminate a Native American symbol in 1970. Its 'Little Red' mascot had been a traditional part of the school's athletics since the 1940s. It was followed in 1972 by Stanford University and the University of Massachusetts.[18] However, the practice remains widespread and Native Americans and other individuals have been campaigning to stop American sports team names, mascots and logos containing references to Native American culture as they consider them to be disparaging, racially discriminatory, to create racially hostile environments and to perpetuate racial stereotypes.[19]

The controversy surrounding the use of Native American names and images in sports teams' names, mascots and logos has led to boycotts, protests and demonstrations by Native Americans and their supporters. The national public debate on these issues intensified when on 4 April 1994, following intense protest over the Cleveland Indians' use of 'Chief Wahoo' as their mascot, President Bill Clinton declined to wear a cap featuring the controversial mascot when invited to throw out the first pitch in the inaugural game at Jacob's Field. Instead, he wore an alternate cap embroidered with a large 'C' rather than the 'Chief Wahoo' emblem.[20] On the one hand of the debate, supporters of maintaining registered trade marks that use objects of Native American culture as mascots and team names argue that (i) the original intent behind the selection of Native American mascots or team names was to honour Native Americans; (ii) Native American culture embodies the virtues athletics teams want to emulate; (iii) team names have been in place for a long time; and (iv) forcing athletic teams to change their name would destroy their ability to market merchandise. On the other hand, Native Americans and their supporters argue that trade marks containing Native American names and images that are often sacred to their communities are disparaging and should therefore be cancelled from the national register.[21]

In the United States, it is estimated that sales of professional team apparel

---

in 1996, the Sioux City Iowa 'Soos' and the Marquette University 'Warriors'. See Hughey Rachel Clark (2004), 'The Impact of *Pro-Football, Inc. v. Harjo* on Trademark Protection of Other Marks', *Fordham Intellectual Property, Media & Entertainment Law Journal*, 14, 327–8.

[18] See American Indian Sports Team Mascots, Chronology: 30 Years of Effort Addressing the Use of American Indian Related Sports Team Mascots, at http://www.aistm.org/1chronologypage.html.

[19] See Masters Brooke A., 'Creative Legal Tactics Used Against Teams With Indian-Themed Names', 11 April 1999, *Houston Chronicle*, 17.

[20] See Rhode John B. (1994–5), 'The Mascot Name Change Controversy: A Lesson in Hypersensitivity', *Marq. Sports L. J.*, 5, 141.

[21] See Dennie Christian (2005), 'Native American Mascots and Team Names: Throw away the Key; The Lanham Act is Locked for Future Trademark Challenges', *Seton Hall J. Sports & Ent. L.*, 15, 201–2.

generate over a billion dollars each year and that several major college teams earn millions each year in licensing agreements. In a *New York Times* article of 31 January 1993, it was pointed out that in 1992 alone, estimates suggested that Major League Baseball sold about 2.4 billion in licensed merchandise, the National Football league sold about $2.1 billion and the National Basketball Association sold about $1.4 billion.[22] Similarly, many college and university teams rely on licensing their trade marks for revenue to enhance the visibility of the athletics program and to produce additional merchandise sales and it was estimated that in 1992 college merchandising sales reached nearly $1.5 billion. Florida State University, for example, was reported to earn as much as $1.8 million each year selling merchandise with its team name and mascot.[23]

Some high profile examples of uses of Native American names and images as teams' names, mascots and logos in professional sports include the team name of the Atlanta 'Braves' professional baseball organisation and a fan ritual called the 'Tomahawk Chop', which was considered by Native American protestors to be offensive and to perpetuate negative stereotypes,[24] the Cleveland 'Indians" professional baseball team name and 'Chief Wahoo' mascot, which were strongly opposed because they were considered to be derogatory and racially offensive[25]

---

[22]   See Sims Calvin, 'It's Not Just How Well You Play the Game . . .', *New York Times*, 31 January 1999, 5.

[23]   See Hughey, *supra* note 17, 330.

[24]   See Behrendt, *supra* note 16, 393–4. Since the early 1990s, the 'Tomahawk chop' has been performed by the Atlanta Braves as a rallying cry, by moving their arms up and down in accordance with a rhythmic chant, to imitate the swinging of a tomahawk. Often, the cry is also performed by the fans with foam tomahawk toys. Tomahawks are a popular symbol of Indian culture. The cheer became a target of protest by Native Americans and other individuals, who argued that it belittled Indian people and their history. According to Clyde Bellecourt, a protest leader and executive director of the American Indian Movement, Indians should not be treated as mascots. He expressed his concerns about sports fans mocking Native American rituals by asking 'Why not name the team the "Atlanta Bishops" and handout crucifixes to everyone who entered the stadium.' See '"Indians", "Braves" and "Redskins", A Performative Struggle for Control of an Image' (1999) *Quarterly Journal of Speech*, 85, 188. Atlanta Braves fans on the other hand argue that their conduct is part of a celebration and that their performance is out of respect for the team. They feel that fan rituals are harmless and that the team name honours Native Americans. See Behrendt, *supra* note 16, 394.

[25]   See Behrendt, *supra* note 16, 395. Supporters of Chief Wahoo say that the mascot was not created to offend Native Americans, but to honour them since both the team name and Chief Wahoo pay homage to an early baseball player, Louis Sockalexis, who was one of the first Native Americans to play professional baseball. On the other hand, opponents of the Cleveland 'Indians' team name and especially of 'Chief Wahoo' perceive the team's moniker and Chief Wahoo logo, which depicts a red-faced, hooked-nosed, grinning caricature of a Native American, to be disparaging to Native American

and the use of the word 'Redskins' by the Washington professional football team.[26]

The Redskins Dispute

The Redskins dispute involves six trade marks owned by Pro-Football Inc., the corporate owner of the Washington football team, which include the word 'Redskin' and were all used in connection with goods and services related to its football team, including merchandise and entertainment services.[27] The oldest, 'The Redskins', written in a stylised script, was registered in 1967. Three other trade marks were registered in 1974, another in 1978 and the sixth, the word 'Redskinettes', was registered in 1990.

In 1992, seven Native Americans[28] representing various tribes filed a complaint with the Trademark Trial and Appeal Board (TTAB) to cancel the registration of the six marks, claiming that they had disparaged Native Americans at the times of registration and had thus been registered in violation of Section 2(a) of the Lanham Act. They asserted that the word 'redskin(s)' 'was and is a pejorative derogatory, denigrating, offensive, scandalous, contemptuous, disreputable, disparaging and racist designation for a Native American person'.[29] This complaint became the case *Harjo v Pro-Football Inc.*[30]

---

culture. Opposition escalated when on 10 April 1998, opening day for the Cleveland Indians baseball team, protestors burned an effigy of Chief Wahoo and were arrested by Cleveland police on charges of aggravated arson. Although the city did not prosecute the protestors, they sued the city, the arresting officers and their commanders for civil rights violations stemming from their allegedly baseless arrest and detention. Ultimately, the case went to the Supreme Court of Ohio, which decided that the right to free speech was not violated by arrest of the protestors after burning an effigy where the municipality's interest was to preserve public safety. See *Bellecourt v Cleveland*, 104 Ohio St. 3d 439.

[26]   Other notorious examples include the Chicago 'Blackhawks' professional hockey organisation, the Cleveland 'Indians' professional baseball organisation, the Kansas City 'Chiefs' professional football organisation, the Florida State University 'Seminoles', the University of Illinois 'Fighting Illini' and the University of North Dakota 'Fighting Sioux'.

[27]   The Redskins football team was named in 1933 in honour of the team's head couch 'Lone Star' Dietz, a Native American. It became the Washington Redskins after the team moved from Boston to Washington in 1937.

[28]   Suzan Shown Harjo, Raymond D. Apodaca, Vine Deloria, Jr., Norbert S. Hill, Jr., Mateo Romero, William A. Means, and Manley A. Begay, Jr.

[29]   See *Harjo v Pro-Football Inc.*, 50 USPQ 2d 1705 (TTAB 1999) 1708.

[30]   *Harjo v Pro-Football Inc.*, 50 USPQ 2d 1705 (TTAB 1999).

The Trademark Trial and Appeal Board's Decision

The claimants argued that the 'Redskins' trade mark and other variations of that trade mark were *void ab initio* and that the word 'redskin(s)' is and has been deeply offensive, humiliating, and a degrading racial slur. They contended that a substantial composite of the general public considered 'redskin(s)' to be offensive and that the inherent nature of the word 'redskin(s)' and the defendant's use of it perpetuated the devastating and harmful effects of negative ethnic stereotypes. Further they contended that Native Americans have understood and still understand the word 'redskin(s)' to be a disparaging racial epithet that brings them into contempt, ridicule and disrepute.[31] More specifically, the claimants argued that the TTAB must consider evidence regarding the historical setting in which the word 'redskin(s)' has been used, the present societal relations of Native American culture with other cultures and the linguistic and written use of the word 'redskin(s)'.[32]

The defendant argued among other things that laches barred the Native Americans' claim. It contended that the claimant's evidence was biased and flawed and that it did not focus on either the appropriate time period or population and contained other specified inadequacies. The defendant denied that the term 'redskin(s)' was disparaging, offensive and derogatory. It contended that the initial use of the term 'redskin(s)', the modern context of the term and the spoken and written use of the term, in connection with a sports team name, were neutral designations that honoured Native Americans.[33]

Evidence included dictionary entries for 'redskin(s)', book and media excerpts from the late nineteenth century through the 1940s that used the term 'redskin(s)' and portrayed Native Americans in a pejorative manner, a study that found derogatory use of the term in Western-genre films from before 1980, the claimant's testimony about their views of the term, results from a 1996 survey of the general population and Native Americans that asked whether the various terms, including 'redskin(s)', were offensive, newspaper articles and game program guides from the 1940s onward using Native American imagery in connection with Washington's football team and testimony and documents relating to Native American protests.

The TTAB examined whether at the time the defendant was issued each of the challenged registrations, the defendant's registered marks consisted of or comprised scandalous matter, or matter which may disparage Native American persons, or matter which may bring Native American persons into contempt or disrepute.

---

31   Ibid. at 1719.
32   Ibid. at 1719–20.
33   Ibid. at 1720–21.

Scandalous matter

In deciding whether the trade mark 'Redskins' was scandalous, the board adopted the 'Per Se Rule'. Thus it looked at the mark in isolation, without taking into consideration the fact that 'Redskins' is attached to a football team.

On the basis of a dictionary definition of the word 'scandalous' contemporary to 1946, when the Lanham Act was adopted, the board looked at whether the mark was giving 'offence to the conscience or moral feelings; exciting reprobation, [or] calling out condemnation'.[34] The Board examined whether the mark was scandalous 'from the standpoint of not necessarily a majority, but a substantial composite of the public'. It carried out a two-step analysis to determine whether 'Redskins' was scandalous. First it looked at 'the likely meaning of the matter in question' and second, whether in view of the likely meaning, 'the matter is scandalous to a substantial composite of the general public'.[35]

The Board decided that the meaning of the matter in question, namely the word or root word 'redskin', clearly carried an allusion to Native Americans, and that this allusion was reinforced by the design elements in the registered marks incorporating the profile of a Native American and a Native American spear. However, the Board found that the claimants had not established by a preponderance of the evidence that the marks in the respondent's challenged registrations consisted of or comprised scandalous matter.[36]

Matter which may disparage

In order to determine whether the trade marks were disparaging, the Board focused on the ordinary and common meaning of the word 'disparage'. It described the applicable test as whether in relation to identified 'persons, living or dead, institutions, beliefs, or national symbols', such matter may dishonour, deprecate, degrade or affect or injure by unjust comparison.[37]

The Board based its analysis on a two-step process. First, it asked 'What is the meaning of the matter in question, as it appears on the marks and as those marks are used in connection with the services identified in the registrations'. In answering this question, the Board determined that 'redskin(s)' had acquired a secondary meaning as the name of a professional football team. However, it found that the trade marks also carried the allusion to Native Americans inherent in the original definition of that word.[38] Second, the Board asked whether the meaning was 'one that may disparage Native Americans'.

---

[34] Ibid. at 1735.
[35] Ibid. at 1736.
[36] Ibid. at 1748.
[37] Ibid. at 1738.
[38] See ibid. at 1741–2.

In this respect, the Board considered the question whether the word 'redskin(s)' as well as the graphics of the spear and the Native American portrait may disparage Native Americans by reference to the perception of Native Americans. In doing so it followed *In re Hines* and reiterated the principle that the views of the referenced group were to determine whether a trade mark was disparaging. Consequently, it examined whether, as of the relevant times, a substantial composite of Native Americans in the United States perceived this subject matter as disparaging. With respect to the spear design and the portrait of a Native American in profile, the Board noted that there was not enough evidence to conclude that these two logos may disparage Native Americans. With respect to the word 'redskin(s)' on the other hand, the Board concluded that 'the word 'redskin(s),' as it appears in the defendant's marks in those registrations and as used in connection with the identified services, may disparage Native Americans, as perceived by a substantial composite of Native Americans'.[39] The Board reached this decision based on the cumulative effect of the entire record of evidence, and not on one single item of evidence or testimony alone.[40]

The Board ordered each of the registrations to be cancelled under Section 2(a) on the grounds that the subject marks may disparage Native Americans and may bring them into contempt or disrepute. However it denied cancellation on the ground that the subject marks consisted of or comprised scandalous matter.[41]

The District Court's Decision

Following the TTAB's decision, Pro-Football filed suit in the US District Court for the District of Columbia,[42] seeking reinstatement of its six registrations on the grounds that: (i) laches barred the Native Americans' petition; (ii) the TTAB's finding of disparagement was unsupported by substantial evidence; and (iii) section 1052(a) of the Lanham Act violated the First and Fifth Amendments to the US Constitution both facially and as applied by the

---

[39]   See ibid. at 1743.

[40]   Evidence included a survey on how the public perceived the word 'redskin', dictionary evidence on the connotation of the word 'redskin' and linguistic evidence about the pejorative meaning of the word 'redskin' throughout history. See *Harjo* at 1743–7.

[41]   See ibid. at 1749.

[42]   Although the Federal District Court for the District of Columbia is normally a court of first instance, in this instance, it was acting in an appellate capacity. The District Court determined that the appropriate standard for reviewing the Board's findings was that derived from the Administrative Procedure Act. Therefore it would reverse the Board's findings only if they were unsupported by substantial evidence.

TTAB.[43] Without reaching conclusion on the constitutional issues, the District Court granted summary judgment to Pro-Football on 30 September 2003 reversing the Board's decision on the alternate grounds that laches barred the Native Americans' petition and that the TTAB's conclusion of disparagement was unsupported by substantial evidence.[44]

The lack of substantial evidence

The District Court found that the TTAB's decision that the marks at issue 'may disparage' Native Americans was not supported by substantial evidence, was logically flawed and failed to apply the correct legal standards to its own findings of fact.

In order to determine disparagement, the Board applied the *In re Hines* two-part test, according to which claimants must show that (i) the trade mark is reasonably understood to refer to the claimants; and (ii) the 'substantial composite' associated with the mark must find it disparaging.[45] The Court did not challenge the standard articulated by the TTAB for evaluating a disparagement claim and confirmed that only the perception of persons in that identifiable group are relevant to determining if the designation is disparaging. Therefore it stressed that the burden to prove that a substantial composite of all Native American Indians regarded the term 'redskin(s)' as disparaging as of the dates of the challenged registrations rests with the claimant. In addition, the court emphasised that the issue was not whether there was evidence that the term 'redskin(s)' was a disparaging or derogatory term in the abstract, but rather whether it was disparaging when used as a trade mark in relation to a pro football team. The court observed that the Board made relatively few findings of fact and simply presented the evidence of the parties in the form of summaries without making clear which of these facts formed the basis for its conclusion that the 'Redskins' marks were disparaging.[46]

The Court found that the evidence brought forward was insufficient to conclude that the 'Redskins' trade marks disparaged Native Americans or brought them into contempt or disrepute. Consequently it decided that the TTAB's findings were based solely on the 'cumulative effect of the entire record' and granted summary judgment to Pro-Football.[47]

---

[43]   See 284 F Supp. 2d 96, 68 USPQ 2d 1225, 102.

[44]   Ibid. at 145.

[45]   Ibid. at 128–9.

[46]   According to the District Court, the Board made specific findings of fact in only two areas: (i) linguists' testimony and (ii) survey evidence

[47]   See 284 F Supp. 2d 96, 68 USPQ 2d 1225, 135–6.

The laches defence

Laches is an equitable defence that prevents a trade mark holder from suing an alleged infringer after a long delay. Under this principle, the claimant has a duty to act promptly in seeking a preliminary injunction. Undue delay in seeking such relief once the claimant has, or should have, knowledge of the infringement might result in its denial.[48]

The Court stated that the laches defence would apply 'if (1) the Native Americans delayed substantially before commencing their challenge to the 'Redskins' trademarks; (2) the Native Americans were aware of the trade marks during the period of delay; and (3) Pro-Football's ongoing development of goodwill during the period of delay engendered a reliance interest in the preservation of the trademarks'.[49]

On the first prong of the test, the Court found that the defendants substantially delayed in bringing their challenge to the marks. It pointed out that in the case of the first trade mark, the defendants waited over 25 years to bring their case.[50] On the second prong of the test, the court found that the defendants had actual and constructive notice of the trade marks as well as of the widespread use of Pro-Football's trade marks. In addition, 25 years had passed since first notice of the mark and the defendants had failed to provide sufficient excuse for the delay.[51] Finally, on the third prong of the test, the court found that cancelling the trade marks would subject Pro-Football to undue economic prejudice.[52] It stressed that Pro-Football was entitled to rely on the security of the trade marks at issue and that the 25-year delay, where Pro-Football had heavily invested in the marks, would clearly result in economic prejudice.[53]

Although the District Court reversed the decision of the TTAB to cancel the trade marks, it based its analysis on the insufficiency of the evidence. It did not hold that any other mark using Native American terms could not be cancelled as disparaging. In other words, other marks may still be attacked.

---

[48]   See Gilson Jerome (1974), *Trade Mark Protection and Practice*, Lexis Nexis, Newark, §14.04[1] (Rel.50–12/03).

[49]   See *Pro-Football, Inc. v Harjo*, 284 F Supp. 2d 96 (DDC 2003), 136–7. The Court articulated a general three-prong test for laches on the basis of the test that the Court of Appeals for the District of Colombia Circuit articulated in *NAACP v NAACP Legal Defense & Educational Fund, Inc.*, 753 F2d 131, 137 (DC Cir. 1985).

[50]   See Pro-Football at 139–40.

[51]   See ibid. at 140–1.

[52]   The Court referred to *Hot Wax, Inc. v Turtle Wax, Inc.*, 191 F3d 813, 824 and pointed out that economic prejudice arose from investment in and development of the trade mark and that the continued use and economic promotion of a mark over a prolonged period added weight to the evidence of prejudice. In addition, it added that where the length of time was great in bringing the claim, prejudice would be more likely to have occurred and less proof of prejudice would be required. See *Pro-Football* at 79.

[53]   See *Pro-Football* at 144.

The Court of Appeal's Decision

On 15 July 2005, the US Court of Appeal for the District of Columbia remanded the Redskins case to the district court for further consideration of the issue of laches.[54] The Court of Appeal agreed with the Native Americans that the District Court mistakenly applied the doctrine of laches to one of the claimants, Mateo Romero, who was only one-year old in 1967, when the District Court started the clock for laches. It ruled that, as to Romero, the District Court's approach ran counter to the 'well-established principle of equity that laches runs only from the time a party has reached his majority'.[55]

The Court explained that laches is an equitable doctrine 'founded on the notion that equity aids the vigilant and not those who slumber on their rights'. It stressed that this defence, which Pro-Football has the burden of proving, 'requires the proof of (i) lack of diligence by the party against whom the defence is asserted, and (ii) prejudice to the party assessing the defence'.[56]

Pro Football argued that a ruling in favour of the claimants would mean that trade mark owners 'could never have certainty, since a disparagement claim could be brought by an as yet unborn claimant for an unlimited time after a mark is registered'.[57] The Court however was not moved and pointed out that even if registrations of some marks would remain perpetually at risk, it was unclear why this fact authorised – let alone required – abandonment of equity's fundamental principle that laches only attach to parties who have unjustifiably delayed in bringing suit.[58] Romero had brought his own claim and there was no reason why the laches of others should be imputed to him.

While retaining jurisdiction over the case, the Court of Appeal decided to remand the record to the District Court for the purpose of evaluating whether laches barred Romero's claim. In particular, when assessing prejudice, the District Court was instructed to address both trial and economic prejudice.[59]

---

[54] See 75 USPQ 2d 1525, 50.

[55] Ibid. at 48.

[56] Ibid. at 47.

[57] Ibid. at 49.

[58] 'Why should equity elevate Pro-Football's perpetual security in the unlawful registration of a trade mark over the interest of a Native American who challenged this registration without lack of diligence? Why should laches bar *all* Native Americans from challenging Pro-Football's "Redskins" trade mark registrations because *some* Native Americans may have slept on their rights?'. See ibid.

[59] As to trial prejudice, the Court was directed to consider the extent to which Romero's post-majority delay resulted in a 'loss of evidence or witnesses supporting [Pro-Football's] position'. As to economic prejudice on the other hand, the Court was encouraged to take briefing on whether economic prejudice should be measured based on the owner's investment in the marks during the relevant years, on whether the owner

CONCLUSION

Irrespective of their final outcome, the Redskins cases have shown the relevance of trade mark law in protecting traditional names and images, in particular where their registration as trade marks by third parties can cause offence. Generally speaking, trade marks can offer a quick, practical and effective solution to the protection to traditional names and images without the need to create a new *sui generis* IP or IP-related system, which would take a long time to establish. Indeed, it has been shown that trade mark law can be used as such or with minor adaptations to protect against some forms of exploitation of traditional names and images. However, trade marks do not provide an ideal system for the protection of traditional names and images, as such a system can only apply to offensive uses in connection with registered trade marks. Trade marks will therefore not prevent the offensive use of traditional names and images where the user does not seek to register them as a trade mark. Consequently, revocation of the Redskins trade marks will not prevent the owners from continuing to use the name and logo. However, it will end the protected status and, given the financial stakes, loss of the trade mark registration is likely to induce the owners to rename the team.

---

would have taken a different course of action (e.g. abandoned the marks), had the claimant acted more diligently in seeking cancellation, or on some other measure. See ibid. at 50.

Index